EVOLUTION OF INTERNATIONAL AVIATION

Evolution of International Aviation
Phoenix Rising
Second Edition

DAWNA L. RHOADES
Embry-Riddle Aeronautical University, USA

ASHGATE

Published by
Ashgate Publishing Limited
Wey Court East
Union Road
Farnham
Surrey GU9 7PT
England

Ashgate Publishing Company
Suite 3-1
110 Cherry Street
Burlington, VT 05401-3818
USA

www.ashgatepublishing.com

British Library Cataloguing in Publication Data
Rhoades, Dawna L., 1958-
  Evolution of international aviation : phoenix rising. - 2nd ed.
  1. Aeronautics, Commercial 2. Aeronautics, Commercial -
  History 3. Airlines - Economic aspects 4. Aeronautics,
  Commercial - Law and legislation - International
  cooperation
  I. Title
  387.7

  ISBN: 978-0-7546-7389-7

Library of Congress Cataloging-in-Publication Data
Rhoades, Dawna L., 1958-
  Evolution of international aviation : phoenix rising / by Dawna L. Rhoades. -- [2nd ed.]
    p. cm.
  Includes index.
  ISBN 978-0-7546-7389-7 (hardback) 1. Aeronautics, Commercial--History. 2. Aeronautics, Commercial--Law and legislation--History. 3. Airlines--United States--History. 4. Airlines--Deregulation--United States. 5. Airlines--Finance--Case studies. 6. Strategic alliances (Business)--Case studies. I. Title.

  HE9774.R48 2008
  387.7--dc22
                                                                2008022332
Reprinted 2013

Printed and bound in Great Britain by
the MPG Printgroup

Contents

List of Figures

List of Tables

Acknowledgements

No book is truly the work of a single individual even though the title page may not reflect the contributions of these other individuals; this is the role of the acknowledgement section. I would like to thank my colleague, Sveinn Gudmundsson, for inspiring the first edition of this book. I doubt that it would ever have been started without him. I also owe a debt of thanks to my colleagues and students at Embry-Riddle Aeronautical University for their support during the writing of this work. They not only supported me during the frantic days of writing and editing, but inspired me to write a text that would help to make aviation accessible to all interested parties. Aviation is a forward-looking industry and the aviation students of today will be the leaders of tomorrow. I hope that we have prepared them well.

I am indebted to the many fine scholars who have gone before me in the quest to understand and explain the aviation industry. Their work is cited throughout this book. There are three individuals who deserve special mention—Brian Graham, Narwal Taneja, Tae Oum, George Williams, and Dipendra Sinha. Their work proved to be especially valuable.

Finally, I would like to thank my husband, John, and two children, Deanna and Be Rhoades. They inspire me to achieve great things as an example to them of what hard work and persistence can accomplish. Their understanding and support have also been greatly appreciated during this hectic time.

Preface to the Second Edition

The writing for the first edition of this book was completed a little over a year from the events of 11 September 2001. There is little doubt that this single event has had deep and enduring effects on the aviation industry. It is also clear now from the recovery that some sectors and regions of the industry were better positioned to come back from these events than others. The reality is that the airline sector has struggled from its inception to make a long-term, consistent profit. It seems a great irony that airlines can not make the kind of profits necessary to attract investment in such a capital intensive business when the number of people traveling by air continues to rise. The demand exists, but airlines seem unable to match supply to that demand. In fact, the industry is perpetually in a condition of either oversupply or undersupply. When there are too many seats available, then airlines are forced to lower prices to fill them, often selling below costs. This downward pressure leads in many cases to bankruptcy for the weakest carriers who then place even more pressure on the industry by using bankruptcy to lower prices even further. Cutting capacity is supposed to help fill seats and allow airlines to raise prices. Of course, after 11 September 2001, the traditional carriers such as American Airlines, Delta, and British Airways did cut capacity only to see low-cost carriers such as Southwest, JetBlue, and Ryanair add planes, increase seats, and enter new markets. Seats are filling up, but prices have not risen as many carriers had hoped. Pricing power was supposed to lift the industry out of the losses following 11 September 2001, but it has not been the magic bullet that airline executives hoped and other events have further threatened the airlines.

US airlines alone use approximately 53.4 million gallons of jet fuel per day for a total of 19.5 billion gallons per year. With rising fuel prices, fuel now constitutes 20–30 percent of the total operating costs of an airline, surpassing labor as the single largest expense (Air Transport Association, 2007). This fuel use is giving rise to another problem, carbon emissions. The cover story on the 19 December 19 2006 issue of *USA Today* was entitled "Concern grows over pollution from jets: Aviation emissions will take off along with worldwide air travel." The story noted that a commercial jet on a flight from New York City to Denver would generate between 840 and 1,600 pounds of carbon dioxide per passenger, roughly the same amount of carbon that would be generated by a Sports Utility Vehicle (SUV) in a month. Due to the projected increases in air travel over the coming decades, aircraft emissions could become one of the largest contributors to global warming by 2050 (Stoller, 2006). In Europe during the same month, the European Commission proposed including emissions from civil aviation into the European Union (EU) Emissions Trading Scheme (ETS). Emissions from all flights within the EU would be covered by 2011 and all flights to and from EU airports would be covered by 2012, including foreign aircraft operators. Although the Air Transport Association, a US trade organization, has listed the environment as one of its top five issues for the past two years, they are strongly opposed to any type of emissions trading (Pilling and Thompson, 2007).

Five years is a relatively short time in the life of a redwood tree or a Galapagos tortoise, but it is an eternity for an airline in the volatile aviation industry, hence, it was time to re-examine this book, updating the details and making new projections based on "what we know now." It also seems appropriate that this book expand its focus to look at the broader aviation industry. After all, airlines are but one part of this industry. They are the primary customers for the aircraft and engine manufacturers. These manufacturers represent the largest exporters in their respective regions, generating plenty of jobs and new technology. When the airlines struggle, the manufacturers also struggle, but they have some advantages over their airline customers in that they are truly global in their marketing. This means that if US airlines are struggling they can always hope to sell to Middle Eastern airlines that are expanding. While the number of competitors in the manufacture of large commercial aircraft (LCA) is very small—Boeing and Airbus at present—the match is fiercely fought and a complacent company can find itself in serious trouble or with a new rival. The announcement by the Chinese government that they intend to create a new aircraft manufacturing company might be greeted with the same derision that the industry gave when the Europeans announced their intentions to enter the industry if Airbus had not proved so successful.

Airplanes carry more than just people; they also transport a growing amount of freight. In fact in a globalizing, just-in-time world, air cargo and express services have experienced significant demand. The so-called integrators—UPS, FedEx, TNT, and Deutsche Post—have consolidated and expanded to provide customers end-to-end shipping services. In many cases, they are even taking over the management of entire supply chains for their customers. At the same time, airlines are entering into cargo alliances to maximize the cargo revenue they carry underneath those increasingly price conscious passengers. The just-in-time manufacturing systems that gained popularity in the latter part of the twentieth century relied on the ability of air cargo to get supplies there when they needed them and not a moment before. Meanwhile, consumers have become accustomed to enjoying fresh fruit from Latin America and Africa during the height of winter thanks to temperature controlled containers.

Finally, a new challenge is facing the industry in the twenty-first century and threatening its ability to meet future demand. While consumers have enjoyed satellite TV and radio for years, the aviation industry has continued to rely on a World War II era system of ground radar and radio communication for air traffic control. Replacing this aging system with a new satellite-based, internet system that links aircraft together, provides all users with integrated data on weather, airport conditions, other aircraft, and security issues to achieve better utilization of the airspace, safer skies, and safer ground movement. Better fuel efficiency is possible and can be achieved but at a cost. The technology exists but there is no consensus on who should pay for this new system.

In short, this new edition is a significant change, and I hope, an improvement over the first edition. It should help tie together developments in a number of areas of the aviation industry and provide a better overall understanding of the challenges and promises of the aviation industry as it moves into the twenty-first century.

Dawna L. Rhoades
1 May 2008

References

Air Transport Association (2007), 'US Airlines Support Development of Alternative Fuels', *ATA Issue Brief.* Available at: www.airlines.org/government/issuesbrief/alt+fuels.htm.

Pilling, M. and Thompson, J. (2007), 'Carbon Storm', *Airline Business*, February, pp. 54–6.

Stoller, G. (2006), 'Concern Grows Over Pollution From Jets: Aviation Emissions Will Take Off Along With Worldwide Air Travel', *USA Today*, December 19, pp. 1A–2A.

Chapter 1
Phoenix Rising

Of Phoenixes and Airlines

According to the most famous legend of the phoenix, the phoenix was a bird of brilliant red and gold plumage whose death in a fiery blaze gave rise to a new phoenix. Like the phoenix, the airline industry seems to have established it own cycle of destruction and renewal. From its very inception, the airline industry has been at the mercy of the business cycle, experiencing soaring profits in the upturn and rapidly falling into losses when the market turns down. The so-called new economy that combined technological innovation, globalization, and abundant venture capital began transforming the US economy and others around 1995. This new economy was predicted to end the business cycle or at least smooth it out so that the booms were not so high and the busts so low. Under this new era of prosperity, the US economy grew at about 4.4 percent a year while unemployment dropped to near 4 percent. At the same time, productivity rose at an annual rate of 2.8 percent (Mandel, 2000). In short, growth, productivity, and employment seemed on an unstoppable path upward. As the US economy teeters on recession, it appears that the death of the business cycle was greatly exaggerated. The newest question on the mind of policy makers and economists is whether the rest of the world is decoupling from the US economy.

In any event, the boom times for airlines have always meant adding capacity through new aircraft acquisitions, opening new routes to unserved destinations, and negotiating bigger labor contracts (or contracts that gave back what was lost in the last downturn). The bust has always been a downward ride into declining profits, falling load factors, and destructive price wars. Unfortunately, even before the events of 11 September, the US airline industry was facing the return of its most dreaded foe, the business cycle, and US airlines were expected to post a $3 billion loss (Air Transport Association, 2002). While the rest of the airline world was not yet expecting losses of this magnitude, the US downturn was expected to have an effect on those carriers with a sizable percentage of traffic to North America (Sparaco and Wall, 2001). Post 9/11, the downturn became even steeper as many carriers struggle to avoid bankruptcy, a valiant struggle that failed for many of the major carriers in the US. The US airline industry would not return to profitability until 2006, just in time to watch the 2007 rise in oil prices (Air Transport Association, 2007).

The airline industry is no stranger to bankruptcy. In the United States, the first passenger on a regularly scheduled airline flew from Tampa Bay to St. Petersberg, Florida on January 1, 1914. The airline chalked up another first when it folded four months later after running into financial difficulty (Wells, 1994). In Europe, war and financial crisis in the 1930s and 1940s led to the nationalization of many of the continent's premier carriers as a means of insuring their survival (Graham, 1995; Sinha, 2001). Back in the US, aviation continued to expand in fits and starts aided by airmail contracts from the US Postal Service, however, since the deregulation of the US airline industry in 1978, the industry has experienced a financial crisis in the early years of each decade. The losses in the early 1990s were nearly $10 billion (Rosen, 1995). The losses for the industry in 2001 alone were $7.7 billion and are expected to be approximately $8 billion for 2002 (Foss, 2002). The International Air Transport Association (IATA) has estimated the US airline losses for 2001–05 at US$42.4 billion (IATA, 2005).

A Special Case

The aviation industry has long been treated as a special case in international business, subject to different rules and held to different standards. In fact, international aviation has been "a serious problem in international relations, affecting the way governments view one another, the way individual citizens view their own and foreign countries, and in a variety of direct and indirect connections the security arrangements by which we live" (Lowenfeld, 1975). There are several reasons for the special status and serious problems associated with international aviation. Originally, the most compelling was national defense. Under programs such as the US Civil Reserve Air Fleet (CRAF) plan, civilian fleets could be used during times of military action to ferry troops and supplies. It was, therefore, vital to insure the existence and health of this civilian reserve. In the case of CRAF, the US government gets a reserve fleet for times of emergency without the cost of maintaining it and the airlines get paid a rate that during Desert Storm was 1.75 times the seat mile or cargo mile rate (Kane, 1998). National defense was also cited as the reason for insisting on home country ownership of these airlines and the manufacturers on the premise that home country nationals would or could be made to cooperate in the defense of their country. As we will see, the connection between civilian and military technology at the manufacturer's level has always been close; the innovations in technology first deployed and tested on military aircraft were quickly applied to the commercial fleet. In a number of countries such as the US, funding for research and development for these "military" innovations came from the government and went to firms who also had sizeable civilian operations, a situation that has led foreign competitors to charge "unfair subsidy."

The second most cited reason for special treatment has been the economic impact of aviation. According to the Air Transport Action Group, the world's airlines carried over two billion passengers in 2007 and transported 40 percent of the world's manufactured exports. The industry provided employment for over 29 million people worldwide. The global economic impact of the industry was over US$2,960 billion. The aviation industry is also a key component of the travel and tourism industry, generating 6.7 million direct tourism jobs in 2007 (Air Transport Action Group, 2008). Passenger traffic grew on average 6 percent per year during the decade of the 1980s and early 1990s driven by a number of factors: falling real costs of air travel, increasing economic activity, intensifying international trade, increasing disposable incomes, political stability, relaxation of travel restrictions, expanding ethnic ties, increasing leisure time, tourism promotion, air transport liberalization, and growth in emerging regions and countries. Historically, air traffic has grown at about twice the rate of gross domestic product (GDP) and during the period 1960–90, 80 percent of traffic growth could be explained by growth in GDP. Beginning in the 1990s, falling real prices (fares) played a greater role in traffic growth. As air travel grows, the direct (value of airline and on-airport activities) and indirect (value of off-airport activities of passengers and shippers) economic impact grows as well. In addition, there is an induced impact from the successive spending of recipients of these direct and indirect benefits. In short, the economic impact of the air transport industry makes its health a major concern of governments, businesses, and passengers around the world and keeps it from being seen as "just another industry."

The third reason for aviation's special status is the link that exists in the minds of many between aviation and national achievement and pride. International airlines "carry the flag" around the world. This reason should not be underestimated as a driver of individual and government perception. When the bankruptcy and subsequent grounding of the Swissair fleet forced the Swiss football team to fly the Russian carrier Aeroflot to a qualifying match in Moscow, one article reported this event as a "further humiliation for the Swiss flag carrier" (Hall, Grant, Done, Cameron, and, 2001). The uproar that occurred in Great Britain over the replacement of the Union Jack on the tail of many British Airways planes by the so-called ethnic tails intended to show British Airways as the airline of the world was motivated by similar nationalistic sentiment (BBC News, 1999b). Likewise, the debate in Belgium over the bankruptcy of Sabena and the need for a national carrier to serve the interest of the people of Belgium has more to do with nationalistic pride than airline economics (BBC News, 1999a; Sparaco, 2001). At the manufacturing level, nations have also mourned the loss of their aviation pioneers. One of the key arguments for the European formation of Airbus was the dominance of manufacturing by US firms. According to Aris (2002), the Airbus project was seen by the French as "*Un Grand Projet*: one of those brilliant combinations of technological skill and political will that serve to remind the French themselves—and everybody else – just what a great nation they are" (16). To the Germans, Airbus was the chance to rebuild an aerospace industry that had contributed many early innovations in aviation. In short, all things aviation have been linked to national pride in their technological achievement and visionary leadership. In the US, the announcement that the US Air Force had chosen Northrop Grumman and European partner EADS, parent of Airbus, for a refueling tanker deal worth US$35 billion was greeted with anger and calls for political investigation. In the US House of Representatives, Todd Tiahrt whose district includes facilities of the losing bidder Boeing, has said that the US "should have an American tanker built by an American company with American workers" (Tessler, 2008: 2). In fact, this last example brings together all of the reasons why aviation is a special case – defense, economic impact, and national pride.

Changing Times

Even without the defense, economic, and national pride arguments, aviation/ aerospace is not likely to be seen as "just another industry." It is the stuff of dreams and has fired the imagination of much of the world's population. Alvin Toffler (1970) noted in his bestselling book *Future Shock* that in 6000 BC the fastest transportation available to mankind was the camel caravan that averaged 8 miles per hour. By 1600 BC the chariot had raised this speed to approximately 20 miles per hour. The first mail coach in England began operating in 1784 at an average of only 10 miles per hour and the first steam locomotive was capable of a mere 13 miles per hour. In fact, it was not until the invention of an improved steam engine that mankind was able to reach a speed of 100 miles per hour. It took almost 8,000 years to go from the 8 mile an hour camel to the 100 mile an hour train. However, in only fifty-eight years, men in aircraft were exceeding the 400-mph line. Twenty years later that limit doubled. By the 1960s aircraft were approaching speeds of 4,000 mph, and space capsules were circling the earth at 18,000 mph.

The history of aviation/aerospace is filled with larger-than-life figures. These men and women were the entrepreneurs of Joseph Schumpeter (1949) who took on the thankless job of building and shaping an industry because "there is the dream and the will to found a private kingdom, usually, although not necessarily, also a dynasty ... . Then there is the will to conquer: the impulse to fight, to prove oneself superior to others, to succeed for the sake, not of the fruits of success, but of success itself ... . Finally, there is the joy of creating, of getting things done, or simply of exercising one's energy and imagination" (pp. 93–94). After all, the Wright brothers started their business career as the owners of a bicycle shop before the dream of aviation led them in a different direction. Their innovation in heavier-than-air flight would start an industry and in many ways illustrates the promises, challenges, and pitfalls of aviation.

Whatever the challenges, there have always been individuals drawn to aviation. The stories of these individuals, the planes they flew, and the companies they founded still fascinate us today. While the level of innovation has slowed, the manufacturers are continuing to face new challenges in design and performance. One of the greatest of these challenges will be increasing the fuel efficiency and improving the emissions profile of aircraft in a world of increasing oil prices and concerns about global warming. As the demand for air travel increases, other challenges are facing the industry. There is a lack of capacity at many of the airports worldwide and crowding of the airspace in many countries demands new systems of traffic management and optimization such as the use of satellites for navigation.

Expanding capacity requires long-term planning and sizeable investment from national and local government as well as private industry. Globalization has brought a tremendous increase in air cargo, particularly between China and the US. Here too capacity is a key issue as well as the one-way direction of the trade.

Sadly, despite the glories of the past, the worldwide airline industry has not fared well in recent years. It is now in the mature stages of its lifecycle, displaying all of the four basic characteristics of such an industry. First, growth slows or diminishes. Second, there are few new, key technologies that can provide an advantage to the first competitor to deploy it as was true in the days when newer, better, faster, and safer were changing with each new innovation. The few new technologies to be deployed by the airlines in recent years have provided only some short-term advantage because they were easily and quickly imitated. Third, the experience (or learning) curve no longer provides an advantage to one competitor over another. Finally, there are few new forms of differentiation and competition is largely based on price. The issue of price is critical because industries in this stage find that their profits are very sensitive to price, price advantages are short-lived, customers begin to expect lower prices, and customers shop for low price rather than value or benefits (Miller, 1998). Alfred Kahn, the Father of US airline deregulation, wrote about the possibility of destructive competition within an industry as a result of fixed and sunk costs that represent a high percentage of total cost and long sustained and recurrent periods of excess capacity (1988). He did not anticipate this occurring in the airline industry, but, in fact, it has come to pass.

Stephen M. Wolf, then Chairman of United Airlines, blamed the financial crisis of the early 1990s on three issues: overcapacity, international competition, and the lack of infrastructure. On the question of overcapacity, he said that in a truly free market overcapacity is temporary, but that liberal US bankruptcy laws allowed carriers "to operate literally for years without repaying their debt obligations; consequently, their capacity is retained in the system and the result is economic havoc for all" (1995: 19). While Wolf would undoubtedly blame the bankruptcy of his current airline, US Airways, on the events of 9/11 and the failure of the US government to approve his United–US Airways deal, his comments regarding overcapacity and bankruptcy remain true. Allowing carriers, any carrier, to continue to operate while receiving the benefits of bankruptcy protection not only fails to reduce overcapacity, but spreads the "bankruptcy virus" to other carriers who are disadvantaged by the competition from this protected carrier.

Warren Buffet, Chairman of Berkshire Hathaway, is "world famous as the greatest stock market investor of modern times" and a man who speaks his mind (Bianco, 1999). When he was asked several years ago about the stock market, particularly the internet stocks, he compared the internet industry to "two other transforming industries, auto and aviation" (Loomis and Buffet, 1999). His statements on aviation present a bitter truth. According to Buffet, the early aviation industry was full of promise and home to many young, vibrant companies, most of whom are a distant memory. Likewise, he cited some 129 airlines that have filed for bankruptcy in the last twenty years. The reason, he says, is clear: the industry as a whole has not made money overall in the long run. Buffet brutally suggested that a farsighted and public-spirited individual would have done the world's investors a favor by shooting down the Wright Flyer in 1903.

Like Joseph's Dream of Egypt, the aviation industry seems condemned to experience years of plenty followed by years of famine. Unlike the Egyptians, however, airlines do not save in years of plenty to survive the coming famine. Instead, they buy planes, expand route systems, and sign ever sweeter labor contracts. It is as though they are convinced that the airline that fattens up the most in the good times will simply outlast the others in bad times. In a truly free market, this strategy might work, but as Wolf and others have noted, the airlines do not operate in such a market. The events of 9/11 did not create this situation, but they made the situation worse for the airlines and those that supplied them. Just as many of the world's airlines had come through the dark post-9/11 days and returned to profitability, oil prices began to rise and fuel became the number one category of expense for many carriers. Unfortunately, fuel is an expense that airlines have very limited control over, other than hedging. Airlines that had hedged well as fuel began to rise such as Southwest and JetBlue managed to continue their profitability. As these hedges run out, however, there will be less room to maneuver.

Ironically, other segments of the aviation industry have recovered much more quickly from the events of 9/11. Manufacturers are posting healthy international sales from rapidly growing regions in Asia and the Middle East. Airlines that can afford to do so are purchasing more fuel efficient aircraft as a long-term means of dealing with higher oil prices. The emergence of very light jets (VLJs) has become a significant driver of general aviation manufacturing. Other aviation suppliers are benefiting from the trend of the large aircraft manufacturers to outsource a growing percentage of work. Efforts to create a twenty-first century airspace have opened opportunities for many firms to design, build, and deploy new technologies for everything from satellite navigation to groundside surveillance security. Airports are becoming intermodally connected shopping hubs, many with landside revenues far exceeding any generated by the airside.

As Buffet pointed out, air travel has transformed the way we live and do business. It is itself in the process of transforming; it is *becoming* something new. A debate has raged in the fields of paleontology, genetics and evolutionary biology over whether change in living organisms takes place in a gradual, step-by-step manner or in periods of rapid, major change followed by stasis. The latter theory is called punctuated equilibrium (Gould and Eldredge, 1977). This theory has been adapted and applied to the evolution of technology (Tushman and Anderson, 1986, 1990) and to the lifecycle and evolution of organizations and their industries (Hannan and Freeman, 1984). The idea of punctuated equilibrium or discontinuous change has caught on in so many areas because it "seems to fit" the observed evidence. In other words, investigators in all of these fields have been unable to trace a slow, clear development from one form to the next. Instead, they see periods of relative stability and little change interrupted by sudden, radical alterations in form. In the evolutionary sciences, these periods of sudden change are usually connected to mass extinctions of older, existing life-forms. In the areas of technology and organizations, startling innovations have arisen that make the technology and know-how that came before obsolete. For organizations, these periods of rapid change have been hardest on the firms of the prior age, firms that developed, grew, and adapted to life in another time. This is the traditional stockbrokerage coping in the new world of the internet or the corner bookseller competing with Amazon.com. The question in the minds of organizational theorists is whether these old age firms can change quickly enough to survive in the new age. If not, they will become the dinosaurs of this new age, dying out to make room for the newer, faster, smaller mammals.

It is possible that the airline industry is entering just such a period of discontinuous change. In the United States, post-9/11 airlines reduced their schedule by 3.5 percent and retired some 350 aircraft. US carriers who had traditionally derived a large percentage of their revenue from domestic operations redeployed many remaining aircraft to international routes where the revenue (yields) were higher. Meanwhile, low-cost carriers witnessed better than usual growth, moving into markets abandoned by the traditional carriers. As traffic has recovered to pre-9/11 levels, first outside the US, load factors (the proportion of aircraft seating capacity that is actually sold and utilized) began to rise; however, pricing power did not recover as quickly. As prices continued to fall and costs continued to rise, the breakeven load factor rose to 77 percent (Air Transport Association, 2002). Fortunately, most of the carriers in developed nations where growth has been slowest have resisted the temptation to dramatically increase fleets, keeping capacity up.

Where Do We Go?

The introduction began with a twisted quote from Lewis Carroll's classic the *Jabberwocky*. This passage begins "The time has come... to talk of many things." Indeed, the time has come for the aviation industry to reexamine itself and insure that what rises out of the ashes is better and more beautiful. In the aftermath of 9/11 it may seem callous to evoke the image of the phoenix rising from the ashes, but while this image may be one that many would like to forget, it remains a viable description for the airline industry. After all, the early international aviation system began to take shape in the time between the two world wars of the twentieth century. The global framework that continues to govern much of the system today emerged from the rubble of World War II. The aviation system was again thrown into turmoil by the deregulation of the US airline industry and the growing movement toward liberalization and economic integration in Europe and Asia. While the world struggles to come to terms with the meaning and implications of 9/11, the aviation industry must again find a way to cope with its losses while finding a new path for the future.

Because the aviation industry is a special case for all the reasons stated earlier, it is important for the people of the world to be involved in this debate. We are the tourists that fly to our long-awaited vacation, the businessmen that fly to important meetings, the shippers that send out goods around the world, the customers that buy grapes from Chile and wine from France, and the citizens that count on the airline industry and all the industries it helps support for a growing, healthy economy. The purpose of this book is twofold. First, the book explores the foundations of the industry (1903–50), looking at the forces that shaped the international aviation industry in terms that can be understood by anyone interested in aviation. Starting with the first trans-border crossing in a lighter-than-air balloon, it will trace the technological innovations, the international conferences, the government interventions, and the opportunities that shaped the industry that entered the era of deregulation and liberalization (1951–2000). This era changed all the rules. Second, the aviation industry in general and the international aviation industry in particular faces many interesting and difficult choices ahead (2001 and beyond). These choices include many dichotomies: pulling back from the trend toward liberalization or embracing the liberalization trend, merging in search of profitability or fragmenting the industry in search of economies, embracing a role in addressing global warming or fighting inclusion in the post-Kyoto regime, building a twenty-first century airspace or muddling along with an aging World War II infrastructure. Because this book is intended for both the interested amateur and the more serious student, references are provided in the text and at the end of each chapter to allow for more in-depth study. The book is NOT intended to be a definitive work on the aviation/aerospace industry; it would require a series of books to even attempt such a feat. The book does try to include most of the major sectors of the industry in order to give the reader an overall understanding of this complex industry. Perhaps the only major sector left out is the airport. It is obviously vital to the industry but airports vary widely within a country much less across nations and regions. Even within sectors such as the aerospace manufacturers, the book only touches on the major players. There is a vast group of aviation suppliers that range in size from Honeywell and GE to small mom-and-pop operations dealing with maintenance and repair of select avionics. Unless otherwise stated, the views expressed in this book are those of the author and do not represent those of the airline industry, any governmental organization or private institution associated with aviation.

The book has been organized into three parts. The first part will address the early development of the aviation system. Chapter 2 will explore the inventions and innovations in aviation technology that laid the foundation for commercial success. This period saw the start of heavier-than-air flight, the first use of the airplane in military action, and the foundations of passenger travel. The implications and possibilities of this new technology would come to hold greater sway in the minds of individuals and governments in the years ahead. Chapter 3 will explore the role of airmail and freight in shaping the industry. Chapter 4 will discuss early aviation conferences and the beginning of the struggle between the proponents of free markets and those favoring tight national control. Chapter 5 will examine the most famous international aviation meeting, the 1944 Chicago Conference. This conference resulted in the Chicago Convention which spells out the rights and obligations of states in international aviation, the creation of the international body responsible for establishing the rules and standards governing international aviation, and numerous technical drafts on recommended practices. Chapter 6 will examine in more detail the structure and role of the new International Civil Aviation Organization (ICAO) in developing the standards and practices of international aviation. If the world had not already learned at the Chicago Conference that aviation could not be divorced from its economic and political consequences, it came to learn these lessons over time in the operation of ICAO. In fact, any illusion that ICAO could deal with these technical problems on their own merit was quickly dispelled when accidental shootdowns of civil aircraft and a growing number of brutal hijackings and criminal attacks against civil aviation came to dominate the agenda of the ICAO council and its subordinate bodies (Sochor, 1991). This chapter will also address the development of another international organization, the International Air Transport Association (IATA), and its role in shaping the international aviation system through the setting of international fares.

Part II of the book explores the period between 1950 and 2000. The industry was growing up, maturing. Chapter 7 will return to the story of the manufacturers in an era in which air travel was becoming available to a growing number of consumers. Chapter 8 will look at another time of dramatic change for the airline industry, domestic deregulation. Domestic deregulation changed the rules of the game allowing competition based on price as well as market-based decisions on routes served and the level of service quality provided. It also freed up the industry for greater competition through the relaxation of rules for air carrier entry. This chapter will explore the link between domestic deregulation and efforts to liberalize international aviation markets. Chapter 9 will discuss the view from Europe and Asia. In Europe, aviation would become part of a greater effort to create an integrated free market system among the European Union nations. While the Europeans disagreed with the pace and implementation of deregulation in the US market, they have taken the concept of aviation liberalization further than their US counterparts by opening up domestic markets to foreign competition. The vast geographical diversity of the Asian region makes sweeping generalizations; however, most of this region has witnessed substantial growth in air transportation as part of its overall economic growth. Chapter 10 examines the alliance movement whose initial impetus was overcoming the national restrictions on air transportation. In an environment of heavy international regulation, the alliance became the airline tool of choice for serving new markets and extending the global reach of your alliance. There have been and will continue to be obstacles to the use of the alliance. In the post-9/11 world, the alliance can either become more important or more irrelevant to international aviation. Chapter 11 will outline some of the remaining legal blocks to international aviation while Chapter 12 explores the question of airline and alliance quality in an increasingly competitive industry. The final chapter in Part II, Chapter 13, will look at the air cargo industry in the new era of the logistics revolution.

In the final part of the book, the future of international aviation will be examined in light of changes in the environment before and after 9/11. Chapter 14 explores the industry's search for profitability in the wake of 9/11 and the growing threat of continuing high fuel prices. Chapter 15 will examine the trend in market liberalization that began with the 1978 deregulation of US domestic markets and has continued in Europe and Asia. Will deregulation and liberalization bring more competition or more losses? Chapter 16 will address the uneven development of international aviation and the regions that have yet to benefit from the economic promises of aviation, particularly those in Africa. Chapter 17 looks at the aviation industry in an era of concern about global warming. In Chapters 18 and 19, we revisit the manufacturing and air cargo industry to see where each of them is heading in the new century. Chapter 20 looks at the infrastructure that will support aviation as it moves forward, the technology, the costs, and the controversies. Finally, Chapter 21 will summarize where we are and where we appear to be going.

Imagining the Future

The airplane and the industry that it fostered have captured the imagination of generations around the world. It is time to apply that imagination to creating a viable, stable environment for international aviation that delivers on the great promise of air travel to link the world together in peace and prosperity. Thomas L. Friedman has said of his work that he hopes that it will evoke one of four reactions from his readers: I didn't know that, I never looked at it that way before, you said exactly what I feel, but I didn't know how to express it, or I hate you and everything you stand for (1999: xi). These reactions seem a worthy goal for any book that attempts to examine and explain complex issues. Even if the book evokes the last reaction at least it should foster a debate on the ideas. It is time to begin the debate on the future on international aviation. I believe that you will find it an exciting and challenging journey.

References

Air Transport Association (2007), 'Quarterly Cost Index: US Passenger Airlines', Available at: http://www.airlines.org/economics/finance/Cost+Index.htm.

Air Transport Association (2002), *State of the Airline Industry: A Report on Recent Trends for U.S. Air Carriers*, Air Transport Association.

Air Transport Action Group (2008), 'Facts & Figures', Air Transport Action Group, Switzerland, Available at: http://www.atag.org/content/showfacts.asp?folderid=430&level1=2&level2=430&.

Anderson, P., and Tushman, M. (1990), 'Technological Discontinuities and Dominant Designs: A Cyclical Model of Technological Change', *Administrative Science Quarterly* 35, no. 1 (March): pp. 604–33.

Aris, S. (2002), *Close to the Sun: How Airbus Challenged America's Domination of the Skies*, Arum Press, London.

BBC News (1999a), 'Belgian National Airline Bankrupt,' BCC News online edition, November 7, www.bbc.co.uk.

BBC News (1999b), 'BA to Fly Flag Again'. BBC News Online Edition, June 6, www.bbc.co.uk.

Bianco, A. (1999), 'The Warren Buffet You Don't Know: Ace Stockpicker, of course-and now, an empire-builder', *Business Week*, July 5, pp. 55–66.

Foss, B. (2002), 'Airlines Expect to Lose $8 billion', Associated Press Wire Service, September 26.

Friedman, T.L. (1999) *The Lexus and the Olive Tree*, Farrar, Straus, 7 Giroux, New York.

Gould, S.J. and Eldredge, N. (1977), 'Punctuated Equilibria: The Tempo and Mode of Evolution Reconsidered', *Paleobiology*, vol 3, pp. 115–51.

Graham, B. (1995), *Geography and Air Transport*, John Wiley & Sons, New York.

Hall, W., Grant, J., Done, K., and Cameron, D. (2001), 'Swissair Grounding Causes Travel Chaos', October 2.

Hannan, M.T. and Freeman, J. (1984), 'Structural Inertia and Organizational Change', *American Sociological Review*, vol. 49, pp. 149–64.

IATA (2005), 'Economic Briefing: Airline Profitability: US vs. Rest of World', December 7, Available at: http://www.iata.org/economics.

Kahn, A.P. (1988), *Economics of Regulation*, Wiley & Sons, New York.

Kane, R.M. (1998), *Air Transportation*, Kendall/Hunt Publishing Company, Dubuque, Iowa.

Loomis, C. and Buffet, W. (1999), 'Mr Buffet on the Stock Market', *Fortune*, Special Issue, vol. 140 (10), pp. 212–20.

Lowenfeld, A. (1975), 'A New Take-off for International Air Transport', *Foreign Affairs*, vol. 54, p. 47.

Mandel, M.J. (2000), 'The Next Downturn', *Business Week,* October 9, pp.173–80.

Miller, A. (1998), *Strategic Management* (3rd ed), Irwin-McGraw-Hill, Boston, MA.

Rosen, S.D. (1995), 'Corporate Restructuring: A Labor Perspective' in Peter Cappelli (ed.), *Airlin Labor Relations in the Global Era: The New Frontier*, ILR Press, Ithaca, New York, pp. 31–40.

Schumpeter, J.A. (1949), *The Theory of Economic Development*, Harvard University Press, Cambridge, MA.

Sinha, D. (2001), *Deregulation and Liberalization of the Airline Industry: Asia, Europe, North America, and Oceania*, Ashgate Publishing, Aldershot.

Sochor, E. (1991), *The Politics of International Aviation*, University of Iowa Press, Iowa City.

Sparaco, P. and Wall, R. (2001), 'Europeans Map Airline Survival', *Aviation Week and Space Technology,* September 24, pp. 35–6.

Sparaco, P. (2001), 'The Curtain Falls on Sabena', *Aviation Week and Space Technology*, November 12, pp. 43–4.

Tessler, J (2008), 'Northrop, EADS win $35B Air Force deal', *The Associated Press*, Available at: http://abcnews.go.com/print?id=4367303.

Toffler, A. (1970), *Future Shock*, Bantam Books, New York.

Tushman, M.L. and Anderson, P. (1986), 'Technological Discontinuities and Organizational Environments', *Administrative Science Quarterly,* vol. 31, pp. 439–65.

Wells, A.T. (1994), *Air Transportation: A Management Perspective,* Wadsworth Publishing Company, Belmont, CA.

Wolf, S.M. (1995), 'Where Do We Go from Here: A Management Perspective', in P. Cappelli (ed.) *Airline Labor Relations in the Global Era: The New Frontier*, ILR Press, Cornell.

PART I
In the Beginning (1903–1950)

Chapter 2
Invention to Commercial Success Inventions

Innovations and Commercializations

An idea is said to have been invented when it has been proven to work. It "becomes an 'innovation' only when it can be replicated reliably on a meaningful scale at practical costs. If the idea is sufficiently important, such as the telephone, the digital computer, or a commercial aircraft, it is called a 'basic innovation' and it creates a new industry or transforms an existing industry" (Senge, 1990). Senge (1990), author of *The Fifth Discipline: The Art & Practice of the Learning Organization*, goes on to note that ideas move from invention to innovation by combining different technologies, often from isolated developments in diverse fields. Until these diverse components come together in the right combination the product is not truly able to achieve its potential as a successful commercial product (commercialization). Until it is able to prove itself safe and reliable it may capture the imagination of the daring, those first movers who are willing to try anything new and different, but it will not capture the market, the laggards who are not interested in thrills but in performance and cost. The first fifty years of heavier-than-air flight would lay the groundwork for the conquest of the laggards and a new commercial aviation industry.

First, of course, an idea needs pioneers and aviation had more than its share of larger-than-life characters. There are accounts dating back to the twelfth century BCE. of people in China riding in balloons. The quintessential Renaissance Man himself, Leonardo Da Vinci, sketched images in the sixteenth century of craft he believed capable of supporting a man in flight. However, it was not until 1783 that history has its first confirmable account of a manned lighter-than-air flight. Jean-Francois Pilatre de Rozier and Francois d'Arlandes flew over Paris for 25 minutes while the residents of the city watched and wondered. However, simply floating with the wind was not enough; a way needed to be found to direct these lighter-than-air craft. Thus was born the dirigible and the name forever linked in the minds of many with these dirigibles is Count Ferdinand von Zeppelin whose airships were carrying passengers and mail on regularly scheduled trips by 1914. However, even without the tragic 1936 disaster of the Hindenburg in Lakehurst, New Jersey, it is doubtful that the dirigible could have held anything more than a minor place in aviation besides the new heavier-than-air craft that took to the sky in the first decade of the twentieth century (Carlson, 2002).

Orville Wright became the first person to pilot a powered heavier-than-air craft on the fateful day of December 17, 1903. He remained aloft for 12 seconds and covered a distance of only 120 feet, but this single event would change the way people around the world viewed the sky; heavier-than-air flight had been invented. For the next thirty years, the new industry would struggle through a series of experiments in search of the right combination of component technologies to make it a viable, commercial product. At first much of the focus was on the development of military aircraft, then airmail/cargo aircraft, but more was needed for viable commercial passenger travel. Finally, the Douglas DC-3 would demonstrate the right combination of features to make passenger air travel safe, comfortable, and economical to operate. The DC-3 combined five key innovations—variable-pitch propellers, retractable landing gear, lightweight molded body construction, radial air-cooled engine, and wing flaps—to produce a plane that was aerodynamic and economical to operate (Senge, 1990). This chapter traces the beginning of this journey from invention to commercially viable product. The airplane will go from a barnstorming thrill to an essential tool of military operations to a transportation mode for the well-to-do, time-sensitive, risk-taker.

Visionaries

During the three years after their historic flight, the Wright brothers worked to improve the reliability, range, and maneuverability of their design, receiving US patent 821,393 in 1906 (Paradowski, 2002). By 1908, the Wright brothers were working under a contract with the US War Department to build aircraft for the Army (Tischauser, 2002). In 1909, the Wright Company was incorporated in Dayton, Ohio and over the next several years, would pursue a lawsuit against another aviation pioneer, Glenn Curtiss, claiming that he violated their patent for ailerons, devices to control the roll of an aircraft during flight. In fact, the Wright technology involved wing-warping rather than the use of separate attachments to the wing that would achieve the same thing, however, in the early days of aviation these distinctions were lost to most people outside the industry.

Today, the Curtiss White Wing is cited as the first United States plane to take off on wheels and use ailerons to control roll in turns, the point of contention with the Wrights. Another Curtiss aircraft, the June Bug, would set a new speed record in 1909 at the first great international air competition in Rheims, France and become the first flight filmed and witnessed by the press. Curtiss would go on to set a number of firsts including the first US licensed pilot, the first person to land an aircraft on the deck of a ship in 1910, and the designer of the first aircraft to cross the Atlantic. He founded the Curtiss Aeroplane and Motor Company before World War I and engaged both in aircraft design and flight training for the US Army and Navy. In addition to the legal battles over the invention of ailerons, Curtiss would side with Albert Zahn, Director of the Smithsonian Institute in Washington, DC, suggesting that Samuel Langley, not the Wright Brothers, actually invented the airplane. Even though the courts would eventually side with the Wrights on the question of ailerons granting some money to Orville, the surviving brother, and the Smithsonian would recognize the Wrights as first in flight, Orville would sell out all of their patents by 1915 and the company that they founded in 1909 would be bought by Glenn Curtiss in 1929 and become known as the Curtiss-Wright Corporation (Niemann, 2007; Tischauser, 2002).

Two other aviation pioneers would get their start before World War I, William Boeing and Donald W. Douglas. On July 15, 1916, Bill Boeing would incorporate the company founded the previous year, Pacific Aero Products. The company would begin by producing a seaplane copied from a Martin aircraft. They would also work on an aircraft later called the Model C that they hoped to sell to the US Navy (50 would be ordered with the start of WWI). This contract and one to manufacture the Curtiss HS-2L would occupy the company through the war (Serling, 1992). Meanwhile, Donald Douglas would go to work for the Glen L. Martin Co. as a chief engineer where he would design the Martin MB-1 bomber, the first US-designed bomber to enter production (Boeing Chronology, 2007).

On the other side of the Atlantic, other visionaries were hard at work. In 1909, Louis Blériot became the first pilot to cross the English Channel in a craft he designed himself called the Blériot XI. Two years later, this plane would go to war with the Italian forces in North Africa (Allaz, 2004). Another pioneer, Anthony Fokker, started his first aviation company at the age of 21 and built his first aircraft, called the Spin, in 1910. Both the Spin I and Spin II would crash. Spin III, however, would be sold to the German army. Fokker would go on to design the tri-plane made famous by Manfred von Richthofen, the Red Baron, in World War I.

Airplane in War

The US government intervened in the lawsuit between the Wright brothers and Curtiss as the US entered World War I. The Curtiss Company would go on to become the largest US aircraft manufacturer in World War I, supplying over 10,000 aircraft to the war effort. The US Navy for whom Curtiss began building planes in 1911 would also use the Curtiss NC-4 to make the first trans-Atlantic flight in 1919 (Marchman, 2002; Roseberry, 1991). The French and the English entered World War I with the English-Channel-crossing Bleriot XI. The English also deployed the BE.2 designed by Geoffrey de Havilland prior to the war. These aircraft started the war classified as scouts and many would end the war with the same designation, however, Fokker would introduce his *Eindecker* series of monoplanes equipped with fixed, synchronized, forward-firing machine guns during this war and they would become known on the Western Front as the 'Fokker Scourge' (McDermott, 2002; Milstein, 2002). In addition to the famous Red Baron tri-plane, the British took to the skies in an aircraft designed by Royal Aircraft called the Sopwith Camel, the favorite aircraft of Snoopy from the Charlie Brown cartoons. Other aircraft such as the DH-4 were used in battle as bombers or in support of advancing ground forces. Another important force in the world of aviation, Rolls-Royce, would find the wartime experience invaluable in staking its claim to the future. Rolls-Royce came out of WWI ready to take its place as one of the foremost manufacturers of aircraft engines.

In short, the aircraft that emerged from World War I would be sleeker, faster, more powerful, and better armed. World War I saw the introduction of the low-wing aircraft, the all-metal body, and the thickened cantilever wing, however, most of the aircraft that entered the war would not emerge; the attrition rate on all sides would be very high. The mass production of aircraft needed to supply the war effort had supported many of the newly emerging aviation companies. With the end of the war, most of these companies had to find other means of support although the military was still the best game in town and the lucky few would continue to research and produce the newest weapon in the military arsenal (Allaz, 2004).

Back to Business

In the years immediately after WWI, the fledgling US aircraft manufacturers continued to focus on the military side of the market with some initial forays into aircraft designed for the growing airmail market. Both Boeing and Douglas introduced an airmail plane during 1925, the Model 40 and M-1 respectively. When Boeing replaced the old Liberty engines with the new Pratt & Whitney 425-horsepower, air-cooled Wasp engine, the Model 40 not only became a reliable cargo craft but the addition of two passenger seats made it Boeing's first commercial passenger aircraft. This new engine made it superior to its competitors—the Douglas M-2 and the Curtiss Carrier Pigeon—which continued to use the Liberty. Boeing bid for and won one of the early airmail routes and established its first subsidiary, Boeing Air Transport, to handle the growing airmail business (Serling, 1992).

In 1927, Boeing purchased Pacific Air Transport (PAT) and introduced the Model 80 and 80A trimotors equipped with Pratt & Whitney Hornet engines and capable of carrying 18 passengers attended by a registered nurse who acted as a flight attendant. It should be noted that the engines of the 80A were enclosed in streamlined cowlings that improved their performance. In 1929, the Boeing/Pratt & Whitney relationship grew even closer when the two companies merged to form United Aircraft & Transport Corporation. The new company acquired several other aircraft companies including Stearman Aircraft, Northrop Aircraft, and Sikorsky. The new holding company purchased several airlines including Varney, Stout, and National Air Transport which it combined with BAT to form United Air Lines (UAL), Inc. While the company was consolidating, it was also working on its next major entry into the market, the B-247. This aircraft started the familiar Boeing numbering scheme. Given the company structure, it is not surprising that United Air Lines took delivery of the first 60 B-247s, leaving the other carriers to look for their own answer to the fleet question (Johansen, 2002; Serling, 1992). The airmail scandal that resulted in the Air Mail Act of 1934 hit Boeing very hard. Airline executives who had participated in the illegal 'division' of mail contracts with the US Post Office were prohibited from holding office in an airline and no airline that had participated could bid on an air mail contract. Further, aircraft and engine companies were prohibited from owning airlines. This scandal would break up the holding company of United Aircraft and Transport and destroy one of William Boeing's great dreams (Serling, 1992).

For the Boeing Company, the exclusive deal with United also proved to be a very bad move, but for the Douglas Aircraft Company it started a wonderful thing (Serling, 1992). Trans World Airlines (TWA), anxious to replace its Fokker-10 trimotors after the fatal 1931 crash involving Knute Rockne, was looking for a plane. The first plane they considered was the B-247, but the UAL order pushed the TWA delivery date well into the future. After the TWA Technical Committee examined several other proposed aircraft, it chose the Douglas Aircraft Company and the DC-1. The DC-1 introduced in 1933 would be the first of a series of aircraft destined to dominate the industry for many years (Rummel, 1991). The DC-2 released the following year was capable of carrying 14 passengers for 1,000 miles. With the introduction of the DC-2 even United would race to sell its 247s for less than half their original price (Serling, 1992). In 1935, the best known plane in the series, the DC-3, would be released. With 14 seats capable of folding into sleeping berths, the DC-3, first sold to American Airlines, would set a new standard in passenger travel. By the 1940s, approximately 90 percent of the passenger aircraft flying in the US would be either DC-2s or DC-3s (Clouatre, 2002).

Another legendary US manufacturer, Lockheed Aircraft, would be incorporated in the years between the wars. Lockheed, founded by Allan Loughead and Jack Northrop, began work on a Northrop designed aircraft later called the Vega. Wiley Post used the Vega to set his around-the-world record of 8 days, 16 hours in 1931. Lockheed was purchased in 1929 by Detroit Aircraft Company. Jack Northrop left to found Avion Corporation, later known as Northrop Corporation. Detroit Aircraft went into bankruptcy during the Great Depression and emerged after a buyout in 1932 as the Lockheed Aircraft Company. Lockheed went on to build the Electra in which Amelia Earhart would make her last flight (McCoy, 2002).

In Europe, Anthony Fokker incorporated his aircraft company in the Netherlands in 1919 and released the F.II, one of the first passenger transport aircraft in 1920. Although he became the main supplier of KLM, the Dutch airline, his passenger aircraft would fall out of favor when Douglas introduced his all-metal aircraft with retractable undercarriages (Milstein, 2002). In England, de Havilland continued to focus on his single and two-seat bi-plane powered by the Gipsy engine. First came the Gipsy Moth, the Tiger Moth, the Hornet Moth, and then the Moth Minor, a low wing, wooden monoplane. De Havilland, like Fokker, would continue to produce cutting-edge aircraft for military and civil use through both wars and beyond.

A Strange, yet Beautiful, Relationship

The aviation industry has always been imperfect by economic standards. First and foremost, it is characterized in both the manufacturing and the airline sides of the industry by small numbers. Perfect competition, according to Adam Smith, is possible when there are many buyers and many sellers. It is assumed that such a market will drive prices down toward costs. Even in the early days before crisis would fuel consolidation and market power would come to rival innovation, there were a limited number of buyers and suppliers. This has not meant that there has been no competition between manufacturers or within the airline and manufacturing sectors, but at times it has led to some very strange relationships—at some times too close for comfort and at other times as antagonistic as a divorcing couple. Airlines would come to play one manufacturer off against another while at the same time cooperating closely on design and specifications. They would threaten to 'go to the competitors' and then seek out special first delivery rights. For their side, the manufacturers will come to the airlines with concepts seeking orders for yet-to-be-built planes, promising first delivery for key orders, and, eventually, using political clout of all forms to make the sell. These patterns started early.

The story of the DC-1 illustrates this close but imperfect relationship. Frustrated with the progress of his Technical Committee, Jack Frye, the TWA Chief Executive Officer (CEO), would write directly to the manufacturers saying the airline was interested in purchasing ten or more aircraft meeting an attached specification and performance. He requested them to give notice of interest and approximate date of first delivery. His requirements: capacity for 12 or more passengers, 1,080 mile range at 150 miles per hour and a one-engine-out ceiling of 10,000 feet. Three companies would respond—Sikorsky, General Aviation, a subsidiary of General Motors who had purchased the troubled Fokker, and Douglas Aircraft. TWA would now proceed with a series of visits, reviews, and expert analyses that would pit each aircraft maker against the other to improve performance, reduce costs, and speed up delivery dates (Rummel, 1991).

The Next War

The decade of the 1930s saw the beginning of a race in military aviation between the Great Powers of Europe. In Germany, Junkers, Dornier, Messerschmitt, Focke-Wulf, and Heinkel emerged as leading aircraft manufacturers turning out a series of aircraft that would lead the Germany Luftwaffe into World War II. The Heinkel He-178 became the first turbojet aircraft to fly successfully in 1939 and began a new era of aerial warfare. Other notable achievements of these manufacturers include the Me-262 Komet which utilized a thrust rocket motor to travel at almost 600 miles an hour and the Ju-287 which sported forward-swept wings over back-swept wings, the Messerschmitt P-1011 with a swept-wing design later used in the

Us on the F-14, and the Blitz, a twin-engine Arado 234B bomber capable of speeds of up to 461 miles per hour (Graetzer, 2002).

In Great Britain, the defense industry tripled its employment between 1930 and 1936 even as the industry struggled to adapt its manufacturing methods to mass production. Still, the Hawker Hurricane, Spitfire, and Lancaster bomber would prove the value in the coming war (McCoy, 2002). The Spitfire gained fame during the famous Battle of Britain. By the end of the war, the Spitfire version equipped with the Rolls-Royce Griffon engine would reach speeds of 460 miles per hour (Wheeler, 2002).

In the US, Boeing had continued work despite the airmail controversy on two aircraft designs that would be critical to the war effort—the B-17 Flying Fortress and the B-29 Superfortress. Although these two aircraft represented only 17 percent of all US bombers, they were responsible for 46 percent of the ordinance dropped on Germany during the war. Further, the B-17 has been credited with shooting down 67 percent of the enemy fighters in the European theatre of operations. At the height of production, Boeing was producing 363 B-17s a month for the Army Air Corp (Johansen, 2002; Serling, 1992).

Seeing the Enemy

The airplane had grown far more deadly in the decade leading up to World War II, but another invention was to be the salvation of Britain during the early years of the war. Radar, an outgrowth of the radio experiments of the 1930s, sent radio waves out into the atmosphere and measured the time that elapsed before the signal reflected off of a solid object and returned to the receiver. Great Britain had begun deploying this new technology along their coast before the start of the war and its use during the early years of the war would help Britain beat back the waves of German bombers that would stream across the Channel. In addition to detecting incoming aircraft, the system could be used to direct intercepting aircraft to their target, help aircraft determine their height from the ground, and identify friendly and enemy aircraft with the use of small broadcasting beacons. The "enemy" would eventually deploy radar as well, but the invention of the microwave-cavity magnetron which generated a high-power radio wave and required a smaller antenna would continue to give the British the advantage during the war. Of course, this new technology had civilian applications and would become the backbone of the civil aviation systems that developed after the end of World War II. In fact, the system currently in use today to track, identify, and direct aircraft is not very different from this early system, a fact that we will discuss in Chapter 20 as the industry searches for a twenty-first century solution.

Conquering the Civilian Market

During its first fifty years of life, the aviation industry witnessed a number of high profile firsts (Table 2.1) and captured the imagination of a whole generation, but it had not yet conquered the traveling public, ordinary citizens who would pay to ride on a flight from point A to point B. The airplane had proven its value in war and was being mass produced on a large scale by the end of World War II. The basic elements of a successful and viable product had been invented and tested in the heat of war. Still, the airplane probably still looked in 1950 like the playground of the rich and the daring; it was not yet the transportation mode of choice for visiting grandma in Iowa or Ontario. The task of creating a commercial aviation industry that would attract this kind of a market would be left to the pioneers of the next fifty years who would make flying a commonplace occurrence, even a necessity (Chapter 7). First, the industry would conquer the cargo market, specifically airmail. Chapter 3 will discuss the development of this industry and how it came to shape the future of the US airline industry. The tale of how a few daring individuals would be thrown on top of the mail will have to wait, but it would come.

Table 2.1   Aviation firsts

Date	Event
1903	First heavier-than-air flight Wilbur and Orville Wright
1906	First European flight Alberto Santos-Dumont
1908	First airplane fatality Lt Thomas E. Selfridge
1909	First cross-channel flight Louis Blériot
	First international aviation competition Rheims, France
1910	First licensed woman pilot Baroness de la Roche
	First aviation conference Paris, France
1913	First multi-engine aircraft Igor Sikorsky
1914	First aerial combat
1917	First black combat pilot Eugene J. Bullard
1918	First regular US airmail

Table 2.1   *Concluded*

1919	First transatlantic flight Lt Cmdr Albert Read
1921	First naval vessel sunk by aircraft
1924	First round-the-world flight Maj. Frederick Marin
1927	First solo non-stop transatlantic flight Charles A. Lindbergh
1931	First non-stop transpacific flight Hugh Herndon and Clyde Pangborn
1932	First woman transatlantic flight Amelia Earhart
1933	First round-the-world solo Wiley Post
1937	First successful helicopter flight Hanna Reitsch
1939	First turbojet flight He-178
1947	First piloted supersonic flight Capt. Charles E. Yeagar

Source: Information gathered from Infoplease. www.infoplease/ipa/A0004537.html

References

Allaz, C. (2004), *The History of Air Cargo and Airmail from the 18th Century*, Christopher Foyle Publishing, Paris.

Carlson, R.V. (2002), 'Dirigibles' in Tracy Irons-Georges (ed.) *Encyclopedia of Flight*, pp. 211–5, Salem Press, Pasadena, CA.

Clouatre, D. (2002), 'DC Plane Family' in Tracy Irons-Georges (ed.) *Encyclopedia of Flight*, pp. 205–7, Salem Press, Pasadena, CA.

Graetzer, D.G. (2002), 'World War II' in Tracy Irons-Georges (ed.) *Encyclopedia of Flight*, pp. 779–85, Salem Press, Pasadena, CA.

Johansen, B.E. (2002), 'Boeing' in Tracy Irons-Georges (ed.) *Encyclopedia of Flight*, pp. 154–6, Salem Press, Pasadena, CA.

Marchman, J.F. (2002), 'Glenn H. Curtiss' in Tracy Irons-Georges (ed.) *Encyclopedia of Flight*, pp. 203–4, Salem Press, Pasadena, CA.

McCoy, M.G. (2002), 'Lockheed Martin' in Tracy Irons-Georges (ed.) *Encyclopedia of Flight*, pp. 420–423, Salem Press, Pasadena, CA.

McDermott, D.P. (2002), 'World War I' in Tracy Irons-Georges (ed.) *Encyclopedia of Flight*, pp. 774–9, Salem Press, Pasadena, CA.

Milstein, R.L. (2002), 'Fokker Aircraft' in Tracy Irons-Georges (ed.) *Encyclopedia of Flight*, pp. 275–8, Salem Press, Pasadena, CA.

Niemann, G. (2007), *Big Brown: The Untold Story of UPS*, John Wiley & Sons, San Francisco, CA.

Paradowski, R.J. (2002), 'WrightFlyer' in Tracy Irons-Georges (ed.) *Encyclopedia of Flight*, pp. 786–8, Salem Press, Pasadena, CA.

Roseberry, C.R. (1991), Glenn Curtiss: Pioneer of Flight, Syracuse University Press, Syracuse, NY.

Rummel, R.W. (1991), Howard Hughes and TWA, Smithsonian Institution Press, Washington.

Senge, P.M. (1990), The Fifth Discipline: The Art & Practice of the Learning Organization, Doubleday, New York.

Serling, R.J. (1992), Legend and Legacy: The Story of Boeing and its People, St. Martin Press, New York.

Tischauser, L.V. (2002), 'Wright Brothers' in Tracy Irons-Georges (ed.) *Encyclopedia of Flight*, pp. 785–6, Salem Press, Pasadena, CA.

Wheeler, H (2002), 'Spitfire', in Tracy Irons-Georges (ed.) *Encyclopedia of Flight*, pp. 625–6, Salem Press, Pasadena, CA.

Website

Boeing, (www.boeing.com/history/chronology)

Chapter 3
The Other Source of Revenue

Following the Money

The first non-mail cargo flight took place on November 7, 1910 from Dayton to Columbus, Ohio. Commissioned by Max Morehouse to celebrate the annual autumn sale of his Home Dry Goods Store, the Wright Model B carried the 200 pounds of silk and ribbon 70 miles to successfully deliver its goods. While this delivery is a noteworthy first, it should probably be considered an even more successful marketing and publicity event (Allaz, 2004). In the beginning, airmail and air cargo were more novelty and show than serious business. In fact, 1911 marked the first airmail exhibition in which souvenir cards and stamps were flown around a local area in India and then sold to collectors. Other such events followed in Great Britain, France, Germany, and the United States. In 1911, The Grahame-White Aviation Company carried 130,000 cards and letters between London and Windsor Castle as part of the celebration for the coronation of George V (Glines, 1990).

While, the idea of airmail and air cargo fired the imagination of aviators and some businessmen around the world, it was the William Randolph Hearst announcement of the creation of a $50,000 prize to the first pilot who could fly coast to coast in the US within 30 days that set off efforts to prove this new technology. Calbraith P. Rodgers was one of the pilots determined to collect the prize. He eventually completed the coast-to-coast flight, crashing only 16 times. Unfortunately, it took him 55 days and he was unable to collect the Hearst prize (Glines, 1990). Others would follow, but it was not until the US government got involved that regularly scheduled, transcontinental airmail became a reality in the US. In Europe, sporadic efforts would be interrupted by the First World War.

Officially Speaking

India not only holds the honor of having the first airmail exhibition but the first official airmail flight on February 18, 1911, however, like so many other efforts this first flight did not translate into a regular service (Allaz, 2004). In the US, the Post Office Department had asked for $50,000 in 1911 to explore airmail delivery, but it was not until 1916 that funds were made available. By 1918, Congress was prepared to authorize $100,000 for an experimental airmail route between Washington and New York. It was left up to Major Reuben H. Fleet of the Army Air Service to make this air service work despite the fact that there was

1) a shortage of pilots, 2) almost no pilots with cross-country flying experience, 3) no adequate maps, 4) few experienced mechanics, and 5) no planes modified to carry airmail. Still, with President Wilson set to attend the official take-off, Glen Curtiss was contacted and asked to modify his Curtis JN6H to leave out the front seat and front controls and add a second gas tank. While this experiment had its share of mishaps and lost pilots, it was deemed a success and the US Post Office Department officially took over the service in August 1918, buying their own planes and hiring their own pilots. According to official records, the Army Air Service delivered 193,021 pounds of mail completing 92 percent of their scheduled flights. They flew 128,255 route miles without a fatality. Ben Lipsner who had officially organized the experiment for the Army Air Service became the first Superintendent of the United States Aerial Mail Service. One of his first tasks upon assuming his position was to commission the design of the first aircraft specifically for airmail delivery. This plane, the Standard Aero-mail, was designed by the Standard Aircraft Company of Elizabeth, New Jersey. It was powered by a 150 horse power engine and had a load specification of 180 pounds. It could travel at speeds of 100 miles per hour and climb to a height of 6,000 feet in 10 minutes. The next task was to begin transcontinental service with the first leg from New York to Cleveland followed over the next two years by New York–Chicago, Chicago–Omaha, Chicago–St Louis, Chicago–Minneapolis, and Omaha–San Francisco. On 1 July 1924, regular transcontinental service was inaugurated. In 1923 and 1924, the Airmail Service received the Collier Trophy for "the greatest achievement in aviation in America" (Glines, 1990).

The US Post Office would gradually close down its Airmail Service with the passage of the Kelly Act of 1925 entitled "An Act to Encourage Commercial Aviation and to Authorize the Postmaster General to Contract for the Mail Service." US Representative Clyde Kelly who sponsored the act believed that private operators, not the government, should assume the risks and reap the rewards of the airmail business. With this act, advertisements were placed in newspapers asking for bids on eight feeder airmail routes to be awarded by the Postmaster General. By 1926, 12 airmail contracts had been awarded. The last flight of the Post Office was conducted in 1927 (Kane, 1998). In order to qualify for these routes, individuals had to be US citizens backed by at least 75 percent US controlled capital stock. Aircraft had to qualify for airworthiness certificates and pilots had to produce certificates of fitness (Glines, 1990).

Table 3.1 lists the route number and the company receiving the award. There are several items of note in this list. First, the first route to be put into operation was Ford Air Transport. This company was another venture by a man more associated with the automobile, Henry Ford. Ford Air Transport manufactured a plane designed by William B. Stout. This aircraft was an all-metal monoplane with internally stressed wings and a liberty engine. A later version, the Ford Trimotor, would go on to become one of the great classic airplanes of the period. Second, Western Air Express which had the airmail route from Los Angeles to Salt Lake City would become one of the first carriers to try to boost revenues by carrying passengers. In 1927, Western received a grant from the Daniel Guggenheim Fund to purchase passenger aircraft. A slightly later effort to combine cargo and passengers was Transcontinental Air Transport (TAT). TAT planned to use train by night and air by day to offer luxury passenger service. The venture lost almost $3 million in the first year and a half. TAT would later merge with several other carriers to become Transcontinental & Western Air (TWA). Eventually, the name would become Trans World Airlines (Glines, 1990). Third, it should be noted that the original list of contract airmail (CAM) awards includes carriers that would go on to form the nucleus of familiar US major and national carriers. National Air Transport and Pacific Air Transport would go on to combine with a later CAM awardee, Boeing Air Transport, to form United Airlines (Davies, 1998). Varney Speed Lines would go on to become Continental Airlines (Davies, 1984). Robertson Aircraft Corporation would become one of eighty carriers merged to form American Airlines (Bedwell, and Wegg, 2000). All American Aviation who would receive a CAM in 1939 would go on to become US Airways (Jones and Jones, 1999). This consolidation would not occur by accident. As the TAT and Western experiments proved, passengers could provide good additional revenue; airmail revenue was essential. Fourth, these routes would establish a basic pattern of air transportation in the US that would continue to this day. Creating this pattern of trunk routes, large coast-to-coast operations flowing east to west, would be the "mission" of Walter Brown.

Table 3.1   The first contract airmail routes

Route Number	Company
Cam 1	Colonial Air Lines
Cam 2	Robertson Aircraft Corp.
Cam 3	National Air Transport
Cam 4	Western Air Express
Cam 5	Varney Speed Lines
Cam 6 and 7	Ford Air Transport
Cam 8	Pacific Air Transport
Cam 9	Charles Dickenson
Cam 10	Florida Airways Corp.
Cam 11	Clifford Ball
Cam 12	Western Air Express

Source: Kane, R.M. Air Transportation

In 1929, Walter Folger Brown was appointed postmaster general. Brown would work diligently for the passage of the Air Mail Act of 1930, also known as the McNary-Watres Airmail Act, which gave the postmaster total control over the airmail bidding process. He believed that an airline business model should be based on passenger revenue, not excess airmail payments (Glines, 1990). According to Brown, the aviation industry suffered from four problems: "1) being unwilling to invest in new equipment, 2) operating obsolete aircraft, 3) demonstrating questionable safety performance from cost cutting, and 4) maintaining marginal operations with no growth" (Kane, 1998: 107). To remedy this situation, Brown eliminated the competitive bidding process for contract airmail routes in favor of a system that granted awards to large, well-financed operators. Only these large operators were invited to attend the so-called spoils conferences that were held in Washington, DC to award contracts. In essence, the US government through the postmaster forced small carriers to merge in order to obtain the lucrative airmail contracts (Glines, 1968). Brown envisioned an air map of the US with three transcontinental routes–a northern, a central, and a southern. These routes would be connected by shorter, regional north-south routes (Glines, 1990). A look at a map of the early airmail routes and stops (http://www.airmailpioneers.org/) will show that he succeeded to some extent, creating a long east-west trunk route with shorter north-south legs. This general structure would be the backbone for the airline networks that followed. Unfortunately, this heavy-handed "indirect" intervention did not set well with many stakeholders. Certainly, the carriers left out of the spoils conferences had ample reason to complain and they did.

By 1932, charges of graft and collusion led US President Franklin Roosevelt to cancel all contracts and return responsibility for the airmail to the US Army. It was decided that the Army Air Corps would operate only 12 of the 26 civilian routes. Unfortunately, even this reduction was not enough for the Corps which had a limited number of pilots and even fewer with night flying or instrument experience. Their aircraft often did not have landing, navigation or cockpit lights nor were they equipped with the new gyro instruments or radios. Given these deficiencies, it is not surprising that the Corps quickly ran into trouble. After a series of accidents, the airmail service was returned to private operators by 1 June 1934 (Glines, 1990). The Airmail Act of 1934, also known as the Black-McKellar Act provided for a return to the competitive bidding process of the past and prohibited awards to carriers involved in the supposed collusion. Three of these carriers American Airways, Eastern Air Transport and Transcontinental & Western Air changed their names respectively to American Airlines, Eastern Airlines, and Transcontinental & Western Air Inc. to avoid this restriction and continue in the airmail business. The administration of contracts would be divided between the Post Office, Interstate Commerce Commission, and the Department of Commerce. Beginning in 1938, rates would be set by the newly created Civil Aviation Bureau (Kane, 1998).

Mail, Morale, and War

In Europe, the years just before World War I saw a number of efforts to start airmail services. In 1911, Henri Pequet transported 6,500 letters and postcards from Allahabad to Naini Junction in France while in Italy a similar shipment was made between Bologna and Venice. In 1912, both Germany and Japan celebrated their first official airmail flight, however, as World War I approached the balloons of Paris, which had operated during the Prussian siege of the city between 1870–71, remained the only example of a regularly scheduled airmail service (Allaz, 2004). Europe would have to wait until the end of the war to achieve this milestone, however, military airmail was established between several areas of the continent during the war. For the most part, these services utilized military aircraft, but allowed some civilian correspondence.

As the First World War wound down, aircraft had a new cargo and a new mission in the form of humanitarian relief. In 1919, an airlift was established between Folkestone and Ghent to provide bedding, medicine, and food. In France, similar efforts were organized between Paris–Lille, Paris–Maubeuge–Valenciennes, Paris–Longwy, Paris–Mulhouse, Paris–Strasbourg, and Paris–Brussels. Most of these efforts were short-lived, but they did give a number of individuals and firms experience in airmail and air cargo. This experience combined with the flying experience of former soldiers would prove useful after the war when nations moved to re-establish their commercial aviation systems. As we will discuss in Chapter 4, Europe would move quickly in association with the Universal Postal Union (UPU) to integrate airmail into the postal system of Europe.

Like in the US, airmail would continue to receive priority in the air cargo business of Europe until after the Second World War, however, several airlines did attempt to expand into other forms of cargo. By 1938, Deutsche Lufthansa was already the world's leading scheduled carrier for freight, a position that it continued to hold in 2008 according to the latest Air Cargo World survey (Air Cargo World, 2008). It would introduce the first long-haul transoceanic freight charter in 1939. According to Allaz (2004) a total of 57,000 tonnes of cargo was shipped by air in 1938. As is still true today, the most common items of shipment were highly perishable, urgent, and high value. These included newspapers, bank notes, perfumes, spare parts, and the occasional live animal. With the introduction of new aircraft designed with cargo operations in mind such as the Junkers W33 and the Ju52, the volume and size of cargo improved lowering the cost. By 1940 TACA (Transportes Aéreos Centroamericanos) was the world's leading all-freight company, shipping 12,640 tonnes of goods throughout Central America. In other regions with poor or challenging surface transportation features, the idea of offering bulk, low rates for air shipment was considered and tried, however, the volumes of air freight would continue to be relatively minor in the period between the First and Second World War.

A Brown Beginning

In 1899, eleven-year-old Jim Casey went to work to help support his family. His first job was with the delivery department at Bon Marche, a Seattle department store. From here, he would go on to start several of his own businesses in the area including a messenger and telephone service. American Messenger Company was founded in 1907. It would later merge with the Motorcycle Delivery Company to become Merchants Parcel Delivery. This new company would handle outsource department store delivery with a small fleet of brown trucks. After World War I, the company would begin the process of expanding down the US west coast. They would purchase the Motor Parcel Company in Oakland, California and change the name again to United Parcel Service (UPS).

These early years would lay the foundation for many of the features that would later "define" UPS. The first, of course, was the color of their delivery vans, selected so that the original department store customers would not see them as a threat. Second, the early years established the pattern of learning the intimate details of an area and utilizing this knowledge to provide better, faster, time-definite service. Third, each new merger, acquisition, or key hire would bring more people into the family that would become UPS. These employees would be seen as the backbone of their success. When the company expanded to Los Angeles, it would advertise their delivery men as the type "you yourself would hire" and they would become known for their neat appearance and prompt, courteous service.

Evert "Mac" McDabe, one of the UPS partners, was an early enthusiast of the airplane. Eventually, he would convince the others to form United Air Express in 1929. United Air Express contracted with three air companies to fly packages delivered by UPS to selected airports. At the same time, UPS was looking to expand its delivery business into the New York City area. The Curtiss Aeroplane ad Motor Company which had recently merged with Wright Aeronautical to form the Curtiss-Wright Corporation made an offer to UPS to buy the company for $2 million and 600,000 shares in Curtiss Aeroplane. The UPS partners would remain with the company and were guaranteed management control for five years. This deal seemed a perfect way to expand the business to the east coast, but the financial collapse that followed the 1929 stock market crash ended the deal and UPS' first foray into the air service business (Niemann, 2007).

Conclusion

It has been noted that the first decade of aviation in the US was synonymous with airmail. In part, this was due to the drive of Otto Praeger who became the second Assistant Postmaster General in 1915 and Walter Folger Brown, Postmaster General beginning in 1929 who was determined to "create" the airline industry in the US. Even after the Post Office officially left the airmail delivery business to the private sector, its indirect influence was substantial and far-reaching. While the accomplishments of the early airmail pilots were significant steps in establishing airmail and air cargo as viable modes of transportation, it was probably the 1927 flight by Charles A. Lindbergh, himself an airmail pilot, that truly captured the imagination of the world and the attention of serious business investment. One month after the historic New York to Paris flight, there was a 20 percent increase in mail on contract mail routes (Glines, 1990).

Thirty-five years after the first air cargo flight, the world had not yet fully accepted the concept but had seen enough evidence of potential in air cargo to set the stage for the post-World War II industry that was to come. Like all things aviation, World War II would be a turning point. The technical innovations and individual and collective achievements that occur during this war will change the nature and shape the popular perception of the industry as it moves into the second half of the twentieth century. However, it would be the logistics revolution and the globalization movement of the latter part of the twentieth century that would make air cargo a force to be reckoned with in the aviation industry (Chapter 13). For now, the fantasy of the balloon would give way to the cold, hard calculation of governments and businessmen. These calculations are the subject of the next three chapters.

References

Air Cargo World (2008), 'Air Cargo World Survey: Air Cargo Excellence', March 2008, pp. 29–33.

Allaz, C. (2004), *The History of Air Cargo and Airmail from the 18th Century*, Christopher Foyle Publishing, Paris.

Bedwell, D. and Wegg, J. (2000), *Silverbird: The American Airlines Story*, Plymouth Press, Boston.

Davies, R.E.G. (1998), *Airlines of the United States Since 1914*, Smithsonian Institution Press, Washington, DC.

Davies, R.E.G. (1984), *Continental Airlines: The First Fifty Years*, Pioneer Publications, The Woodlands, TX.

Glines, C.V. (1990), *Airmail: How it all Began*, TAB Aero, Blue Ridge Summit, PA.

Glines, C.V. (1968), *The Saga of the Airmail*, D. Van Nostrand, Princeton, NJ.

Jones, G. and Jones, G.P. (1999), *U.S. Airways*, Ian Allan, Shepperton, England.

Kane, R.M. (1998), *Air Transportation*, 13th ed., Kendall/Hunt Publishing, Dubuque, IA.

Niemann, G. (2007), *Big Brown: The Untold Story of UPS*, John Wiley & Sons, San Francisco, CA.

Chapter 4
A Dangerous Idea?

Imagined Possibilities

On January 7, 1785, less than two years after the first recorded balloon flight, Jean-Pierre Blanchard and John Jeffries became the first individuals to cross above a national border when they flew their balloon across the English Channel to France. This event was not viewed at the time as an "invasion" but a triumph of mankind. While experimentation with lighter-than-air flight continued, the balloon inspired thoughts of fancy, not fear. Even the development of the dirigible, an elongated balloon with a system of propulsion and guidance, did not change the general view of lighter-than-air flight. Still at the mercy of the winds, the balloon did not seem to pose the threat or hold the promise of heavier-than-air travel. It is true that the French used balloons in a military setting as early as 1793 when they provided reconnaissance during conflicts following the French Revolution and that the first recorded air-to-air combat occurred in 1870 between a French and a Prussian balloonist during the siege of Paris, but the balloons of war were quickly replaced by their heavier-than-air cousins. It was the airplane that raised concerns and careful calculations among the nations of the world (Glines, 1990; Wirth and Young, 1980).

The world's governments, however, would not wait for the aircraft to enter battle before acting. By 1910, they had already seen enough to know that the airplane was no passing fancy but a new technology with great promise and dangerous potential. New regulations were needed to insure the development of international aviation and to protect the interests of nations. This was the goal of the Paris Conference. This conference would not achieve the goals that its organizers had hoped, but it did make one thing abundantly clear: international aviation would not be divorced from politics and national interest (Sochor, 1991).

Let the Conferences Begin

The French government convened the first ever conference on aviation in 1910 to draft a convention on air navigation. The conference was attended by the representatives of 19 European countries. It quickly became apparent that there were conflicting opinions among the delegates present over the rights and privileges of flying. The French and German delegations favored a system of extensive freedom based on the Freedom of the Seas model of Hugo Grotius. The British insisted on complete state sovereignty and control over the airspace above a country's land borders. This fundamental disagreement prevented the conference from achieving its principal goal of establishing a broad framework for international aviation, however, the convention did identify many of the key terms, concepts, and technical provisions that would become standard in later conferences. In the absence of agreement over an international framework, the British became the first nation to declare its sovereignty over the airspace above their country in 1911. The British Aerial Navigation Act gave the Home Secretary full power to regulate the entry and activities of aircraft into its airspace. The other European nations quickly followed suit in the years prior to World War I (Sochor, 1991). The debate over freedom of the skies would resume at the 1913 Madrid Conference which would also fail to reach consensus (Allaz, 2004).

The Peace Conference at the end of World War I faced two key aviation issues. The first was the disposition of the military and civilian fleets of the defeated countries. The second issue was to complete the work begun in 1910. The meeting, known as the Convention Relating to the Regulation of Aerial Navigation, accepted the US position that permitted German civil aviation development within their national borders while eliminating all of the military aspects of aviation. The conference also produced the so-called Paris Convention of 1919. The first article of the Convention declared the complete and exclusive sovereignty of each nation over its airspace. It went on to call for 1) prescribed national registration of aircraft, 2) the restricted movement of military aircraft, 3) prescribed rules of airworthiness, that is, certification that an aircraft is safe to fly through a range of operations, 4) regulation of pilots, and 5) establishment of police measures. A permanent commission was established in Paris to continue the study of international aviation legal issues, the International Commission on Air Navigation or ICAN (Kane, 1998; Sochor, 1991). The Paris Convention was eventually ratified by 26 countries, the most notable exceptions being the United States and Russia who both chose to distance themselves from international affairs after the end of World War I. The US did later sign the Commercial Aviation Convention, also known as the Havana Convention, in 1928. This convention resulted from the Sixth International Conference of the American States and differed from the Paris Convention in several key respects. The Havana Convention did not seek to establish a uniform international standard on aviation for aircraft or pilot regulation nor did it contain any provision for influencing future aviation development such as ICAN (Groenewedge, 1996).

Postal Agenda

The Universal Postal Union (UPU) was established in 1874 on the initiative of Heinrich von Stephan, the Director General of Post for Prussia (later Germany). The primary concern of the UPU was the free transit of international mail and Article I of the Universal Postal Convention considered all the countries under the treaty a single territory over which the UPU imposed fixed transit fees for sea and rail. In 1920, the UPU met in Madrid and began the process of incorporating air services into the Convention. This proceeded in three phases: recognition (1920–27), integration (1927–38), and full incorporation (1938–). Article 4b—Aerial Services was inserted into the Convention. It stated that:

> Aerial services established for the conveyance of correspondence between two or more countries are considered as analogous to the extraordinary services to which Article 4, section 6 refers. The conditions of conveyance are settled by mutual consent between the Administrations concerned. The transit charges applicable to each aerial service are, however, uniform for all Administrations which use the service…

As an extraordinary service, however, there was no uniform regulation common to all companies or air routes. A special conference called by the UPU at the Hague in 1927 would change this status including aerial conveyance under all the articles covering other modes of conveyance and establishing a basic and surcharge rate based on weight. It would also require that the classic blue label *"Par Avion"* be applied to the outside of correspondence. Three further conferences were held prior to the outbreak of World War II: Brussels in 1929 and 1931 and Cairo in 1934. The unstated goal was to eliminate the surcharge. No official action was taken but a number of European postal administrators began to unofficially remove it beginning in the 1930s. The surcharge was officially removed in the Brussels Conference of 1938 (Allaz, 2004).

Domestic Developments

While the international aviation community remained divided on the general question of freedom versus sovereignty, the course of domestic aviation development diverged as well in the years leading up to the Second World War. Direct governmental intervention became the most frequent method of promoting the growth and development of domestic aviation. Governments either provided direct subsidies and/or assumed full or partial ownership of domestic air transport companies. British Airways and Air France are two classic examples of this strategy. A privately owned British Airways was formed in 1935 from the merger of several smaller British carriers. British Airways and Imperial Airways were merged and nationalized to form British Overseas Airways Corporation (BOAC) in 1939. BOAC and British European Airways (BEA) would be merged under the name British Airways in 1974 and remain under government ownership until 1987 (Marriott, 1998). Air France was founded in 1933 through the merger of five smaller French carriers and negotiated with the French government to become the country's national carrier. In 1948, the government assumed a 70 percent ownership stake in the newly reincorporated Air France. All four of the government owned airlines of France were merged in 1990 into the Air France Group (Gross, 2002). By the mid-1950s, most of the carriers of Europe were wholly or partly owned by their respective governments (Graham, 1995). Although many of Asia's national carriers were formed after their European counterparts, the pattern of government ownership was widespread there as well (Sinha, 2001).

This direct intervention did not suit the philosophical and political tastes of US lawmakers and officials. This did not mean the US government did not feel that it had a stake and a role to play in the development of domestic aviation. As noted in Chapter 3, the early development of US aviation was closely tied to airmail and it was largely at the urging of the US Post Office that experimentation with airmail delivery and route creation was begun. After the transition from government to private airmail delivery prompted by the Kelly Act of 1925, the Postmaster General would unofficially continue to intervene in the private airlines that emerged to shape the aviation industry. While this intervention was later deemed illegal, it provided the financial support and strategic vision that shaped the industry that went to war in World War II.

By the beginning of the Second World War, the domestic aviation environment of the Americas and Europe was in place, although the strain of the Great Depression was putting pressure on these systems. Government ownership was the preferred method of domestic support and development in most of the world's nations while the US government intervened in equally significant, though indirect ways to create a large, stable aviation system. A question occasionally arises from aviation interested individuals from outside the US as to what factors account for the different, that is, indirect path taken toward the development of domestic aviation by the US government. There are probably a number of concrete economic and geographical explanations, but the more intuitive and less obvious answer may lie in the basic, shared attitude of many of the individuals that were originally colonized and later immigrated to the US, namely a general distrust of organized government. This distrust grows in direct proportion to the distance that government is from the individual or individuals in question. It has been said in a number of slightly varying ways that citizens in the United States tend to believe that their government was invented by geniuses to be run by idiots (Friedman, 2000). These sentiments are clearly and forcefully expressed by such economists as Hayek, Milton Friedman, and other individuals associated with the so-called Chicago School. Simply put, government intervention distorts the functioning of free market forces preventing the efficient allocation of resources and the establishment of natural prices (Friedman, 1980, 1982; Hayek, 1960, 1980, 1994; Yergin and Stanislaw, 2002). Clearly such an attitude does not predispose the average US citizen to favoring greater government involvement in their daily life. The federalization of airport screening in the wake of 9/11 probably reflects the confusion, shock, fear, and uncertainty created by those events far more than it represents a true belief that the government can perform this function better than private enterprise. It is likely that within a few years there will be increasing pressure to "privatize" that which was once "federalized" for just these reasons. Likewise, the US reluctance to privatize airports and air traffic control service, like so much of the rest of the world would do so in the latter part of the twentieth century, has more to do with entrenched political forces and powerful labor groups than it does with a belief in the efficiency and effectiveness of governments, although airports in the US tend to be run by local (city, county) governments who do meet the "closer-to-me" test of the US citizen and thus get a slightly higher level of trust.

Lessons of War

During the first half of the twentieth century, the world would experience two great wars. The airplane would play a role in both of these conflicts. Although the airplane first went to war in 1911 with the Italian forces in North Africa, its role was to provide reconnaissance. In World War I, it would assume an offensive role first as a bomber and later in aerial combat with mounted machine guns. The airplane that went into the First World War was propelled by an engine capable of about 90 horse power and 75 miles per hour. By the end of the war, Rolls-Royce and American Liberty engines were producing 360 and 400 horse power, speed had doubled, and innovations such as cantilever wings and all metal fuselages were in place (Allaz, 2004). While World War I evokes images of flying aces such as Manfred von Richthofen, commonly called the Red Baron, twisting and turning in an aerial ballet with his opponents, the war also saw the first large-scale bombing of such cities as London. On June 13, 1917 alone, the Germans dropped 118 high-explosive bombs on the city of London. The airplane had clearly arrived as a weapon of war.

If World War I saw the airplane become more than an observer of the action, then World War II saw it become an integral, vital part of the grand strategy of nations and allies. The war itself began with the *Blitzkrieg* of Poland and later much of Europe. The aircraft made these lightning strikes possible and devastating. The desperate Battle of Britain demonstrated the important role of aircraft for both offensive and defensive purposes. The aircraft in fact took several major leaps forward in design and performance during the war years. One of the most significant developments was the turbojet aircraft. Germany followed this innovation with the Messerschmitt (Me-262), which was capable of carrying 550-pound bombs installed on the aircraft's wing racks as well as 12 R4M rockets fitted under the wings. The Me-163 Komet was fitted a rocket motor that could propel it at almost 600 miles per hour and climb vertically at 11,810 feet per minute. Other advances during the war included the use of rocket boosters for short take-offs, pressurized cabins, four-engine aircraft, forward-swept wings mounted over swept-back wings to establish stability at low speeds, and drag-resistant body designs (Badsey, 1990; Cooksley and Robertson, 1998).

Aircraft were not the only beneficiaries of the wartime push to innovation. The British development of radar discussed in Chapter 2 was critical to the defense of Britain and the Allies' ability to avoid detection during bombing raids over Germany. This innovation led to early efforts at reducing aircraft detection, stealth technology, through the use of deflected radar beams and radar-absorbing materials. Work was also begun on the use of thinner, flatter, heat-resistant materials for aircraft construction. Finally, unmanned, armed aircraft and guided missiles would make their appearance toward the end of the war (Cooksley and Robertson, 1998).

In short, the aircraft came out of these two conflicts as a more powerful and deadlier device. As has always been the case with aviation, however, the innovations developed for military application can also have important impacts on the civilian sector. By 1946, aircraft such as the Douglas DC-6 would be carrying 102 passengers at 20,000 feet in a pressurized cabin (Badrocke and Sunston, 1999). Commercial aviation was coming of age and prepared to launch the world on a path to globalization.

Coming Out with Different Agendas

As World War II was coming to an end, the Allied powers would turn at least some of their attention back to the issue of creating an international aviation system. This interest would result in the Chicago Conference (Chapter 5), but the countries attending that conference had been changed by the years of war in ways that would echo through the halls in Chicago. It has been said that the United States was the only country to emerge from World War II richer. In fact, the US gold reserves at the end of the war totaled $20 billion, two-thirds of the world's total (Matloff, 1959). The US would be responsible for more than half of the total manufacturing production of the world and account for one third of the production of all types of goods (Ashworth, 1975). In the aviation area, the United States production of aircraft had risen by 1945 to 49,761 per year, up from 5,856 in 1939. It would account for more aircraft per year than the combined manufacturing of Britain and the USSR (Overy, 1980).

For its part, the USSR had not only lost 20–25 million citizens between 1941 and 1945, it had lost a substantial portion of its infrastructure (Hosking, 1985). It is estimated that in the transportation sector alone the USSR "was hit by the destruction of 65,000 kilometers of railway track, loss of or damage to 15,800 locomotives, 428,000 goods wagons, 4,280 river boats, and half of all the railway bridges in the occupied territory" (Nove, 1969; 285). The losses to infrastructure were devastating in the nations of other Allied and Great Powers as well. In 1946, German national income and output was one-third of its 1938 level (Landes, 1969). Japanese real income had fallen to only 57 percent of its 1934–36 levels and exports were only 8 percent of the 1934–36 figures (Allen, 1981). Italy's gross national product had declined by 40 percent to its 1911 level (Ricossa, 1972). The Allied Powers, with the exception of the US, had not fared any better. By 1944, years of war and occupation had left France with a situation where "most of the waterways and harbors were blocked, most of the bridges destroyed, much of the railway system temporarily unusable" (Wright, 1968; 264). The French national income in 1945 was half of its 1938 level. In Great Britain, years of bombing had severely weakened the industrial base and damaged the overall civilian infrastructure. Exports had fallen to 31 percent of their 1938 figures with a resulting surge in the British trade deficit (Kennedy, 1981).

It is with this backdrop that the Allied and Neutral powers would meet in Chicago to decide the shape of the post-war international aviation system. The fact that the meeting would take place even before the conclusion of the war was an indication of the importance this young industry had gained in the eyes of world governments and their citizens. While the industry itself was young, the arguments heard in Chicago were old. The aviation community had heard them before Chicago and would hear them again over the subsequent years. The successes and failures of Chicago would live on in the international aviation system of today.

References

Allen, G.C. (1981), *A Short Economic History of Japan*, St Martin's Press, New York.

Allaz, C. (2004), *The History of Air Cargo and Airmail from the 18th Century*, Christopher Foyle Publishing, Paris.

Ashworth, W.A. (1975), *A Short History of the International Economy Since 1850*, London.

Badrocke, M. and Sunston, B. (1999), *The Illustrated History of McDonnell Douglas Aircraft from Cloudster to Boeing*, Osprey, Oxford.

Badsey, S. (1990), *Modern Air Power: Fighters*, Gallery Books, New York.

Bedwell, D. and Wegg, J. (2000), *Silverbird: The American Airlines Story*, Plymouth Press, Boston.

Cooksley, M.K. and Robertson, B. (1998), *Air Warfare: The Encyclopedia of Twentieth Century Conflict*, Frank Cass, London.

Friedman, M. (1980), *Free to Choose*, Harcourt Brace Jovanovich, New York.

Friedman, M. (1982), *Capitalism and Freedom,* University of Chicago Press, Chicago.

Friedman, T.L. (2000), *The Lexus and the Olive Tree*, 2 ed., Farrar, Straus & Giroux, New York.

Glines, C.V. (1968), *The Saga of the Airmail*, D. Van Nostrand, Princeton, N.J.

Graham, B. (1995), *Geography and Air Transport*, John Wiley & Sons, New York.

Groenewedge, A.D. (1996), *Compendium of International Civil Aviation,* International Aviation Development Corporation, Quebec.

Gross, P.M. (2002), 'Air France' in Tracy Irons-Georges (ed.) *Encyclopedia of Flight*, pp. 52–4, Salem Press, Pasadena, CA.

Hayek, F.A. (1960), *The Constitution of Liberty*, University of Chicago Press, Chicago.

Hayek, F.A. (1980), *Individualism and Economic Order*, University of Chicago Press, Chicago.

Hayek, F.A. (1994), *Hayek on Hayek: An Autobiographical Dialogue*, University of Chicago Press, Chicago.

Hosking, G.A. (1985), *A History of the Soviet Union*, Fontana Press, London.

Jones, G. and Jones, G.P. (1999), *U.S. Airways*, Ian Allan, Shepperton, England.

Kane, R.M. (1998), *Air Transportation*, 13th edition, Kendall/Hunt Publishing, Dubuque, IA.

Kennedy, P.M. (1981), *The Realities Behind Diplomacy*, Routledge, London.

Landes, D. (1969), *The Unbound Prometheus: Technological Change and Industrial Development in Western Europe from 1970 to the Present*, Cambridge.

Marriott, L. (1998), *British Airways Book*, 2nd ed., Plymouth Publishing, Plymouth, MI.

Matloff, M. (1959), *Strategic Planning for Coalition Warfare, 1943–1944*, Washington, DC.

Nove, A. (1969), *An Economic History of the USSR,* Harmondsworth.

Overy, R.J. (1980), *The Air War, 1939–1945*, Europa, New York.

Ricossa, A. (1972), 'Italy 1920–1970' in C. Cipolla (ed.) *The Fortuna Economic History of Europe*, London.

Sinha, D. (2001), *Deregulation and Liberalization of the Airline Industry: Asia, Europe, North America, and Oceania*, Ashgate Publishing, Aldershot, UK.

Sochor, E. (1991), *The Politics of International Aviation*, University of Iowa Press, Iowa City.

Tischauser, L.V. (2002), 'Wright Brothers', in Tracy Irons-Georges (ed.) *Encyclopedia of Flight*, pp. 785–6, Salem Press, Pasadena, CA.

Wirth, D. and Young, J. (1980), *Ballooning: The Compete Guide to Riding the Winds*, Random House, New York.

Wright, G. (1968), *The Ordeal of Total War, 1939–1945*, New York.

Yergin, D. and Stanislaw, J. (2002), *The Commanding Heights: The Battle for the World Economy*, Simon & Schuster, New York.

Chapter 5
Chicago, the Windy City

Crosswinds

The wind can be a friend or a foe to the air traveller. A strong headwind can add time to your journey. A strong tailwind can help speed you along your way. Crosswinds, however, are unpredictable, often dangerous. At the very least they can make it very difficult to maintain your planned course and reach your planned destination. Chicago has long been called the Windy City and anyone who has ever looked out over the lakefront on a fall day can understand the nickname. It is perhaps fitting that Chicago was the chosen site for the most famous aviation conference in history. The events that happened and didn't happen at Chicago still echo in the events of today. To understand the forces that created the international aviation landscape of today, you must understand Chicago.

Even as US President Franklin D. Roosevelt and British Prime Minister Winston Churchill were meeting in Quebec to plan the cross-channel invasion of Normandy and turn the tide of war in Europe, the topic of a general meeting to discuss the future of air transportation came up as an issue. US politicians had already begun to explore the nature of a post-war aviation system. Henry Wallace, the US Vice-president, proposed a global network of air routes and international airports under the envisioned United Nations while Clare Boothe Luce denounced this notion as "globaloney" in her maiden address to the US Congress. Edward Warner, the vice-chairman of the US Civil Aviation Bureau, envisioned air navigation agreements that would prevent the "return to the evil days when air transportation was regarded with caution and suspicion" (Sochor, 1991: 4). The British had also been considering the issue of aviation. At the 1943 Dominion and Empire Conference and a May 1944 meeting of the Dominion ministers there were discussions about creating some system of reciprocal rights. In a White Paper shortly after the 1944 meeting, the British proposed an international regulatory body with the power to decide on routes, frequencies, and fares. Clearly, the crosswinds would be blowing in Chicago.

Setting the Table

When the delegates arrived in Chicago on November 1, 1944, they found four proposals awaiting them on shaping the international environment. The opening message of President Roosevelt called on the delegates "not to dally with the thought of creating great blocs of closed air, thereby tracing in the sky the conditions of future war" (Sochor, 1991: 8). His call was for an open sky that could be exploited for the good of all mankind. Not surprisingly, the US proposal called for a system of complete market access without restrictions on routes, frequency, and fares. The British who rightly feared that the large, undamaged aviation infrastructure, commercial fleet, and manufacturing capacity of the US would dominate the war-ravaged systems of Europe saw the US proposal as self-interest masquerading as philosophical principle. The British plan reiterated their earlier White Paper calling for a tightly regulated system governed by an independent international regulatory body. The Canadian proposal attempted to offer a compromise between the US and British positions by creating a multilateral regulatory body that would allow for limited competition within the system. The last proposal, jointly sponsored by the Australians and New Zealanders, called for the international ownership and management of all international air service. Committee I of the Chicago Conference would clearly have its work cut out for it.

Meanwhile, the other three committees worked on the technical issues of the conference eventually completing work on the Interim Agreement on International Aviation, the Chicago Convention on International Civil Aviation, and the International Air Transport Agreement. The first treaty or convention established a temporary organization called the Provisional International Civil Aviation Organization to operate until the permanent organization created in the second document came into effect, the International Civil Aviation Organization (ICAO). The third convention is also known as the Five Freedoms Agreement (Table 5.1 lists the freedoms of the air including the subsequently added sixth to ninth freedoms). The first two freedoms are known as technical freedoms. The remaining freedoms deal with the commercial rights of aviation to pick up and discharge passengers and cargo to, from and through foreign nations.

While the technical committees were concluding their work, Committee I was deadlocked. Despite several exchanges between Roosevelt and Churchill on the issues facing the Committee and a series of private meetings between the key players, there would be no compromise on the basic positions of either the US or Great Britain. The US might have the planes to fly, but without landing rights they had only half the resources needed for a viable international system of carriers. They needed landing rights and Great Britain had potential landing sites galore. In fact, as the conference was opening the British publicized a "plan" for creating an all-Commonwealth airline called the All-Red Line after the cartographic practice of showing Commonwealth nations in red. This All-Red Line would be given exclusive rights to land on Commonwealth territory. In a world in which the sun never set on the British flag, the All-Red Line was a reminder that the British did not come to the table empty-handed nor would they allow a system of international aviation to be put in place that created serious disadvantages for Britain and other small aviation nations.

Table 5.1   The freedoms of the air

Freedom	Description
First	The right to fly over the territory of a contracting State without landing
Second	The right to land on the territory of a contracting State for non-commercial purposes
Third	The right to transport passengers, cargo and mail from the State of registration of the aircraft to another State and set them down there
Fourth	The right to take on board passengers, cargo and mail in another contracting State and to transport them to the State of registration of the aircraft
Fifth	The right to transport passengers, cargo and mail between two other States as a continuation of, or as a preliminary to, the operation of the third or fourth freedoms
Sixth	The right to take on board passengers, cargo and mail in one State and to transport them to a third State after a stopover in the aircraft's State of registration and vice versa
Seventh	The right to transport passengers, cargo and mail between two other States on a service which does not touch the aircraft's country of registration
Eighth	The right to transport passengers, cargo and mail within the territory of a State which is not the aircraft's State of registration (full cabotage)
Nineth	The right to interrupt a service

Just as it began to seem that nothing would be achieved in Committee I, the Netherlands broke the deadlock by suggesting that the British might join in an agreement on the first two freedoms of overflight and technical landing or stopover. The Netherlands then moved immediately to guarantee these rights as part of a multilateral agreement. The British agreed to this proposal which became the fourth treaty or convention to come out of the Chicago Conference. The International Air Services Transit Agreement would eventually be signed by all of the participants and come into effect on June 30, 1945. It is now recognized by over 100 nations. The International Air Transport Agreement which contained the remaining commercial freedoms would be signed by 19 of the participants, but nine, including the US, would subsequently denounce it. The remaining nations would not endorse it, primarily for its fifth freedom condition. One final document would come out of the Convention. This form, the Bilateral Agreement for the Exchange of Routes and Services, would be adopted as part of the Final Act and serve to move the international aviation community forward in the absence of a broader, multilateral agreement on commercial aviation rights. The gavel fell on December 7, 1944 ending the Chicago Conference and the governmental delegates went home with their treaties and the bilateral form to decide on the next steps in the process of creating an international aviation system.

Not all of the individuals present in Chicago, however, went home immediately. Airline executives who had attended the conference as delegates or advisors to their national governments had quickly realized the implications of a failure by the conference to reach a broad multilateral agreement on commercial rights and fares. Showing admirable restraint, they waited until 6 December to begin discussions on the formation of a trade association for international carriers. This new association would be their voice in the international system and they hoped that it would fill the void left in the commercial aviation system by the events in Chicago. The newly formed International Air Transport Association (IATA) called its first meeting in Havana in April 1945.

A Bilateral World

Without a multilateral agreement, it was left to the national governments of the world to begin the process of negotiating bilateral air service agreements. In fact, the United States had opened bilateral talks with the Dominions, Chinese, and Russians even before the conference began and quickly returned to this process after the conference, signing a bilateral agreement with Spain on December 2, 1944, Denmark and Sweden on December 16, 1944, Iceland on January 27, 1945, Canada on February 7, 1945, and Switzerland and Norway on July 13, 1945 (Kane, 1998). However, it was not until 1946 that the United States and Great Britain were ready to sit down again and discuss the aviation issues that had not been resolved at Chicago. The agreement that emerged from these talks would be called the Bermuda Agreement and would, by agreement of both governments, become the model for all of the future agreements either side would negotiate. This form would henceforth replace the Chicago form as the world's standard Air Service Agreement.

The United States agreed to accept the British position on fares and rates which allowed the airlines to mutually set these matters subject to prior approval by both governments. The United Kingdom agreed to allow airlines to unilaterally set their own capacity, that is, aircraft size and service frequency subject to subsequent review for unfair practices. Other key features of the agreement included designated (or named) routes and multiple carrier designation. In total, "the Agreement clearly favored the United States which then accounted for about 60 percent of the world's passenger airline traffic and which had the largest and most efficient international airlines" (Toh, 1998: 61). This may reflect the fact that the British were also in negotiations with the US over a US$3.75 billion loan to rebuild its economy and thus had to negotiate from a position of some weakness (Sochor, 1991). As a concession to the British, the United States did agree to allow the International Air Transport Association (IATA) to set international fares and cargo rates. They also decided to limit their pursuit of fifth freedom rights which are seen in aviation circles as placing a foreign carrier in too close a competition for domestic traffic with a state's national carriers (Toh, 1998). By 1947, over 100 bilaterals had been signed around the world and the fare-setting power of IATA accepted in subsequent aviation accords (Sochor, 1991).

The last bilateral between the US and UK illustrates the key points of bilaterals as well and the specific and restrictive nature of such air service agreements (Air Transport Association of America, 2001). Under the portion of the air service agreement entitled "United Kingdom Routes: Atlantic combination air service" are shown in the following list in Table 5.2.

In addition to the Atlantic combination air service, lists are provided of named routes for Atlantic regional combination air service, Atlantic combination air service via Canada, Atlantic combination air service beyond Mexico City, Atlantic combination air service beyond to South America, Atlantic combination service beyond to Japan, Atlantic combination service beyond to the Pacific,

Table 5.2   US-UK bilateral agreement

(A) UK Gateway Points	(B) Intermediate Points	(C) Points in US Territory
London, Manchester, Prestwick/Glasgow, Belfast. Any UK point, excluding London.	Points in Luxembourg, The Netherlands and the Republic of Ireland. Points in Belgium, France and Germany.	Atlanta, Boston, Charlotte, Chicago, Detroit, Houston, Las Vegas, Los Angeles, Miami, New Orleans, New York, Orlando, Phoenix, Philadelphia, San Diego, San Francisco, Seattle, Tampa, Washington/ Baltimore. Up to two points to be selected and notified to The United States.

Atlantic combination service beyond to Australia, Pacific combination service, Pacific combination service via Tarawa, Bermuda combination service, Caribbean combination service, Caribbean combination air service, Atlantic all-cargo service, Atlantic all-cargo service beyond to South America, Atlantic all cargo service beyond to Mexico, Pacific all-cargo services, Pacific all-cargo service via Tarawa, Bermuda all-cargo service, Caribbean all-cargo service, and Caribbean all-cargo air service.

Conversely, the principle of reciprocity demands that similar lists of named routes be included for US passenger and all-cargo service. Table 5.3 shows a list of United States Routes: Atlantic combination service.

These excerpts demonstrate the reciprocal exchange of named routes as well as the application of fifth freedom (beyond) rights between the US and the UK. By the old bilateral standards, the US-UK agreement was considered liberal in that it did not include capacity (aircraft size and route frequency) restrictions.

As an example of further restrictions, the US-Japanese bilateral distinguished between incumbent carriers which were provided for by the 1952 agreement (Northwest and United Airlines for the US and Japan Airlines and All Nippon Airways for the Japanese) and non-incumbent carriers (Delta Air Lines, American

Table 5.3   US–UK bilateral agreement

(A) US Gateway Points	(B) Intermediate Points	(C) Points in UK Territory	(D) Points Beyond
Anchorage, Atlanta, Boston, Charlotte, Chicago, Cincinnati, Dallas/Ft Worth, Detroit, Houston, Los Angeles, Miami, Minneapolis/St. Paul, Newark, New York, Philadelphia, Pittsburgh, Raleigh-Durham, San Francisco, Seattle, St. Louis, Washington/ Baltimore. Up to 3 points to be selected and notified to the United Kingdom.	Shannon	London, Prestwick/ Glasgow. Any UK point excluding London.	Berlin, Frankfurt, Hamburg, Munich, Oslo. One point in Western Europe to be selected.

Airlines, and Continental Airlines) in naming routes. It also included sections on restricted frequency routes. In this case, non-incumbent airlines are permitted to operate up to 42 additional aggregate weekly round-trip frequencies on the following city-pair markets: Tokyo–New York, Tokyo–Chicago, Tokyo–San Francisco, Tokyo–Los Angeles, Tokyo–Honolulu, Tokyo–Guam/Saipan, Osaka–Los Angeles, Osaka–Los Angeles, Osaka–Honolulu, Nagoya–Honolulu, and Fukuoka–Honolulu (Air Transport Association of America, 2001).

Looking Back

Looking back on the Chicago Conference, it is clear that no compromise could have bridged the gap between the basic US and British positions. In the tug-of-war between free markets and political reality, political reality was the victor. Ironically, the lever that had allowed the British to hold off the US push for open skies would not long survive the end of World War II. The British Empire would be replaced by a much looser Commonwealth of independent nations with the right to determine the disposition of their own landing rights. Unfortunately, the system created by the major aeronautical players to meet their needs would not give these newly emerging nations a great deal of clout in the international system even if it did recognize their sovereign rights to control their own airspace.

The United States for all of its philosophical preaching on open skies was not willing to grant more open access to the US market as it proved later when it renounced the International Air Transport Agreement rather than grant foreign carriers greater fifth freedom rights through the US (Sochor, 1991). This was seen as an admission by the US that there could be no stable commercial aviation system without reciprocity between countries (de la Rochère, 1971). While the United States was able to use its power and prestige following the war to sign a number of bilateral agreements advantageous to the US carriers, it did so by giving up the right to allow the markets to determine price. The US would again be accused of abandoning philosophical principle in favor of commercial and political reality when it began to take up the cause of open skies again after airline deregulation (Chapter 8). Frederik Sorensen of the European Commission Air Transport Policy Unit has said that "open skies is an American term which, as we see it, is synonymous with a free for all system depending on the good behavior of air carriers and only partial opening of the market" (1998: 125).

Looking Ahead

Out of the ashes of the post-World War II world, the phoenix of international aviation took off. If it did not fly as high as some would have liked or take the paths its creators envisioned, it did at least fly. The winds blowing out of Chicago did not make its flight either smooth or steady, but it has remained aloft. The next decades would see less dramatic but no less significant progress in the world of international aviation. The two international organizations born in Chicago, ICAO and IATA, would build on the framework laid out there (Chapter 6) only to have many of the structures set in place challenged by deregulation of the US airline industry (Chapter 8) and liberalization in European and Asian markets (Chapter 9). The events of the past would come back to challenge the future and demand that the world community grapple with them again.

The preamble to the Convention on International Civil Aviation laid out the goals of the Chicago Convention as follows:

> WHEREAS the future development of international civil aviation can greatly help to create and preserve friendship and understanding among nations and peoples of the world, yet its abuse can become a threat to the general security; and

> WHEREAS it is desirable to avoid friction and to promote that cooperation between nations and peoples upon which peace of the world depends;

> THEREFORE, the undersigned governments having agreed on certain principles and arrangements in order that international civil aviation may be developed in a safe and orderly manner and that international air transport services may be established on the basis of equality of opportunity and operated soundly and economically; (Reprinted in Sochor, 1991).

This vision of international aviation as a global force for peace was perhaps utopian, but air travel has certainly brought the world closer together in time and space. Unfortunately, the events of 9/11 temporarily replaced this unifying vision with a grimmer reality. This reality too is overstated. An airplane was merely the tool used to perpetrate the destruction of 9/11. Like any tool, it serves the wishes of its user; the terrorists used their tool to drive the world apart. Others continue to use it to bring the world together. While the vision of ICAO has proven elusive, the goals have also presented their own challenges. As we will see in the next chapter, ICAO would work hard to create a safe, orderly, and economical air transportation system and, by-and-large, they will achieve this goal.

The difficulty lies in the basis for this system: equality of opportunity. Free markets guarantee all the right to participate. They do not guarantee that the opportunities are equal or that the outcomes are equitable. In fact, free markets are about access, not success and neither of these commodities is equally distributed. In a free market the opportunities of large, wealthy nations are greater than those of small, poor nations. The chances of success are also greater for the large and wealthy. Equity is about fairness, impartiality, and justice. Free markets are about competition and winner-take-all. Governments intervene in the market to provide opportunity and equity. All governments intervene to some extent. The level of intervention or regulation has been a subject for debate in economic and policy circles since Adam Smith. The push for liberalization in the airline industry would raise these issues once again for policy makers and the people they represent.

References

Air Transport Association of America (2001), 'Air Service Rights in US International Air Transport Agreements: A Compilation of Scheduled and Charter Service Rights Contained in US Bilateral Aviation Agreements', Washington, DC.

De la Rochère, J.D. (1971), *La Politique des Etats-Unis en matière d'aviation civile*, Libraire de Droit et de Jurisprudence, Paris, pp. 30–36.

Kane, R.M. (1998), *Air Transportation*, 13th edition., Kendall/Hunt Publishing, Dubuque, Iowa.

Sochor, E. (1991), *The Politics of International Aviation*, University of Iowa Press, Iowa City.

Sorensen, F. (1998), 'Open Skies in Europe', in U.S. Department of Transportation (ed.), *FAA Commercial Aviation Forecast Conference Proceedings: Overcoming Barriers to World Competition and Growth*, pp. 125–32, Office of Aviation Policy and Plans, Washington, DC.

Toh, R.S. (1998), 'Toward an International Open Skies Regime: Advances, Impediments, and Impacts', *Journal of Air Transportation World Wide*, vol. 3, pp. 61–70.

Chapter 6
Shaping the World

First Chicago, Then the World

The interim Agreement on International Civil Aviation established the framework for a provisional International Civil Aviation Organization (PICAO), which functioned until 1947 when the required number of countries ratified the agreement to create a permanent organization. Over the coming years the International Civil Aviation Organization (ICAO) would work to develop the standards and practices followed by much of the world's aviation community. They would do so amidst the push and pull of the Cold War, the rapid development of aviation technology, and the limited funding often available to organizations associated with the United Nations. Like the United Nations, their actions could not be enforced on the world community, but could only be considered advisory. ICAO would thus struggle like the UN to achieve a consensus that would allow it to foster and develop the aviation system while balancing the needs of a diverse and fractious constituency.

The other organization born in Chicago, the International Air Transport Association, would receive recognition of its role at the 1946 bilateral talks between the US and UK. It would not suffer from the kind of tension that divided ICAO. Its members, international airlines, would set about the task of setting the fares, dividing the world's international routes, establishing the standards for interlining (transfer between carriers), and devising the methods of revenue sharing that would govern the international aviation system until these powers were slowly eroded by domestic air transport deregulation and international liberalization (Chapter 8). ICAO and IATA would work together on many issues related to safe air transport operation, standardization of documentation and procedures, and the development of legal agenda such as the Warsaw Convention on airline liability. Together these two organizations would shape the post-World War II international aviation system.

Setting the Standards

The International Civil Aviation Organization (ICAO) is composed of appointed representatives of all nations interested in international civil aviation (at the time of writing totaling 188 contracting states). ICAO is governed by a sovereign body, the Assembly, which meets at least once every three years. Each nation represented has one vote on key matters and majority rules. The governing body of ICAO is the Council. The Council is elected from the Assembly for a three-year term and is composed of 36 members elected from three categories of ICAO general members. The first category is states of chief importance to air transport. The second is states that make the largest contribution to the provision of air navigation facilities. The final category is composed of states designated to insure that all of the regions of the globe are represented. Table 6.1 provides a list of the nations currently serving on the Council.

These nations maintain a permanent presence at ICAO's headquarters in Montreal, Canada where they are responsible for the day-to-day operations of the organization. The Council adopts the Standards and Recommended Practices (SARPs) and approves the Procedures of Air Navigation Services (PANS) that are the heart of the work of ICAO. Assisting the Council are the Air Navigation Commission which is responsible for technical matters, the Air Transport Committee responsible for economic matters, the Committee on Joint Support of Air Navigation Services, and the Finance Committee. Proposals to amend or add new SARPs come from ICAO-sponsored international meetings, deliberative bodies within the organization itself, the Secretariat, the United Nations or other interested international organizations. ICAO works closely with such organizations

Table 6.1   ICAO council membership

Argentina	Mexico
Australia	Namibia
Brazil	Nigeria
Cameroon	Republic of Korea
Canada	Romania
China	Russian Federation
Dominican Republic	Saudi Arabia
Ecuador	Singapore
Egypt	South Africa
El Salvador	Spain
France	Switzerland
Germany	Tunisia
Ghana	Uganda
Iceland	United Arab Emirates
India	United Kingdom
Italy	United States
Japan	Uruguay
Malaysia	Venezuela

as the World Meteorological Organization, the International Telecommunications Union, the Universal Postal Union, the World Health Organization, the International Maritime Organization (all UN affiliated), the International Air Transport Association, the Airports Council International, the International Federation of Air Line Pilots, and the International Council of Aircraft Owner and Pilots Association (all non-governmental organizations).

Once an issue is brought to ICAO for consideration, it is referred to the Air Navigation Commission, which is composed of fifteen persons who have "suitable qualifications and experience in the science and practice of aeronautics." These individuals are nominated by Contracting States and appointed by the Council. The Commission is assisted by the Air Navigation Bureau and panels and working groups nominated by Contracting States and appointed by the Commission. These individuals serve based on their personal expertise and not as representatives of any Contracting State. Once the Commission submits a SARP to the Council, a two-thirds vote of its members is required for adoption. If a majority of the Contracting States do not disapprove it, the SARP becomes effective on the established date. SARPs are considered binding, although States that cannot comply can file a "difference" that is published by ICAO in Supplements to Annexes. This process takes roughly five to seven years to reach completion which means that the work of ICAO progresses slowly. PANS are developed in a similar way, however, they are not binding and no difference needs to be filed. Table 6.2 lists the annexes and areas, which are covered by ICAO.

Other activities of ICAO include joint financing of navigation services on the high seas or in areas where no nation can be charged with the responsibility. Iceland and Greenland are examples of the latter. Considering that their own aircraft represent less than three percent of the transatlantic traffic, the burden for navigational services is shared by other nations. The Legal Affairs Committee prepares drafts for key international conferences related to aviation such as the Geneva (1948) and Rome (1952) Conventions. ICAO's Technical Co-operation Programme works with the United Nations Development Programme (UNDP) on projects aimed at developing the aviation system of developing nations. The Trainair programme provides assistance to national and regional civil aviation training institutes. Finally, ICAO provides expert services such as site selection and design of airstrips and design of air traffic control systems. The magnitude of work of ICAO seems overwhelming, particularly in light of their limited funding. Much of their efforts depend on the support, both technical and monetary, that comes from the Contracting States (ICAO, 2002).

The key to understanding ICAO is in realizing that, like the United Nations in general, it has *no* independent enforcement power; it can not make its members implement any of its standards. Its main bodies may act to support or condemn certain actions by members that relate to aviation, but this is an exercise in public relations and free expression. When or if a vote is taken on the issue of SARPs or PANS, it is the perfunctory end to months or years of consensus building at ICAO. If consensus is not initially achieved on certain issues, then all parties

Table 6.2　　Annexes to the ICAO convention

Annex	Subject
1	Personnel Licensing
2	Rules of the Air
3	Meteorological Service
4	Aeronautical Charts
5	Units of Measurement to be used in operations
6	Operation of Aircraft
7	Aircraft Nationality and Registration
8	Airworthiness of Aircraft
9	Facilitation
10	Aeronautical Telecommunications
11	Air Traffic Service
12	Search and Rescue
13	Aircraft Accident Investigation
14	Aerodromes
15	Aeronautical Information Service
16	Environmental Protection
17	Security
18	Safe Transport of Dangerous Goods

revise, rework, or reframe the issue until consensus is obtained. It is a painstaking process, but it has and is producing some very positive results. After years of debate, ICAO established in January 1999 the Universal Safety Oversight Program which "consists of regular, mandatory, systematic, and harmonized safety audits carried out by ICAO in all 187 countries ... it has proven effective in identifying and correcting safety deficiencies in areas of personnel licensing and airworthiness and operations of aircraft" (ICAO, 2002: 1). The program has been expanded to include air traffic service and airports. ICAO has been requested to help in the resolution of deficiencies through educational activities, funding and technical coordination, and the creation of a Quality Assistance Function. Given the politically sensitive nature of safety for governments and airlines, the Universal Safety Oversight Program was a great victory for ICAO in their efforts to further advance the cause of international aviation. Most recently, ICAO has been directed by its Assembly to establish a Universal Security Oversight Audit Programme that would assess the implementation of ICAO security-related SARPs (ICAO, 2002).

Setting the Fares

Under the 1945 Articles of Association, the aims of the International Air Transport Association are:

> To promote safe, regular, and economical air transportation for the benefit of the peoples of the world, to foster air commerce, and to study the problems connected therewith;

> To provide means for collaboration among the air transport enterprise engaged directly or indirectly in international air transport service;

> To cooperate with the newly created International Civil Aviation Organization and other international organizations (IATA, 2002).

In the early years, IATA worked on such issues as the Multilateral Interline Traffic Agreements, Passenger and Cargo Services Conference Resolutions, and Passenger and Cargo Agency Agreements & Sales Agency Rules. The Interline Agreements involved insuring acceptance of other carriers' tickets and waybills. The Conference Resolutions prescribed standard formats and specifications for tickets and waybills. The Agency Agreements governed the relationships between IATA airlines and their accredited agents. A Clearing House was also established in 1947 to handle debt settlements between carriers largely arising from interlining, that is, when a passenger changes from one airline to another at point B during a trip from A to C. The Clearing House insures that each carrier is paid the cost of the segment that they flew.

It was the role of IATA's Traffic Conferences that would eventually come under intense scrutiny by a liberalizing world air transportation system. Under the Bermuda Agreement of 1946, IATA was delegated the role of establishing fares and rates subject to government approval. According to IATA, the goal of the system was to establish "coherent fares and rates patterns." Such a system would avoid "inconsistencies between tariffs affecting neighboring countries – and thereby avoiding traffic diversion" (IATA, 1996). In effect, there was a set fare for any given international route that any IATA member was expected to charge. If there continued to be an imbalance in the revenues earned by the designated carriers on such a route, then a revenue-sharing or pooling agreement could be worked out to equalize the revenues of both sides (Taneja, 1988). There were intermittent efforts in ICAO to question the tariff (fare)-setting role of IATA, but during the last such effort ICAO concluded that "at present, there is no justification for ICAO to undertake specific studies and other economic work on the subject of airline tariffs" (Sochor, 1991: 17).

Following the events discussed in Chapter 8, IATA would be forced to reconsider its role in fare setting. It did so first by establishing a "two-tier" system. Under this system, the IATA Trade Association became responsible for technical, legal, financial, and traffic services. The Tariff Coordination became responsible for fares and rates. An airline could participate in the Trade Association without participating in the Tariff Coordination activities. Over time, IATA has placed increasing emphasis on the trade association activities and come to derive much of its funding from the educational and product marketing activities of the Association. For all intents and purposes, the new IATA does not engage in fare or rate setting but allows these activities to be the domain of the airlines themselves.

A New Day Dawning

IATA and ICAO would emerge from the Chicago Convention to shape the aviation system that would develop after World War II. This system would preside over an aviation era in which air travel would come to be seen as a safe and reliable mode of transportation, but it would not yet be seen as a transportation mode for the masses; achieving this goal would require fares to fall to levels that the "common man" could afford. This vision of air travel was the goal of deregulation. Markets and competition, not governments, would determine fares, destinations, and service levels (Chapter 8). First, the manufacturers and the airlines that they supplied would have to get back to the business of civil aviation and establish the industry that would be turned on its head in the late 1970s. Few people in the international aviation system would realize that the "end of an era" was coming, but the passage in the United States of the Airline Deregulation Act of 1978 would be such a watershed. For the cozy system of routes and fares set up by IATA, it would mean radical change. For ICAO, this new era would mean more issues of safety and security would be added to their already full plate of issues.

References

International Air Transport Association (2002), electronic edition, www.iata.org.
International Air Transport Association (1996), 'Early Days', electronic edition, www.iata.org.
International Civil Aviation Organization (2002), electronic edition, www.icao.int.
International Civil Aviation Organization (2002), 'Meeting Caps Most Productive Triennium in Recent ICAO History', News Release, 9 October, pp. 1–4.
Sochor, E. (1991), *The Politics of International Aviation*, University of Iowa Press, Iowa City.
Taneja, N.K. (1988), *The International Airline Industry*, Lexington Books, Lexington.

PART II
The Industry Grows Up (1950–2000)

Chapter 7
Taking Off

Back to Business

For obvious reasons, civil aviation in Europe was placed on hold during World War II. In the US, civil aviation continued on a somewhat limited basis, while the manufacturers thrived under government orders for military equipment. As the war approached a recognizable end, a number of manufacturers began to shift more focus back to the civilian market and anxiously waited to be released from government obligation. Within days of the events at Hiroshima and Nagasaki, others found their government contract cancelled and quickly had to shift gears back to a more civilian manufacturing position (Rummel, 1991). Most companies had prospered during the war, racing to keep up with demand. Many would struggle with the end of the war, converting aircraft built or partially built at contract cancellation to civilian use. Only part of the concern was the end of lucrative government contracts; the volume of war surplus aircraft also threatened to depress possible civilian orders (Rummel, 1991; Serling, 1992). Still, civil aviation was about to reap the benefits of all of that wartime innovation. The amazing feats of aerial combat and the list of aviation achievements had captured the imagination of the population. Now the industry needed to convince the general public that aviation was a safe, affordable, comfortable travel experience. The rise in passenger traffic indicates that they were successful; people around the world were getting ready to take to the skies. Airlines and the manufacturers would work closely together to create the planes that would attract new flyers, the kind that were not looking to push the envelope as first movers in a new and untried field but the more cautious followers. During the second half of the twentieth century, aviation would grow up.

First Out of the Gate

Lockheed and Douglas would be two of the first manufacturers released by the US government. Both would begin working on projects to bring the pressurized cabin to civil aviation. The DC series for Douglas and the Lockheed Constellations (popularly known as "Connies") would compete with Convair (General Dynamics) to offer bigger and faster aircraft to the airlines. Two goals fuelled the competition: "fastest coast-to-coast" service and a transatlantic non-stop range (Rummel, 1991). Both companies would compete aggressively to sell their aircraft to the major carriers: United, American, TWA, and Pan Am. In this race, a few more feet in length (L1049) or more efficient engines and propellers (DC-7) were the selling points, although in some cases the delivery schedule became a make-or-break issue. The DC-6, first released in 1946, would feature a pressurized cabin and 102 passenger seating configuration. It would regularly be used in around-the-world flights by the major international airlines and become the first US presidential aircraft (President Harry Truman). The next Douglas aircraft, the DC-7, would become the first aircraft to fly non-stop from New York to Los Angeles (Clouatre, 2002). Despite some early problems with the Constellation series, TWA and a number of other international airlines would make the aircraft a fondly remembered part of aviation history (McCoy, 2002; Rummel, 1991).

In 1950, the Farnborough Air Show would showcase the "wave of the future", the de Havilland Comet. The Comet which had made its maiden flight the previous year was set to enter commercial airline service in 1952 and become the first operational commercial jet transport. One of the people attending the air show would be Ron Allen, CEO of Boeing. Allen was convinced that Boeing could develop a better aircraft and would return to Seattle to get his engineers working. At the April 22, 1952 meeting of the Boeing Board, tentative approval would be given to proceed with the design and construction of a jet transport which would become the B707. The plane would feature sweptback wings and engine pods. Seating for 100 passengers would compete well with the Comet's more limited 36 seat size. Development of the 707 would prove far more costly than the original Boeing estimate and the breakeven point far higher, but Pam Am agreed to be the launch customer. Meanwhile the rest of the industry appeared to be choosing the DC-8, the planned Douglas entry into the world of commercial jet transport. The DC-8 was only a "paper aircraft at this stage, that is, it was still in the very preliminary stages of design, but Douglas had a family of aircraft and a proven record of success. These factors gave them an edge and guaranteed that airlines would listen when they suggested that their aircraft would have greater range, power, and size than the Boeing aircraft for less money" (Serling, 1992).

On January 10, 1954, the industry was shaken when a BOAC Comet exploded in mid-air over the Mediterranean. A second Comet would disappear soon afterwards on a flight from Rome to Cairo. The cause of both crashes was explosive decompression of the fuselage caused by metal fatigue cracks, a result of the pressurization and depressurization of the cabin. This phenomenon was known from military jet aircraft. Fortunately, both Boeing and Douglas were aware of the problem and working on solutions. In fact, at the rollout of the B707 prospective customers were shown a film entitled *Operation Guillotine.* The film showed the results of explosive decompression and the solutions that Boeing had implemented. These solutions included triple-strength windows rounded at the corners, thicker-gauged skin braced with metal stripping, and small stopper straps running the length of the fuselage. The result was that the cabin remained intact after being deliberately pierced by several blades. The Comet did convince Boeing that more pilot training would be needed to fly the faster, more unforgiving jet aircraft (Serling, 1992).

With the 1959 release of the DC-8 jet, the future of air transportation appeared clear to almost all. The DC-8 was equipped with four engines and capable of over 600 miles per hour. An extended fuselage allowed for the seating of 260 passengers (Clouatre, 2002). Of course, not all airlines were convinced. Despite being impressed by the barrel roll of the Dash-80 (demonstration model for the B707), Eddie Rickenbacker, former World War I flying ace and CEO of Eastern Airlines, preferred the propeller-driven craft which he viewed as safer and more reliable. This kept Eastern out of the jet era until the early 1960s when his successors began a buying spree to catch up that left the airline heavily in debt going into deregulation (Bernstein, 1999). While the new jets did prove to be fuel hogs, guzzling more fuel on take-off than the Spirit of St Louis consumed crossing the Atlantic, the new jet engines proved far safer and more reliable (Serling, 1992). In fact, the introduction of the jet engine would dramatically lower accident rates. These rates would experience a sharp decline in the 1950s and 1960s, primarily attributable to the widespread introduction of the jet engine and improvements in jet engine reliability (Barnett and Higgins, 1989). In their study, Oster and Zorn (1989) found an overall decline in accidents of 54 percent with a 71 percent reduction in accidents attributed to equipment failure.

Too Big to fly?

Pan Am wanted a bigger plane and the B707 could not be stretched any further. The answer was the B747. In their letter of intent, Pan Am called for a 400 passenger aircraft with a range of 5,000 miles and a cruising altitude of 35,000 feet. The plane had to be able to take off in no more than 8,000 feet fully loaded and be capable of cargo nose loading. It seemed a very tall order for a company that did not even have a building large enough to construct such a plane. Nevertheless, three years after this letter, the first B747 would be rolled out. Building the aircraft would strain Boeing to the breaking point. The company laid off 5,000 people in a single week in 1970. By the end of that year, office staff had dropped from 24,000 to 9,000. Hourly workers declined from 45,000 to 15,000. This crisis inspired the famous billboard in Seattle asking "Will the last person leaving SEATTLE – Turn out the lights" (Serling, 1992). The first flight of the B747 from New York to London would take place on January 22, 1970. Of course, anyone who has flown internationally in recent decades knows that the B747 would become the symbol of international aviation. The B747 would go through a number of variants over the years that would reflect extended range and capacity as well as special purpose, for example, as a freighter. The latest is the -800 series. The B747 would eventually prove to be one of the best selling planes in history and the only plane in its "class" until the launch of the A380.

Down But Not Out

The idea of supersonic commercial flight became part of the dream list of aeronautical engineers and their companies within a decade of the 1947 flight of the Bell X-1. Reaching a speed of 700 miles per hour, Captain Charles "Chuck" Yeager officially achieved Mach 1.06, breaking the sound barrier. By 1953, the Douglas Skyrocket would break Mach 2, but Douglas would drop out of the US race for a commercial aircraft fairly early in the design competition in the US (Marchman, 2002). Boeing established its own small supersonic transport (SST) design team in 1957 and started building a supersonic wind tunnel three years later. In 1963, the Federal Aviation Administration announced plans to invite US aerospace companies to submit plans for an SST (Lynn, 1998). Boeing's US competitors were Lockheed and North American. North American and its Curtiss Wright engine would eventually drop out of the race. In 1966, Boeing unveiled its $11 million mock-up to the media. Later that year, the FAA proclaimed the Boeing-GE design the SST winner, but years of work would not result in an American SST; the US Senate would refuse to fund further development in 1971. Still, the dream would live on and be revived at Boeing briefly as the SonicCruiser before the decision was made to proceed with the plane that would become the B777 (Serling, 1992).

Over in Europe, Sud Aviation unveiled a scale model of a medium-range SST named the Super Caravelle at the 1960 Paris Air Show. By 1962, the French and British had signed the Anglo-French Supersonic Aircraft Agreement to jointly develop an SST following a decision by the FAA and US companies not to consider a partnership with the British to design an aluminum SST. The Anglo–French alliance (and the Germans joined later) would eventually result in the Concorde but the project was not without significant challenges. In addition to numerous technical challenges, the cost of the project continued to rise to well over ten times the original estimate, threatening to create a political backlash in each of the key countries. The French would ask Henri Ziegler, war hero, resistance fighter, head of Air France, and proponent of a very different concept in aerospace design, later called Airbus, to rescue the supersonic effort. The Concorde would make its maiden flight in March 1969, two months after the Soviet SST became the first SST into the air. The Soviet aircraft, the Tu-144, would crash in 1973 at the Paris Air Show. Meanwhile, the Concorde would not make it into commercial service until 1976 with its maiden voyage from London to Bahrain. While TWA and Pan Am in the US had taken options to pursue the Concorde, both would eventually back out leaving British Airways and Air France as the only commercial operators. Despite safety concerns in the development stages, the Concorde would fly accident-free until the 2000 crash of AF 4590 on take-off from Paris. Unfortunately, the premium pricing for the very narrow-bodied Concorde and the high operating costs would never make the aircraft a money-winning proposition, sadly confirming the predictions of Henri Ziegler that the plane would not sell and amounted to little more than a remarkable technical achievement in aviation (Aris, 2002; Serling, 1992; Shuman, 2002).

Ziegler was particularly concerned that the Concorde would take away the European focus from the one project that he did believe had the potential to re-establish Europe in the commercial aviation industry—Airbus. Airbus Industrie would be headquartered in France, but the final product of its labor would come from the assembly of parts designed and manufactured all over Europe. Establishing common rules and standards would prove simple compared to the logistics involved in moving large aircraft parts from one end of Europe to another. Although many thought that the concept of a wide-body, 200 passenger, twin engine airplane was madness, the Airbus A300 would be launched in 1972 and begin commercial service in 1974. By 1978, the A310, a shortened version of the A300 seating 218 passengers, had been launched. The Airbus family continued to grow with the A320, a single-aisle 130 to 170 passenger aircraft, the A321, a lengthened version of the A320 seating 180 to 200 passengers, the A330, a twin-engine 235 passenger aircraft, and the A340, an ultra-long, four-engine aircraft seating 295 passengers. Table 7.1 shows clearly the members of the Airbus family, basic seating number, release date of first aircraft, and total number of aircraft delivered. Several features distinguished the Airbus family from the start. First, the flight deck was standardized across models making training and operation more simple and less costly. Second, there was a two-person cockpit design, also a cost saver. Finally, the aircraft utilized the latest technology including the fly-by-wire controls which replaced the old mechanical systems with their cables attached to pulleys; these were later aided by hydraulics as the size of rudder and flaps increased with computers systems that would send electrical impulses to the moveable surfaces. Fly-by-wire had been used before in military aircraft and on the Concorde, but there was resistance to the new technology, particularly from pilot groups. Boeing would not take the plunge into fly-by-wire for another decade.

Table 7.1   Airbus family of aircraft

Aircraft	Seating	Released	Delivered	Backlog
A300	266–285	May 1969	561	0
A310	210–250	Jul 1978	255	5
A320	189	Mar 1984	2915	269
A321	185–220	Nov 1989	422	243
A330	375	Jun 1987	515	355
A340	239–475	Jun 1987	348	41

Breaking the Mold

In the book *Twenty-first Century Jet: The Making and Marketing of the Boeing 777*, (Sabbagh, 1996) Chapter 1—Why a new plane—begins with a quote from Alan Mulally who eventually took over as general manager of the 777 team when Phil Condit was promoted to President of the Boeing Company. His answer to the question was that airlines wanted an airplane bigger than the B767 but smaller than the B747. Boeing first tried several scenarios for stretching the 767 but the aerodynamics did not work well. In fact, the design was dubbed a "chipolata sausage"—very long and skinny–by unnamed representatives of a British airline. Design issues were not the only driver of a new plane; the 767 project was launched in 1978 and first delivered in 1982 and the technological advances since then seemed to argue for a new redesign rather than retrofit of an older one. The 777 would represent a number of firsts for Boeing including the first paperless design, the first fly-by-wire, first experiments in design-build teams and a new employee relationship, and first efforts to involve customers early in the process. In the early days of manufacturing, a plane was designed on paper and then a full-scale mock-up was used to catch any "conflicts" in the design, for example, a call button placed where an air duct was also planned. Computer-aided design (CAD) allowed the process to take place virtually. The 777 would use fly-by-wire like the Airbus aircraft on the market, but would rely on a back-up system written separately to avoid the possibility of a "computer glitch" in the first software being re-created in the back-up, a possible safety problem. Two new concepts would emerge with the 777: Working Together and design-build teams (DBTs). Working Together embodies the idea that the 777 team create an environment where everyone came together in "a shared thought, a shared vision, a shared appreciation, a shared understanding of what it is we're really going to try to accomplish together" (Sabbagh, 1996: 66). For a company with a history of tense labor relations, lay-offs, and union strife, the concept was a departure. Equally novel for Boeing was the Japanese concept of design-build teams linked vertically and horizontally to one another by a common team member. The DBTs were to insure that communications did occur between the design teams so that "interferences" were reduced. The program eventually had 250 DBTs coordinating design. The final new element was the Boeing effort to involve customers early and often. In the past, "Boeing policy had been to dream up a new plane, design it, make it, and then sit around and hope that enough people would buy it" (Sabbagh, 1996: 27). The costs and uncertainties made this old approach too risky even for Boeing who had "bet the farm" on projects such as the 707 and the 747. The 777 would become everything that the designers hoped that it would be after some early issues with its twin-engine design. Since the aircraft range was intended to allow extended over-water operations, there was some concern that the failure of one engine would create a safety hazard over water. This issue was resolved and the aircraft has proved to be remarkably successful, and safe (Sabbagh, 1996).

Table 7.2   Boeing family of aircraft

Aircraft	Seating	Released	Delivered	Backlog
B707	141	July 1954	1,010	0
B717	106	Oct 1995	155	0
B727	106–125	Nov 1962	1,831	0
B737	110–215	Jan 1967	5,626	2,072
B747	416–500	Sep 1968	1,397	125
B757	200	Jan 1978	1,049	0
B767	224–409	Aug 1981	960	51
B777	279–550	Oct 1990	693	353

Let the Mergers Begin

As Boeing was struggling with the cost of bringing the B747 to market, Donald Douglas was slipping further out of control at Douglas Aircraft, spending more and more time with his mistress, Peggy Tucker, who came to virtually control the company. By the middle of the 1960s, the company had amassed huge losses and was ripe for a take-over by McDonnell of St Louis, until then primarily a weapons manufacturer. Although the new McDonnell-Douglas would re-enter the commercial market with the DC-10, it would never achieve its former glory (Lynn, 1998). The main competitor for the DC-10 was the Lockheed L-1011 Tristar, Lockheed's first jetliner. Lockheed would sell 250 L-1011s, but the cost of developing the aircraft at the same time as the C-5, military cargo transport, would drive the company to the brink of bankruptcy, an event averted by a US government credit guarantee to lenders. The L-1011 would lose some $2.5 billion by the time it was retired in 1981 (Newhouse, 2007). At McDonnell-Douglas, things were not much better. By the 1990s, employees of the Douglas unit would complain that the company pencils were designed so that when they were sharpened the Douglas disappeared. The DC-10 was in fact inferior to the L-1011 in a number of ways and would prove to be the last commercial aircraft produced by the company. It would increasingly rely on its military aircraft and weapons development for profit (McCoy, 2002; Newhouse, 2007).

It became clear to even those outside the industry that McDonnell-Douglas was struggling in 1992 when the company posted a 51 percent drop in earnings overall with a 62 percent drop for the Douglas unit. By 1996, Douglas Aircraft had only 40 new aircraft orders. Without a viable commercial business, the company had to commit to an all-out effort to win the Joint Strike Force (JSF) fighter project for the

US combined forces' aircraft of the future, estimated to be worth approximately $300 billion in future sales. When McDonnell-Douglas was "deselected" by the Pentagon in 1996, there appeared to be little future for the company. Boeing would pay $13.3 billion for this former competitor in 1997. This move was not widely popular within Boeing's Commercial Division who felt that the Douglas unit was even weaker than projected and that the two cultures would clash. Strategic reasons that favored the merger were that the combined company better balanced the commercial and military sides of the industry (Newhouse, 2007). Whether it will face the kind of long-term tension that arose from the inability of the McDonnell-Douglas merger to forge a common culture and identity remains to be seen.

Another commercial aviation pioneer, Fokker, was to disappear during this era. The company began struggling in the 1970s and briefly explored a collaboration with McDonnell-Douglas in 1981. The company received a financial bail-out from the Dutch government in 1987 as development costs for their new line of aircraft soared. One condition of the government was that they seek out new partners for the company. DASA, the parent company of Daimler-Benz, was that partner. Their decision to focus on core operations in 1996 forced Fokker into bankruptcy. Stork Aerospace took over the repair and maintenance business while various interests have continued to raise the prospects of a re-entry into the civil aviation market. Thus, a decade after Airbus entered the commercial airline industry, there were only four major players in the market with Boeing in the top spot. Lockheed and McDonnell-Douglas, as noted above, would continue to decline under the weight of their own mistakes. This would set the stage for the new kid-on-the-block, Airbus, to emerge as the dominant threat in the large commercial aircraft (LCA) market, but the major players would ignore a segment of the market that other companies would target, the small regional jet market.

Small is Beautiful?

In 1986, a Canadian company founded in 1942 to manufacturer tracked vehicles for transport over snow bought Canadair, a leading Canadian aircraft manufacturer. This company, Bombardier, purchased Short Brothers in 1989, de Havilland in 1992 (51 percent stake and remaining 49 percent in 1997), and LearJet in 1995. Aviation was part of a broader diversification into transportation that included bus, rail, and water vehicles as well as services such as FlexJet and Skyjet. Bombardier would develop a line of commercial vehicles ranging from the 37 seat Dash 8 to the 145 seat C130 (see Table 7.3). A second entrant into this segment of the commercial industry was Embraer, a Brazilian company that began in the 1960s with general aviation and military aircraft. They too would go on to offer a line of commercial aircraft ranging from 30 to 122 seats. These aircraft are referred to in the industry as regional jets and have flourished on the wave of the strategic changes at the major carriers to move toward point-to-point service and/or a hubbing structure; these smaller aircraft are used to serve less dense routes that are channeled into the major carrier hubs where traffic is concentrated and placed on larger aircraft to the final destination. From a major carrier perspective, they can fill smaller aircraft and serve these markets more frequently. From an airport perspective, this has often resulted in more flights but little increase in overall passengers or revenue. This will become a bigger problem at heavily congested airports in the northeast US. From a passenger perspective, it often meant more cramped seating and less overhead space. From the perspective of the LCA manufacturers, it represents a potential, but unrealized, source of future competition.

Table 7.3   Regional jet families

Aircraft	Seating	Released	Delivered	Backlog
Bombardier				
Dash-8	37	1980	299	0
Q200	37	1980	100	5
Q300	50	Mar 1986	251	13
Q400	70–78	Jun 1996	175	89
CRJ100 (below)				
CRJ 100/200	50	Mar 1989	1,017	19
CRJ700/705	70	Jan 1997	271	10
CRJ900	86	Jul 2000	127	94
C110	110–125	*	*	*
C130	130–145	*	*	*
Embraer				
EMB120	30	1985	352	0
ERJ135	37	1995	108	0
ERJ140	44	1995	74	0
ERJ145	50	1995	682	51
Embraer 170	70–80	Oct 2001	137	26
Embraer 175	78–88	2002	46	60
Embraer 190	98–114	2002	99	292
Embraer 195	108–122	2002	10	42

* C Series entry anticipated in 2013.

Source: Various company websites

Powering the Planes

Pratt & Whitney, the company that had been founded in 1925 and formed one leg of William Boeing's vision of a fully integrated air transport company, would continue to produce engines for both military and civilian use as part of the United Aircraft Corporation. The company would change its name in 1975 to United Technologies Corporation (UTC). UTC would eventually become a diversified company with business units such as Otis Elevator, Hamilton Sundstrand, Carrier Heating and Air Conditioning, Pratt & Whitney, and Sikorsky Helicopter. In 1996, Pratt & Whitney would form an alliance with another engine manufacturer, General Electric (GE), to begin work on an engine that would power the world's largest commercial aircraft, the A380. Table 7.4 provides an overview of the Pratt & Whitney commercial engine family (Pratt & Whitney website, 2008).

GE, the company that first entered the "aviation business" in 1917 in response to the US government's search for a way to boost engine power at high altitude would go on to produce the nation's first jet engine in 1942, the I-A. Further development would result two years later in the J33 which would power the US Air Corps' first operational jet fighter. Building on years of expertise in the military market, GE would move into the civilian area in 1971 with the CF6, a high bypass turbofan engine first installed on the DC-10. The same year GE

Table 7.4   Large commercial aircraft engines

Manufacturer	Engine	In-Service Date	Aircraft Example
Pratt & Whitney	JT8D	1964	B737-100
	PW2000	1994	B757
	PW4000	1987	B747
	V2500	1988	A319
General Electric	CF34	1983	Bombardier CRJ-100
	CF6	1971	A300
	CFM56	1981	B737
	CT7	1978	Saab 340
	GE90	1995	B777
Rolls-Royce	RB211	1966	L-1011
	Trent 700	1995	A330
	Trent 800	1996	B777

Source: Company websites

began its partnership with Snecma, a French engine firm. The partnership was formalized in 1974 with the formation of CFM International, a 50/50 joint venture. CFM International would become one of the most successful aviation partnerships in history. Over the years, CFM engines would grab an increasing share of the short- to medium-range commercial aviation market and become the exclusive powerplant for the long range A340 (General Electric website, 2008).

Rolls-Royce, a company better known at the time for its cars, had entered the civilian market in the early 1950s with the Dart for the Vickers Viscount, the Avon for the Comet, and the Conway for the B707. By 1966, the main British engine makers, de Havilland, Bristol Siddeley, Blackburn, and Napier Aero Engines, had merged into Rolls-Royce. Unfortunately, this was the same year that Lockheed began work on its first jetliner, the L-1011 Tristar, which would feature the Rolls-Royce RB211. The high cost of development would drive Lockheed to the brink of bankruptcy while costs and early problems with the engine would lead Rolls-Royce into state ownership in 1971. The car divisions would be separated in 1973 and Rolls-Royce would return to the private sector in 1987. In 1990, Rolls-Royce would form an aero engine joint venture with BMW, a venture they assumed full control of in 2000 (Rolls-Royce website, 2008).

Conclusion

As the twentieth century came to an end, there were only two manufacturers Airbus and Boeing, left standing in the LCA market. However, rather than competition being reduced, it would intensify in the twenty-first century. The events of 11 September would naturally impact the manufacturing firms, but this time there would be a difference; the US domestic market no longer dominated the industry or the thinking of the aerospace manufacturers. The global airline industry would recover much more quickly than their US counterparts who would struggle to stay out or get out of bankruptcy. Meanwhile, the phenomenal growth in Asia would be reflected in their aviation industry as well. China and India would lead the region while airlines in the Middle East, notably Emirates and Qatar Airways, would expand to position themselves as the link between Europe and Asia.

Even more noteworthy is that the twenty-first century would become the stage for a new battle between Airbus and Boeing, a battle of visions. These two companies would begin to diverge sharply in their strategic vision of the future of the aviation industry. Boeing would plan for a future where point-to-point traffic would become the growing and driving force behind air travel. Airbus would envision a future in which aircraft even larger than the B747 would carry air travelers to the major international hubs. These visions would have a definite effect on the products each planned to release in the first decade of the new century and their fortunes would be measured by how the "market" appeared to be validating their vision.

References

Aris, S. (2002), *Close to the Sun: How Airbus Challenged America's Domination of the Skies*, Arum Press, London.

Barnett, A. and Higgins, M.K. (1989), 'Airline Safety: The last decade'. The Institute of Management Sciences 35 (1), pp. 1–21.

Bernstein, A. (1999), *Grounded: Frank Lorenzo and the Destruction of Eastern Airlines*, Beard Books, Washington, DC.

Clouatre, D. (2002), 'DC Plane Family' in Tracy Irons-Georges (ed.) *Encyclopedia of Flight*, pp. 205–7, Salem Press, Pasadena, CA.

Lynn, M. (1998), *Birds of Prey: Boeing Vs Airbus – A Battle for the Skies*, Four Walls Eight Windows, New York.

Marchman, J.F. (2002), 'Supersonic Aircraft' in Tracy Irons-Georges (ed.) *Encyclopedia of Flight*, pp. 645–7, Salem Press, Pasadena, CA.

McCoy, M.G. (2002), 'Lockheed-Martin' in Tracy Irons-Georges (ed.) *Encyclopedia of Flight*, pp. 420–423, Salem Press, Pasadena, CA.

Newhouse, J. (2007), *Boeing versus Airbus: The Inside Story of the Greatest International Competition in Business*, Alfred A. Knopf, New York.

Oster, C.V. and Zorn, C.K. (1989), 'Is it Still Safe to Fly?' in Moses, L.N. and Savage, I. (eds), *Transportation Safety in an Age of Deregulation*, Oxford University Press, New York.

Rummel, R.W. (1991), *Howard Hughes and TWA*, Smithsonian Institution Press, Washington, DC.

Sabbagh, K. (1996), *Twenty-First Century Jet: The Making and Marketing of the Boeing 777,* Scribner, New York.

Serling, R.J. (1992), *Legend and Legacy: The Story of Boeing and its People*, St. Martin's Press, New York.

Shuman, R.B. (2002), 'Concorde' in Tracy Irons-Georges (ed.) *Encyclopedia of Flight*, pp. 190–93, Salem Press, Pasadena, CA.

Websites

General Electric, http://www.geae.com/aboutgeae/history.html
Pratt & Whitney, http://www.utc.com/units/pw.htm
Rolls-Royce, http://www.rolls-royce.com

Chapter 8
A Brave New World

New Deal

In 1976, the British gave notice to the US government that it was terminating Bermuda I. According to the British, Bermuda I gave American carriers a disproportionate share of the traffic in large measure due to the liberal fifth freedom rights granted to US carriers. It had been thirty years since the events at Chicago and the signing of Bermuda I. The world was now a very different place. The Asian miracle saw, first Japan, then other Asian nations achieve double-digit levels of economic growth. Between 1950 and 1973, the Japanese gross domestic product grew at a rate of 10.5 percent a year. By the 1970s, the Japanese were producing over half the world's tonnage of shipping and as much steel as their US counterparts (Kennedy, 1987). In Europe, most of the nations were back to their pre-war levels of output by 1950. Between the period 1950–1970, European gross domestic product grew on average 5.5 percent a year while industrial product rose 7.1 percent (Landes, 1969). By contrast, the US economy had lost the relative advantages it possessed coming out of World War II. At the Bretton Woods conference in 1944, the world monetary system had been established pegging all major currencies to the US dollar. Unfortunately, US policies to finance both the war in Vietnam and domestic, social spending without increasing taxes had led the government to print more money, that is, increase the money supply. This in turn led to inflation and put pressure on the international monetary system. This system was abandoned in 1973 (Solomon, 1982). Rising inflation, declining shares of exports, and new foreign competition at home were taking their toll on the US economy.

For the British, the time appeared right to make a change. For their part, the US government, fearing a complete breakdown of the commercial air traffic with Great Britain, agreed to sign what became known as Bermuda II in 1977. This bilateral agreement virtually eliminated multiple carrier designations, established capacity limitations, and redressed the imbalance in fifth freedom rights. Bermuda II was seen as a major policy setback by the US government and a direct challenge to competitive markets.

Not Taking it Laying Down

To demonstrate its commitment to air transport liberalization, the US initiated three actions in 1978. The first action was to issue a statement entitled "Policy for the Conduct of International Air Transportation." This statement declared the US intention to "trade competitive opportunities, rather than restrictions" in order to expand competition and reduce prices (US Congress, 95th Congress, 1978). This policy was a denunciation of Bermuda II and a clear challenge to the rest of the aviation community. Shortly afterwards, the US Civil Aeronautics Board (CAB) issued an order to IATA to "show cause" why they should not be considered an illegal cartel as prohibited by US antitrust law. Since IATA membership was restricted to international carriers whose major tasks included setting fares and capacity, there was little argument of violation. This was also a warning to US carriers that their participation in the tariff- and capacity-setting activities of IATA would not be acceptable. Finally, in late 1978, the US became the first nation in the world to deregulate its air transport industry with the passage of the Airline Deregulation Act (Toh, 1998).

The purpose of the Airline Deregulation Act was "to encourage, develop, and attain an air transportation system which relies on competitive market forces to determine the quality, variety, and price of air services, and of other purposes." The Act phased out the CAB with its market control of entry/exit, pricing, and service levels. The proponents of deregulation argued that regulation forced competition based solely on service quality and thus created fares that in many cases were 50 percent higher than comparable intrastate (unregulated) fares. Studies had concluded that regulation also forced carriers to accept low, uneconomical load factors, raised labor costs, protected inefficient carriers, and prevented them from establishing economies of scale that would allow them to lower unit prices (Caves, 1962; Douglas and Miller, 1974; Jordan, 1970; Kahn, 1971). It should be noted that several studies found that the average cost per passenger did not fall as firm size increased which tended to indicate that airlines were not natural monopolies that should be subject to regulation (Eads, Nerlove, and Raduchel, 1969; Straszheim, 1969; White, 1979). On the other hand, larger aircraft and increasing density (increased frequency of flights, additional seats in existing flights) did appear to lower unit costs (Caves, Christensen, and Thetheway, 1984; Graham and Kaplan, 1982). Overall, deregulation was expected to improve service to the public, lower fares, allow carriers to achieve higher profits, and create a more competitive airline industry through the entry of new carriers as well as the freer regulatory environment afforded to existing competitors (Kane, 1998). These proponents have noted that there are more carriers flying today than in 1978 and that prices have fallen. Morrison and Winston (1997) have estimated that airfares fell 33 percent in real terms between 1976 and 1993. They attribute at least 20 percent of this decline to deregulation itself which increased competition and reduced costs at large and medium airports. A recent study of international carriers found that the major US carriers as a whole are most cost competitive than all but some of the lower wage Asian carriers (Oum and Yu, 1998).

While the impact of deregulation is still under debate, it is clear that following deregulation many US carriers were forced to undergo a painful process of restructuring that not all of them completed successfully. The financial crisis in the early 1980s hit all of the US carriers hard and led to industry consolidation and the creation of the hub-and-spoke system. In addition to the disappearance of such pre-deregulation carriers as Eastern Airlines and Pan Am, more than 200 new-entrant carriers have started and failed. By the early 1990s, another financial crisis had led the industry to develop complex holding structures, expand non-airline and/or discrete services, and race to create global seamless service through a network of strategic alliances (Rosen, 1995). Studies show that although there are more carriers flying, the top six carriers account for an increasingly large proportion of the total traffic. In 1985, the top six accounted for 62 percent of the domestic US traffic. By the early 1990s, these same six controlled 86 percent (Kim and Singal, 1993). Several studies have even suggested that real prices fell faster under regulation than they did in the post-deregulation period (Dempsey and Goetz, 1992; Dempsey and Gesell, 1997). In addition, it has been suggested that deregulation did not benefit all consumers in terms of the level of service or price. Small, outlying communities have in fact lost some portion of the service they enjoyed prior to deregulation and the fact that they may be linked to a single dominant hub may also increase their fares (Goetz and Dempsey, 1989; Jones, 1998). While there are no studies examining the pre- and post-deregulation levels of service quality among US carriers, there is a general consensus that it has declined significantly following deregulation and US carriers are conspicuously absent from surveys ranking the service quality of international carriers (Kahn, 1990; Dempsey and Goetz, 1992; Towers and Perrin, 1991; Zagat, 1992).

The benefits and costs of domestic regulation can and have been the subject of an entire book (or series of books) and are mentioned here only because freeing domestic markets added philosophical and economic pressure to the liberalization of international markets. The arguments briefly presented here are also intended to suggest some of the effects that might occur in a truly deregulated international market. Deregulation in the US market did appear to result in overall declines in fare prices and the appearance, at least temporarily, of new-entrant carriers. These pressures forced the industry to restructure to lower costs as noted above by Oum and Yu (1998). Whatever the successes or failures of deregulation in the long run, the US was now ready to push forward on the international scene with new initiatives designed to open international markets to greater competition and more market-based controls.

Encircling the World

In 1979, the US passed the International Air Transportation Competition Act which set out three goals for future US aviation policy. First, the US would push for multiple carrier designations, permissive route authority, and no operational restrictions on capacity and frequency. Second, air fares would be freed to respond to consumer demand. Finally, the US would work to eliminate discriminatory practices preventing US carriers from effectively competing in international markets. Some of the practices targeted for change included foreign computer reservation systems that favored other national carriers, government user fees at international airports that appeared excessive compared to domestic only airports, (the contention being that national governments were using these fees to subsidize smaller, local airports), and policies that required exclusive contracts for ground handling and other services (Toh, 1998).

The US would now pursue its new open skies policy through the application of two levers. The first lever was laid out by the Director of the Bureau of Pricing and Domestic Aviation and the CAB. The so-called Encirclement Strategy called for the US to bring pressure on smaller market countries to sign open skies agreements as a means of diverting traffic from larger aviation markets. The strategy was based on the assumption that open skies would lower fares between those countries involved in the bilateral agreement and cause passengers to change their traveling patterns in pursuit of lower fares. Two nations were primarily targeted for encirclement—Japan and Great Britain—because they represented the key entry ports for US travelers to Asia and Europe respectively (Levine, 1979). The US first targeted smaller market countries that generated very little third and fourth freedom traffic (to and from the US) since these countries stood to gain by simply getting greater access to US destinations. There could also be no question of exchanging domestic opportunities (cabotage) with these nations since they had little or no domestic markets to exchange for the sizable US domestic market.

The second lever to open skies came through the application of the US Department of Transportation's (DOT) policy on approving airline alliances. This policy based approval on either the coverage of the rights under existing bilateral or proven benefits to the US (Gellman Research Associates, 1994). In addition, the US DOT has granted immunity from antitrust enforcement to alliances between carriers from open skies countries (see Chapter 10 for a further discussion). The arguments being that there were proven benefits to the US deriving from these agreements. Antitrust immunity allowed competitors to coordinate on issues of pricing, capacity, and scheduling. Thus, they were able to achieve greater levels of operational integration, cut costing, and improved quality through coordination (Oum and Park, 1997).

Opening Up

Table 8.1 lists the open skies agreements signed by the US prior to 2001 and the dates of their signing. It is interesting to note the momentum that was building in the US efforts prior to 11 September. In part, this momentum represents the liberalization focus of the Clinton presidency as well as the growing international movement toward liberalization. Following 11 September, security issues dominated the aviation agenda. When aviation liberalization returned to the agenda, the issue that took center stage was the proposed multi-lateral agreement with the European

Table 8.1   Open skies agreements

Year	Month	Country	Year	Month	Country
2001	10	France	1997	7	Aruba
	9	Oman		2	Brunei
	5	Poland		10	Chile
	11	Sri Lanka		4	Costa Rica
				4	El Salvador
2000	11	Benin		4	Guatemala
	2	Burkina Faso		4	Honduras
	5	Gambia		6	Malaysia
	3	Ghana		12	Nether. Antilles
	10	Malta		5	New Zealand
	10	Morocco		5	Nicaragua
	2	Namibia		3	Panama
	8	Nigeria		12	Romania
	10	Rwanda		1	Singapore
	12	Senegal		3	Taiwan
	1	Slovak Republic			
	3	Turkey	1996	11	Jordan
				2	Germany
1999	8	Argentina			
	5	Bahrain	1995	5	Austria
	12	Dom. Republic		5	Belgium
	4	Pakistan		12	Czech Republic
	12	Portugal		5	Denmark
	10	Qatar		5	Finland
	11	Tanzania		5	Iceland
	4	UAE		5	Luxembourg
				5	Norway
1998	11	Italy		5	Sweden
	4	S. Korea		5	Switzerland
	5	Peru			
	2	Uzbekistan	1992	10	Netherlands

Union. This very complex and contentious agreement would take precedent over single country open skies.

Table 8.1 also illustrates the advance of the Encirclement Strategy which dictated that the countries approached first were small market nations. To understand the difference open skies has made in the bilateral process, it is interesting to note that the length of the bilateral agreements discussed in Chapter 5 between the US–Great Britain and US–Japan were sixteen pages in length. The US–Netherlands agreement is one page. Under routes, there appeared the following (see Table 8.2).

There is no mention of pricing, capacity or frequency restrictions in these agreements. Clearly, open skies agreements have been helpful in saving the world's trees. One might ask whether they have achieved the goals set forth by US policy and whether the consumers of the world have benefited from these new bilateral agreements.

Conspicuously absent from the open skies list in Table 8.1 are two countries: Japan and Great Britain. Understanding the reasons for their absence illustrates several key issues in international aviation. To those outside the industry it may be surprising to discover that not all the disagreement during the course of the bilateral negotiations between these countries took place between national governments; airlines on both sides of the debate disagreed among themselves and thus did not present a unified voice to their respective governments. The 1952 agreement between the US–Japan had given broad rights to three carriers: United, Northwest, and Japan Airlines. The remaining US carriers and All Nippon Airlines (ANA) received limited access in the 1980s due to a series of Memoranda of Understanding between Washington and Tokyo. Although Northwest, an incumbent carrier, supported open skies, United Airlines did not favor such an agreement,

Table 8.2   US–Netherlands open skies agreement

	Netherlands
A	The Netherlands via intermediate points to a point or points in the United States and beyond.
B	The Netherlands Antilles via the intermediate points Santo Domingo, Port au Prince, Kingston, Montego Bay, Camaguey, and Havana, to Miami.
C	The Netherlands Antilles to New York.
D	The Netherlands Antilles to San Juan.
	United States
A	The United States via intermediate points to a point or points in the Netherlands and beyond.
B	The United States via intermediate points to Aruba, Curacao, and St. Maarten and beyond (Air Transport Association of America, 2001).

which would have allowed more US competition into the Japanese market. From a policy perspective, the non-incumbent US carriers would have received more access under a "not-quite-open-skies" agreement and felt that the US should not push for open skies if that push jeopardized an overall agreement (Goldman, 1997). Similar issues surfaced in the open skies negotiations between the US and UK As part of their Oneworld alliance, American Airlines and British Airways had asked the US government for antitrust immunity which would only be granted in the presence of an open skies agreement. As Richard Branson, Chairman of Virgin Atlantic Airways, has noted, "they thought they had the British Department of Transport in their pocket, which unfortunately at the time was probably true. They also thought that the US Department of Transportation would be so eager to get rid of the Bermuda II disagreement, that it would be blind to the dire consequences such an alliance would hold for competition on the North Atlantic." (Branson, 1998: 100).

As this quote indicates, the competitors in both countries were generally more interested in simply gaining more access to US and UK markets than pursuing a broad open skies agreement. Carriers such as British Airways and American saw open skies initially as the only way to gain even more from the system. However, even these two carriers began to have doubts when they realized the price that the European Union intended to extract for its approval. Access to Heathrow Airport in London, the number one destination airport for North Atlantic passengers, is tightly constrained. In order to free up landing slots for new-entrant carriers, European officials have sought ways to encourage incumbent carriers to give up slots. It should be noted that, unlike in the US, slots can not be sold as an asset. In Europe, a carrier either uses a slot or loses it. The price of European approval was the surrender of 300 landing slots by British Airways and American (Phillips, 1999). British Airways "apparently decided the price for opening up Heathrow to new competition might not be offset by revenues gained from a full alliance with American" (Morrocco, 1998: 45).

If opening up Japan and the United Kingdom were the key goals of open skies, then the policy has not yet been a complete success, however, the example of US–Japan and US–UK internal divisions illustrates the interplay that occurs in free market systems where competitors look to individual profit and advantage over mutual, assured benefits. According to Adam Smith, the Father of market economics, individuals each acting in their own self-interest was supposed to result in a more perfect distribution of good and determination of price. In the case of airlines, market operation is never separated from government intervention. In a broader sense, open skies has helped to spread a more liberal environment for international pricing and capacity. In 1984, the US signed a multilateral agreement with the European Civil Aviation Conference that created zones of reasonableness for each fare class allowing individual carriers latitude in setting prices. The US also pushed for the inclusion of language within bilateral agreements that disallowed fares only with the mutual disapproval of the two parties to the agreement. This new pricing freedom placed tremendous pressure on IATA members to find ways around the IATA set fares. Many IATA members resorted to illegal discounting of fares through extra commissions to travel agents (Toh, 1998). These "bucket shops" sold blocks of tickets at prices more competitive with US carriers, but without sales receipt documentation that would be evidence of violation. Over time the zones of reasonableness became so broad that for all intents and purposes the market ruled in matters of pricing and IATA abandoned its role in fare setting.

Several studies by the US Department of Transportation (DOT) have concluded that open skies bilateral agreements have been effective in lowering fares. In the 1999 report *International Aviation Developments: Global Deregulation Takes Off*, the DOT reported that fares in open skies markets dropped 17.5 percent between 1996 and 1998 compared to only a 3.5 percent drop in non-open skies markets. Fares increased slightly in non-open skies gateway-to-gateway markets, but dropped 11.1 percent in open skies markets. In the 2000 report *International Aviation Developments: Transatlantic Deregulation – The Alliance Network Effect*, the DOT concluded that average fares to open skies countries declined by 20 percent overall compared to 1996, and approached 25 percent in connecting markets beyond European gateways. Significantly, double-digit fare reductions have occurred even in gate-to-gate markets in open skies countries (3). This report goes on to suggest that the link between open skies and strategic alliances have created an "alliance network effect" that has further lowered prices. In fact, it concludes that "alliance-based networks are the principle driving force behind transatlantic price reductions and traffic gains" (5).

The Next Step

The US deregulation of air transportation and the concomitant push for open skies would slowly erode the old system of international aviation set up in the post-World War II era. The liberalization and economic integration of Europe and Asia (Chapter 9) would further press the cause of liberalization. However, the fact remains that the system remained far from open. Branson (1998) has observed that the Virgin retail division in the US "has a rapidly growing chain of Megastores in this country (US) selling CDs, books, computer games, etc. We employ several thousand US staff and the increased competition our stores have brought clearly benefits the consumer. No one stands in our way when we want to invest … What a difference from aviation, where if Virgin wanted to establish a US airline we would be restricted to a mere 25 percent of the voting shares, and thus prevented from exercising any form of control." (101).

The events of 9/11 propelled the already slumping international airline industry to the brink of one of its greatest disasters, but in every crisis there is also the possibility of creating new futures. Some of these possible new futures will be the subject of Part III. First, we will look at the progress of deregulation and liberalization in Europe and Asia (Chapter 9). Then, we will look at the way airlines attempted to create global seamless networks that extend their reach throughout the world before liberalization took hold (Chapter 10).

References

Air Transport Association of America (2001), *Air Service Rights in U.S. International Air Transport Agreements: A Compilation of Scheduled and Charter Service Rights Contained in U.S. Bilateral Aviation Agreements,* Air Transport Association of America, Washington, DC.

Branson, R. (1998), 'Luncheon Address', *FAA Commercial Aviation Forecast Conference Proceedings: Overcoming Barriers to World Competition and Growth*, March 12–13, pp. 99–102.

Caves, R.E., Christensen, L.R., and Tretheway, M.W. (1984), 'Economies of Density versus Economies of Scale: Why Trunk and Local Service Airline Costs Differ,' *Rand Journal of Economics*, vol. 15, pp. 471–89.

Caves, R.E. (1962), *Air Transport and Its Regulators: An Industry Study*, Harvard University Press, Cambridge, MA.

Dempsey, P. and Goetz, A. (1992), 'Airline Deregulation and Laissez Faire Mythology'.

Dempsey, P. and Gesell, L. (1997), 'Airline Management: Strategies for the 21st Century'.

Douglas, G.W. and Miller, J.C. (1974), *Economic Regulation of Domestic Air Transport: Theory and Policy,* The Brookings Institution, Washington, DC.

Eads, G., Nerlove, M. and Raduchel, W. (1969), 'A Long-Run Cost Function for the Local Service Airline Industry: An Experiment in Non-Linear Estimation,' *Review of Economics and Statistics*, vol. 51, pp. 258–70.

Gellman Research Associates (1994), 'A Study of International Airline Codesharing', report submitted to Office of Aviation and International Economics, Office of the Secretary of Transportation, U.S. Department of Transportation, Washington, DC.

Goetz, A.R. and Dempsey, P.S. (1989), 'Airline Deregulation Ten Years After: Something Foul in the Air,' *Journal of Air Law and Commerce,* vol. 54, pp. 927–63.

Goldman, M. (1997), 'Negotiating not-quite-open-skies', *The Journal of Commerce*, November 1, p. 4.

Graham, D.R. and Kaplan, D.P. (1982), 'Airlines Deregulation is Working,' *Regulation*, vol. 6, pp. 26–32.

Jones, J.R. (1998), 'Twenty Years of Airline Deregulation: The Impact on Outlying and Small Communities,' *Journal of Transportation Management*, vol. 10, pp. 33–43.

Jordan, W.A. (1970), *Airline Regulation in America: Effects and Imperfections*, Johns Hopkins University Press, Baltimore, MD.

Kahn, A.E. (1990), 'Deregulation: Looking Backward and Looking Forward,' *Yale Journal of Regulation*, vol. 7, pp. 325–354.

Kahn, A.E. (1971), *The Economics of Regulation*, John Wiley & Sons, New York.

Kane, R.M. (1998), *Air Transportation,* 13th edition, Kendall/Hunt Publishing Company, Dubuque, IA.

Kennedy, P. (1987), *The Rise and Fall of the Great Powers,* Random House, New York.

Kim, E.H. and Singal, V. (1993), 'Mergers and Market Power: Evidence from the Airline Industry', *American Economic Review*, vol. 83, pp. 549–69.

Landes, D. (1969), *The Unbound Prometheus: Technological Change and Industrial Development in Western Europe from 1970 to the Present*, Cambridge University Press, Cambridge, UK.

Levine, M.E. (1979), 'Civil Aeronautics Memo by Michael E. Levine', *Aviation Daily*, March 8, pp. 1–7.

Morrison, S.A. and Winston, C. (1997), 'The Fare Skies: Air Transportation and Middle America,' *The Brookings Review*, vol. 15, pp. 42–5.

Morrocco, J.D. (1998), 'Open Skies Impasse Shifts Alliance Plans', *Aviation Week and Space Technology*, November 9, pp. 45–6.

Oum, T.H. and Yu, C. (1998), *Winning Airlines: Productivity and Cost Competitiveness of the World's Major Airlines*, Kluwer Academic Press, Boston, MA.

Oum, T.H. and Park, J. (1997), 'Airline Alliances: Current Status, Policy Issues, and Future Directions', *Journal of Air Transport Management,* vol. 3, pp. 133–44.

Phillips, E.H. (1999), 'Oneworld Late, But Powerful', *Aviation Week and Space Technology*, August 23, pp. 63–4.

Rosen, S.D. (1995), 'Corporate Restructuring: A Labor Perspective', in P. Cappelli (ed.), *Airline Labor Relations in the Global Era: The New Frontier*, pp. 31–40, ILR Press, Ithaca.

Solomon, R. (1982), *The International Monetary System*, Harper & Row, New York.

Straszheim, M.R. (1969), *The International Airline Industry*, The Brookings Institution, Washington, DC.

Toh, R.S. (1998), 'Towards an International Open Skies Regime: Advances, Impediments, and Impacts', *Journal of Air Transportation World Wide*, vol. 3, pp. 61–70.

Towers and Perrin (1991), *Competing in a New Market: Is Airline Management Prepared?,* Towers and Perrin, San Francisco, CA.

U.S. Congress (1978), *Hearings before the Subcommittee on Aviation of the Committee on Commerce, Science and Transportation*, United States Senate, 95th Congress Second Session on S.3363, pp. 19–20.

U.S. Department of Transportation (1999), *International Aviation Developments: Global Deregulation Takes Off*, Department of Transportation, Office of the Secretary, Washington, DC.

U.S. Department of Transportation (2000), *International Aviation Developments: Transatlantic Deregulation - The Alliance Network Effect,* Department of Transportation, Office of the Secretary, Washington, DC.

White, L.J. (1979), 'Economies of Scale and the Question of 'Natural Monopoly' in the Airline Industry,' *Journal of Air Law and Commerce*, vol. 46, pp. 545–73.

Zagat, W. (1992), *Zagat United States Travel Survey*, Zagat, New York.

Chapter 9
A Different View?

Different Markets, Different Views

As the US struggled with its Big Bang deregulation and pressured the rest of the world to open up its markets, Europe and Asia proceeded to follow their own path to deregulation and liberalization. In Europe, the process of aviation liberalization would be a part of a much bigger effort to integrate the countries in the European Community (EC) into the European Union (EU); aviation would be but one of the industries that would have to adjust to the changing times. In Asia, the story of liberalization and deregulation would be more mixed, but, in any event, international politics probably guaranteed that the rest of the world would not fall in line with the US position. Independence needed to be demonstrated. Still, some of the variations in attitudes and approaches had their roots in the fact that different regions and nations were faced with very different historical, geographic, and economic realities that inevitably shaped their approach to these issues.

The View from Europe

From a historical and geographic standpoint, Europe can be said to include all the nations west of the Russian Ural mountains, however, this chapter will focus primarily on the nations of the European Union (Table 9.1) with a brief look at the other nations that have asked to be considered for membership in the European Union (Table 9.2). These nations represent a very diverse set of languages, cultures, histories, and geographies. As Table 9.1 shows, the landmass of the EU countries ranges from 316 square kilometers for Malta to 547,030 square kilometers for France. Likewise, the population of EU countries ranges from 401,880 for Malta to 82,400,996 for Germany. This diversity in size and population is reflected in the level of aviation infrastructure within these countries as well as the importance of aviation to domestic travel and commerce. The geographic location of nations also influences the ability of potential hub city airports to attract traffic. The countries requesting consideration for admission to the EU under enlargement plans also show considerable diversity in size and population, ranging from Macedonia with an area of 25,333 square kilometers and 2,055,915 people to Turkey with an area of 780,580 square kilometers and 71,158,647 people.

There are a number of key differences between the air transport market in Europe and the US that have influenced the development of and approach to domestic deregulation and international liberalization. The Chicago Convention of 1944 led to the adoption of a one-airline policy in most of the nations of Europe. This airline, the *de jure* flag carrier, was seen as more of an instrument of state policy than a moneymaking enterprise (Graham, 1995). The typical European carrier was to be completely or partially owned by the state which would provide direct financial assistance to carriers "(1) to compensate airlines for the imposition of a public service obligation; (2) to develop and operate domestic service; (3) to provide service to economically underdeveloped regions; (4) to encourage the acquisition and operation of specific airplanes; or (5) simply to cover an airline's operating losses" (Taneja, 1988: 59). This flag carrier would develop its national hub, usually at the nation's capital, and dominate that hub accounting for over 50 percent of the departures (Borenstein, 1992). The network of airline routes would reflect national requirements and former colonial ties. As a whole, the old European air transport market would be characterized by low productivity, high unit costs, and high fares. In contrast, the US domestic market was substantially larger than that of any single EU nation and benefited from a number of privately owned carriers throughout its history, although it too received government assistance in its early development from airmail rates (Graham, 1995; Sinha, 2001).

Another feature that distinguishes the European market from that of the US is the higher level of intermodal competition from automobiles and high-speed trains. The average length of a haul in Europe is 750 kilometers, half the US average length of a haul. This increases the competition from other modes of transportation and has limited the ability of airlines to develop hub-and-spoke systems like their US counterparts. This in turn has limited consumer ability to achieve reduced fares by accepting indirect routing over direct flights to destination. With the exception of the northeastern corridor of the US, train service does not offer a viable substitute to air travel for US consumers (Graham, 1995; Sinha, 2001). European carriers also face competition from a well-developed air charter market. In the early 1990s, charter services in the US accounted for less than two percent of all passenger miles, but more than 25 percent of the passenger miles in Europe. These European charter passengers were predominantly leisure travelers, leaving scheduled carriers to serve business travel needs (Sinha, 2001). Finally, there is a significant difference in the product mix between US and European carriers. For US carriers, only 15.4 percent of the departures in 1990 were international while international departures represented 52.9 percent of the departures of European carriers (Sinha, 2001). In short, it was neither feasible nor probably possible to institute US style deregulation in Europe.

The European Way

When the European Economic Community, a predecessor of the current European Union, was formed in 1957, it established a Common Transport Policy, but failed to include aviation in the original draft (Button, 1997). This oversight was corrected in a 1986 ruling by the European Court of Justice which declared that air transport would henceforth be subject to the competition rules of the Treaty of Rome. The

Table 9.1   Information on European Union nations

Country	Area*	Population**	Airports (paved)
Austria	83,870	8,199,783	55 (25)
Belgium	30,528	10,392,226	43 (27)
Bulgaria	110,910	7,322,858	214 (131)
Cyprus	9,250	788,457	16 (13)
Czech Rep.	78,866	10,228,744	122 (45)
Denmark	43,094	5,468,120	91 (28)
Estonia	45,226	1,315,912	19 (12)
Finland	338,145	5,238,460	148 (76)
France	547,030	60,876,136	476 (292)
Germany	357,021	82,400,996	550 (331)
Greece	131,940	10,706,290	81 (66)
Hungary	93,030	9,956,108	46 (20)
Ireland	70,280	4,109,086	34 (15)
Italy	301,230	58,147,733	132 (101)
Latvia	64,589	2,259,810	42 (21)
Lithuania	65,200	3,575,439	87 (30)
Luxembourg	2,586	480,222	2 (1)
Malta	316	401,880	1 (1)
Netherlands	41,526	16,570,613	27 (20)
Poland	312,685	38,518,241	123 (83)
Portugal	92,391	10,642,836	66 (44)
Romania	237,500	22,276,056	61 (25)
Slovakia	48,845	5,447,502	35 (20)
Slovenia	20,273	2,009,245	14 (6)
Spain	504,782	40,077,100	133 (85)
Sweden	449.964	8,876,744	255 (147)
UK	244,820	59,778,002	470 (332)

* Square Km. ** Estimated July 2007 figures. Data on airports from 2007

Source: Central Intelligence Agency (CIA) Factbook

Table 9.2   Information on selected EU enlargement countries

Country	Area*	Population**	Airports (paved)
Croatia	56,542	4,493,312	68 (23)
Macedonia	25,333	2,055,915	17 (10)
Turkey	780, 580	71,158,647	117 (90)

* Square Km. ** Estimated July 2007 figures. Data on airports from 2007
Source: CIA Factbook

following year, the Council of Ministers adopted the so-called First Package which allowed multiple designation of carriers on country-to-country routes and high volume city-to-city routes, fifth freedom rights on city-to-city routes up to 30 percent of capacity, automatic approval of discount fares up to 55 percent, and double approval of full fares. The Second Package, adopted in 1990, included a double-disapproval provision for full fares and an extension of fifth freedom rights to city-to-city routes up to 50 percent of capacity. Protection was also granted for routes designated as public service obligations. The Third, and final, Package was implemented in 1993 and ended on April 1, 1997. This package granted full access to all routes including cabotage which came into effect on April 1. It removed all restrictions on fares subject to the right of the European Commission to intervene in matters of predatory pricing and seat (capacity) dumping. All distinctions were removed between charter and scheduled carriers and freedom was granted to start an airline provided it was 1) EU owned, 2) financially sound, and 3) in compliance with all safety requirements (Graham, 1997, 1995; Sinha, 2001).

Overall Results

There have been few studies to date on the effects of the three packages. The early packages, combined with the more liberal bilateral agreements signed during the 1980s, do appear to have increased the frequency on some routes and reduced leisure (but not business class) fares, particularly where multiple carrier designation allowed new market entry (Button and Swann, 1989; Graham, 1995). Morrell (1998) has found that the number of cross-border routes served increased by 11 percent between 1989 and 1992. This number rose to 25 percent between 1992 and 1995. The number of flights operated also increased during these periods by 14 and 18 percent respectively. The average frequency on all intra-EU routes increased from 13.9 departures per week in 1989 to 15.5 in 1992. Seat capacity did not increase between 1989 and 1992, but did go up after 1992 on routes that were served by three or more carriers. A 1995 study by the Civil Aviation Authority of Great Britain also found that consumers only gained from lower fares, better service, and better connecting flights when there were at least three competitors on a given route. In effect, actual, rather than threatened, entry was essential to realizing benefits from liberalization (Abbot and Thompson, 1989; Humphreys, 1996). A study by the European Commission (1996) concluded that competition had little effect on routes run as a monopoly or duopoly. Unfortunately, approximately 94 percent of the intra-EU routes fall into this category.

The effect of liberalization on established EU carriers has until recently been relatively limited. Carriers such as British Airways and KLM worked to improve their long-haul market and hub system more than their intra-EU system (Civil Aviation Authority, 1995). While one of the key features of the first two packages was the extension of fifth freedom rights, evidence indicates that few carriers exploited these rights (Graham, 1995). Some of the peripheral EU countries did initially attempt to exploit the intra-EU opportunities of cabotage, but many of these services were discontinued due to limited profitability (Morrell, 1998). Thus, there was generally little third carrier entry in many markets, certainly not by the traditional flag carriers.

Another goal of deregulation and liberalization is the creation of new entrants. Between 1992 and 1995, there was a net gain of six carriers (Morrell, 1998). The most successful of these carriers are Ireland's Ryanair, the UK's easyJet and Virgin Express. In 2001, these carriers posted significant profits compared to their traditional counterparts in the EU. In fact, it appears that 2001 was to be a turning point for the low-cost European entrants. Industry experts had expected them to increase their share of intra-European passenger traffic from 7 percent in 2001 to over 14 percent over the next five years, however, analysts were somewhat divided over the extent to which low-cost carriers could continue to post gains in the EU market given some of the EU's more unique problems (Binggeli and Pompeo, 2002; R2A, 2002). Ryanair has proved many of the analysts wrong, going from 11 million passengers in 2001 to 42.5 million in 2006 (Air Transport Intelligence, 2008). As with US low-cost carriers (LCCs), the events of 11 September created new opportunities in Europe for this model of aviation business.

With liberalization, particularly the implementation of the Third package, charter operators in the EU were presented with a number of options. They could now (1) enter scheduled service in a head-to-head competition with EU flag carriers; (2) enter scheduled service on leisure routes; or (3) stay in the core charter market and develop their long-haul operations. The evidence to date shows that option 1 was not very successful for these operators (Air Europe, Dan Air, Trans European). Some carriers did have limited success on certain routes (Maersk Air, Transwede, Transavia), but generally charter operators have not provided a serious challenge to the established carriers (Morrell, 1998). Wallace, M., Tiernan, S., Rhoades, D.L., and Linck, T (2008) found that, despite a good deal of consolidation in the charter industry, most of the chapter companies have lost passengers since 2001 while the LCCs appear to be major winners.

UK experience   Among the EU countries, the UK has attempted to apply a policy of liberalization in its domestic markets for the longest period of time. British

Airways continues to cling to its status as the dominant carrier, but change was coming into the British aviation world where "inequalities of opportunity" had long existed among the UK carriers. Richard Branson of Virgin Atlantic Airways has been very vocal in complaining that British Airways has the British Department of Transport in their pocket (Branson, 1998). According to Graham (1995), the New Right which dominated UK politics during the 1980s when British Airways was privatized insisted that privatization could not damage the airline's international competitive strength and so "the consequent protection of BA's position, and the reconstruction of its finances prior to privatization in 1987, not only exacerbated the long-term problems created by the airline's dominance of the UK air transport industry but, simply, were factors incompatible with the stimulation of competition" (148). He suggests that three other factors prevented the Civil Aviation Authority from achieving its goals of greater liberalization. The first factor was business failure and consolidation. The same phenomena also occurred in the US market and limited the level of competition in many areas. The second factor was the "goal" of developing a UK carrier to serve the secondary London airport, Gatwick, to relieve congestion at Heathrow. The final factor is BA itself dominating at the UK airport of Heathrow which continues to be the primary airport of London. Despite these problems, the UK managed to maintain a higher level of viable internal competition than other EU countries during this period. Barrett (1999) has reported that the productivity on routes between Ireland and the UK resulted in higher levels of traffic and faster falling fares than that of the 14 other airlines of the Association of European Airlines. Liberalization and competition allowed UK carriers to achieve lower unit costs and higher productivity than their EU counterparts (Alamdari, 1998).

The Netherlands   With a total area of only 41,526 square kilometers and a population of 16,570,613 (Table 9.1), the Netherlands does not have a significant domestic market. Not surprisingly, the focus of KLM, the Netherlands flag carrier, was primarily on international markets. As the airline of the first country to sign an open skies agreement (Table 8.2), KLM focused its attention on long-haul operations across the North Atlantic, forming a strategic alliance with the US carrier Northwest. KLM and Northwest were the first to receive antitrust immunity from the US government based on the existence of an open skies agreement. This allowed them to coordinate closely on issues of schedules, pricing, and capacity which in turn has resulted in a financially strong network with a high level of network density (frequency) and a market presence greater than its geographic scope would suggest (Merrill Lynch, 1999).

Remaining Obstacles

The EU faced a number of hurdles in its efforts to liberalize. First, there was the continuing issue of airline subsidies. In 1993 alone, six EU carriers, Air France, Olympic, Iberia, TAP-Air Portugal, Alitalia, and Aer Lingus, required government subsidies to remain in business (Graham, 1995). Most recently, the Belgium government stepped in to salvage something of its flag carrier, Sabena. These subsidies, while approved by the European Commission, were vigorously opposed by other members of the EU. This apparent preference of governments for national carriers flies in the face of the objective to remove such barriers to free trade in the EU as a whole. It also keeps excess capacity in the European market in a way similar to the liberal bankruptcy laws of the US In both cases, artificial barriers prevent the market from adjusting quickly in market demand downturns and spread the problem to other carriers.

The EU has not yet seen the level of new entrants into liberalized markets that the United States witnessed after deregulation. In part this is a function of the slot allocation problem in Europe. Under the IATA-agreed rules accepted by the EC, slots must be allocated on a non-discriminatory basis, but historic rights may be considered. Given the pattern of European air transport development, the traditional flag carriers have superior access to slots at the major airports which tend to be those that face capacity restrictions. If slots cannot be sold, which has been historically true in the EU, it was in the best interest of airlines to maintain rights to these slots by exercising at least the minimum number of departures. Thus, it was very difficult for new entrants to gain the landing slots required to offer competition at these hubs. The European Commission attempted to open up slots as a prerequisite for approving exemptions from competitive rules for airline alliances, but this has not been enough at many airports. Low-cost carriers like Ryanair have attempted to bypass major hubs but Europe has far fewer secondary airports than the US.

Low-cost new entrants face other problems as well. First, the low-cost segment in Europe has been smaller than in the US and there is overlap between the charter carriers who may sell up to a third of their seats without the hotel package that normally accompanies it and the traditional flag carriers who offer discounted weekend travel. Second, if the US pattern holds, then the first entrant into the markets (route) will be able to stimulate new growth and capture the markets share. Later entrants with similar costs structures will find it more difficult to generate traffic. At the moment, there are still a number of routes not served by low-cost carriers so there is some room for growth, but the surge by Ryanair and easyJet may be a sign that grown potential will slow soon. From the EU consumer perspective, low-cost carriers have lowered prices. Like Southwest in the US, many of these entrants have adopted a no-frills, secondary airport strategy that is gaining momentum, although Ryanair appears to be set on making Southwest look like a luxury carrier. This has provoked some backlash from consumers, but not enough to slow its growth (Creaton. 2004). Like Southwest, analysts continue to predict that their growth will be limited in the future due to a lack of routes with sufficient origin and destination traffic to support entry (Morrell, 1998).

Future EU Liberalization

It seems likely that the EU will admit most, if not all, of the countries in Table 9.2. Like the original 15 EU nations, the recently admitted and proposed nations share many of the same structural and historic problems that have inhibited greater liberalization of their air transport markets. Preparing for entry into the EU, the air transport industry of these nations began to reorganize by 1) placing new organizational and management structures into place including privatization, strategic alliances, and joint ventures with western firms, 2) attempting to reorient their networks westward to attract the tourism markets, 3) acquiring more western aircraft, and 4) upgrading their infrastructure (Graham, 1995).

While it does not appear to be productive to argue over whether the approach to deregulation and liberalization taken by the EU was better than that of the US, the evidence to date suggests that consumers in the EU have not yet benefited to the same extent as consumers in US markets (Sinha, 2001). This may simply be a function of time, however, a number of authors have suggested that there is reason to believe that the EU will never achieve the level of fares or the connectivity of US markets. Taneja (1988) argued that two factors were likely to keep fares higher in Europe than those in the US. The first was the policy of EU governments to maintain inefficient EU carriers with subsidies and other benefits. This not only keeps excess capacity in the marketplace, but allows inefficient carriers to continue to operate using more expensive equipment, less efficient route structures, and less productive labor. The second reason was the overall higher cost structure of EU airlines that is partly a function of higher input costs such as labor, but is also the result of shorter average lengths of flights. Graham (1995) went on to argue that the hubbing patterns in the EU created a "considerable degree of inertia" (154). In connection with hubs, he cited two factors that inhibit the connectivity of EU markets. First, these hubs continued to be national in nature and dominated by the flag carrier. Second, regional carriers tended to operate in connection with these national carriers. This meant that "peripheral regions were likely to be linked by direct flights to national air hubs, but not more widely to the EU itself" (167). As noted in the previous chapter on the US market, smaller, outlying areas often experienced declines in service levels and higher fares caused by routing to a major hub dominated by a single carrier (Goetz and Dempsey, 1989; Jones, 1998). The very unevenness of the population within the EU means that the traffic demands on some routes will not support significant frequency. This could continue to hinder connectivity patterns and necessitate transfers across hubs (Graham, 1995).

The View from Asia

According to the ICAO regional classification, the Asia–Pacific is composed of 34 nations covering 16,000 kilometers. It extends from Afghanistan in the west to Tahiti in the east and from Mongolia in the north to New Zealand in the south.

The Asia–Pacific accounted for roughly 50 percent of the total world population and was responsible for 25 percent of the world's scheduled passenger traffic in 2001 (ICAO, 2002). ICAO has projected that the region could increase its share of traffic to 42 percent by 2020 (Sinha, 2001). This growth is obviously tied to the rapid economic development of the region and the rising level of income, both of which are closely linked to aviation activity.

According to Taneja (1988), the growth in Asian–Pacific aviation can be attributed to a number of factors including high-growth, export-oriented economies, productive, lower-cost airlines, and coordination and cooperation between airlines and their respective governments. He also cited the pro-competitive policies of the governments of the US and Asia for some of this growth. The Asian financial crisis slowed the growth rates in both economic and aviation terms, but growth has since returned. Passenger numbers are predicted to grow annually through 2011 at 5.9 percent for the region as a whole (IATA, 2007; ICAO, 2002). While there is a great deal of variation in the general approaches of the countries in the Asia–Pacific region, they too have been on a path toward greater deregulation and liberalization even if the pace has been somewhat slower and more uneven than the North American and European markets.

Variations on a Theme

Graham (1995) divides the Asia–Pacific into five categories: (1) China, (2) the wealthy states of the West-Pacific Rim: Japan, Brunei, South Korea, Singapore, Taiwan, and Hong Kong as well as Thailand, Malaysia, Indonesia, and the Philippines, (3) the East Asian low-income nations of Vietnam, Cambodia, Laos, and Myanmar, (4) Australia, New Zealand, and the Southwest Pacific islands, and (5) the South Asian nations of India and Pakistan. These divisions will be used to explore the aviation environment in Asia.

China   With a population of almost 1.3 billion and an area of 9,596,960 square kilometers (Table 9.3), China can not be left out of any discussion of aviation even if it had not experienced some of the highest economic growth rates of the past decade. Until 1988 China had only one state airline, CAAC, which was a division of the Civil Aviation Administration of China. This same division also ran the air traffic control system and administered airports in China. In 1998, the CAAC created six regional airlines—Air China, China Eastern, China Southern, China Northern, China Northwest, and China Southwest—which were expected to run as more or less independent carriers by 1995 (Aviation Daily, 2001). In April 2001, the CAAC announced plans to merge nine airlines under its control into three larger groupings—China Southern Airlines Group, China Eastern Airlines Group, and Air China Group (Centre for Asian Business Cases, 2002). Air China, originally designated as the international division, took over China Southwest in 2002. Also in 2002, China Eastern took over China Northwest. In 2003, China Southern absorbed China Northern. In addition to Cathay Pacific and its subsidiary

Dragonair, Hong-Kong-based carriers that have now reverted to Chinese authority, there were roughly 60 other airlines or air cargo operators in China as of 2007 (Air Transport Intelligence, 2008). In other efforts to restructure Chinese aviation, the CAAC has announced plans to overhaul the domestic air route network, permit ticket discounting, encourage airport alliances, and raise air transport service fees (Centre for Asian Business Cases, 2002; Aerospace Daily, 2001). Although passenger traffic has been predicted to grow at a rate of approximately 11 percent a year through 2010, this still represents a small percentage of the domestic Chinese market (Graham, 1995). In order to meet the expected demands, China and the CAAC are focusing on improving the infrastructure within China.

Several factors hindered the growth of civil aviation in China during this period. First, the country remained a relatively low-income nation which limits the internal demand for air travel, even if there were no restrictions on travel imposed by the Chinese government. Second, while inbound traffic has increased with economic growth, there was not a corresponding growth in outbound traffic (again, largely reflecting the policies of the Chinese government). Third, a number of crashes by Chinese carriers led to questions about the overall system safety. Fourth, there was a shortage of experienced airline pilots. Finally, the air traffic control system and the airport infrastructure needed major upgrading requiring a good deal of investment from government or private sources (Graham, 1995). Despite its potential, China has yet to embrace a more liberal domestic or international policy in regard to aviation and is not likely to achieve anything like its true potential until it does, but even without such a policy the number of Chinese passengers is likely to experience significant growth over the next two decades fueled mainly by rising standards of living.

The West Pacific Rim   This area not only includes the Asian Tiger economies of South Korea, Singapore, Taiwan, and Hong Kong, but the all-important North American gateway of Japan. It is also home to some of the strongest and largest carriers in the Asian region, notably Singapore Airlines, Thai Airways, Korean Airlines, and Japan Air Lines (JAL). Differing views on privatization are reflected in the fact that carriers in this area range from wholly owned government operations such as Garuda to partially owned carriers such as Singapore and Malaysian to private carriers such as JAL. Whether privately or governmentally owned, Asian carriers continue to be treated as flag carriers by and large, receiving preferential government treatment in matters of international aviation. International routes tend to be highly competitive both within the region and to Europe and North America. Five of the countries in this area have open skies agreements with the United States—Singapore, Taiwan, Malaysia, Brunei, and South Korea. Of these countries, Singapore, Taiwan, and Brunei have little or no domestic markets. The focus of growth has been almost exclusively long haul international travel, making open skies a good option.

Singapore Airlines, partially privatized sixteen years ago, has consistently been rated one of the best international carriers in the world. It flies one of the most modern fleets in the industry to over 40 countries (BBC News, 1999). Until 2001, it was also a consistently profitable carrier as well. In fact, the airline not only weathered the Asian financial crisis well but used its assets to good advantage purchasing stakes in other financially troubled Asian carriers such as Air New Zealand (BBC News, 2001a). In 2000, Singapore Airlines purchased 49 percent of the British carrier, Virgin Atlantic (BBC News, 1999). The economic slowdown that began prior to 9/11 combined with the aviation slump following the terrorist attacks led the carrier to post profits for the period April to November 2001 that were 90 percent below the prior year. Despite these problems, they continue to remain one of the strongest competitors in Asia (BBC News, 2001a). They opened a low-cost subsidiary, Tiger Airways, in 2003 and jointly purchased 24 percent of China Eastern in 2007. They were the launch customer for the A380.

Thai Airways who along with Singapore Airlines is a member of the Star Alliance was even harder hit by the aviation crisis that followed 9/11. In September 2001, the board of Thai was forced to resign amid labor disputes and bomb threats that capped off a year of carrier losses. Thai debt at the time was estimated to be roughly 18 times its equity and the airline was considered to be overstaffed with a total workforce of 25,000 compared to 14,000 at Singapore Airlines. The Thai government reduced its stake in the carrier from 93 percent to 70 percent by offering shares to the general public (BBC News, 2001b). Of the Asian carriers included in the Oum and Yu (1998) study of cost competitiveness, Thai had the lowest input costs in the region but was twice as inefficient as the next worst carrier in the region.

South Korea has two major international carriers, Korean Airlines and Asiana, both of which are privately owned. Beginning in 1992, the government ceased to set fares, although Korean domestic air travel has not seen significant drops in fares. The entry of Asiana in 1988 did begin to increase passenger enplanements but again had little or no effect on fares. In effect, the Korean government allowed a collusive duopoly to form following changes made in 1994 (Sinha, 2001).

Korean Airlines and Asiana were hard hit by the Asian crisis, however, these problems were overshadowed in many ways by the decision of the US Federal Aviation Administration to downgrade them from a Category 1 to a Category 2, meaning that they failed to meet the minimum international safety standards set by ICAO. As a result of this action, Asiana, the second largest carrier in South Korea lost its code-sharing pact with American Airlines costing it an estimated US$16 million. Korean Airlines had earlier lost its international alliance with the US carrier Delta Air Lines after a series of accidents in 1999. The Korean government temporarily banned it from international flights in 1999. Following joint efforts by the Korean government and the FAA, Category 1 status was renewed. Korean Airlines made a series of changes that allowed it to rejoin the SkyTeam alliance with Delta and Air France (BBC News, 2001d).

Malaysia and Indonesia were two other countries hit very hard by the Asian crisis. Malaysia Airlines suffered like many Asian carriers during the Asian financial crisis, 11 September the fall-off in demand after 11 September, and the

Table 9.3   Information on selected Asia–Pacific countries

Country	Area*	Population**	Airports (paved)
Australia	7,686,850	20,434,176	461 (317)
China	9,596,960	1,321,851,888	467 (403)
Cook Islands	240	21,750	9 (2)
East Timor	15,007	1,084,971	8 (3)
Fiji	18,270	918,675	28 (3)
India	3,287,590	1,129,866,154	346 (250)
Indonesia	1,919,440	234,693,997	652 (158)
Japan	377,835	127,433,494	176 (145)
Malaysia	329,750	24,821,286	116 (36)
New Zealand	268,680	4,115,771	121 (41)
Pakistan	803,940	147,663,429	120 (85)
Philippines	300,000	91,077,287	255 (84)
Singapore	693	4,553,009	8 (8)
Taiwan	35,980	22,858,872	41 (38)
Thailand	514,000	65,068,149	106 (65)
Vietnam	329, 560	85,262,356	44 (37)

*Square Km. ** Estimated July 2002 figures. Data for airports from 2001
Source: CIA Factbook

bird flu scare. Major restructuring over the last two years has helped to place the airline firmly back in the black for 2007 (Ionides, 2008). Indonesia's carriers have not done quite as well. During the financial crisis, Garuda, one of the two Indonesian international and government-owned carriers, nearly collapsed. Garuda struggled to return to profitability by rationalizing its fleet and cutting unprofitable routes and was scheduled to begin the process of privatization in 2003, however, this was not to be. Another international carrier, Merpati Nusantara Airlines, once a subsidiary of Garuda that had been delinked in 1997, took over the domestic routes of Garuda. In 2007, the EU placed all Indonesian carriers on their list of banned airlines (Air Transport Intelligence, 2008).

As you will remember from Chapter 8, the United States policy of encirclement in Asia was aimed at opening up the Japanese market, the key Asian market from North America at the time. This policy was less than successful. Japanese policy was marked by a strict regulation of the aviation system after the so-called "aviation constitution" was adopted in 1972 dividing the market among the three Japanese carriers, Japan Air Lines (JAL), All Nippon Airways (ANA), and Japan Air Systems (JAS). JAL was to serve the main domestic truck routes and the international market. ANA was assigned short-haul international charter flights and other domestic trunk routes. JAS was to serve primarily on local routes. Little or no competition was allowed between these carriers. In 1986, the Council for Transport Policy recommended the privatization of JAL, the introduction of greater domestic competition, including new-entrant carriers, and the end of JAL's international monopoly. In 1996, a zone fare system was introduced allowing carriers to offer a discount up to 50 percent of the minimum fare, however, fares for all carriers operating on the same routes were to be the same. Although new entrants were allowed in the market, restrictive regulations and limited airport capacity hindered the development of more carriers for a number of years (Graham, 1995). One of the surviving new entrants from the post-1996 market is Skymark who applied for several new routes following the decision of ANA to abandon them as part of a re-thinking of its domestic route structure. Skymark flew 2.9 million passengers in 2006 on its four domestic routes but has failed in recent years to make a net profit (Air Transport Intelligence, 2008). The ANA re-thinking was triggered by the decision of the Japanese government to allow JAL and JAS to merge under a new holding company, Japan Airlines Systems Corporation (Reuters, 2002). JAL rebranded itself in 2004 as Japan Airlines International and officially joined the Oneworld alliance in 2007. The JAL group includes the following regional or low-cost carriers: Hokkaido Air System, JAL Express, JALways, Japan Air Commuter, Japan Asia Airways, Japan Transocean Air, J-Air and Ryukyu Air Commuter. ANA struggled for a number of years to recreate itself as a more international carrier, but losses in 2000 temporarily forced it to suspend some services. They rebranded themselves in 2002 and became the launch customer for the B787. In 2006, ANA carried approximately 50 million passengers to some 52 destinations. The ANA airline group includes the following carriers: Air Central, Air Hokkaido, Air Japan, Air Next, Air Nippon, Air Nippon Network and ANA & JP Express (Air Transport Intelligence, 2008). Overall, Japanese consumers have not yet fully benefited from the more liberal policies of the government, although there is some evidence that airlines have been able to lower their own costs (Sinha, 2001). Internationally, JAL and ANA have suffered from higher input costs and lower efficiency than most of their US and European competitors and all but Thai Airways in Asia. According to Oum and Yu (1998), these carriers were 52.7 and 63.5 percent less cost competitive in 1993 than the benchmark US carrier American Airlines.

East Asian Nations Three characteristics define this group of nations. First, they all are among the poorest nations in the world. Second, they have all experienced war and civil unrest that have left their economies and their transportation systems in ruins. Finally, they will each require substantial foreign investment to rebuild their economies and their airlines (Sinha, 2001). These nations have sadly been left out of the Asian miracle. With the exception of Vietnam which is showing some sign of recovery, there does not appear to be much room for hope in the near future.

Australia and New Zealand　　The first act regulating aviation in Australia was the Navigation Act of 1920, but confusion over the role of state and Commonwealth governments in air transport regulation led to an amended Air Navigation Act in 1936. According to this act, the Commonwealth was authorized to control air transportation with other countries and within the two territories of Australia. It was left to the states to control intra-state air transportation, although this did not keep the Commonwealth government from attempting to regulate intra-state aviation.

One of the most significant aviation policies of the Australian government occurred in the 1950s when then Prime Minister Robert Menzies decided that it was essential to prevent a monopoly from developing in Australian domestic airline service. The Two Airline Policy became official in 1952 with the passage of the Civil Aviation Agreement Act. Henceforth, there would be two carriers in Australia. Trans-Australian Airlines (later Australian Airlines), the state-owned carrier, would operate alongside the privately owned Australian National Airways (later Ansett). The government guaranteed the loans of Australian National up to a specified limit and later loosened the requirement that all government employees fly Trans-Australian. International service would be the province of Qantas. In 1957, the government further declared that two and only two trunk carriers would exist in Australia and established a Rationalization Committee composed of a member of each airline and a coordinator nominated by the Transport Minister. The Airlines Equipment Act of 1958 authorized the government to restrict the size of each carrier's fleet. In 1961, two additional acts authorized the Rationalization Committee to establish timetables, frequencies, aircraft types, capacity, fares, freight levels, and overall load factors on groups of routes.

By 1981, criticism of the Two Airline Policy led to the Holcroft Inquiry which recommended a pricing policy based on cost that would be nationally consistent and allow discounted fares to be determined by the airlines. This same year Trans-Australia Airlines was made a public company, although the government continued to maintain effective ownership. Other actions in 1981 created an Independent Air Fares Committee to review fares, approve discounts, and change fare formulas to consider cost and efficiency and strengthened the government's ability to control the capacity of regional and cargo carriers through licensing of aircraft imports (Sinha, 2001).

Overall, limited information suggests that while the Two Airline Policy did create a stable aviation system of high yield, profitable carriers with an excellent safety record, it was characterized by higher costs and lower productivity (Kirby, 1979; Sinha, 2001). The perception of Australian consumers was that it also resulted in higher fares than the deregulated market of the US. Under pressure, the Australian government decided in 1990 to deregulate its domestic market. In the first year of deregulation, the Australian market experienced a growth of 66 percent and average air fares dropped 41.3 percent, however, both of these numbers have fluctuated in the years since then in part due to the entry and failure of new carriers. Forsyth (1991) has argued that entry into the Australian market was destined to be difficult because of the advantages incumbent carriers possessed, particularly in terms of airport and terminal access. In a further effort to foster competition, the Australian government proposed a single trans-Tasman aviation market with New Zealand, granted Air New Zealand greater fifth freedom rights, and opened up the international market to other carriers (after allowing Qantas to purchase Australian). Two new carriers entered the Australian domestic market, Impulse Airlines and Virgin Blue (owned by Richard Branson of Virgin Airlines) which led to price wars on the main routes temporarily lowering fares to Australian consumers. In 2001, the Australian Competition and Consumer Commission approved the acquisition of Impulse Airlines by Qantas who has also signaled its intent to improve fleet allocation and costs to more effectively compete against the lower-cost Virgin Blue (Cahners Publishing Company, 2000; M2 Communications Ltd., 2001a; M2 Communications Ltd., 2001b). Virgin Blue continues to operate on 25 routes including some short-haul international routes and hopes to introduce long-haul international service in 2008 (Air Transport Intelligence, 2008).

Airline deregulation in New Zealand actually predates that of Australia having begun in 1983 with the abolishment of domestic fare and entry controls. The flag carrier, Air New Zealand, was privatized in 1989 and Australian-based Ansett was invited to set up a subsidiary to serve the New Zealand domestic market, however, internationally the market continued to be restricted, particularly between New Zealand and its near neighbor Australia. Beginning in 1992, there was some movement to provide greater flexibility in pricing, fares, and capacity in international service between the two countries. Like the Australian market, New Zealand has found it difficult to retain new entrant carriers. Kiwi Airlines started service in 1995 between Australia and New Zealand, but halted operations in 1996. After Ansett New Zealand and its parent company began to experience financial difficulty, Qantas considered making a financial investment in the New Zealand carrier. When this deal fell through Qantas New Zealand was allowed to begin domestic service (Sinha, 2001). In an interesting twist on Australian-New Zealand aviation relations, Air New Zealand went on to purchase Ansett Australia in 2000 only to cut it loose on September 12 when it was placed in voluntary administration (bankruptcy). Following allegations that they had stripped Ansett of assets before its collapse, Air New Zealand agreed to pay the administrators of Ansett NZD180 million (M2 Communications, 2001, 2002). Singapore Airlines had purchased 25 percent of Air New Zealand, but this share was reduced to 4.3 percent after the New Zealand government renationalized the carrier in October 2001(BBC News, 2001c). During 2002–2004, there were talks about a major alliance between Quantas and Air New Zealand that would have seen Qantas invest $550 million in Air New Zealand, assuming a 15 percent stake in the company

(M2 Communications Ltd, 2002). These were eventually abandoned and Qantas sold its remaining stake in ANZ in 2007 (Air Transport Intelligence, 2008).

South Asia   The South Asian region includes India, Pakistan, Bangladesh, Sri Lanka, and the small Himalayan states of Nepal and Bhutan. India is second only to China in population and since the 1991 crisis triggered by the collapse of the Soviet Union, a major trading partner of India, has been on a path toward economic liberalization. Until the early 1990s, the Indian government maintained a virtual monopoly on the airline industry with the market divided between Indian Airlines who served the domestic market and Air India who provided international service and limited connecting flights. Under the Air Corporation Act of 1953, these two government-owned carriers were the only ones permitted to offer air service in India. The open skies policy introduced in 1990 allowed air taxi operations, charters, and new entrants to begin serving the domestic market. In 1993, Indian Airlines was allowed to begin international operations to the Gulf countries where many expatriate Indians worked. Indian Airlines continued to serve the bulk of the domestic markets, however, their share declined to only about 46 percent as of 2000 due to new carrier competition. In 2007, the Indian government announced that it had approved the merger of Air India and Indian Airlines under the Air India name (Air Transport Intelligence, 2008).

Jet Airways and Sahara Airlines were two of the high profile new-entrant carriers. Jet Airways continues to thrive, flying over 10 million passengers in 2006, but Sahara Airlines, with a fleet of only seven aircraft, was not as successful and has since ceased flying. Other new entrants also did not fare well. The list of failed carriers includes Modiluft, a joint venture between the Modi group of India and Lufthansa, Air Asiatic, Continental Air Link, UB Air, Damania, East West, and NPEC. These failures have been attributed to several factors including overexpansion, high debt, and continued government control over routes served, aircraft imported, and feeder service requirements. In addition to these burdens, carriers were prohibited from exiting loss-making routes and required to purchase state controlled aviation fuel at almost twice the world price. The Indian market continues to suffer from a lack of infrastructure, particularly in the areas of air traffic control and airport facilities (Sinha, 2001). Despite suggestions by Sinha and Sinha (1997) that the Indian market could surpass the potential of China in areas of aviation, it continues to wait for the kind of major increase in domestic passenger traffic that has propelled other developing markets. According to Gallagher and Jenkins (1996), the Indian market is more price and income elastic than the developed nations of the West. Therefore, traffic growth responds more favorably to changes in fares rather than changes in income. The Indian market has recently seen a number of low-cost carriers that might help to stimulate domestic demand including Deccan (2003), GoAir (2005), and SpiceJet (2005). Several other carriers are in the planning stage including City Air and Easy Air, both low-cost carriers (Air Transport Intelligence, 2008).

Resuming Growth

Passenger traffic for all of Asia was flat for 2001 unlike world figures overall which posted a negative growth rate of 2.9 percent. IATA is projecting that the global passenger traffic for the Asia–Pacific will grow to 27 percent of the world total by 2011. The Asian growth rate of 5.9 percent is second only to the growth of the Middle East (IATA, 2007: 9). The principal generator of traffic in Asia has been trade which is closely tied to economic growth and Asian policies of export-oriented development, however, tourism has increasingly been used as a means to development both nationally and regionally (Hodder, 1992; Hitchcock, King, Parnwell, 1993). The extent to which the rest of Asia continues on a path toward further liberalization will determine which Asian carriers emerge and/or remain world competitive (Graham, 1995).

Looking Backward and Forward

Although both Asia and Europe have been latecomers to the liberalization and deregulation of aviation markets, they have both made great strides in developing their aviation systems and reducing fares while increasing services. Although both areas were affected by 11 September and the other crises that followed, many of their carriers have emerged far stronger than their US counterparts. Heading into the new century, the problems of infrastructure, competition, and costs will continue to challenge these regions, but there appear to be hopeful signs.

References

Abbott, K. and Thompson, D. (1989), *Deregulating European Aviation: The Impact of Bilateral Liberalization,* Center for Business Strategy Working Paper Series no. 73, London.

Aerospace Daily (2001), 'CAAC Readies for Airport, Carrier Alliance,' October 30, Aviation Week Group.

Air Transport Intelligence (2008), Available at: www.rati.com.

Alamdari, F. (1998), 'Trends in Airline Lobor Productivity and Costs in Europe,' *Journal of Air Transportation World Wide*, vol. 3, pp. 71–88.

Aviation Daily (2001), 'Six China Carriers Join Forces, Will be Fourth Largest Group,' June 21, Aviation Week Group.

Barrett, S.D. (1999), 'Peripheral Market Entry, Product Differentiation, Supplier Rents, and Sustainability in the Deregulated European Airline Market – a Case Study,' *Journal of Air Transport Management*, vol. 5, pp. 21–30.

BBC News (1999), 'Branson sells 49% of Virgin Atlantic,' BBC News wireservice, December 20.BBC News (2001d), 'South Korea to probe airline industry,' BBC News wireservice, August 20.

BBC News (2001c), 'Air New Zealand Renationalized,' BBC News wireservice, October 4.

BBC News (2001a), 'Singapore Airlines Sees Profits Slide,' BBC News wireservice, November 26.

BBC News (2001b), 'Thai Airways May Collapse,' BBC News wireservice, November 16.

Binggeli, U. and Pompeo, L. (2002), 'Hyped Hopes for Europe's Low-cost Airlines,' *McKinsey Quarterly*, no. 4.

Borenstein, S. (1992), 'Prospects for Competitive Air Travel in Europe,' in W.J. Adams (ed.), *Singular Europe: Economy and Policy of the European Community After 1992*, University of Michigan Press, Ann Arbor.

Branson, R. (1998), 'Luncheon Address,' *FAA Commercial Aviation Forecast Conference Proceedings: Overcoming Barriers to World Competition and Growth*, U.S. Department of Transportation, Washington, DC.

Button, K.J. (1997), 'Developments in the European Union: Lessons for the Pacific Asia Region,' in C. Findley, C.I. Sien, and K. Singh (eds), *Asia Pacific Air Transport: Challenges and Policy Reform*, Institute of Southeast Asian Studies, Singapore.

Button, K.J. and Swann, D. (1989), 'European Community Airlines-Deregulation and its Problems,' *Journal of Common Market Studies*, vol. 37, 259–82.

Cahners Publishing Company (2000), 'Virgin Blue Launches Service; Second Route to Debut Sept. 7,' Gale Group wireservice, September 4, www.findarticles.com.

Centre for Asian Business Cases (2002), *Preparing for China's Entry to the WTO: China's Airline Industry*, The University of Hong Kong School of Business, Hong Kong.

Civil Aviation Authority (1995), *CAP 654 The Single Aviation Market: Progress So Far*, Civil Aviation Authority, London.

CIA Factbook (2007), www.odci.gov/cia/publications/factbook.

Creaton, S. (2005), *Ryanair: How a Small Irish Airline Conquered Europe*, Arum Pres, London.

European Commission (1996), *Impact of the Third Package of Air Transport Liberalization Measures COM 96*, European Commission, Brussels.

Forsyth, P. (1991), 'The Regulation and Deregulation of Australia's Domestic Airline Industry,' in K.J. Button (ed.) *Airline Deregulation: International Experiences*, David Fulton, London, pp. 48–84.

Gallagher, T. and Jenkins, D. (1996), 'Going When the Price is Right,' *Airfinance Journal*, February, pp. 38–40.

Goetz, A.R. and Dempsey, P.S. (1989), 'Airline Deregulation Ten Years After: Something Foul in the Air,' *Journal of Air Law and Commerce*, vol. 54, pp. 927–63.

Graham, B. (1997), 'Air Transport Liberalization in the European Union: An Assessment,' *Regional Studies*, vol. 31, pp. 87–104.

Graham, B. (1995), *Geography and Air Transport*, John Wiley & Sons, New York.

Hitchcock, M., King, V.T., and Parnwell, M.J.G. (1993), 'Introduction,' in M. Hitchcock, V.T. King, and M.J.G. Parnwell (eds), *Tourism in South East Asia*, Routledge, London, pp. 1–31.

Hodder, R. (1992), *The West Pacific Rim: An Introduction*, Belhaven Press, London.

Humphreys, B. (1996), 'The UK Civil Aviation Authority and European Air Services Liberalization,' *Journal of Transport Economics and Policy*, vol. 3, pp. 213–20.

IATA (2007), 'IATA Economic Briefing: Passenger and freight Forecasts 2007–2001', October, Available at: 222.iata/economics.

ICAO (2002), 'One Year After 11 September Events ICAO Forecasts World Air Passenger Traffic will Exceed 2000 Levels in 2003,' Press Release of International Civil Aviation Authority, September 10, Montreal.

Ionides, N. (2008), 'MAS Upbeat After Record High 2007 Profits', February 28, Available at: Air Transport Intelligence, www.rati.com.

Jones, J.R. (1998), 'Twenty Years of Airline Deregulation: The Impact on Outlying and Small Communities,' *Journal of Transportation Management*, vol. 10, pp. 33–43.

Kirby (1979), 'An Economic Assessment of Australia's Two Airline Policy,' *Australian Journal of Management*, vol. 5, pp. 105–18.

M2 Communications Ltd (2001a), 'Air New Zealand Denies Stripping Ansett Assets,' Gale Group wireservice, November 13, www.findarticles.com.

M2 Communications Ltd (2001b), 'Virgin Blue may be able to Open Review into Qantas' Takeover of Impulse Airline,' Gale Group wireservice, September 7, www.findarticles.com.

M2 Communications Ltd (2002), 'Air New Zealand Increases Flights in Asia after Ansett Collapse,' Gale Group wireservice, www.findarticles.com.

Merrill Lynch (1999), *Global Airline Alliances: Global Alliance Brands Create Value*, Merrill Lynch, Pierce, Fenner & Smith, Inc.

Morrell, P. (1998), 'Air Transport Liberalization in Europe: The Progress so Far,' *Journal of Air Transportation World Wide*, vol. 3, pp.42–60.

Oum, T.H. and Yu, C. (1998), *Winning Airlines: Productivity and Cost Competitiveness of the World's Major Airlines*, Kluwer Academic Publishers, Boston.

R2A (2002), Unisys R2A Scorecard: Airline Industry Cost Measurement, Unisys Corporation.

Reuters (2002), 'Skymark Plans to Double Domestic Routes,' Reuters Newswire, October 25.

Sinha, D. (2001), *Deregulation and Liberalization of the Airline Industry: Asia, Europe, North America, and Oceania*, Ashgate, Aldershot.

Sinha, T. and Sinha, D. (1997), 'A Comparison of Development Prospects in India and China,' *Asian Economics*, vol. 27, pp. 123–6.

Taneja, N.K. (1988), *The International Airline Industry: Trends, Issues and Challenges*, Lexington Books, Lexington, MA.
Wallace, M., Tiernan, S., Rhoades, D.L., and Linck, T (2008), 'European Tour Operators and Low Cost Carriers: Strategic Options in a Changing Marketplace', *Journal of Air Transportation*, 12 (3).

Chapter 10
The Defining Deal of the Next Century?

A New Model?

While the United States circled and the Europeans attempted to integrate the economies of 15 different countries, the airlines looked for ways to provide global service in a bilateral world. Part of the push for global networks is based on studies that indicate that consumers choose an airline based on schedule first rather than price and prefer to fly with an airline serving a large number of cities (Tretheway and Oum, 1992). Consumers also prefer non-stop or single carrier connecting service to non-interline connecting service. Interlining refers to the situation whereby a consumer changes from one carrier to another. Carriers with interlining agreements are expected to provide for the seamless service of joint ticketing and baggage transfers while non-interline connecting service requires the consumer to make all of these arrangements (Dempsey, 2001). If bilateral agreements prevented carriers from achieving non-stop or single carrier connecting service, then carriers needed to find ways to imitate this service to attract consumers. The strategic alliance seemed to offer an answer.

Less than a decade ago, conventional wisdom suggested that the primary business decision corporations had to deal with was to "make or buy." In other words, do we engage in arms-length contractual relationships to obtain important resources or do we internally develop and/or purchase the resources to carry out our strategic plan? The arms-length contractual choice created so-called transaction costs, costs of buying and selling. These costs included the time and financial resources involved in selecting partners, negotiating the deal, and monitoring the relationship to insure contract compliance. These costs could be substantial depending on the number of suppliers to be considered, the reputation of suppliers, and the information available on actual supplier costs. These costs multiplied exponentially for corporations with many suppliers. Not surprisingly, firms also felt at the mercy of suppliers when it came to guaranteeing deliveries and quality. These costs and the lack of control led many to adopt the "GM model." The "GM model" was a vertically integrated company that sought to do it all, making its own spark-plugs, radiators, lights, ballbearings, and so on. Ownership eliminated transaction cost uncertainty and provided greater control of the operational aspects of the relationship. This obsession with "owning" in the United States led to the merger mania of the 1980s and the takeover mania of the 1990s. During the three busiest years of the 1990s (1998–2000), merger deals totaled almost 44 trillion which was more than the preceding 30 years combined (Henry, 2002). Greater economic integration in Europe has also led to an increase in owning, often fueled by economic crises that create deals out of stressed companies in many industries. However, evidence has indicated that this obsession may be waning in many industries and regions. A *Business Week* study indicates one reason why the trend is declining. According to their study, 61 percent of the "buyers" actually destroyed shareholder wealth by picking bad acquisitions and paying too much for them (Henry, 2002).

According to *Business Week*, "the defining deal for the next decade and beyond may well be the alliance, the joint venture, the partnership" (Sparks, 1999: 106). This article argued that alliances provided more flexibility, speed, informality, and economy than traditional business arrangements. These qualities seem to make them ideal in rapidly changing business environments. Industries cited as embracing the alliance movement include media, entertainment, airlines, financial services, pharmaceuticals, biotech, and high tech. However, there is a large body of evidence citing instability in alliances across industries. As we will see, this instability can be attributed to a number of factors including poor selection, governance (control), and failure to meet expectations. It is possible that the alliance landscape is now shifting competition to a higher level of abstraction as alliance groups compete on price, choice, and brand. It is also possible that liberalization of markets and ownership rules will cause some to rethink the "make-or-buy" decision once again in light of the instability and complexity in alliances.

Defining the Terms and Conditions

A strategic alliance can be defined as a "relatively enduring interfirm cooperative arrangement, involving flows and linkages that utilize resources and/or governance structures from autonomous organizations, for the joint accomplishment of individual goals" (Parkhe, 1991: 581). In other words, a strategic alliance is an agreement between two independent firms to share resources in a jointly governed project that helps each individual firm achieve specific, not necessarily shared, goals. While the old business model equated control with ownership, control in alliance arrangements is gained through one of three means. The first means of control is through active participation in the management of the enterprise or operation. The second means of exercising control is through withholding or threatening to withhold some resource or capability vital to the success of the overall operation and/or desired by the other partner. The final means of control is through legal or de facto prohibitions on the actions of alliance partners. Areas where firms might seek control include daily operations, quality of products or services, physical assets, brand name, tacit knowledge of procedures and processes, and codified knowledge such as computer reservation systems (Contractor and Kundu, 1998).

The international joint venture (IJV) used to be the preferred mode of conducting international business, but a joint venture is a legally separate entity with a mission and administration separate from that of its parents. The alliance, on the other hand, can be formed and dissolved quickly and "entail little if any paperwork–maybe only a handshake" (Sparks, 1999: 134). According to Jürgen Weber, CEO of Lufthansa Airlines, the Star alliance started with a two-and-a-half-page contract stating that its members "will cooperate forever as long as we like it" (Feldman, 1998: 27). This sounds very similar to a comment made by Leo Mullin, CEO of Delta Air Lines. Mullin declared that Delta was "extraordinarily committed to the Atlantic Excellence Alliance" (Flint, 1999: 33). Delta was so committed in fact that, less than a year later, they announced the termination of its involvement and its new partnership with Air France (Hill, 1999).

One issue that appears repeatedly in the popular accounts of airline alliances is the level of time and coordination required by many alliance arrangements. There are several issues involved. First, alliances often involve information sharing and/ or the "outsourcing" of some activities to alliance partners. This requires trust. As Jürgen Weber, CEO of Lufthansa, has noted, a key issue in many alliances is trust and the willingness to sell the other's seats as forcefully as your own (Feldman, 1998). According to past research, trust is a function of three factors: ability, benevolence, and integrity. Trust develops when the trustor believes that the trustee has the ability to do what they promise, the desire to do good for the trustor, and the value set that is consistent with that of the trustor (Cook and Wall, 1980; McFall, 1987; Sitkin and Roth, 1993). Mayer, Davis, and Schoorman (1995) have suggested that the perceived integrity of a partner is more important early in the relationship when other information is not available. Benevolence develops in a relationship over time. In fact, the outcome of prior trusting behavior will influence a partner's perception of the ability, benevolence, and integrity of other parties in a relationship. A second key factor is differences in corporate culture and philosophy. Atlantic Excellence members found that different philosophies on service quality, pricing, and other important operational issues created problems. Strong personalities and size differences between members also contributed to the perception and resolution of problems (Feldman, 1998). A third factor affecting coordination is the number of partners involved. As noted above, the more parties involved in a negotiating situation the more potential there is for disagreement and gamesmanship. A fourth factor is the compatibility of partner systems. The final factor relates to the very real limitations placed on international airlines by laws restricting foreign ownership and limiting the scope of allowed activities. Initial results from the earlier mentioned survey of international airlines confirm these problems in alliance governance. The most frequently cited problem with alliance partners was incompatible systems, policies or procedures. The second most frequently cited problem related to differences in national and/or corporate culture and the effect of these differences on communications (Rhoades, Waguespack and Marett, 2000).

The result of these limitations is that airline alliances are coordinated or managed by committee; agreement is achieved by arriving at the lowest common denominator or minimally acceptable standard to all members (Feldman, 1998). The Star alliance has struggled with governance arrangements. They have reduced the number of coordinating committees from 25 to 15 and established a policy group to oversee the activities of these committees. At the highest level, the management board consists of the CEOs of each partner airline (Feldman, 1998; Nelms,1999).

Alliances in the Airline Industry

According to Oum and Yu (1998), the first international alliance of the modern era was between Air Florida and British Island in 1986. It was not until the mid-1990s, however, that alliances in the airline industry began to soar. Table 10.1 summarizes the alliance activity documented by *Airline Business* over the seven years prior to 2001 and the 9/11 events that temporarily halted much of the new alliance activity in the industry. There are several striking trends in these numbers. First, the total number of alliances has risen almost 45 percent from 1994 to 1999 (see Figure 10.1). Second, the majority of alliances do not involve equity stakes and those that do are declining. Third, between one-fourth and one-sixth of the reported total yearly alliances are newly created. Finally, the number of airlines participating in some form of alliance was steadily increasing.

The term "strategic alliance" covers a multitude of different forms or types of arrangements in the airline industry, possibly more than in any other industry. To understand the airline alliance, it is necessary to understand that alliance activities can range from a simple, single route codeshare or bundle of codeshares all the way to the so-called "mega-alliances" created by international groups of competing airlines such as Star, Oneworld, and SkyTeam. Table 10.2 lists the most common types of alliance activities and a basic definition of each.

Not only is there a wide range of alliance activities or types in existence, there is also a large number of type combinations that can be created between any two or more carriers. However, not all types are equally likely to occur. Several studies have reported that the most common types of alliances involve code sharing,

Table 10.1   Alliance summary 1994–2000

	1994	1995	1996	1997	1998	1999	2000
Number of Alliances	280	324	389	363	502	3	579
With Equity Stakes	58	58	62	54	56	53	-
Without Equity	222	266	327	309	446	460	-
New Alliances	21	34	26	56	84	79	72
Number of Airlines	136	153	159	177	196	204	220

Source: *Airline Business* (see under 'Gallacher, J.' in the References) June 1994–June 2000. Reporting of equity change in 2000

Figure 10.1   Number of alliances, 1994–1999

block space/franchising/feeding agreements, joint marketing, and joint service agreements (Table 10.3). Least common are alliances involving the sharing and/ or adoption of information technology systems, including computer reservation systems (CRS). This is probably not surprising given the proprietary nature of such information in the airline industry (Rhoades and Waguespack, 2000; Zwart, 1999).

An airline's choice of alliance partner and alliance type is a function of its objectives which are believed to center around four strategic drivers. The first and traditionally most popular driver has been the need to gain entry into international markets restricted by bilateral agreements. Alliances allow foreign carriers to "serve" international destinations without obtaining the right through country-negotiated bilateral agreements, a political process that many carriers have found difficult to influence. The second driver is the desire to build a global, seamless network that allows consumers to reduce travel costs, take advantage of expanded frequent flyer programs, and obtain better services. The third driver of alliance formation is cost reduction. Cost reduction can be achieved in several ways. Alliances can be used to enter and develop a new market without an actual "presence" in that market. In this case, the entering carrier may rely on its alliance partner to provide the aircraft, ground handling, maintenance, customer service personnel, and other services in the new market. Carriers may also seek to reduce costs through arrangements creating joint activities such as marketing, maintenance, insurance, parts pooling, and so on. These joint activities not only reduce redundancy but may create cost savings through economy of scale effects. A fourth driver can be the desire to maintain market presence in an area whose traffic pattern and growth make it unprofitable to serve alone (Merrill, Lynch, Pierce, Fenner & Smith, Inc., 1998; Oum and Yu, 1998). For many airlines, their alliance activity is driven by more than one objective and clearly carriers may have a different set of objectives for each market or region that they serve. This diversity of objectives can make the scope and depth of interaction important issues in negotiating and governing an alliance.

Table 10.2   Definition of airline alliances

Alliance Type	Definition
Codeshare	One carrier offers service under another carrier's flight designator
Blockspace	One carrier allocates to another carrier seats to sell on its flight
Revenue Sharing	Two or more carriers share revenues generated by joint activity
Wet Lease	One carrier rents the aircraft/personnel of another
Franchising	One carrier 'rents' the brand name of another for the purpose of offering flight service but supplies its own aircraft/staff
Computer	One carrier shares and/or adopts the reservation
Reservation System	system of another
Insurance/parts Pooling	Two or more carriers agree to joint purchase
Joint Service	Two carriers offer combined flight service
Management Contract	One carrier contracts with another carrier to manage some aspect of its operation
Baggage Handling/maintenance	One carrier contracts with another to provide services/personnel/facilities at specified sites
Joint Marketing	Two or more carriers combine efforts to market joint services/activities
Equity Swap/governance	Two or more carriers swap stock and/or create joint governance structures

Table 10.3   Alliances by type

Alliance Type	Description	Percentage of Total
Type I	Codeshare	29%
Type II	Block space	15%
Type III	CRS/Accting/IT	2%
Type IV	Pooling	6%
Type V	Joint Service	13%
Type VI	Commercial Agreements	3%
Type VII	Facilities/Ground Handling	9%
Type VIII	Marketing	16%
Type IX	Equity	7%

Source: Zwart, M.L. (1999), 'Duration and Stability of Strategic Alliances in the Airline Industry'

Unstable Creations

Unfortunately, strategic alliances have also been defined as arrangements "characterized by inherent instability arising from uncertainly regarding a partner's future behavior and the absence of a higher authority to ensure compliance" (Parkhe, 1993: 794). Doorley (1993) found that 60 percent of the alliances he examined had a survival rate of only four years. Less than 20 percent survived for ten years. An Anderson Consulting survey found that 61 percent of corporate partnerships were either outright failures or performing below expectations (Sparks, 1999). Michael Porter of Harvard University believes that we should not be surprised by these numbers since he sees alliances as transitional rather than stable arrangements that rarely result in sustainable competitive advantage (Porter, 1990). Hamel (1991) has even suggested that many alliances are simply a race to learn in which the winner will eventually establish dominance in the partnership or dissolve it before its partner can catch up.

Whichever means of control partners select, the fact remains that most interfirm alliances involve attempts by competitors to cooperate in some aspect of their operation. It has been suggested that such firms have an "inalienable de facto right to pursue their own interests" (Buckley and Casson, 1988: 34). This perception, however, may make it inevitable that problems will arise as partners seek to control the alliance to their own benefit. Another reason for instability in alliance arrangements may be the failure of partners to clearly define objectives and establish means of measuring performance. A surprising 49 percent of alliances in the *Business Week* survey did not have formal performance guidelines (Sparks, 1999).

The first step in understanding the issue of stability is achieving a consensus on the meaning of the terms of business. From an alliance point of view, failure occurs when one or all parties fail to achieve their objectives. Obviously, it is possible for one member to achieve their goals when other parties do not. This type of failure can occur either because of a problem in the objective-setting process or because of deliberate action on the part of one member. A more ominous reason for failure is the possibility that one or more partners enter an alliance seeking to gain competitive advantage (Buckley and Casson, 1988; Hamel, 1991). Given this definition, a terminating alliance is only unsuccessful if it is "unplanned and premature from the perspective of either or both partners" (Inkpen and Beamish, 1997: 182). Duration simply refers to the length of time between the initiation of an alliance and its termination.

Researchers have defined instability in terms of changes in equity and/or governance control, termination, and duration (Franko, 1971; Killing, 1983; Kogut, 1988). From a theoretical perspective, instability should be separated from duration and termination. If a stable relationship is defined as one in which there have been no major changes in the relationship design to either increase or decrease the linkages between firms, then an alliance could terminate without experiencing instability. Actions which would indicate instability include changes in strategic direction, renegotiation of contracts or agreements, and reconfiguration of ownership and/or management structure (Yan, 1998). It would not include alliance termination. A stable alliance may terminate when the strategic goals of partners have been met or when the strategic needs of partners change. By the same token, an unstable alliance will not necessarily end in termination. Instability may arise because partners are adjusting their expectations or objectives. It may indicate that partners have decided to commit themselves to even higher levels of interaction or to a longer-term strategy to disengage from or de-emphasize the relationship.

Lasting Relationships

Given the high failure rates already cited, it is reasonable to ask what factors contribute to longevity. Bleeke and Ernst (1995) have categorized alliances based on three factors—market strength of partners, motivation of alliance partners, and alliance outcome—to create six classes or types of alliances. These six types are: 1) collisions between competitors, 2) alliances of the weak, 3) disguised sales, 4) bootstrap alliances, 5) evolutions to a sale, and 6) complementary equals. According to their typology, an alliance between a weak firm and a strong firm can be either a disguised sale, that is, it will result in the weaker firm failing to gain strength and being acquired (and, hence, the alliance terminated) by the stronger firm or a bootstrap alliance in which the weaker firm increases its strength and dissolves the alliance. In their typology, only one type of alliance, the complementary equals, will survive longer than the median age of seven. This alliance involves two firms with truly complementary skills, assets and/or resources. Unfortunately, many alliances are entered in the belief that partner complementarity exists. It is usually only in the process of implementing the alliance that partners discover incompatibility. The other weakness of the Bleeke and Ernst (1995) typology is that it is post hoc: it classifies alliances after the outcome of the alliance is known. It does not predict which alliances will succeed nor does it lay out conditions for success.

Park and Cho (1997) examined the market strength of code sharing partners and its effect on market share performance, presumably a goal of such alliances. They found that the most successful alliances occurred between partners of equal size. They also reported that the performance effects were greater in growing markets with few competitors and flexible market share changes. Here, at least, we have two factors that might be useful in selecting partners and/or predicting alliance outcome.

Khanna, Gulati and Nohria (1998) offer us another way. They focus not on the strengths of alliance partners but on the nature of the benefits arising from alliance activity. They suggest that alliances create two types of benefits—common and private. Common benefits "accrue to each partner in an alliance from the collective application of the learning both firms go through as a consequence of being part of the alliance" (195). By contrast, private benefits can accrue to a firm that can pick up partner skills and apply them to areas unrelated to alliance activity. In the case of an alliance with purely common benefits, "all firms must finish learning in order for any of them to derive the common benefits" (197). Thus, such an alliance may be expected to last longer and result, even if terminated, in a successful alliance from the viewpoint of all parties. The alliance with purely private benefits is indeed a race to see which partner can finish learning first. That partner will then have no further incentive to incur alliance costs and will terminate the relationship. In reality, most alliances are a combination of both types of benefits. It is the ratio of private to common benefits that will affect a firm's decision to stay in or quit an alliance. All things being equal, the greater the scope of the alliance relative to the total market scope of the partners, the greater the common benefits and the lower the private benefits. In this regard, the mega alliances with their increased alliance scope relative to firm scope should create more common benefits and last longer than their narrow alliance scope competitors. In connection with learning in alliance arrangements, Simonin (1999) has suggested that the more ambiguous and tacit the information to be transferred the longer the process will take. In other words, it should be more difficult for a Singapore Airlines to transfer the rich, experience-laden knowledge that has made it an industry leader in service quality than to train alliance partners in line maintenance procedures.

A number of studies have examined the role of resource commitment to alliance duration. Resource commitment involves dedicating assets to a particular use in such a way that their redeployment to other uses would result in some level of cost to the firm. By limiting strategic flexibility and acting as a barrier to exit, the willingness to commit resources lessens the perception of opportunistic behavior on the part of other alliance members (Parkhe, 1993). The more non-recoverable, alliance-specific the investment, the greater the potential effect on alliance duration.

Resource commitment can also have a positive effect on alliance stability and performance (Freeman, 1987; Heide and Johns, 1988; Smith and Aldrich, 1991). Resource commitment effects stability for much the same reason as it increases duration, namely that it creates incentives to stay in the relationship rather than quit. Its effect on performance is due to the link between resource commitment, firm control, and involvement in operations. The higher the level of commitment by the firm, the more likely it is to exercise control in the alliance and seek involvement in decision making (Anderson and Gatignon, 1986; Root 1987). On the other hand, high levels of commitment are often associated with more alliance complexity. The more complex the relationship, the greater the "fundamental problem of cooperation" (Ouchi, 1980: 130). Alliances that involve greater coordination and integration of resources require a level of trust and interaction that is generally foreign to competitive firms. The more highly concentrated the industry, the more unstable the relationship may be, particularly when the scope of the venture involved marketing and after-sales service (Kogut, 1988). The need for higher levels of coordination and integration is also likely to increase problems relating to incompatible systems, procedures, training, and organizational/national cultures.

According to Yan (1998), four forces act to destabilize alliance arrangements: unexpected changes in the environment, undesirable alliance performance, obsolescing bargain effects, and interpartner competitive learning. Clearly, changing environmental conditions and poor performance can cause partners to reevaluate/restructure their relationship. The obsolescing bargain occurs when the foreign partners relative bargaining power erodes over time as it invests increasing, unrecoverable resources in a local economy. Finally, the race to learn can lead to various strategic maneuvering in an alliance. Yan (1998) also cites four factors that can increase alliance stability: the political and legal environment at founding, the initial resource mix, the initial balance of bargaining power, and the interpartner, pre-venture relationship. As we have discussed earlier in this book, the airline industry is currently facing a series of challenges to the existing political and legal structure that has governed the industry since the end of World War II. When this challenge is added to alliance-specific differences in resource mix, balance of power, and pre-venture relationships, the results can be volatile.

Scott (1992) has noted that the forms organizations establish at founding are likely to persist over their lifespan. This is called structural inertia. The initial form may reflect the task environment (Stinchcombe, 1965), the characteristics of executives (Mintzberg and Waters, 1980) or top management team (Eisenhardt and Schoonhoven, 1990) or institutional factors such as laws, organizational or national culture (Meyer and Scott, 1983). The initial resources and bargaining power partners bring into an alliance can also create stability as can a pre-alliance relationship of trust and respect. The stability of the alliance depends on the delicate balance between these eight forces.

A Balancing Act

In a 1997 article in the *Journal of Air Transportation Management*, Rhoades and Lush proposed an alliance typology that involved another delicate balancing act. Their typology was based on the premise that airline alliances could be classified according to two dimensions: commitment of resources and complexity of arrangement. In general, the typology predicted that the level of resource commitment should increase both the duration and stability of alliances while the complexity of the alliance arrangement should decrease both duration and stability. These predictions are consistent with theory and research in other industries. The difficulty lies in assessing the interaction effects of these two dimensions on duration and stability. For example, what is likely to happen to an alliance that involves a low level of resource commitment to a complex task requiring partners to integrate different systems, cultures, or tasks? Rhoades and Lush (1997) attempted to address this difficulty by assigning each of the activities defined above in Table 10.2 based on the level of resource commitment and complexity. Figure 10.2 outlines a refined version of the typology used in a test of the model. Type I alliances involve low levels of resource commitment and complexity. The relatively simple nature of the activity should make them more stable and lasting. However, these types of code sharing arrangements are normally driven by the desire for market access and/or market presence in a restricted or undeveloped market. The lasting nature of Type I alliance could change if liberalization continues and carriers can enter markets freely in their own right. On the other hand, financial crisis in the wake of 9/11 has seen cost-cutting carriers withdraw from increasingly marginal routes in favor of alliance partners.

Diagonally across from Type I alliances is Type IX. These alliances involve multiple activities, complex integration efforts, extensive resource commitment, shared decision making, and, often, equity investment. High resource commitment makes the exit cost of these alliance types high. On the other hand, the complex nature of the tasks to be coordinated and integrated will make these alliances unstable as well. On balance, resource commitment should provide Type IX partners with greater incentives to work through complexity. Type III alliances involving low complexity and high resource commitment should make these alliances some of the most durable. On the diagonal from Type III are Type VIII alliances that tend to involve low levels of resource commitment and high complexity. These types of arrangements should experience some of the highest failure rates. An increasing focus on quality may make the potentially undesirable outcomes of some of these complex and important activities too great to bear. Of course, it is possible that the cost savings benefits of these arrangements and/or airport specific restrictions on facilities or eligible grand handling firms will override the destabilizing effects of complexity.

This typology was tested for its duration predictions using data from the *Airline Business* surveys. Gudmundsson and Rhoades (2000) found that alliances in general were at greater risk of termination in year 2. The rate of termination decreased from years 3 to 6. Four types of alliance arrangements demonstrated a lower risk of termination: Type IV-pooling, Type VIII-marketing, Type II-block space, and Type I-code sharing. Type V (joint service) and Type VII (ground/ facilities) showed a significant relationship with higher risk of early termination. Type IX (equity) alliances were also associated with high risk of termination. The remaining two types of alliances, Type III (CRS/IT) and Type VI (commercial agreements) contained too few cases to test. While this study did not provide unqualified support for the typology, it does demonstrate that different alliance activities are at greater risk for termination.

The Gudmundsson and Rhoades (2000) study also found that the more extensive the alliance, that is, the more types of activities involved, the lower the risk of termination. Since each additional alliance activity adds incrementally

		COMPLEXITY −	+	
+	**Type III (IT)** Accounting services CRS links Data processing Freight IT IT Development	**Type VI (Management)** Commercial agreements Commercial support mgmt Management Contract MOU Spares mgmt cooperation Strategic Partnership	**Type IX (Equity)** Equity	**+**
R E S O U R C E S	**Type II (Block-Space)** Block seat agreements Block space agreements Feeding agreement Franchise agreement Revenue sharing Wet Lease	**Type V (Joint-Service)** Cargo cooperation Freight handling Joint cargo terminal Joint flight Joint freighter flight Joint route development Joint venture Schedule coordination Shared routes	**Type VIII (Marketing)** Coop on Sales Gen sales agency Joint Mkt Joint FFP Joint advertising Mkting agreement Mkting alliance Reservations	D U R A T I O N
−	**Type I (Code-Share)** Cargo code-share Code sharing	**Type IV (Pooling)** Fuel purchasing Financial access arrangements Joint insurance purchase Freight return pool Joint purchase Pool agreement Revenue Pooling Space swap	**Type VII (Ground Facilities)** Slot-sharing Maintenance Catering JV Joint check-in Ground handling Shared Terminal Shared lounge Through check-in	**−**
	+	DURATION	−	

Figure 10.2 Alliance activity by type

to the level of resource commitment, this finding is supportive of the general proposition that resource commitment increases duration. The attempt by mega-alliances to increase the breadth and scope of partner activity also supports the contention of Khanna, Gulati, and Nohria (1998) that the higher the level of common benefits to private, the more likely the alliance is to survive. In the case of the mega-alliances, resource commitment appears to outweigh complexity as a factor in alliance duration. In the case of Type IX equity alliances, the troubles of shared governance and organizational control have created instability in a number of alliances, notably KLM-Northwest and Northwest and Continental, although it has not necessarily resulted in termination of the overall alliance.

To date, there has been no test of the stability predictions of the typology. As Rhoades and Lush (1997) noted in their original article, "instability in and of itself is not necessarily a "bad thing." It can be an indication that the parties in the alliance are committed to establishing a successful partnership" (113). On the other hand, too much instability should have a negative effect on an alliance's ability to function and produce profitable returns. Testing the stability predictions would require a careful year-by-year survey of changes (major and minor) within alliances. A related area of study would be to examine the possibility of sequencing as it relates to alliance stability and duration. For example, are alliances that begin their relationship with relatively simple, low resource activities and then move to more complex arrangements more successful than those who jump right into equity and/or other complex activities?

Strategic Actions

As noted earlier, airlines that serve a large number of destinations tend to be preferred by consumers because such an airline can minimize their travel time and offer a higher quality of service (Tretheway and Oum, 1992). Responding to this preference, carriers sought to develop extensive domestic, continental, and international service networks. In the US following deregulation, carriers consolidated and created hub-and-spoke networks to achieve continental coverage. Achieving international coverage, however, proved more difficult. American Airlines initially attempted to apply the domestic model of network coverage to foreign markets by creating foreign spokes to their US hubs. They encountered two problems: legal barriers created by the bilateral system and high financial costs. We have already discussed many of the legal barriers to establishing an efficient foreign network (Chapter 8). In regard to the financial costs, Oum, Taylor, and Zhang (1993) have estimated that the potential revenues of a "successful" global network would be more than $30 billion. This is at least twice the revenue level of the largest existing mega-carriers. They argued that a single carrier simply could not marshal the financial resources to establish such a network. Whether a single carrier could administer such a network is a matter we will address later.

Given these problems and the legal restrictions on international mergers and acquisitions, strategic alliances became the method of choice in global network construction. They allowed individual carriers to compensate for strategic weaknesses in their operations or route structure. The savings in cost and time over internal development could be substantial. In fact, outsourcing to alliance partners was the easiest way to control costs, but there were additional problems with this approach. First, it was difficult to restart an activity once it is discontinued. So, if the alliance fell apart or the quality of the work did not meet standards, bringing that activity back in-house would be expensive. Second, such cost savings required more airline integration than many carriers were currently willing to accept (Feldman, 1999).

As far as route construction, Oum and Park (1997) envisioned the following future for airline alliances. First, global alliances would consist of a two-tier system of super-hub anchor carriers on each continent and junior spoke carriers feeding the continental super-hubs. Second, the number of major global alliances, constrained by the limited number of major continental carriers, would be no more than five or so. Finally, carriers left out of the "system" would be forced to become niche players. By and large, these predictions have come to pass with the formation of three major mega-alliances (Star, Oneworld, and SkyTeam) and the announcement of secondary and tertiary carriers (Merrill Lynch, Pierce, Fenner & Smith Inc.,1999). Further consolidation in the North American and European airline industry, however, has resulted in shifts in current alliance partnerships, that is, the end of the KLM–Northwest alliance. What remains to be seen is the level of integration these mega-alliances will seek and achieve.

Research on competitive behavior suggests that it is driven by both the ability to compete and the motivation to engage in competition (Chen, 1996). Global networks give alliances the ability to compete in numerous markets. The motivation to compete (or not to compete) is based on other considerations including expected retaliation by competitors. Research at the firm level indicates that multi-market contact "gives a firm the option to respond to an attack by a rival not only in the challenged market, but also in other markets in which both compete" (Gimeno, 1999: 102). In the United States, major airlines seek to maintain some presence in all their competitors' markets. Those that are successful "are able to simultaneously: (a) enjoy lower intensity of price competition from their rivals, (b) display less intense competitive behavior of their own, and (c) maintain a higher equilibrium market share" (Gimeno, 1999: 122). Retaliation in an attacker's hub has been shown to be a powerful and effective response to attacks on one's own hub (Nomani, 1990). Assuming that competition eventually moves from the airline to the alliance level, then multipoint alliance contact will gain increasing importance. This also assumes that a liberalizing global aviation system allows for the development of such a framework. Merrill Lynch, Pierce, Fenner & Smith Inc., (1999) have examined the market presence of the mega-alliances in thirty world markets. Of these thirty markets, fifteen have an alliance with 50 percent or more market share. This indicates the basic framework of a multipoint system that, given regulatory freedom, it would allow one alliance group to respond to an attack in their dominant market by acting in the attacker's market.

A New Level

The discussion of multipoint competition links structure to behavior. Research points to other behavioral possibilities in alliance strategic action. At the firm level, organizational size has been positively associated with economies of scale, experience, brand name recognition, and market power (Hambrick, MacMillan, and Day, 1982; Kelly and Amburgey, 1991). Small firms tend to be more flexible, faster, innovative, and risk-seeking. Such firms initiate more competitive moves and implement them quicker than their larger rivals (Chen and Hambrick, 1995; Fiegenbaum and Karnani, 1991; Hitt, Hoskisson, and Harrison, 1991; Katz, 1970). Large firms initiate fewer actions, tend to be slower to implement agreed upon actions, and are less likely to change core features (Chen and Hambrick, 1995; Kelly and Amburgey, 1991). However, as Chen and Hambrick (1995) found they respond quickly to perceived attack. This rapid response to attack may indicate a greater need to protect their reputation (Fombrun and Shanley, 1990), to signal stakeholders (Pfeffer, 1982) and competitors (Axelrod, 1984) that they are not passive, and to deter further attack (Chen and MacMillan, 1992).

As we have noted earlier, the size of an organization or alliance necessary to establish a successful global network is tremendous (Oum, Taylor, and Zhang, 1993). There are already signs that administering these networks is proving time consuming, frustrating, and cumbersome. British Airways has estimated that its alliance staff spends two-thirds of their time attending or traveling to meetings. The Star alliance reduced the number of alliance committees from 25 to 15 and is rethinking the overall alliance structure. Even apparently simple decision making such as joint airbag purchase has proved difficult (Feldman, 1998). Alliances run the risk that their alliance structure may in fact become too great a burden and allow quicker, more nimble competitors to overtake them.

Strange Bedfellows

While airlines appear committed to the idea of an alliance world, there are many problems facing alliances as they try to provide the seamless service that their founders hope to achieve. If the negotiating and governance process looks complex, then imagine the complexity of day-to-day activity. Micheal E. Levine, the Executive VP-Marketing for Northwest Airlines has said that "the hardest thing in working on an alliance is to coordinate the activities of people who have different instincts and a different language, and maybe worship slightly different travel gods, to get them to work together in a culture that allows them to respect each other's habits and conviction, and yet work productively together in an environment in which you can't specify everything in advance" (Levine, 1993: 69). Resolving these human issues as well as the legal issues surrounding alliances is one of the chief challenges of the alliance movement and one of the causes of instability in alliance arrangements.

References

Anderson, E. and Gatignon, H. (1986), 'Modes of Entry: A Transaction Cost Analysis and Propositions', *Journal of International Business Studies*, vol. 17, pp. 1–26.

Axelrod, R. (1984), *The Evolution of Cooperation,* Basic Books, New York.

Bleeke, J. and Ernst, D. (1995), 'Is Your Strategic Alliance a Sale?', *Harvard Business Review*, vol. 73, pp. 97–105.

Buckley, P. and Casson, M. (1988), 'A Theory of Cooperation in International Business', in F.J. Contractor and Peter Lorange (eds) *Cooperative Strategies in International Business*, D.C. Heath & Company, Lexington.

Chen, M.J. (1996), 'Competitor Analysis and Inter-firm Rivalry: Toward a Theoretical Integration,' *Academy of Management Review*, vol. 21, pp. 100–134.

Chen, M.J. and Hambrick, D.C. (1995), 'Speed, Stealth, and Selective Attack: How Small Firms Differ from Large Firms in Competitive Behavior', *Academy of Management Journal*, vol. 38, pp. 453–82.

Chen, M.J., and MacMillan, I.C. (1992), 'Nonresponse and Delayed Response to Competitive Moves: The Role of Competitor Dependence and Action Irreversibility,' *Academy of Management Journal*, vol. 35, pp. 359–70.

Contractor and P. Lorange (eds.), *Cooperative Strategies in International Business*, Lexington Books, Lexington, pp. 31–54.

Contractor, F.J. and Kundu, S.K. (1998), 'Modal Choice in a World of Alliances: Analyzing Organizational Forms in the International Hotel Sector', *Journal of International Business Studies*, vol. 29, pp.325–58.

Cook, J. and Wall, T. (1980), 'New Work Attitude Measures Trust, Organizational Commitment and Personal Need Fulfillment,' *Journal of Occupational Psychology*, vol. 53, pp. 39–52.

Dempsey, P.S. (2001), 'Carving the World into Fiefdoms: The Anticompetitive future of International Aviation', Working Paper, McGill University, Montreal, Quebec.

Doorley III, T.L. (1993), 'Teaming Up for Success', *Business Quarterly*, vol.57, pp. 99–103.

Eisenhardt, K. and Schoonhoven, C.B. (1990), 'Organizational Growth: Linking Founding Team Strategy, Environment, and Growth among Semiconductor Ventures, 1978–1988', *Administrative Science Quarterly*, vol. 35, pp. 504–29.

Feldman, J.M. (1999), 'Disappearing Act', *Air Transport World*, February, pp. 25–30.

Feldman, J (1998), 'Making Alliances Work', *Air Transport World,* June, pp. 27–35.

Fiegenbaum, A. and Karnani, A. (1991), 'Output Flexibility – A Competitive Advantage for Small Firms,' *Strategic Management Journal*, vol 12, pp. 101–24.

Flint, P. (1999), 'Alliance Paradox', *Air Transport World*, April, pp. 33–6.

Fombrun, C. and Shanley, M. (1990), 'What's in a Name? Reputation Building and Corporate Strategy,' *Academy of Management Journal*, vol. 33, pp. 233–58.

Franko, L. (1971), *Joint Venture Survival in Multinational Companies*, Praeger, New York.

Freeman, R.E. (1987), 'Review of the Economic Institutions of Capitalism, by O.W. Williamson', *Academy of Management Review*, vol. 12, pp. 385–7.

Gallacher, J. (1994), 'Airline Alliance Survey', *Airline Business*, June, pp. 25–53.

Gallacher, J. (1995), 'Airline Alliance Survey', *Airline Business*, June, pp. 26–53.

Gallacher, J. (1996), 'A Clearer Direction', *Airline Business*, June, pp. 23–51.

Gallacher, J. (1997), 'Partners for Now', *Airline Business*, June, pp. 26–67.

Gallacher, J. (1998), 'Hold your Horses', *Airline Business*, June, pp. 42–81.

Gimeno, J. (1999), 'Reciprocal Threats in Multimarket Rivalry: Staking Out Spheres of Influence in the U.S. Airline Industry,' *Strategic Management Journal*, vol. 20, 101–28.

Gudmundsson, S.V. and Rhoades, D.L. (2001). Airline Alliance Survival: Analysis, Strategy, and Duration, *Transport Policy*, 8(3) p. 209–18.

Hambrick, D.C., MacMillan, I.C., and Day, D.L. (1982), 'Strategic Attributes and Performance in the BCG Matrix-A PIMS-based Analysis of Industrial Product Businesses," *Academy of Management Journal*, vol. 25, pp. 510–31.

Hamel, G. (1991), 'Competition for Competence and Inter-partner Learning within International Strategic Alliances', *Strategic Management Journal*, vol. 12, pp. 83–104.

Heide, J.B. and Johns, G. (1988), 'The Role of Dependence Balancing in Safeguarding Transaction-specific Assets in Conventional Channels', *Journal of Marketing*, vol. 52, pp. 20–35.

Henry, D. (2002), 'Mergers: Why Most Big Deals Don't Pay Off', *Business Week*, October 14, pp. 60–70.Hill, L. (1999), 'Global Challenger', *Air Transport World*, December, pp. 52–4.

Hitt, M.A., Hoskisson, R.E., and Harrison, J.S. (1991), 'Strategic Competitiveness in the 1990s Challenges and Opportunities for U.S. Executives', *Academy of Management Executive,* vol. 5, pp. 7–22.

Inkpen, A.C. and Beamish, P.W. (1997), 'Knowledge, Bargaining Power, and the Instability of International Joint Ventures', *Academy of Management Review*, vol. 22, pp. 177–202.

Katz, R.L. (1970), *Cases and Concepts in Corporate Strategy*, Prentice-Hall, Englewood Cliffs.

Kelly, D. and Amburgey, T.L. (1991), 'Organizational Inertia and Momentum: A Dynamic Model of Strategic Change,' *Academy of Management Journal*, vol. 34, pp. 591–612.

Khanna, T., Gulati, R, and Nohria, N. (1998), 'The Dynamics of Learning Alliances: Competition, Cooperation, and Relative Scope', *Strategic Management Journal*, vol. 19, pp. 193–210.

Killing, J.P. (1983), *Strategies for Joint Venture Success*, Praeger, New York.

Kogut, B. (1988), 'Joint Ventures: Theoretical and Empirical Perspectives,' *Strategic Management Journal*, vol. 9, pp. 319–32.

Levine, M.E. (1993), 'Interview', *Air Transport World*, January, pp. 69–70.

Mayer, R.C., Davis, J.H., and Schoorman, F.D. (1995), 'An Integrative Model of Organizational Trust,' *Academy of Management Review*, vol. 20, pp. 709–34.

McFall, L. (1987), 'Integrity', *Ethics*, vol. 98, pp. 5–20.

Merrill Lynch, Pierce, Fenner & Smith (1999), *Global Airline Alliances: Global Alliance Brands Create Value*, Merrill Lynch, New York.

Merrill Lynch, Pierce, Fenner & Smith Inc. (1998), *Global Airline Alliances: Why Alliances Really Matter from an Investment Perspective*, Merrill Lynch, Pierce, Fenner & Smith Inc., New York.

Meyer, J.W. and Scott, W.R. (1983), *Organizational Environments: Ritual and Rationality*, Sage, Beverly Hills.

Mintzberg, H. and Waters, J.A. (1982), 'Tracking Strategy in an Entrepreneurial Firm', *Academy of Management Journal*, vol. 25, pp. 465–499.

Nelms, D.W. (1999), ' Getting Their Acts Together', *Air Transport World,* April, pp. 27–36.

Nomani, A.Q. (1990), 'Fare Warning: How Airlines Trade Price Plans', *Wall Street Journal*, October 9, pp. B1–B10.

Ouchi, W.G. (1980), 'Markets, bureaucracies, and Clans', *Administrative Science Quarterly*, vol. 25, pp. 129–42.

Oum, T.H. and Yu, C. (1998), *Winning Airlines: Productivity and Cost Competitiveness of the World's Major Airlines*, Kluwer Academic Publishers, Boston.

Oum, T.H. and Park, J.H. (1997), 'Airline Alliances: Current Status, Policy Issues, and Future Directions', *Journal of Air Transport Management,* vol. 3, pp. 133–44.

Oum, T.H., Taylor, A.J., and Zhang, A. (1993), 'Strategic Airline Policy in the Globalizing Airline Network', *Transportation Journal*, vol. 32, pp. 14–30.

Park, N.K. and Cho, D. (1997), 'The Effect of Strategic Alliance on Performance', *Journal of Air Transport Management*, vol. 3, pp. 155–64.

Parkhe, A. (1991), 'Interfirm Diversity, Organizational Learning, and Longevity in Global Strategic Alliances', *Journal of International Business Studies*, vol. 22, pp. 579–601.

Parkhe, A. (1993), 'Strategic Alliance Structuring: A Game Theoretic and Transaction Cost Examination of Interfirm Cooperation', *The Academy of Management Journal*, vol. 36, pp. 794–829.

Pfeffer, J. (1982), *Organizations and Organizational Theory*, Pitman, Boston.

Porter, M.E. (1990), *The Competitive Advantage of Nations*, Free Press, New York.

Reuters (2000), 'KLM, MAS in quite intensive Wings Talks, March 15.

Rhoades, D.L., Waguespack, B., and Marett, P. (2000), 'The Mating Habits of International Airlines: Alliance Formation and Governance', Working paper, Embry-Riddles Aeronautical University.

Rhoades, D.L. and Waguespack, B., Jr. (2000), 'Divorce Airline Style', Working paper, Embry-Riddle Aeronautical University.

Rhoades, D.L. and Lush, H. (1997), 'A Typology of Strategic Alliances in the Airline Industry: Propositions for Stability and Duration', *Journal of Air Transportation Management*, vol. 3, pp. 109–14.

Root, F.R. (1987), *Entry Strategies for International Markets*, Lexington Books, Lexington.

Scott, W.R. (1992), *Organizations: Rational, Natural, and Open Systems' 3rd ed.,* Prentice-Hall: Englewood Cliffs.

Simonin, B.L. (1999), 'Ambiguity and the Process of Knowledge Transfer in Strategic Alliances', *Strategic Management Journal*, vol. 20, pp.595–624.

Sitkin, S.B. and Roth, N.L. (1993), 'Explaining the Limited Effectiveness of Legalistic "Remedies" for Trust/Distrust,' *Organizational Science*, vol. 4, pp. 367–92.

Smith, A. and Aldrich, H.E. (1991),'The Role of Trust in the Transaction Cost Economics Framework', Paper presented at the annual meeting of the Academy of Management, Miami.

Sparks, D. (1999), 'Partners', *Business Week*, October 25, pp. 106–12.

Stinchcombe, A.L. (1965), 'Organizations and social structures'. In James G. March (ed.) *Handbook of Organizations*, Rand McNally, Chicago.

Tretheway, M.W. and Oum, T.H. (1992), *Airline Economics: Foundation for Strategy and Policy*, The Centre for Transportation Studies, University of British Columbia.

Yan, A. (1998), 'Structural Stability and Reconfiguration of International Joint Ventures', *Journal of International Business Studies*, vol. 29, pp. 773–96.

Zwart, M.L. (1999), 'Duration and Stability of Strategic Alliances in the Airline Industry', Dissertation at Maastricht University.

Chapter 11
The Slippery Legal Slope

Legally Speaking

One of the first issues that any student of international relations must deal with is the fact that there is no nice body of "law" for most things international. In this sense, the student of international aviation is better positioned to accept this reality because that student has already grappled with the bilateral system of treaties that governed (and still governs) airline affairs between nations. In international law, treaties (bilateral and multilateral) are negotiated and signed (or not signed) by the parties involved in the negotiation and they set out how the system in question works, what the rules are, and with whom (or how) disputes are resolved. As discussed in Chapters 5 and 6, aviation law still rests firmly on the Chicago Convention and ICAO. Just as a reminder of what this means, let's go back to Chapter 6 for the following quote:

> The key to understanding ICAO is in realizing that, like the United Nations in general, it has *no* independent enforcement power; it can not make its members implement any of its standards. Its main bodies may act to support or condemn certain actions by members that relate to aviation, but this is an exercise in public relations and free expression. When or if a vote is taken on the issue of SARPs [Standards and Recommended Practices] or PANS [Procedures of Air Navigation Services], it is the perfunctory end to months or years of consensus building at ICAO. If consensus is not initially achieved on certain issues, then all parties revise, rework, or reframe the issue until consensus is obtained. It is a painstaking process, but it has and is producing some very positive results.

In short, if a nation or a firm from a given nation violates the international rules set down by treaty, there may be little recourse for the aggrieved party except international mediation and dispute resolution by a body that both parties recognize (Abeyratne, 2002).

Within any given country's boundaries, the rules and laws of that nation, however they came into existence, are in force. In only rare occasions can a firm from one country operating in another country avoid complying with that country's laws. While one country may attempt to extend its laws beyond its borders (extraterritoriality), such attempts are widely frowned upon by the rest of the world. A case in point is the 1977 Foreign Corrupt Practices Act (FCPA) which prohibited US companies from making illegal payments to foreign government officials with the purpose of influencing their decisions in matters of business. Many saw this act as an attempt by the US to impose its own standards on the rest of the world and objected. This example also illustrates the problem with "international law." In 1997 the Organization for Economic Co-operation and Development Convention on Bribery was signed by 36 of the nations that had addressed these issues. Any nation not signing the treaty is not obligated to abide by it and even nations that did sign it can renounce it, should they choose to do so. So while it is possible to discuss the question of aviation or aerospace law in an international context, we will either be talking about "domestic laws" relating to (or applied to) aviation or international treaties relating to aviation/aerospace. Whole texts have been written and courses have been taught on these subjects. The goal of this chapter is simply to introduce some of the broad legal areas affecting aviation, aerospace, and strategic alliances—liability issues, environmental issues, and economic issues, particularly antitrust or competition policy.

A Bumpy Ride

It is not surprising that one of the first issues to concern the aviation industry was liability in event of a crash. The Warsaw Convention of 1929 was the first to address this matter in an attempt to protect the newly forming airlines from the possibility that a single crash would put them out of business. The Warsaw Convention, article 17, states that a carrier is liable for "damage sustained in the event of the death or wounding of a passenger, if the accident which caused the damage so sustained took place on board the aircraft or in the course of any of the operations of embarking or disembarking." Over the years, legal experts have debated the meaning of "accident" and wounding, whether passengers are duly notified of the opportunity to pursue liability insurance (and/or have the opportunity to do so), the meaning of willful misconduct and negligence, and the limits to liability. New issues to be resolved are the liability in case of pulmonary embolism, lack of medical equipment, and contaminated cabins and the spread of disease such as SARS (Severe Acute Respiratory Syndrome) (see Abeyratne, 2002 for more discussion). The Warsaw Convention set a damage limit of US$8,300 per person. The Chicago Convention avoided this issue deferring to the agreement in Warsaw. Warsaw, however, did not settle the matter. Developing countries complained that the limit was too high and, over time, developed countries have considered the limit too low. The Hague Protocol of 1955 sought to examine the issue again. This was followed by the Montreal Agreement (1966), the Montreal Convention (1971), and a second Montreal Convention in 1999. The limit for liability was progressively raised, but the last agreement stated that the new limit (100,000 in special drawing rights) could not be exceeded if the carrier could prove that neither it nor its agents had been negligent or committed a wrongful act or omission (Abeyratne, 2002). The events of 11 September obviously raised the issue of airline liability (and insurance) again as we will discuss in Chapter 14.

Environmental Impacts

Like any other industry, aviation is subject to the rules and regulations in place to "protect" the environment and the health and wellbeing of the citizens within that environment. The set of rules that applies depends on the location, not the nationality of the firm involved. When American Airlines is in London, it is the rules of the UK and the broader European Commission that apply. There are obviously some issues that may be very specific to a firm and/or location such as dumping of toxic wastes or dangerous working conditions. Other issues are much broader in scope such as aircraft noise and aviation-related pollution from aircraft and from airfields. The latter has taken on new meaning with the concern about global warming and carbon emissions. We will discuss this whole issue in Chapter 17. For now, we will examine the question of aircraft noise. This issue took on new meaning with the advent of the jet age. ICAO created the Committee on Aircraft Noise (CAN) to deal with this issue and the national regulatory bodies governing aviation in respective countries have extensive rules and procedures for addressing noise that attempt to establish acceptable decibel levels, hours of operation, distances involved, remediation efforts, and so on. A good deal of effort has been expended to determine what level of noise is harmful, physically and mentally. Is excessive noise an annoyance? Does it negatively impact the "quality of life"? What can and must be done to address the problem? Noise concerns limited the landing rights of the supersonic Concorde and are a factor in limiting some operations at major airports such as Heathrow and Frankfurt (Aris, 2002; Michaels, 2008).

The Politics of Antitrust

Perhaps no area of the "law" has bedeviled the aviation industry more than antitrust (competitive policy as it is commonly called in Europe and Asia). Once you understand the concepts involved, it is not hard to see why. Antitrust is that body of principles and statutes whereby governments seek to promote forms of competition that benefit society and consumers. In many cases, this means restraining the use of market power (ability to control prices, supplies, distribution channels, and so on) by firms within an industry or preventing mergers or acquisitions that would create excessive market power. In an industry in which many segments (airline, manufacturing, engines, avionics, air cargo, alliances) may have only a few players or a few players with most of the market share, antitrust questions arise frequently. While all countries have some statutes addressing the behavior of firms within their domestic markets, the background and philosophy of countries regarding business itself, the role of government, and the limits of free enterprise differ. We will examine the background and philosophy of antitrust law and its application to aviation in the United States, Europe, and Asia. We will attempt to chart the future direction of antitrust enforcement and discuss critical issues impacting airline alliances.

In the years following the American Civil War (1861–65), the United States witnessed a renewed westward expansion fueled by the growth of the US railroad industry. As the economy became more integrated, there was an effort by a number of smaller companies to combine their businesses to increase market power. The most notorious effort involved Standard Oil, led by John D. Rockefeller. The Standard Oil "trust" was a device to gain market power by requiring participants to transfer stock from their company to a trustee in exchange for trust certificates. This trustee was then empowered to fix prices, control output, and allocate markets to other trust members. A series of scandals fueled the public perception that "trusts" were designed to drive smaller competitors out of business through the use of predatory tactics. Public outcry led the US Congress to pass a series of acts designed to curb activities that sought to restrain trade or establish excessive market power. Anti-trust legislation was born.

United States

The first US legislation dealing with antitrust was the Sherman Act (1890) which was concerned with "horizontal restraints" that is, agreements between rival firms in the same market or industry that sought to fix prices, restrain output, divide markets, exclude other competitors or erect barriers that impeded free markets. In 1914, the Clayton Act (amended by the Robinson–Patman Act of 1936 and the Cellar–Kefauver Act of 1950) attempted to correct publicly perceived flaws in the Sherman Act by clearly prescribing actions that were deemed "anti-competitive." These actions include price discrimination, exclusionary practices such as exclusive dealing contracts and tying arrangements (tie-in sales agreements), and mergers that may have the effect of reducing competition.[1] The Civil Aviation Act of 1938 applied antitrust specifically to airlines. Section 408 of the Civil Aviation Act, later recreated in virtually unchanged form in the Federal Aviation Act of 1958 and amended by the Airline Deregulation Act of 1978, made it unlawful for 1) two or more carriers to merge, 2) any carrier to control a substantial portion of the properties of another, or 3) any carrier to acquire control of another carrier. Section 414 provided the Civil Aviation Bureau (CAB) with the authority to grant limited immunity (exemption) from antitrust enforcement if it deemed the action to be "in the public interest." With the termination of the CAB in 1985, the Assistant Secretary for Policy and International Affairs in the Department of Transportation was given antitrust responsibility. Antitrust issues for other segments of the industry tend to fall under the Department of Justice and the Federal Trade Commission, although other departments may be consulted.

Domestic airline issues Following US deregulation in 1978, twenty-four US carriers were allowed to merge "in the public interest", a number that has increased since 9/11 with such mergers as US Airways and America West (Note that American Airlines bought key assets of TWA, but this is not considered a merger). The rationale for some of the mergers was the *failing company doctrine*, however, Robert Pitofsky, formerly with the Federal Trade Commission, told the Commerce, Science, and Transportation Committee of the US Senate that some of these mergers were clearly "anti-competitive." He specifically cited the TWA–Ozark merger in his testimony (Pitofsky, 1999). Alfred Kahn, the father of US deregulation, agreed and has commented that "I said we should deregulate the airline industry. I didn't say we should abolish the antitrust laws" (Reno, 2000). The general attitude of the US Republican party which was in power during much of this time was to view most business-related legislation as an interference in the workings of the free market (Clarkson, Miller, Jentz, and Cross, 1992). This view was supported by the so-called Chicago School of antitrust whose members argued that while monopoly pricing hurt consumers, it had little effect on overall economic growth and productivity (Mandel, France, and Carney, 2000). However, these political and economic arguments do not entirely account for the level of consolidation permitted during the 1980s. In an effort to ensure competition, the Federal Aviation Administration and the Department of Transportation became caught in their own trap. When they allowed United Airlines to acquire the Pacific routes of the failing Pan Am, they created a carrier whose large domestic base and extensive, profitable international route system placed domestic rivals with smaller geographic reach at a major disadvantage. So when Northwest petitioned the Department to purchase Republic citing the need to expand their geographic reach in order to counter the United threat, the DOT agreed and so it went as other carriers pressed similar arguments.[2] In effect, the FAA created, somewhat reluctantly, a domestic market dominated by six or seven major carriers, each possessing an extensive continental network (Oum and Park, 1997; Gesell, 1993).

The existence of these large, overlapping network competitors explains in part the failure of US carriers to form the type of joint activity alliances common in Europe. Two cases, one old and the other still pending, explain the government's view that such joint activities are on balance anti-competitive. The first case, *in Re Passenger Computer Reservation System Antitrust Litigation CCH 21 AVI 17, 732*, was brought against US carriers' use of computer reservation systems (CRSs) in booking and marketing. It was charged that these systems, created by individual carriers, restricted competition by 1) displaying flight information in a biased manner, 2) imposing discriminatory fees on competing carriers, 3) using the data to identify travel agents who could be persuaded to divert business to the carrier owning the CRS, and 4) delaying the entry of competitor data. Since the development of computer reservation systems is expensive and beyond the reach of many carriers, such practices were considered an unfair use of market power and proprietary technology. In addition, the courts upheld the decision of the Civil Aviation Bureau in *Republic Airlines vs CAB 756 f.2d 1304 (1985)* to prohibit an exclusivity provision of joint operating agreements between carriers (Gesell, 1993). The American Society of Travel Agents (ASTA) asked the US Department of Justice to take action against 27 US and foreign carriers participating in the development of an industry website for online booking. According to the chief executive of the ASTA, the "joint site is a clear attempt on the part of the airlines to lure consumers onto the Web with lower prices, and drive all their competitors out of business." Action was taken to insure that distance was placed between carriers and the web booking sites (Carey, 2000). Further, the Federal Trade Commission and the Department of Justice issued a joint policy statement (to be discussed later in the chapter) that attempted to consolidate and clarify policy regarding competitor collaboration.

The US Federal Trade Commission and the Department of Justice also began to scrutinize airline mergers and alliances more closely. This did not (and does not) mean that more consolidation is not likely. American Airlines was permitted to go ahead with its acquisition of Reno Air. The rationale behind this acquisition was that American had a very weak position in the California/West Coast market where Reno Airlines was relatively strong, thus, competition was not likely to be harmed. On the other hand, the Department of Justice filed suit when Northwest Airlines announced plans to acquire a controlling stake in Continental. While this case was settled when Northwest agreed to sell its Class A voting shares and retain only a 5 percent non-voting position, it should be noted that the Department of Justice did allow the two carriers to implement a number of their planned marketing activities (Carey and McCartney, 2000). UAL Corp, parent company of United Airlines, announced its proposed $11.6 billion deal to purchase US Airways with great fanfare, but ended its planned merger after consumer groups, fellow airlines, and local governments complained about the scope and nature of the acquisition which would have created an airline with a combined market share of over 30 percent, making it twice as large as its nearest US competitor (Hatch, 2000; Zellner, Carney, and Arndt, 2000). This would have been the first merger between two major US airlines since 1987 when US Air (now US Airways) and Piedmont Aviation were consolidated. It should be noted that a study conducted by Lehn and Kole on 18 airline mergers from 1979 to 1991 found that most resulted in negative long-run stock returns for the acquiring airline, including the US Air/Piedmont merger (Lehn, 2000). Of course, this did not stop US Airways from merging with America West in 2005 or from pursuing a merger with Delta while it was in bankruptcy.

Since deregulation took effect in the US over 200 airlines have started up and failed, a number that is increasing by the week as we will discuss in later chapters (Rosen, 1995). Start-ups contend that major carriers are unfairly using their market power advantages, specifically the ability to control price and capacity, to force them out of profitable markets. This is commonly called predatory behavior. Unfortunately for regional carriers, the record of antitrust cases in the US courts, particularly those involving charges of predatory behavior, has been very poor. In *Brookes Group Ltd v Brown & Williamson Tobacco Corp* (1993), the US Supreme Court ruled that aggressive cost cutting (even selling below costs) benefited consumers. Of the 37 cases to reach the Supreme Court since this decision, not one has prevailed (Carney and Zellner, 2000). The record for other cases of predatory behavior is equally poor (Walker, 1999). There was a renewed effort by the US Department of Justice under the administration of President Clinton to enforce legislation relating to predatory behavior. As part of this new commitment, the US Department of Transportation issued the "Proposed Statement on Enforcement Policy on Unfair Exclusionary Conduct by Airlines." The statement outlined the following situations when the DOT was likely to act on predatory practice complaints: (1) a major airline adds seats and discounts fares reducing "local revenue", or (2) a major airline carries more passengers at the new low fare than the new entrant has capacity, reducing the major's "local revenue", or (3) a major airline carries more at the new low fare than the new entrant carries reducing the major's local revenue. This issue had a number of implications for domestic alliances. First, many regional US carriers had decided to avoid direct competition by entering into franchise agreements with major carriers acting as a feeder service to their hubs. Second, regional carriers themselves had begun to consolidate either through merger or alliance (AvStat, 1998).

International airline issues   As discussed in Chapter 8, the deregulation of the US airline industry was accompanied by a renewed effort to liberalize international markets and antitrust legislation had an important role to play in the US strategy, first as a means to attack the fare-setting power of IATA and then to encourage the spread of open skies bilateral agreements through the promise of antitrust immunity for alliance partners from open skies countries. The first of the "approved" alliances was Northwest and KLM. Four of the approved alliances are no longer in effect due to the failure (merger) of one or more of the carriers involved in the immunized alliance—American with Canadian International Airlines, Delta with Swiss Air, Sabena, and Austrian Airlines (formerly the Qualifyer group), Swissair with American, and Northwest and KLM (PRNewswire, 2000; OIG, 1999). The new US–EU Open Skies promises to increase the pool of immunized alliances.

In December of 1999, the United States Department of Transportation released a report on the benefits of open skies. According to the report, fares in open skies markets dropped 17.5 percent between 1996 and 1998. Non-open skies markets experienced only a drop of 3.5 percent (DOT, 1999). Thus, the United States rationale for waiving antitrust provisions in approved alliances between open skies market partners is that the pro-competitive benefits to consumers of open skies outweighs the possible anti-competitive harm.

Domestic issues in other sectors   Chapter 13 picks up the story of air cargo and notes that UPS struggled state by state with the Interstate Commerce Commission for the right to compete against the US Postal Service (USPS) in the delivery of parcels. UPS pointed to the fact that the USPS was subsidized, paid no taxes, did not show a profit, and was often the subject of hearings and public outcry over mismanagement and incompetence. Their legal arguments centered the value of competition, the lower rates of UPS, and the "benefits to consumers." They were ultimately successful in their struggles but not without years of effort (Niemann,

2007). Obviously, when an entity is owned by the government, whether it is an airline or a postal system, there are incentives to protect it that create conflicts with the stated obligation of that government to protect competition for the benefit of consumers. As noted in the introduction to this book, aviation is often seen as a special case. One of the reasons for this is national defense. Therefore, it is not surprising that there are a number of "activities" that may be exempted from the application of competition rules including any activity approved by the US president on the grounds of national defense (Defense Production Act), activity involving research consortium to develop new computer technology (National Cooperative Research Act) or any activity of a regulated industry that is approved by the regulatory agency in that area (Clarkson, Miller, Jentz, and Cross, 1992). Further, there are "special" circumstances that have led the US government for national security reasons to approve mergers or acquisitions deemed to affect national security. The approval of the Boeing/McDonnell-Douglas merger and the Lockheed-Martin–Marietta merger are two relatively recent examples of aerospace firms (with military as well as civilian activities) that the US government felt merited exception.

International issues in other sectors   "Fair competition", of course, has been the stated reason behind the ongoing battles between Boeing and Airbus. Boeing has claimed that the initial launch aid provided to Airbus represents an "illegal subsidy." In 1992, the US and EU had agreed that governments could provide money for no more that 33 percent of the development costs of a new aircraft. These development costs would be viewed as loans repayable if the plane was actually built, the first 25 percent at government rates and the remainder at commercial rates. Airbus has charged that the aid Boeing receives from the US military amounts to a sizeable "indirect subsidy." Neither side has ever been able to put a specific figure to the amounts of aid, but this has not stopped them from battling over the issue. The US would again revisit this issue at the urging of Boeing in 2004, after Airbus had surpassed Boeing in orders. Both sides eventually filed a complaint with the World Trade Organization. As Airbus went to EU governments for new launch aid, Boeing howled. As Boeing outsourced development costs to the Japanese heavies (supported by their government), Airbus cried foul. This battle continues.

The US engine manufacturers have also lodged complaints about subsidies against UK competitor, Rolls-Royce, who is reported to have received almost 450 million pounds from the UK government who also holds a "golden share" in the company. Pratt & Whitney has noted that the CFM56 was partly funded by the French government in support of GE partner Snecma. The V2500, designed for the A380, by Rolls-Royce and Pratt is another example of development aid in action. Once again, all sides of the debate can charge "indirect subsidy" because of the engine manufacturers' relationships with their respective government defense spending (Newhouse, 2007).

Europe

While each individual European nation has its own legislation relating to competitive activity, we will address the development of antitrust or competitive policy as it is called in Europe from the perspective of European integration.[3] Although a common transport policy was one of the stated goals of the European Community, the Council of Ministers, under their authority to issue block exemptions, chose to exempt transportation from the enforcement of competition rules. In 1986 the Court of Justice ruled in the *Nouvelles Frontières* case that the air transport sector was subject to the general rules of the EEC Treaty. In that same year, the Commission began proceedings against ten Community airlines for violation of various competition rules. The "first package", adopted 14 December 1987, officially included an implementing regulation giving the Commission the authority to investigate alleged violations of the competition rules and fine violators.

Domestic airline issues   The Commission's policy toward airline mergers has been shaped in large part by what they perceive as failures in US policy. According to many European aviation experts, "the experience of deregulation combined with the lack of antitrust enforcement, destroyed many of the benefits of that deregulation" in the United States (Soames, 1990: 82). Mario Monti, a former EC antitrust commissioner, led a concerted effort to crackdown on industries that attempted to set prices or divide markets. While there is a general feeling that cross-border ownership would benefit the EU system by reducing the tendency to favor "local" firms and allow for more economies of scale, the Commission has also been cautious in approving mergers and acquisitions. The Commission's policy was questioned several years ago when Air France/UTA were allowed to merge, however, a series of Commission rulings, including one involving AirTours planned takeover of First Choice, appears to indicate that the Commission is prepared to take a tougher stance in aviation/aerospace mergers/acquisitions (Soames, 1990; Taverna, 1999). Most recently, the EU rejected a proposed merger between Ryanair and Aer Lingus on the grounds that the merger would create a monopoly at Ireland's Dublin Airport. Ryanair CEO, Michael O'Leary, has complained that this decision is at odds with the earlier decision to allow Air France and KLM to merge even though these two carriers would control about 60 percent of the aircraft movements at Charles de Gaulle Airport and Schiphol Airport respectively (Media Limited, 2007). Similarly, a previously suggested merger between British Airways/KLM raised questions over the fact that any merger would place a single airline in control of two of Europe's most important airports—Heathrow and Schiphol. The stated reason for ending the talks was "intractable commercial and regulatory issues", but clearly there were serious concerns over European Commission approval, The US was also concerned because The Netherlands was an open skies country while the UK still had not signed such an agreement (Field, 2000).

While European officials have taken a hard line on the issue of mergers and acquisitions, they have tended to have a more favorable view of cooperative agreements between carriers involving fleet rationalization and network efficiencies. While EC competition rules do not explicitly consider "the public interest", they have often held that these types of agreements "contribute to the promotion of economic progress and to the interests of consumers" (AEA, 1999). Some of the allowed practices include consultation on and coordination of tariffs, joint operations, interline agreements, route planning, coordination of schedules, and linked frequent flyer programs. Perhaps signaling its limits, the European Commission recently conducted a raid on the offices of Scandinavian Airlines and Maersk Air to determine whether Maersk Air stopped operating between Stockholm and Copenhagen "in concert with SAS" following their recent cooperation pact (Dow Jones Newswire, 2000). US officials, on the other hand, have tended to view almost all actions relating to route planning, schedule coordination, and joint operations as violations of antitrust law.

In an address at the 23rd Annual FAA Commercial Aviation Forecast Conference, Frederik Sorenson, Head of the Air Transport Policy Unit, Directorate General of Transport, European Commission, addressed the issue of competitive behavior by stating that the EU did not agree with the US "free for all system depending on the good behavior of air carriers" (Sorensen, 1998: 125). The Commission has acted in several cases of alleged predatory behavior ruling in favor of plaintive airlines (easyJet–KLM, easyJet–BA Go). Most recently, BA's Go has lodged a complaint with the European Commission charging that Deutsche Lufthansa AG was selling tickets below cost (Independent, 2000). Given sufficient protection, many of these carriers may opt to remain independent, niche players rather than franchising feeders for the major airlines. The rapid growth of Ryanair, however, may give this carrier the market power to dampen the growth and development of the low-cost competition that the EU hoped to see from its deregulation and single sky program.

International airline issues   While the US chose to tie alliance approval to open skies, European officials have tied alliance approval to domestic market development. A key issue in alliance approvals has been the willingness of potential partners to relinquish slots at congested European airports (United–Lufthansa and BA–AA, for example). These slots were deemed necessary to the development of viable start-up competitors. The European Commission has argued for a multilateral approach to traffic rights negotiations on the basis of the one market concept and launched a case against eight member states arguing that the bilateral agreements that they signed with the US violated the EU external competence. The 2002 ruling by the European Court of Justice gave the EC the go ahead to "demand" multilateral talks with the US (EurActiv, 2008). In 1991, the EU and the US had agreed to notify and give weight to the competition policies of the other party in instances where their own enterprises were concerned. Most of the notifications involved proposed mergers. Unfortunately, the principle of positive comity has often merely served to highlight the differences between EU–US policy. In particular, US authorities explicitly consider "the public interest" when assessing the benefits of proposed action (AEA, 1999). Given that one part of the new multilateral agreement signed between the US and EU calls for regulatory convergence, it is not clear what criteria will be used for alliance approval in the future (The CalTrade Report, 2007).

Domestic issues in other sectors   In aerospace, the EU did block the proposed GE/Honeywell merger, claiming that the merger would reduce competition. GE and Honeywell had offered to unload some assets in the avionics area, but the European Commission asked that GE either spin off its aircraft leasing unit or sell shares (CNNMoney.com, 2001; CNN.com, 2001). In 1999, the EU rejected another aerospace merger between Honeywell and AlliedSignal on concerns over undue dominance in avionics. Complaints had been lodged several years earlier when the EC had approved French subsidies to Sextant and Smith Industries to build a flight management system for Airbus, a move that some saw as an attempt to reduce Airbus reliance on Honeywell (CNNMoney.com, 1999).

International issues in other sectors   It is not surprising given the battles between Airbus and Boeing that the EC waded into the debate about the Boeing–McDonnell merger, eventually approving the merger after Boeing agreed to give up an exclusive sales agreement with American, Delta, and Continental (Newhouse, 2007). More recently, the EC has agreed to the merger between Travelport and Worldspan which would mean that global distribution systems (GDSs) would be combined. Travelport is the second-largest GDS in the EU. Worldspan, whose subsidiary Orbitz is an online travel provider, ranks fourth in GDS systems. Amadeus and Sabre are the other main players. The EU has stated that although the merged entity would have a very high market share in some of its member states, it did not feel that it would be able to increase prices due to high competition with other providers (Michels, 2008).

Asia

There is no single legal framework for Asia, but most of its countries do have some kind of legislation dealing with monopoly and competition. The difficulty lies in understanding the degree to which these regulations are applied and/or enforced. In Japan, the Anti-Monopoly Act is intended "to eliminate excessive concentrations of business power and to encourage fair and free competition" (Japan External Trade Organization (JETRO), 1999). It prohibits holding companies and places restrictions on share holding, interlocking directorates, mergers and acquisitions. The Fair Trade Commission is responsible for enforcing the anti-monopoly guidelines. The Korean Fair Trade Commission is also charged with promulgating guidelines and enforcing policies of their Monopoly Regulation and Fair Trade Act. Like its Japanese counterpart, the Monopoly Regulation and Fair Trade Act is intended to prohibit excessive concentration, abuse of market power, and unfair business practices. To the outside observer, the Japanese Keiretsus and the Korean Chaebols, forms of tightly linked industrial groupings, appear to violate much of this legislation. Critics have often complained that the legislation is primarily directed at limiting foreign access to domestic markets (Gibney, 1985; Prestowitz, 1988). The recent financial crisis in Asia has put a great deal of pressure on these structures. Indications are that Korea at least is willing to dismantle much of the chaebol structure to improve efficiency and transparency within their market.

Domestic airline issues   Efforts were underway in a number of Asian countries to deregulate aspects of their air transport sectors before the Asian crisis. The Japanese government changed it policy in 1995 to make discounted fares easier and in 1996 created a zone-fare system. On 5 December 1996, the Japanese Ministry of Trade announced an end to the supply–demand balance clauses that had effectively blocked new entry. A 1999 study of the changes, however, had not found a significant shift in market share or reduction in airfares (Yamauchi, 1999). The Korean market continues to be market regulated. The domestic market has traditionally been divided between Korean Airlines (KAL) and Asiana. Internationally, Asiana is primarily restricted to short-haul Asian routes while KAL flies transatlantic and transpacific routes. To date, there is little evidence of domestic alliance development outside the traditional industrial grouping structure.

International airline alliances   As with aviation policy as a whole, there is no consistent "Asian" strategy toward international alliances. Market access through code sharing has been the dominant form of alliance arrangement. The economic crisis that started in Thailand and spread throughout Asia affected all of the region's air carriers. Hardest hit were Thai Airlines, Philippines Airlines, Korean Airlines, Malaysian Airlines, and Garuda. High operating and financing costs combined with outbound and inbound traffic decreases placed severe stress on these and other Asian carriers (Li, 1999). There have been talks of regional consolidation, but little action took place until the 9/11, SARS, and bird flu crises added further pressure to some of the Asia carriers. Many of these talks (and actions) included Singapore Airlines which emerged as one of the strongest of the Asian carriers and has continued an aggressive campaign to improve its already impressive quality and position itself well in the mega-alliance world.

Stumbling Along

It should be clear from the above discussions that the line between politics and legal matters is very fine and frequently shifting. The aviation/aerospace industry is a highly visible, important employer with close ties to national security and defense; this places any matter affecting its profitability squarely into the political arena. In the all-important area of competition, the trend is clearest for the European Union where the Commission appears intent on maintaining a relatively hard line on mergers/acquisitions and predatory behavior. Several factors could slow this trend, but they are unlikely to reverse it. Perhaps the key factor will be the willingness of Europe's national governments and the people they represent to allow cross-border acquisitions. Consolidation is certainly a possibility in a deregulated market and more likely following 11 September. The approval of Air France–KLM certainly indicates that the EC is interested in selected merger activity. As noted above, the Commission has indicated on a number of occasions that it would like to see more consolidation in the relatively fragmented airline and aerospace industry (Sparaco, 1999). If, on the other hand, this consolidation is seen as destroying national flag carriers and/or eliminating jobs within certain countries, then there is likely to develop greater political opposition, as appears to be the case with the Air France–KLM and Alitalia merger. This issue had already been hotly debated in the EU as national governments pondered the failure of Sabena and Swissair and efforts by their governments to salvage some part of these carriers. Any effort by the Italian government to intervene to "keep Alitalia Italian" is likely to meet similar protests.

As for predatory behavior, the EU provided start-up carriers greater protection than is typically afforded them in the US market. This protection could help insure that deregulation increases competition at the route level within Europe. In a new twist, the start-up darling of Europe, Ryanair, is facing increasing charges that it has now begun to practice the kind of market power tactics once used against it to compete against legacy and other start-ups (Creaton, 2005). The pool of start-ups in Europe remains relatively small and it is likely that many of the major European carriers have not felt the need to aggressively engage them. The events of 9/11 hit the major European carriers hard and regional European carriers appear poised to increase their 7 percent share of the intra-European market even more, possibly reaching the 25 percent share achieved by their US cousins (Binggeli and Pompeo, 2002). It is likely that the expansion of Ryanair alone has moved the low-cost carriers very close to this goal. Although alliances found themselves caught up in the effort to promote start-up carriers, a report by the British Civil Aviation Authority found that no more than 7 percent of intra-European city pairs are served by three or more competitors (Sparaco, 1998). Once again, the growth of Ryanair has probably done more to increase competition on intra-EU routes that any government action.

The US, under the Clinton administration, had moved toward stronger enforcement of its antitrust provisions. The Federal Trade Commission and the Department of Justice had jointly issued antitrust guidelines for collaboration among competitors which outlined those agreements that would be considered *per se* illegal from those that would be analyzed under the rule of reason to determine their effect on competition. According to these guidelines, any agreement addressing pricing or capacity was to be deemed *per se* illegal. All other agreements would be analyzed according to the rule of reason policy. The agencies would first define "relevant markets", then calculate "market shares" and concentrations to assess possible market power increases stemming from the agreement. If this raised concerns about anti-competitive harm, they would then assess the degree of independent decision making by partners to the agreement to determine the potential degree of collusion. They would then be interested in the ability and incentives of partners to compete independently. According to the guidelines, the agencies would focus on six factors: (1) the degree of exclusivity in the agreement, (2) the extent of independent asset control, (3) the nature and extent of inter-partner financial interest, (4) the control of competitive decision making, (5) the degree of information sharing, and (6) the duration of the partnership. These guidelines were largely a consolidation and elaboration on existing law. A somewhat more problematic issue concerns weighing anti-competitive harm against collaborative efficiencies and whether these efficiencies are considered pro- or anti-competitive (Federal Trade Commission, 1999). Previous US administrations had tended to accept the argument that pro-competitive benefits outweigh potential harm. In the area of predatory behavior, the failure of the US government in the American Airlines case was but a foretaste of the shifting US government stance on matters of antitrust. The Bush administration, as is typical of Republican administrations, has worked hard to reverse the "excesses of antitrust enforcement" (France, 2002; Hamm, Greene, and Reinhardt, 2002). Current rhetoric suggests that a Democratic administration might reverse policy again and the harmonization efforts with the EU can be expected to influence US action in the future.

Notes

1. Federal antitrust laws are enforced by the Department of Justice (DOJ) and the Federal Trade Commission (FTC). Violations of the Sherman Act fall under the jurisdiction of the DOJ and can be prosecuted as either a criminal or civil case. The Department can ask companies to divest certain holdings or dissolve a partnership. The FTC has the responsibility to enforce the Clayton Act through civil proceedings. In addition, private parties may sue for damages as a result of violation of the Sherman and Clayton Acts. Private parties may also seek an injunction to prevent antitrust violations. It should be noted that European law does not include possible criminal prosecution.

2. I am indebted to Paul V. Mifsud, Vice President, Government & Legal Affairs, US, for KLM Royal Dutch Airlines for his willingness to share his insight and experience.

3. Antitrust legislation was first contained in Articles 4 and 65–7 of the European Coal and Steel Community treaty. It is incorporated in Articles 85–6, 90, and 92–4 of the Treaty of European Union. The European Commission (Directorate-General IV) is responsible for implementing competitiveness policy.

References

Abeyratne, R.I.R. (2002), *Frontiers of Aerospace Law*, Ashgate Publishing, Aldershot, UK.

AEA (1999), *Towards a Transatlantic Common Aviation Area*, Association of European Airlines, Brussels.

Aris, S. (2002), *Close to the Sun: How Airbus Challenged America's Domination of the Skies*, Arum Press, London.

AvStat Associates Inc. (1998), 'Summary of Passenger Service by State', AvStat Associates.

Binggeli, U. and Pompeo L. (2002), 'Hyped Hopes for Europe's low-cost airlines', *McKensey Quarterly*, Available at: www.mckinsey/quarterly.com.

The CalTrade Report (2008), 'US, EU Pact Opens Transatlantic Market', 17 July, Available at: http://www.caltradereport.com/eWebPages/front-page-1178627781.html.

Carey, S. (2000), 'Travel Agents Ask the U.S. to Act Against Web-Site Plan', *The Wall Street Journal*, February 18.

Carey, S and McCartney, S. (2000), 'Antitrust Trial Pressures Northwest Airlines to Cede Controlling Stake in Continental', *Wall Street Journal*, November 7.

Carney, D and Zellner, W (2000), 'Caveat Predator?' *Business Week*, May 22, pp. 116–118. Clarkson, K.W., Miller, R.R., Jentz, G.A. and Cross, F.B. (1992), *West's Business Law: Text, Cases, Legal and regulatory Environment* (5th ed.). West Publishing Company, New York.

CNNMoney (2001), 'GE Pessimistic on Merger', June 14, Available at: http://cnnmoney.com/pt/cpt?action=cpt&title=GE%2C+Honeywell.

CNNMoney (1999), 'EC Probes Avionics Merger', August 30, Available at: http://cnnmoney.com/pt/cpt?action=cpt&title=EC+probes+AlliedSinanl.

CNN (2001), 'EU Kills GE-Honeywell', July 3, Available at: http://cnn.europe.business.com/pt/cpt?dropdown=Y&action=cpt%exp.

Creaton, S. (2005), *Ryanair: How a Small Irish Airline Conquered Europe*, Aurum Press, London.

Department of Transportation, (1999), 'International Aviation Developments: Global Deregulation Takes Off', DOT: Washington, DC. ostpxweb.dot.gov/aviation.

Dow Jones Newswire (2000), 'EU Raids Maersk, SAS In Connection with Cooperation Pact', June 21.

EurActiv (2008), 'EU–US 'Open Skies' Agreement', Available at: http://www.euractiv.com/en/transport.

Federal Trade Commission (1999), www.ftc.gov/opa/1999/9910/jointven.html

Field, P. (2000), 'BA, KLM Ground Merger Plan. Airlines Faced Opposition from Government Which feared Massive Layoffs', *USA Today*, September 22, 1B.

France, M. (2002), 'Uncle Sam's Trustbusters: Outgunned—and Outmoded,' *Business Week*, November 18, pp. 44–5.

Gesell, L.E. (1993), 'Aviation and the Law' (2nd ed.). Coast Aire Publications, Chandler, AZ.

Gibney, F. (1985), *The Fragile Super-Power*, New American Library, New York.

Hamm, S., Greene, J., and Reinhardt, A. (2002), 'What's a Rival to do Now?', November 18, pp. 44–6.

Independent (2000), 'BAs GO Accuses Lufthansa of Unfair Competition', London, February 28, p. 17

International Air Transport Association (1999), 'Competition and Court Cases in Europe', *Airlines International*, vol. 4, p. 58.

Hatch, M. (2000), 'Minnesota Attorney General Letter to the DOJ re US-UA', June 5.

JETRO (1999), www.jetro.go.jp.

Lehn, K.M. (2000), 'Why Airline Mergers are a Disaster – Soaring Labor Costs May Ground Airline Mergers', May 25.

Li, M.Z.F. (1999), 'Asia-Pacific Airlines amidst the Asian Economic Crisis', Presented at the Air Transportation Research Group Conference, Hong Kong, June 1999.

Mandel, M.J., France, M. and Carney, D. (2000), 'The Great Antitrust Debate', June 26, pp. 40–42.

Media Limited (2007) 'EU Steps in on Irish Airline Merger', June 27, Available at: http://www.airport-technology.com/news/news1701.html

Merrill Lynch, Pierce, Fenner & Smith, Inc. (1998), *Global Airline Alliances: Why Alliances Really Matter from an Investment Perspective*, Merrill Lynch, Pierce, Fenner & Smith Inc., New York.

Michels, J. (2008), 'Travelport Completes Acquisition of Worldspan', Aviation Daily, Available at: http://aviationow.com/pt/cpt?action=cpt&title=Aviation+Week%3A.

Michaels, D. (2008), 'Heathrow Makeover to Heat up Airline Wars', *The Wall Street Journal Online,* March 6.

Newhouse, J. (2007), *Boeing versus Airbus: The Inside Story of the Greatest International Competition in Business*, Alfred A. Knopf, New York.

Niemann, G. (2007) *Big Brown: The Untold Story of UPS*, John Wiley & Sons, San Francisco, CA.

Office of Inspector General (OIG) (1999), 'Aviation Safety Under International Code Share Agreements,' 30 September AV-1999-138, Available at: www.oig.dot.gov/item.jsp?id=29.

Pitofsky, R (1999), *The Impact of Recent Alliances, International Agreements, Dot Actions, and Pending Legislation on Air Fares, Air Service, and Competition in the Airline Industry*, 10x Cong., 2 Sess.

Prestowitz, C.V. (1988), *Trading Places: How We Are Giving Our Future to Japan and How to Reclaim it,* Basic Books, Inc, New York.

PRNewswire (2000), 'Northwest Airlines and Malaysia Airlines receive Antitrust Immunity; Approval Represents First Immunized Alliance Between a U.S. and Asian Carrier', November 21.

Reno, R. (2000), 'In Several Ways, United/US Airways Merger Might Not Fly', *STAR TRIBUNE*, June 1.

Rosen, S.D. (1995), 'Corporate Restructuring: A Labor Perspective', in *Airline Labor Relations in the Global Era: The New Frontier*, P. Cappelli (ed.), ILR Press, Ithaca, NY.

Soames, T. (1990), 'Joint Ventures and Cooperation Agreements in the Air Transport Sector', in P.D. Dagtoglou and T. Soames (eds), *Airline Mergers and Cooperation in the European Community*, Kluwer Law and Taxation Publishers, Boston.

Sorensen, F. (1998), 'Open Skies in Europe', in *FAA Commercial Aviation Forecast Conference Proceedings*, U.S. Department of Transportation, Washington, D.C., pp. 125–131.

Sparaco, P. (1999), 'EC Pushes Quick Aviation Accord with U.S.', *Aviation Week & Space Technology*, November 29, pp. 40–41.

Sparaco, P. (1998), 'European Deregulation Still Lacks Substance', *Aviation Week & Space Technology*, November 9, pp. 53–7.

Taverna, M.A. (1999), 'European Rulings Signal Tougher Antitrust Stance', *Aviation Week & Space Technology*, October 4, pp. 42–3.

Walker, K. (1999), 'American Justice', *Airline Business*, July, pp. 66–7.

Yamauchi, H. (1999), 'Air Transport Policy in Japan: Policy Change and Market Competition', Paper presented at the Air Transportation Research Group Conference, Hong Kong, April 1999.

Zellner, W., Carney, D., and Arndt, M. (2000), 'How Many Airlines Will Stay Aloft', *Business Week*, June 19.

Chapter 12
The Quality Question

Know it When You See it

Quality is a very elusive term. Consumers know (or think they know) it when they see it and firms have spent billions trying to get them to articulate their preferences or to convince them that what they get is what they want. A researcher will tell you that you can not measure something until you define it. Unfortunately, the very act of defining and measuring a concept can change the concept itself, marketing's own "Uncertainty Principle." The term quality has been defined as excellence, value, conformance to specification, and so on. The most commonly used definition comes to us from the total quality movement. It defines quality as "meeting and/or exceeding customer expectations." To comply with this definition of quality, companies must first know who their customers are and then continually strive to understand and meet their expectations (continuous improvement). While this sounds simple on paper, many companies find it difficult to put into practice. For airlines, revenue management systems that divided customers by their preferences on booking time, price, class, and so on and frequent flyer surveys of services provided to these customers have often been considered sufficient to comply with this quality definition. However, the growing movement to "brand" airline and alliance service is focusing new attention on issues of quality. This movement is fueled by the belief that "a very real risk exists that the flight will be reduced to a commodity status, and that the individual choice of airlines will be factored out of the buying process" (Fraser, 1996: 61). The answer, as we discussed in Chapter 10, is to create products and services that send images and messages to the consumer that reassure them about quality, convenience, comfort and so on. In short, the very name must separate one airline (one alliance) from another in terms of key consumer expectations whether they are "global reach", "superior service" or "value for the money."

Measuring a Concept

For individual carriers, consumers have three basic sources of information on quality: personal experience (or word of mouth), third-party surveys or secondary reports. Personal experience or the so-called word-of-mouth information that comes to us from friends and strangers alike is clearly a powerful force. For many companies this source calls to mind the old adage that a satisfied customer tells five other people about their experience while a dissatisfied customer tells at least ten. For most firms in the so-called service industries, satisfying customers is a primary goal of the organization. Taking this concept one step further, marketing gurus such as Fred Reichheld (1996) have suggested that *The Ultimate Question* is "Would you recommend us to a friend?" Reichheld believes that the best measure of a firm's success is the size of their net promoter score (promoters less detractors). Reichheld's promoters are the truly loyal customers. Loyal customers repurchase your products or services and recommend them to others.

Loyalty, repurchase, and satisfaction are among the most significant concepts in marketing research and the key to superior performance. Loyalty, repurchase, and satisfaction play an important role for understanding consumer behavior. The academic literature provides a number of research findings on relations between loyalty, repurchase, and satisfaction. However, Szymanski and Henard (2001) report that, despite numerous studies, the research findings are conflicting. Loyalty is a multidimensional construct, which is defined and viewed differently by researchers. Despite the large number of studies published in the area of satisfaction and loyalty, Oliver (1999) stated that loyalty–satisfaction relations are not well defined. The general assumption is that loyal consumers are satisfied. However, several researchers have indicated that satisfaction itself is an unreliable predictor of loyalty. While many researchers consider loyalty and repurchase as highly related concepts, and often use those two terms interchangeably, other researchers identified differences. High repurchase rates do not necessarily indicate loyalty; low repurchase rates do not always indicate disloyalty. Several researchers, including Bloemer and Kasper (1995), have stated that repeated purchasing behavior is the actual re-buying of a product or service, where only the behavior is important, regardless of the customer's degree of commitment. In contrast, loyalty takes into account the actual behavior's antecedents, including the psychological state of a consumer's mind. Many researchers, including Jacoby and Chestnut (1978), distinguish between the psychological aspect of loyalty and the behavioral aspect of loyalty, which is identified with repurchase.

While personal experience and word of mouth clearly influence opinions about quality, real or perceived, surveys are one of the most popular sources for information about products and services. Publicly available surveys involving airlines are typically conducted by such organizations as J.D. Powers, Zagats or Conde Nast utilizing information from frequent flyers to rank or award airlines on quality performance. The 1997 J.D. Powers' survey found that there are ten factors that drive consumer satisfaction with airline quality: on-time performance, airport check-in, schedule/flight accommodations, seating comfort, gate location, aircraft interior, flight attendants, food service, post-flight services, and frequent flyer programs. Specifics in the pre-flight categories include availability of flight when desired, helpfulness of reservations agents, ability to get seat preference, ability to get priority boarding, and frequent flyer qualification levels. In-flight issues judged important by consumers include effective communication on flight delays/cancellations, carry-on luggage space, seating comfort, and helpfulness of flight attendants. In the area of airport activities, consumers want such things as speedy baggage delivery, good connecting flight information, short check-in times, and good airport lounges (Glab, 1997). While surveys are a source of valuable information to consumers, they have several weaknesses from a research perspective. First, it is difficult to compare the surveys from different organizations because the factors included vary between them. Second, the cross-sectional nature (that is, the respondents in 1996 are not the same as in 1998) and changing factors across years for the same organizations limit the ability to evaluate trends in the data. Finally, these surveys do not generally provide an overall ranking of all the airlines included but a category-by-category ranking of the top performers.

The final source of information on airline quality is reported secondary data. This information is gathered either routinely by airlines or is mandated by the regulatory authority in that country (region). This information may or may not be publicly available. If publicly available, it may be provided by the regulatory agency upon request, periodically published, or posted to a publicly accessible website. To illustrate the type, use, and limitation of such data, we will use the US example. The US Department of Transportation has published the *Air Travel Consumer Report (ATCR)* monthly since 1987. The ATCR contains data on areas of service quality of interest to consumers, but has changed somewhat over time as issues such as flight cancellation and animal handling in transport have become more important and problems of smoking on aircraft have declined in importance and occurrence. The data is provided in raw form with no effort made to adjust the data for the size of airline operations. Such adjustment is important for evaluating the performance between airlines and is usually based on either departures, miles, or hours flown. Two groups of US researchers have used the data in the ATCR to explore issues of airline service quality. In 1991, the Aviation Institute at the University of Nebraska published its first *Airline Quality Rating* (AQR) report on the ten major US carriers. The weighted AQR has been revised since its inception to disaggregate service, safety, and financial indicators. The second group of researchers began reporting on airline service in 1998, although they went back to the first publication of the ATCR in 1987 to begin their analysis of service quality (Rhoades, Waguespack, and Treudt, 1998). Service and safety quality were separated from inception to construct two different rankings of airline performance which could be compared for each carrier and the industry overall (Rhoades and Waguespack, 1999, 2004). Further, Rhoades and Waguespack (2000a) examined the service and safety quality of US national and regional carriers whose performance could be compared to the traditional legacy (major) carriers. Comparisons were also made between legacy and low-cost carriers (LCC) (Rhoades and Waguespack, 2001, 2005). In their most recent work, Rhoades and Waguespack (2008) reported on twenty years of US airline service quality.

One of the advantages of secondary data is that it allows for consistent trend analysis. For example, it is possible to say (based on the work of Rhoades and Waguespack) that the industry average service quality for the major carriers improved from 1987 to 1993 and remained relatively stable at around 40 service problems per departure for 1994–97 before it began to climb in 1998 reaching 47 service problems per departure in 2000. This same analysis can apply at the firm level to analyze how a given firm has changed over time. Secondary data is also easy and cheap to obtain. As with anything else, there are also disadvantages as well. First, this secondary data does not specifically ask about many of the areas identified as important by the survey research—food service, legroom, and aircraft interior. The primary focus of the measures in the secondary data is basic service—on-time performance, delays, and baggage delivery. Critics have suggested that amenities are important to flyers and are not considered in the secondary data. A final criticism has to do with the issue of perception.

Perception Versus Reality

The dictionary defines perception as the "recognition and interpretation of sensory stimuli based chiefly on memory" (The American Heritage College Dictionary, 2000: 1014). Since individuals vary in terms of memory, sensory acuity, and cognitive ability, it is clearly possible that no two individuals will perceive a situation or event the same way. Parasuraman, Zeithaml and Berry (1985) have argued that service quality is the difference or gap between customer expectations of performance and customer perceptions of that performance. They used this starting point to develop the SERVQUAL instrument. In the SERVQUAL instrument, quality is defined or operationalised in the form of five dimensions: tangibles, reliability, responsiveness, assurance, and empathy (Parasuraman, Zeithaml and Berry 1988). Cronin and Taylor (1992) have taken the argument one step further to suggest that all that matters is perception of performance; perception equals service quality. Only a few of the studies have attempted to integrate a scale such as SERVQUAL or SERVPERF into the airline service research literature. One such study utilized the SERVQUAL scale adopted for an airline situation in 1994 (Sultan and Simpson, 2000) and found the SERVQUAL factor of reliability (one example: excellent airlines will provide their services at the time they promise to do so) was the most important dimension among air passengers. However, there has been no longitudinal perceptual study on airline service quality published in the academic realm. This lack of follow-up study or an update of the work done is common in much of marketing research, not just airline service quality research. A further issue that deserves study is the relationship between perception and "reality." In other words, how does customer perception compare to some sets of "objective" measures of performance? One of the first attempts to address this question is Tiernan, Rhoades, and Waguespack (2008). They compared survey data asking for the respondents to identify the percentage of certain service failures—lost baggage, delayed flights, cancelled flights, and so on—to the available secondary data for the US and EU. They found that the perception of airline quality was for the most part far worse than the secondary metrics of performance would suggest. Even when secondary service metrics were reaching over 99 percent, respondents reported perceptions of increasingly poor service.

And the Winner is...

In terms of flight delays, late arrivals, cancellations, and other quality indicators, the US airline industry is set to post its worst year since the US Department of Transportation began public reporting. Preliminary figures indicate that the industry has posted on-time arrival rates of only 72 percent, an all-time low (Yu, 2007a) while the rate of mishandled baggage for 2006 rose to 6.5 per 1,000 passengers and shows little signs of improving in 2007 due to the increased number of passengers checking baggage in the wake of the new regulations on liquids (The Associated Press, 2007). Further adding to the quality woes plaguing the industry has been the very public meltdown of carriers such as JetBlue Airways. Bad weather and lean operations resulted in the stranding of over 5,000 passengers during the Valentine's Day holiday. This single event is projected to cost JetBlue US$14 million in refunds and overtime. The cost in terms of reputation and goodwill for a carrier that had been held up as an example of airline excellence is not yet known (Sloan and Ehrenfeld, 2007).

Alliances—Sum of the Parts?

To date, there have been few attempts to evaluate the quality of alliances, but many of the same issues cited for individual carrier quality would apply such as whether the data comes from surveys or secondary sources. Unfortunately, there is no single entity that collects the type of secondary data available in the US and EU for individual carriers. Thus, it is not possible to take data from all of the global members of an alliance, combine them, and compare across alliances. Tiernan, Rhoades, and Waguespack (2008) reported three areas of comparison available across the airline alliance groupings for US and EU carriers only based on reported data from both the US DOT and the EU AEA. Their findings indicate very few statistically significant differences across the main alliance groupings and the three indicators of service quality examined: on-time arrivals, baggage reports and flight cancellations. While there are some yearly differences between each of the alliance groupings it is the overall similarity which is of note.

There have been at least two other attempts to use secondary data to access alliance quality (Chapter 10). Chapter 10 also outlined four basic reasons that carriers form alliances:

1. to gain market access,
2. to build global seamless networks,
3. to reduce costs, and
4. to maintain market presence.

From a consumer perspective, airline cost reduction is only important if it allows the carrier or alliance to reduce consumer costs and/or improve other aspects of airline service valued by consumers. Reasons 1 and 4 relate to the scope and/or depth of the alliances' coverage and the area of schedule/flight accommodation identified above for customer satisfaction with an individual carrier. From an alliance perspective, the more destinations they serve and the more frequently they serve them should be a quality issue for consumers.

This issue of alliance coverage proved to be a key factor in the Merrill Lynch (1999) report on alliances. Merrill Lynch rated the mega-alliances in terms of geographical network, market size, network density, financial strength, and regulatory freedom. This study drew a distinction between geographic scope (number of destinations/departures) and network density (utilization of network or extent of duplication). In this regard, an alliance such as Wings (NW–KLM) outscored the other mega-alliances on network density but ranked lowest on geographic scope. From an alliance point of view, less duplication in the network lowers fears of anti-competitive outcomes and means more overall extension of geographic scope. From a consumer point of view, greater density means more frequency to desired destinations. Thus, the ideal alliance configuration would involve partners having extensive depth within their geographic scope but little network duplication of alliance partner networks. This is not always an easy combination to find. One of the major stumbling blocks to the proposed BA–AA alliance was the extent of network overlap and the fear that such overlap would encourage the alliance partners to "rationalize" their networks (that is, dividing markets between partners in such a way that only one partner would effectively serve a particular route). Anderson Consulting identified three integration platforms in strategic alliances based on the level of control (degree of carrier control over resources) and degree of global coverage (Ott, 1999). According to Anderson, bilateral strings are essentially based on a series of international code shares between partners. These alliances string together a moderate number of international destinations. Andersen Consulting classified US Airways, Japan Airlines, and America West as string airlines. The Regional Cluster is the second type of integration platform. As the name implies, the backbone of this platform is several regional airlines. The geographic coverage is approximately equivalent to the bilateral string, but the level of control is greater. Swissair and the Qualiflyer alliance were examples of this type of platform. The final integration platform is the global skeleton which has greater coverage than the other two and slightly lower levels of control than the regional cluster. Based on their analysis, the four mega-alliances that existed at the time of their study were roughly equivalent in terms of global coverage while the ranking on control was as follows: Wings,

Star, SkyTeam, and Oneworld. The informally named Wings alliance of KLM–Norwest was officially abandoned with the KLM–Air France merger. Andersen Consulting envisioned all three platforms moving toward the Global Network with its maximum global coverage and balance between alliance control and member independence. There appear to be six key areas of development for alliance skeletons. The first area is route overlap or increasing "unduplicated route miles/kilometers." Several studies have shown that complementary (non-overlapping) alliance networks increase overall demand and passenger volumes (Park and Cho, 1997; US GAO, 1995) while parallel alliances decrease demand (Park and Cho, 1997). The problem for airlines and regulators lies with addressing pre-existing alliance overlap. Airlines clearly have some incentives to reduce overlap, especially if the overlap results in decreased demand and/or lower fares. The degree of intra-alliance competition could also damage efforts to build a cooperative alliance arrangement. Regulators are concerned with the degree of competition/cooperation and any action that decreases capacity and increases fares. The second area of development involves "filling the gaps" in overall global coverage and in specific destination departure levels. Given the stated consumer preference for airlines with wide coverage and increased connections, the goal of a superior global alliance is to serve more destinations more frequently than their competitors. All the mega-alliance groups have looked to fill major gaps in Asia, the Middle East, and Africa (Merrill Lynch, 1999; Taverna, 1999). Other alliance groups are also active in courting prospective members (Flint, 1999). In line with this notion of a superior global alliance is the third key area of alliance branding. In addition to the sort of advertising employed by the Star alliance, alliances may seek other areas of alliance integration and standardization such as joint facilities, alliance terminal grouping, harmonized (merged) distribution networks including CRS systems and joint internet booking sites, and common service standards such as seat pitch and reclining angle. The Star alliance has announced their intention to pursue many of these areas, although they have encountered resistance to some of their plans, specifically alliance terminal grouping (Taverna, 1999). The Wings alliance is committed to a single yield and revenue-accounting system and uses a program called Interhost Through Check In to communicate essential passenger information between airlines (Feldman, 1998; Ott, 1999). Oneworld has yet to aggressively brand itself in part because of the BA–AA approval question, but the new multilateral agreement with the EU should change this issue. The major alliances have begun to reduce operating costs through such actions as facility sharing and maintenance and other ground personnel utilization, but there are a number of other fruitful areas to explore including joint purchasing, combined cargo operations, wet-leasing, joint marketing, and so on). There are obvious risks to the development of some types of joint activities. These efforts require more integration of operation, more information sharing, and greater trust. Given the current transient nature of alliance, this entails great risks. The fifth key area of development is the creation of the secondary and tertiary tiers of national/regional carriers whose job it will be to increase feed to alliance hubs. From an alliance perspective, the more developed and exclusive these arrangements, the better they will be able to extract benefits (Berardino and Frankel, 1998). However, such exclusivity raises anti-competitive fears in many countries as we have already discussed in the chapter on antitrust law. The final area of development, and probably the last to receive formal attention, is likely to be multipoint competition.

Coordinating Quality

While the Merrill Lynch index does not provide a comprehensive overview of alliance quality, it is an important first step in the process of understanding alliance quality. From a consumer quality perspective, a more difficult area to address is the issue of "global, seamless service." "Global" is a function of geographic reach, but "seamless" suggests a great deal more. What does it mean to provide seamless service? How do independent airlines provide such service? Let us start at the airline level. Airlines are organized by function: flight operations, engineering and maintenance, marketing, and services. Under marketing, which composes approximately 50 percent of the workforce, there are units concerned with reservations and ticketing, cabin service, ground service, food service, and so on. (Wells, 1994). The consumer view, however, is not segmented into functions. Consumers experience airline service as a series of processes. The order fulfillment process begins with check-in and proceeds to final destination and baggage retrieval (Ekdahl, Gustafsson, and Edvardsson, 1999). When a problem arises during the travel experience, consumers are not interested in fixing the blame on a particular function and they certainly do not wish to stand around while the airline attempts to do so. Consumers want the issue resolved to their satisfaction as quickly as possible by their first contact point. They do not wish to be shuffled from department to department or supervisor to supervisor looking for resolution. One of the greatest drawbacks to a functional structure is that consumers often "feel they are forced into a system characterized by contradictions, redundant or insufficient information, misguided authority, and confusion" (Ekdahl, Gustafsson, and Edvardsson, 1999). In other words, the traditional functional structure often finds it difficult to provide a seamless service. Many companies claim that "quality is everyone's business", but they fail to realize that quality must also be "someone's responsibility."

There are basically two ways to approach the process quality issue. The most obvious way is to restructure the organization on a process basis—order fulfillment, new product development, customer acquisition, and so on. In a process-structured organization, coordination within the process eliminates the "cracks" through which customers often fall. This coordination is usually achieved through the establishment of cross-functional teams that include at least one member from each functional area involved in that process. All elements of the process become the responsibility of the process leader and his team. Their job is to 1) insure that all elements of the process are addressed, and 2) act as liaison to the functional departments, providing input from and guidance to the process. According to SAS, three principles should govern the design of the process: (1) give passengers control, (2) make the process transparent, and (3) empower the staff (Ekdahl, Gustafsson, and Edvardsson, 1999). A related option would be to institute a matrix structure that would in fact overlay the functional structure with a process structure. This type of organizational restructuring was popular in the 1980s but met with resistance from employees who in effect now had two bosses—the function leader and the process leader.

There are many personal and organizational barriers to process restructuring. At the personal level, teamwork requires good interpersonal skills and demands more emphasis on cross-functional skill development. Since many companies tie some portion of an individual's compensation to team results, individuals may also feel a loss of control in this important area of organizational life. If team results are not compensated in any way, then firm's run the risk that team activities will not receive the necessary level of individual attention. Organizationally, team make-up and training are critical. Firms must decide on functional skill requirements for membership, number of representatives from each function, level of functional representatives (for example, customer service manager, vice-president of customer relations), leadership of groups, and so on. These decisions can become very politicized. Functional conflicts over resource allocation and differing goals or objectives require the establishment of some process or procedure for conflict resolution. There are clearly costs associated with such a massive change in structure. There is also likely to be resistance from within the organization.

Quality Function Deployment (QFD) is one way to retain a functional structure while "systematically deploying operations and functions that make up the quality into step-by-step detail" (Akao, 1999). QFD requires companies to identify consumer desires, translate them into specific components, establish standards and procedures for delivery, and follow-up on delivery. For example, consumers want reliability in a number of company-provided areas. One such area is food service. They expect food to be consistent in quality, to taste and look good, to provide a good portion, and to be hot or cold (depending on the type of food). Companies must translate these desires into specific parameters (for example, temperature of food, and size of portions). Then establish and enforce standards on the "function" charged with delivering the item. Finally, there must be feedback and improvement (Barlow, 1999). While there is elaborate software to support the implementation of QFD, it is still a complex process that has yet to be fully embraced outside Japan (see Akao (1990) for a fuller discussion of QFD).

As difficult as process quality can be for individual airlines, it is potentially nothing compared to the prospect of integrating the process across multiple carriers. As Deming, a "father" to the total quality management (TQM) school of thought, and others have pointed out, no two processes are identical (Deming, 1988). Each process will invariably produce a certain amount of random variation (flaws or problems related to the nature of the system(s) in place). Special variations (flaws or problems related to a change in the system such as change in training procedures, receipt of a batch of faulty parts, and so on) also occur from time to time. Management must understand their process well enough to distinguish between random and special variation. Management must act to identify the source of special variation and remove its cause. Random variation, on the other hand, can only be reduced by changing the process itself.

When attempting to integrate the processes of two or more carriers, there are two primary areas of concern. First, are the processes compatible? A case in point is the airline boarding pass. All carriers issue them and most require that they be run through an electronic devise before boarding. However, if the size of these boarding passes differs between carriers such that the boarding pass issued by one carrier will not pass through the system of the other (and customers are required to check in again at the second airline for a new pass), then some of the seamlessness of the process is lost. The same question applies for many other standards and procedures such as upgrade requirements, carry-on specifics, seating assignments, boarding procedures, and so on. To the extent that these differences create snags in the seamless fabric of air travel for consumers, they will detract from perceived quality and can result in loss of business to higher quality alliances. We will discuss strategies for avoiding these snags later.

The second area of concern is potentially more serious and more difficult to resolve. It relates to differences in the quality level (or random variation) of alliance partners. Consumers who book a flight on one airline but find at least one leg of their journey flown by a carrier of lesser quality can develop a negative perception of the alliance as a whole. Obviously, the greater the difference in quality levels, the more severe the problem becomes. In a truly seamless alliance, consumers should perceive no difference in quality levels. The most worrisome difficulty lies in equalizing the quality level of alliance partners. Again, there are no studies examining the overall quality levels of alliance partners or the effects of quality equalization, but a recent study suggests one possible scenario. Research on quality levels at major US carriers indicates that over the last ten years quality levels have begun to converge and now show little variation across the major US carriers (Rhoades and Waguespack, 2000b). In statistical research, the term "regressing to the mean" refers to the tendency for extremes at both ends of a particular phenomenon to move over time toward the mean for that population. In the case of quality levels between alliance partners, there might be a similar tendency for quality levels to converge toward a mean. At the lower end, alliance partners' quality will tend to rise. On the other hand, the alliance quality leaders could see declines in their quality toward the alliance mean. Singapore Airlines would likely find this prospect disturbing.

Of course, this is not the only possible scenario. However, an alliance seeking to brand itself as one of high quality must be aware of the fact that upward equalization of quality standards will not just happen. Higher quality standards will not just "rub off" on alliance partners. This is where "cross-alliance" teams become important in insuring the quality of lateral/cross-airline processes. The Star alliance currently has 15 committees overseen by a policy group that reports directly to a board composed of alliance member chairmen. In addition, working groups are often formed to address specific problems. These groups report to an alliance development committee. Some of the results of this committee work have been manuals to explain members' products and services, common baggage tracking systems, common lounge access, linked frequent-flyer plans, and so on.. However, some issues have proved more problematic, such as joint facilities and integrated information systems (Feldman, 1998). As noted above, there are personal and organizational problems associated with the use of cross-functional, alliance teams. In the early years of their alliance United and Lufthansa found it difficult to agree on something as seemingly simple as the joint purchase of airsick bags (Feldman, 1998). Imagine the potential for disagreement on an issue such as the operation of the Malpensa Airport or yield management integration. At the very least, alliances are finding that coordination takes time and effort. Jürgen Weber, Luftansa CEO, has estimated that alliances consume approximately one-third of his time (Feldman, 1998).

Improving Alliance Quality

There are two important steps in achieving and insuring overall alliance quality. The first factor is conducting pre- and post-alliance audits. In May 1999, US Congressman James Oberstar introduced a bill that would require US carriers to conduct safety audits of code share partners as a condition for approval of the code sharing agreement. Under the existing system, the Office of the Secretary of Transportation (OST) must approve all code share agreements. The OST has a statutory mandate to consider safety as "the highest priority in authorizing air transportation services" (Title 49, section 40101(a)(1)), but has not required such assessments before. Under the guidelines recommended by the Office of the Inspector General (OIG), the safety audit "must demonstrate that foreign carriers have implemented safety procedures in critical areas such as maintenance operations, aircraft airworthiness, crew qualifications, crew training, flight operations, en-route procedures, emergency response plans, security, and dangerous goods" (OIG, 1999: 12). The US Department of Defense and six US carriers have already put such systems in place, although there is as yet no standard process for such an audit.

Given government-mandated safety audits, carriers should establish a similar auditing procedure for the service quality aspects of potential partners. These audits would establish a baseline quality level for each partner. Assuming that each alliance partner understands the needs and expectations of its customers, the next step is to reach some consensus among alliance partners on the level of desired quality and the priority of service quality goals. Finally, a plan must be created that outlines the goals, objectives, and tactics to be used by each carrier to achieve the necessary changes.

The second step is to create a process that "shows one face to the customer."

Alliances, like individual firms, are finding that it is essential "to make it easy for the customer to access resources, products, and services across the horizontal spectrum" (Ashkenas, Ulrich, Jick and Kerr, 1995: 128). When customers can enter into the company or alliance through multiple doors (or portals as they are sometimes called), there are several problems that can arise that have the potential to adversely affect process quality. Without careful coordination, customers may find that the point-of-entry changes the final destination. For example, if alliance members are not familiar with the products and services offered by their partners, then a customer accessing the alliance through one partner may receive different scheduling, information, and service than another customer accessing the "system" from a different partner. A related problem occurs when the parts of the system are not aware of the actions of one another and fail (or are unable) to take these differences into consideration when assisting customers.

In their book, *The Boundaryless Organization: Breaking the Chains of Organizational Structure*, Ashkenas, Ulrich, Jick, and Kerr (1995) outline five warning signs of dysfunctional horizontal boundaries:

1. slow, sequential cycle times,
2. protected turf,
3. suboptimization of organizational goals,
4. the enemy-within syndrome, and
5. customers doing their own integration (115).

Slow, sequential cycle times occur whenever multiple divisions, departments, units, and so on must be consulted one by one to create new products or respond to customers' demands. Whenever protecting one's own resources or power interferes with customer service, quality suffers. The same thing is true when members of a process come into decision-making situations with different, often, conflicting goals such as cost reduction versus higher service level or higher yield versus higher load factor. One of the most damaging problems related to horizontal boundaries occurs when members of a process come to see one another as enemies. Ashkenas, Ulrich, Jick, and Kerr (1995) give an example of an airline where baggage handling at a particular airport was the responsibility of two separate teams. One team handled check-in and ticketing while the other was responsible for loading, transferring, and off-loading. Teams were reluctant to help each other, to accept advice from "them", and frequently argued over which team was responsible for baggage handling errors. Finally, horizontal boundaries can also create problems if it forces customers to do their own integration of products and services. In the airline industry, there are customers who would prefer to customize their own bundle of products and services in order to accommodate special needs in terms of price, scheduling, and destination. On the other hand, there are customer groups that want a one-stop shopping experience. They do not want to be handed from one airline to another because an airline cannot book to a code share partner directly or to be told that seats cannot be assigned through to the final destination.

There are a number of possible solutions to the problems of horizontal boundaries including the close, cross-alliance, cross-functional coordination already mentioned. These efforts need to encourage and teach teamwork, define measures of shared resources success, restructure quickly to meet changing customer needs, and create new mental models that do not see the world as divided by clearly defined borders between functions and companies (Ashkenas, Ulrich, Jick, and Kerr, 1995; Berardino and Frankel, 1998). In addition, many service organizations have created "customer managers" who are responsible for coordinating all the needs of specific customers or specific customer groups. This approach clearly makes sense for major customers.

Several problems can arise on the way to upward equalization. The traditional customers of alliance partners may not have similar expectations. After over twenty years of deregulation, the expectations of many US travelers in, for example, seating comfort, and food, have declined below the expectations of many European and Asian travelers. This difference in expectations may make agreeing on a level of service more difficult. This is further complicated by airline cost, pricing structure, and available resources for quality improvements. Alliance partners may find it necessary to establish inter-alliance programs for training, cost sharing, and other quality improvements. Another stumbling block to success is the need to share more information between partners on service offerings, prices, and amenities. In short, partners may be called upon to share the revenue management information that has traditionally been treated as proprietary or share facilities that certain partners have spent years developing. Such attempts can create three problems for alliance members. The first problem is a legal one: without antitrust immunity, this level of sharing would be deemed illegal in most regions of the world. The second problem relates to the technological difficulties of systems integration. The sheer size and cost of integrating information systems can be very daunting to alliance members. Finally, alliance members must perceive a benefit to such information sharing that is greater than the risk of "giving up" the potentially valuable information on customers and operations. Alliances will need to find ways to track the costs and benefits of joint alliance activities and to maximize joint benefits (Berardino and Frankel, 1998).

In light of the events on 11 September, there are questions about the "quality" of security at airlines and some implications for alliance members. In general, quality is a function of creating a process, standardizing it, and incrementally improving on the process. However, security is an exception in several ways. First, "standardization" should not be the goal, even if the level of standardization is raised. Any "established standard" makes it easier for acts of terror to occur because actions are predictable. The major concern for alliances is the overall "quality" of security among all partners in order to prevent lax security in one partner from jeopardizing security within the alliance as a whole. Second, governments might be willing to relax some aspects of antitrust enforcement if it is perceived to impede the ability of airlines to coordinate on security efforts.

Conclusion

Although it may seem to customers that airlines sometimes forget that they are a service industry, international competition and the pursuit of profit in a tough industry are forcing airlines to pay more attention to issues of quality, customer satisfaction, and customer loyalty. At the carrier and the alliance level, airlines are trying to distinguish themselves from their competitors. At the carrier level, attention to basics is essential but branding requires memorable amenities. At the alliance level, seamless service requires intensive coordination to achieve high quality, and consistent service. To satisfy the desire for global coverage, alliances are taking two basic approaches—weave and throw a wider web or throw a finer web over a smaller area. While avoiding the legal stumbling block of antitrust has been difficult for many alliance partners, it has not been as visible a failure to consumers as the hurdle of achieving seamless service. In large part, the alliance movement is about breaking down the barriers that separate companies from their suppliers, their customers, and, in many cases, their competitors. It is about creating linkages and networks. Alliances are "about spinning a web to catch more customers" (Sparks, 1999: 106).

References

Akao, Y. (1999), 'ISO 900 and 14000 Systems Supported by QFD', in S.K.M. Ho (ed.), *Proceedings of the Fourth International Conference on ISO 900 and TQM*, pp. 325–31.

Akao, Y. (1990), *Introduction to Quality Function Deployment*, JUSE Press.

Ashkenas, R., Ulrich, D., Jick, T., and Kerr, S. (1995), *The Boundaryless Organization*, Josey-Bass, San Francisco.

Associated Press (2007), Airline passengers dissatisfied with service, 15 May, online edition, www.msnbc.com/id/18661797/print/1/displaymode/1098.

Barlow, G.L. (1999), 'QFD within the Service Sector – A Case Study on how the House of Quality was used within Service Operations', in S.K.M. Ho (ed.), *Proceedings of the Fourth International Conference on ISO 900 and TQM*, pp. 332–40.

Berardino, F and Frankel, C. (1998), 'Keeping Score', *Airline Business*, September, pp. 82–7.

Bloemer, J., and Kasper, H. (1995), The Complex Relationship Between Consumer Satisfaction and Brand Loyalty. *Journal of Economic Psychology*, 16, pp. 311–29.

Cronin, J.J. and Taylor, S.A. (1992), 'Measuring Service Quality: a Reexamination and Extension. *Journal of Marketing*, vol. 56 (3), pp. 55–68.

Deming, W.E. (1988), *Out of crisis*, MIT Press, Cambridge, MA.

Ekdahl, F., Gustafsson, A., and Edvardsson, B. (1999), 'Customer-oriented Service Development at SAS', *Managing Service Quality*, vol. 9, pp.403–10.

Feldman, J.M. (1998), 'Making Alliances Work', *Air Transport World*, June, pp. 27–35.

Flint, P. (1999), 'Alliance Paradox', *Air Transport World*, April, pp. 33–6.

Fraser, D. (1996), 'A Personal Approach', *Airline Business*, March, pp. 58–61.

Glab, J. (1997), 'The People's Choice', *Frequent Flyer*, June, pp. 24–8.

Jacoby, J. and Chestnut, R.W. (1978), *Brand loyalty: Measurement and Management*. John Wiley & Sons, New York.

Merrill Lynch, Pierce, Fenner & Smith (1999), *Global Airline Alliances: Global Alliance Brands,* Merrill Lynch, Pierce, Fenner & Smith Inc., New York.

Office of Inspector General (OIG) (1999), 'Aviation Safety Under International Code Share Agreements,' 30 September AV-1999-138, Available at: www.oig. dot.gov/item.jsp?id=29.

Oliver, R. I. (1999), Cognitive, Affective, and Attribute Bases of the Satisfaction, *Journal of Consumer Research,* 20 (3), 451–66.

Ott, J. (1999), 'Alliances Spawn a Web of Global Networks', *Airline Business*, August 23, pp. 52–3.

Parasuraman, A., Zeithaml, V.A., and Berry, L.L. (1988), 'SERVQUAL: A Multiple-item Scale for Measuring Customer Perceptions of Service Quality', *Journal of retailing*, vol. 64 (1), 12–40.

Parasuraman, A., Zeithaml, V.A., and Berry, L.L. (1985) 'A Conceptual Model of Service Quality and its Implications for Future Research,' *Journal of Marketing*, vol. 49 (4), 41–50.

Park, N.K. and Cho, D. (1997), 'The Effect of Strategic Alliance on Performance,' *Journal of Air Transport Management*, vol. 3, pp. 155–64.

Reichheld, F. F. (1996). *The Loyalty Effect: The Hidden Force Behind Growth, Profits, and Lasting Value*. Boston: Harvard Business School Press.

Rhoades, D.L. and Waguespack, B (2008), 'Twenty Years of Service Quality Performance in the US Airline Industry', *Managing Service Quality. 18 (1),* pp. 20–34.

Rhoades, D.L. and Waguespack, B (2005), 'Strategic Imperatives and the Pursuit of Quality in the US Airline Industry', *Managing Service Quality 15 (4)*, 344–56.

Rhoades, D.L. and Waguespack, B. (2004), 'Service and Safety Quality in the US Airlines: Pre- and Post-September 11th,' *Managing Service Quality 14 (4)*, 307–16.

Rhoades, D.L. and Waguespack, B (2001), 'Airline Quality: Present Challenges, Future Strategies' in: Butler, G.F. and Keller, M.R. (eds) *Handbook of Airline Strategy: Public Policy, Regulatory Issues, Challenges and Solutions*, McGraw-Hill, New York, 469–80.

Rhoades, D.L. and Waguespack, B (2000a), 'Judging a Book by its Cover: The Relationship Between Service and Safety Quality in US National and Regional Airlines', *Journal of Air Transport Management* 6, pp. 87–94.

Rhoades, D.L. and Waguespack, B. (2000b), 'Service Quality in the U.S. Airline Industry: Variations in Performance Within and Between Firms', *Journal of Air Transportation World Wide,* vol. 5, pp. 60–77.

Rhoades, D.L. and Waguespack, B. (1999), 'Better Safe than Service? The Relationship Between Service and Safety Quality in the US Airline Industry', *Managing Service Quality 9 (6)*, pp. 396–400.

Rhoades, D.L.,Waguespack, B, and Truedt, E. (1998), 'Service Quality in the US Airline Industry: Progress and Problems', *Managing Service Quality 8 (5)*, pp. 306–11.

Sloan, A. and Ehrenfeld, T. (2007), 'Lessons from Jetblue's Meltdown', *Newsweek MSNBC*, www.msnbc.cim/id/17313450/site/newsweek.

Sparks, D. (1999), 'Partners', *Business Week*, October 25, pp. 106–12.

Sultan, F. and Simpson, Jr., M. C. (2000), 'International Service Variants: Airline Passenger Expectations and Perceptions of Service Quality', *Journal of Services Marketing*, vol. 14 (3), pp. 188–216.

Szymanski, D. M., and Henard, D. H. (2001), ,Customer Satisfaction: A meta-analysis of the Empirical Evidence', *Journal of the Academy of Marketing Science*, 29(1), pp. 16–35.

Taverna, M.A. (1999), 'Star Alliance Approaches Next Phase of Collaboration', *Airline Business*, August 23, pp. 58–60.

Tiernan, S., Rhoades, D.L., and Waguespack, B. (2008), 'Airline Service Quality: An exploratory Analysis of Consumer Perceptions and Reported Operational Performance in the US and EU', *Managing Service Quality*, vol. 18 (3), 212–24.

The American Heritage College Dictionary (2000), 3rd edition, Houghton Mifflin Company, Boston.

US General Accounting Office (USGAO) (1995), 'Airline Alliaces Product Benefits, but Effect on Competition is Uncertain', *GAO/RCED-95*, April.

Wells, A.T. (1994), *Air Transportation: A Management Perspective*, Wadsworth Publishing Company, Belmont.

Yu, R. (2007a), Flight Delays Worst in 13 years, *USA Today* online edition. www.usatoday.com/travel/flights/2007-06-04-airline-delays_N.htm.

Yu, R. (2007b), Airlines Score Lower than IRS in Customer Satisfaction, *USA Today* online edition, www.usatoday.com/2007-airlines-score-lower.

Chapter 13
The Need for Speed

Freight comes of Age

If airmail was the driving force in aviation development in its first decade of life, then the decade of the 1940s and World War II were the time when other types of freight began to become a more prominent element in the air cargo story and to capture the interest of the aviation community. In 1938, freight accounted for only about 17 revenue ton kilometers (RTKs) of the total 53 RTKs of air activity. By 1951, freight RTKs had risen to 870, far outstripping the 230 RTKs for air mail in that year (Allaz, 2004). Military forces around the world would come to recognize the value of air freight in support distant troops and far-flung activities. They would also begin to demand and order aircraft that could deliver these troops and supplies. The Berlin airlift would prove its strategic geopolitical value as the British and Americans would be airlifting over 4,740 tons of cargo a day to Berlin within five months of the start of the blockade (Allaz, 2004).

Beginning in the 1970s, deregulation of domestic industries and liberalization of the rules of international trade began to spread throughout the world. Market forces would now trump the tight rules and standards that once protected firms and employees in their national markets. Firms would begin to look outside for lower-cost labor and the lower-cost manufacturing that came with them. The concepts of outsourcing and just-in-time inventory would capture the imagination of the business community. These new concepts, however, created new dispersed supply chains that demanded a new system of logistics to support them. As computing power rose and IT costs fell, the technology was ready for tracking and optimizing. The decline in transportation costs that came with deregulation, and later, with falling oil prices made it faster and cheaper to ship from distant locations. Further, consumers came to crave customized products delivered door-to-door. Faster, cheaper, and better was the new consumer mantra. This meant that businesses had to find ways to meet these new demands or risk falling victim to a host of new competitors.

These trends continued to pick up speed as the twentieth century approached its end. They also fostered tremendous growth in air cargo operations and operators. Airlines would offer cargo-only flights and order so-called combi-aircraft, half passenger and half cargo, to provide greater cargo capacity and additional revenue. New scheduled and charter cargo operators would come into the market offering to ship everything from letter-sized packages to massive oil drilling equipment (Nelms, 2007). If the jet would make air cargo the transportation choice for speed, then FedEx would make overnight shipping a new business mindset. FedEx and

UPS would lead the way for integrated shipping, that is, door-to-door delivery using multiple modes of transportation. However, before the commercial explosion of air cargo could take place, the industry needed a plane suitable for its purposes. Once it had such an aircraft, it could begin to take advantage of the new rules and the changing nature of business.

The Perfect Plane

From a cargo perspective, the perfect cargo plane would have a fuselage that was rectangular rather than cylindrical. The floor would be sturdy and low lying to accommodate heavy freight with a maximum of vertical capacity. Large doors would be located at the sides and front (preferably) to make loading easy and quick. Using both would reduce loading time. The aircraft would be designed so that different types of cargo could be partitioned and anchored (Allaz, 2004). While cargo had and would continue to be flown in aircraft not specifically designed for cargo, there would often be a cost not only in terms of converting passenger aircraft to cargo use (reinforcing floors, adding anchors, and so on) but in terms of productivity. As in passenger service, cargo operators have to be concerned with load factors. Because operators have little control over the prices they charge, costs are critical and an aircraft that has a low capacity either due to shape or weight constraints represents a problem. Aircraft that require high levels of labor or expensive equipment to load create added costs.

Between 1960 and 1962, freight capacity doubled, both in terms of belly cargo, that is, cargo carried in the belly of passenger aircraft and cargo aircraft. Several factors account for this increase in capacity. First, the new jet aircraft coming on the market had a larger cargo capacity than previous aircraft. Second, as airlines switched to jet aircraft, there was a growing number of used, propeller aircraft on the market and available for use by cargo operators. The first jet aircraft went into service in 1958 under the Pan Am colors, but others would quickly follow (Allaz, 2004). According to Allaz (2004), the Canadair CL-44D was the first modern jet cargo aircraft. It featured a swing tail, unit load devices, and a maximum payload of 28,000kg. Packages were loaded onto pallets fitted with retention nets or into containers. The famous Flying Tigers would be the first to take the CL-44D into service in 1961. With the arrival of the B707-320C and the DC-8F, costs would significantly decline while speed and capacity would dramatically improve.

Of course, the aircraft that would become most closely associated with air cargo would be the B747. The letter of intent signed with launch customer Pan Am specified a 400 passenger airliner with a range of 5,000 miles, a cruise altitude of 35,000 feet, and cargo nose loading. The latter requirement is telling: Juan Trippe, CEO of Pan Am, saw the B747 primarily as a freighter that could also carry passengers. Of course, the B747 would become one of the most popular passenger aircraft in the world and a symbol of international aviation, but this was certainly not clear when the project began (Serling, 1992). In fact, the story of the 747 is a fascinating one. Production problems, redesigns, a launch in 1970 just as the economy began to slow, and the coming oil crisis would put the Boeing company almost into bankruptcy. The plane would not approach breakeven sales until 1978 (Lynn, 1998; Newhouse, 2007). Still, there is no doubt that it set new standards that few others could begin to meet. In the cargo area, the wide-bodied 747 could hold two standard pallets side-by-side on the main deck with nine additional positions in the lower hold for either pallets or containers. Overall, the 747 was capable of carrying 90 tonnes of cargo as compared to 30 tonnes for the 707 and 70–74 for the DC-10 (Allaz, 2004).

Play it Forward

Air freight had come a long way in the years just after the end of World War II, but in some ways it had changed very little from that early 1910 flight (Chapter 3) that carried the 200 pounds of silk and ribbon to Max Morehouse for his Home Dry Goods Store. In fact, a number of things were still true. First, small, often family run firms (also known as "mom-and-pops") still made up a large portion of the air cargo operators. Like the early airlines themselves, cargo operators started flying small piston-powered aircraft from one point to the next on an unscheduled, as-needed basis. They were private firms and many continue to be privately rather than publicly owned companies making it difficult to assess their overall profitability. Second, the firms were essentially a specialized form of forwarder, that is, a carrier that transported freight by air under published freight tariffs. Shippers were responsible for seeing that the freight reached the operator and for arranging pick-up when it arrived at its destination. In some cases, shippers could add a step in the process and use a separate consolidator, someone who took their shipment and consolidated it with those of other shippers to form a "larger" shipment eligible for lower rates. Third, airlines would continue to see freight revenue as supplemental income. In the US, freight would continue to be a very small portion of the overall revenue. In Asia, freight tonnage would growth apace with the emerging economies of the region. What was beginning to change in the cargo world was the size and the scope of the shipments. As the volume increased and shippers began to ship to more markets around the world, pressure increased for industry consolidation. Both of these changes were driven in part by the logistics revolution that was sweeping the world.

Logistics Revolution

Logistics is defined as "the process of planning, implementing, and controlling the efficient, effective flow and storage of raw materials, in-process inventories, finished goods, services, and relevant information from point of origin to the point of consumption" (Boske, 1998). In the capitalist system, the goal is to match supply to demand, but the system has often proven itself given to overproduction. Producers are then forced to carry excess inventory or find some ways to increase sales with discounts, advertising, credit extension, and so on. If the ideal is to carry only the inventory you need and produce only what consumers want, then the producers need accurate, readily available data to make their decisions. Point-of-sale (POS) data provides this type of information. Firms like Wal-Mart began to use computers and scanning equipment to collect this information. This helped Wal-Mart to insure that shelves were stocked with the goods consumers were demanding. As they linked the system to their vendors, vendors were able to see in near real time what was and was not selling which allowed them to adjust production accordingly, including controlling their own inventories. The ubiquitous bar codes are giving way in many areas to radio frequency identification devices (RFID). These devices collect and store (in many cases) lots of information that can be read and analyzed to improve the system. Unfortunately for the producers, there is a snake in the grass; this new system has shifted power to the retailers like Wal-Mart. As the Wal-Marts of the world get bigger so did their requirements and demands: lower prices, more frequent deliveries, chargebacks (fines for failing to meet specifications like misplacing a bar code). For the consumers, the new fast, flexible production system and the close tracking of stock means shelves with "what I want when I want it" (Bonacich, and Wilson, 2007, Castells, 1996; Fishman, 2006; Kumar, 1996).

All of these advances would still not have been enough to create the logistics revolution; it needed two more ingredients: changing regulatory environments and falling transportation costs. Thomas L. Friedman, the popular press advocate of globalization and author of the bestselling books *The Lexus and the Olive Tree* (1999) and *The World is Flat* (2005) has argued that success in the global economy demands that nations put on a golden straitjacket. This straitjacket is made from government and extra-governmental policies that promote 1) an expanding private sector, 2) low inflation and price stability, 3) shrinking government bureaucracy, 4) balanced governmental budgets, 5) low tariffs and the elimination of import quotas, 6) no restriction on foreign investment, and currency conversion and mobility, 7) privatization of state-owned enterprises, 8) deregulation of markets and industries, 9) no domestic sector protection, 10) increasing exports, and 11) labor mobility. Taken together, these policies laid the foundation for a global system in which production could take place wherever conditions favored it (cost of labor, environmental regulation, available resources, and so on), be shipped to wherever consumers demanded it, and be serviced (repair, 24/7 help lines) wherever it was most profitable for the company. Beyond the borders of individual nations, the global trading system advanced from the old Bretton Wood institutions of the World Bank and the International Monetary Fund to the General Agreement on Tariffs and Trade (GATT) and to the World Trade Organization (WTO). Global trading blocks would also emerge such as the European Union (EU), and North American Free Trade Agreement (NAFTA), and MERCOSUR, the Latin American trade area. The goal of these blocks was to reduce or remove the impediments to trade and the flow of goods, services, and people between the member nations.

Transportation was one of the areas that witnessed a wave of deregulation beginning in the US in the late 1970s and early 1980s with the Air-Cargo Deregulation Act of 1977, the Airline Deregulation Act of 1978, the Motor Carrier Act (that is, trucking) in 1980, the Staggers Rail Act in 1980, the Shipping Act in 1984, and the Freight Forwarder Deregulation Act in 1986. As noted in earlier chapters, transportation is considered in most countries to be an area of vital national interest and safety so there are still a great many areas of regulation remaining, however, the focus of transportation deregulation was to allow market forces to determine to a much greater extent issues of pricing, capacity, networks, and service quality. In many nations, deregulation also opened up greater opportunities for intermodal transportation. Intermodal transportation refers to the "process of transporting passengers and freight by means of a system of interconnected networks, involving more than one transportation mode, in which all the component parts in the systems process are seamlessly linked and efficiently coordinated" (Boske, 1998). The technical innovations that helped make the supply chain of Wal-Mart successful—computers, scanning, RFID, and so on—were utilized in intermodal transport systems to insure that goods flowed with minimal delay through the system. Logistics leaders could use this technology to optimize their system based on specific needs: lowest cost,and time to delivery.

There was one final piece of the puzzle that made the transportation and logistics revolution: the container. On April 26, 1956, the *Ideal X*, a converted tanker, became the first ship to have an aluminum truck body lifted onto the deck. The concept was the brainchild of Malcolm McLean, a trucker whose US firm had risen to become one of the ten largest in the nation. He had observed that lots of trucks traveled between the seaports of the Gulf and the East Coast and figured that if he could find a way to reduce the time spent loading and unloading cargo, he could gain an advantage on his competitors (De La Pedraja, 1992). Soon the aluminum container, now standardized to 8×8×20, would be decoupled from the wheels and stacked onto specially designed vessels. Huge port cranes would load and unload containers from larger and larger vessels. These containers would be lifted from the deck of the ship directly onto trailer trucks or railcars. Containerization made shipping cheap; the most expensive part of the process was shifting cargo from sea to land and the occasional need for drayage (transporting freight by truck, usually to link one mode of transport to another because it can not be done directly on the dock). Containerization thrives on volume and the reduction in cost and time of shifting cargo has meant that a doubling of the distance cargo is shipped results in only about an 18 percent increase in shipping costs (Levinson, 2006).

Air cargo is often choice for "high value goods, perishable and emergency shipments, but also electronic equipment, apparel, shoes, printed material, [and] chemicals" (Muller, 1995: 73). It has benefited somewhat less than other modes from containerization because of the size of the standard container. While a B747 airfreighter could be loaded through the nose with an 8×8×40 container, it would only have inches to spare on the door. There is also the question of container-to-fuselage fit; the typical rectangular box container leaves wasted space in the curve. There are specially designed air-surface 8×8×20 containers as well as containers for the lower decks on the B747. A great deal of air cargo still travels on pallets (either 88in×125in or 96in×125in). There are also so-called pallet wings that attempt to utilize the full contour of the lower decks (Muller, 1995). One type of high-value goods that gained increasing popularity in the cargo world was the document and small package shipment. As the pace of global business increased so to did the need and desire of global firms to stay connected.

Expressing it

In 1971, Frederick W. Smith founded Federal Express, based on an idea first developed in his Yale dissertation. The dissertation was not a big success, but the company which began operations in 1973 became the industry leader in the express mail industry. By the end of the twentieth century, FedEx revenues exceeded US$22 billion and its fleet of 600 aircraft and 200,000 employees would be delivering packages around the world (Birla, 2005). Unlike competitor UPS, FedEx would start in the air and then move onto the ground. It would do this first through agreements with trucking and logistics companies such as RPS, Inc., Viking, Roberts, and Caliber Logistics. RPS, Inc specialized in ground delivery of small packages. Viking used the less-than-truckload model to ship one- and two-day packages. Roberts specialized in surface-expedited shipping. Caliber Logistics joined the FedEx family in the late 1990s with its specialized contract logistics services (FedEx website; Aviation Week and Space Technology, 2007).

The FedEx model would be based on five key principles: hub-and-spoke operations, weight and size limitations on shipments, integrated door-to-door service, guaranteed time-definite delivery, and end-to-end traceability. Table 13.1 traces the growth in FedEx over the last five years of the last century. As the table illustrates, FedEx experienced a steady increase in revenues, fleet, employees,

Table 13.1   FedEx growth 1994–1999

	1994	1995	1996	1997	1998	1999
Revenues	10,302	11,720	12,722	14,238	15,873	16,773
Express	1,925	2,248	2,478	2,716	3,026	3,129
Fleet	458	496	557	584	613	634
Employees	88,502	94,201	99,999	145,721	150,823	156,386

Source: FedEx website, www.fedex.com, Annual Reports. Numbers in 000s

and the volume of shipping. Over the coming decades, the weight limits would go higher while the time-definite options and the delivery area would increase. In time, the FedEx hub in Memphis would be the busiest in the world, shipping almost 3.6 million tones a year (Air Cargo World, 2006).

Brown is Back

The company whose first venture into air cargo ended with the 1929 stock market crash would not get back into the air for almost sixty years. When it did finally re-enter the air transport business in 1982 with a new service from its hub in Louisville, Kentucky, it would do so under a very different set of circumstances than competitor FedEx. For one thing, UPS had acquired common carrier status with its early purchase of the Russell Peck Company in California. As a common carrier it was regulated by the Interstate Commerce Commission (ICC) as well as various state commissions. By US law, common carriers were required to serve any shipper, carry any package regardless of size, and deliver to any destination in its region. It also could not commingle wholesale and retail packages. The ICC was the first regulatory agency in US history and expanded from its early mandate to protect against railroad malpractice to all areas of surface shipping. In effect, the ICC defined the rights of shippers and customers, engaging in rate making, regulation, and labor dispute resolution. UPS would fight the ICC for the right to expand its ground services and network one city and one state at a time. While the ICC could become involved in labor disputes involving interstate transport, UPS was unionized relatively early in its history on a local and regional level; the UPS-Teamsters National Master Agreement was not signed until 1979. Its labor relationships were largely positive until the 1997 strike that lasted two weeks and cost the company $750 million. The FAA would grant UPS authorization to operate its own aircraft in 1988 and over the next year UPS would become the fastest growing airline in FAA history, adding 110 aircraft by the end of 1989. These new employees would challenge some of the long held ideas of the "Brown" culture with its notion of working your way up the ladder from part-time to full-time, driver-to-top manager, but Big Brown would adjust (Niemann, 2007).

By 1985, UPS Next Day Air was available in the lower 48 states. The Louisville hub, located on 550 acres at the Louisville International Airport, would become known as Worldport. The UPS facility would grow to four million square feet and explode with activity between 11 p.m. and 4 a.m. with over 5,000 employees engaged in sort, routing, scanning, and loading/unloading. Like competitor FedEx, package tracking and time-definite options would become an essential element to long-term success. As the twentieth century drew to a close, UPS would also see sustained growth (Table 13.2).

Table 13.2   UPS growth 1994–1999

	1994	1995	1996	1997	1998	1999
Revenues	19,576	21,045	22,268	22,458	24,788	27,052
Express	1,867	2,281	2,400	2,488	2,707	2,905
Fleet	462	467	529	555	536	575
Employees	320,000	337,000	338,000	331,000	333,000	344,000

Source: Company website, www.ups.com. Numbers in 000s

Going Postal

A review of the UPS history reveals that its early history was marked by an intense rivalry not with FedEx but with the US Postal Service. All countries have some form of a postal service that is involved, by definition, in the delivery of parcels and small packages. To illustrate the involvement of these postal units in air cargo, a brief look at two companies will have to suffice. The first Postmaster of the United States was Benjamin Franklin, appointed in 1775. The Postal Reorganization Act of 1970 changed the status of the Postal Service to that of an independent unit of the Executive Branch of the US government with a Board of Governors appointed by the President of the United States. Since it started as a unit of the US government, it had an obligation to serve all citizens wherever they were located. Further, it was not expected to make a profit on its operations. The German postal system officially began in 1490. In 1924 Deutsche Reichspost was founded as an independent agency. In 1995, the Posts and Telecommunications Act would reorganize the postal system into stock companies with the federal government holding all the initial shares but with private investment allowed. Deutsche Post would acquire Danzas Holding, a Swiss logistics company, in 1999 and go on to become the largest Initial Public Offering (IPO) in Germany in 2000 laying the groundwork for even greater changes in the coming century (www.dpwe.de).

How the Airlines Do it

In airlines, cargo began its life in the belly of the aircraft, the so-called belly cargo. The airline was simply one more air freight forwarder looking to fill space. For some carriers, cargo became a great deal more than additional revenue. A study on the productivity and cost competitiveness of world airlines found that while passenger revenue accounted for almost 90 percent of the revenue of most US major carriers, a number of international carriers derived between 20 and 40 percent of their revenue from cargo operations (Oum and Yu, 1998). Among the world's top international cargo carriers, three airlines have consistently appeared at or near the top: Korean Air Lines, Lufthansa, and Singapore Airlines (Air Cargo World, 2005). After a rocky start, Korean Air Lines (KAL) was privatized in 1969 and began transpacific cargo services to the US in 1971. KAL would continue to expand its cargo and passenger operations until a series of accidents in the 1990s would threaten their alliance membership and their future (Jeziorski, 1999). Fortunately, KAL would resolve these problems by the end of the decade and begin to post the kind of double-digit cargo growth that would propel them to the top of the cargo airline list in the early part of the new century (Air Cargo World, 2005). Lufthansa began operations in 1926 and carried over 258 tons of cargo in the first year of its operation. By 1966, they had converted a passenger B707 to become their first dedicated freighter and would become the first airline to operate the B747 Freighter in 1972. In 1977, Lufthansa created a cargo division, German Cargo Services (GCS), with a dedicated fleet of B707-220Fs. A dedicated cargo center was completed at Frankfurt Main in 1982. Several events during the 1990s are indicative of the Lufthansa interest in cargo operations: 1) acquisition of an equity stake in DHL, 2) agreement with Deutsche Post for same-day service, 3) launch of Lufthansa Cargo as a wholly owned subsidiary, and 4) founding membership in the first cargo airline alliance WOW with SAS and Singapore Airlines (Lufthansa Cargo website; WOW website). Singapore Airlines was formed after the Singaporean and Malaysian governments decided to separate their joint airline in 1972. By 1978, Singapore was operating cargo services from Singapore to San Francisco. The Singapore cargo division was formed in 1992 using both dedicated and belly cargo options (Chan, 2000).

Catering to Cargo

Given the growth in air cargo operations during the last half of the twentieth century, it is not surprising that airports would begin to seek this business out either in an effort to grow their overall revenue or to compensate for declining passenger traffic. Because cargo shippers often prefer night flights, airports could serve passengers during the day and cargo shippers during the usual nighttime lulls. While it is not surprising that the hub airport for the integrators (for example, UPS, FedEx, DHL) or the major cargo-carrying airlines post sizeable numbers of freight tonnage, a number of other airports are attempting to attract cargo activity. In 2006, the fifteen fastest growing freight airports in Europe did not include the traditional big name hubs; the top three were Leipzig/Halle, Oporto, and Liège. The growth of these smaller airports is attributed to lower costs and improved service at these airports. It is not simply a matter of courting carriers and freight forwarders. Airports like Schiphol in Amsterdam are trying to draw businesses with interests in import/export near the airport itself (Conway, 2007). Of course, to attract cargo to the airport the airport needs the necessary facilities—warehouse space, special services and facilities (refrigeration, Hazmat, customs), cargo handling equipment, and intermodal connections (the closer the better as drayage (short trucking) is one of the most expensive parts of the transportation equation (Muller, 1995). Given the explosive growth of the Asian export-oriented economies and the apparently insatiable appetite of the Western world for these cheap products, airports around the world are ready to play in the cargo game.

Flying High

The second half of the twentieth century would witness explosive growth in the air cargo world as the logistics revolution and globalization pushed firms to seek out better, faster, and cheaper means of shipping. The new century will challenge air cargo as it has not been challenged since the early days of aviation. There will be rising fuel costs, new security rules, and growing competition to battle but for now cargo will enjoy the ride, reveling in rates of growth that exceed passenger growth in many cases and utilizing the new form of information technology and systems to track and manage rising volumes of goods.

References

Air Cargo World (2005), *The World's Top 50 Cargo Airlines*, September, pp. 22–8.

Allaz, C. (2004), *The History of Air Cargo and Airmail from the 18ᵗʰ Century*, Christopher Foyle Publishing, Paris.

Aviation Week and Space Technology (2007), 'Evolution of the Air Cargo Industry: Road Map', *Aviation Week and Space Technology*, 7 May, pp. 47–54.

Birla, M. (2005), *FedEx Delivers: How the World's Leading Shipping Company Keeps Innovating and Outperforming the Competition*, John Wiley & Sons, New York.

Bonacich, E. and Wilson, J.B. (2007), *Getting the Goods: Ports, Labor, and the Logistics Revolution*, Cornell University Press, Ithaca.

Boske, L.B. (1998), *Multimodal/Intermodal Transportation in the United States, Western Europe, and Latin America: Governmental Policies, Plans, and Programs*, Lyndon B. Johnson Schools of Public Affairs, University of Texas, Austin.

Castells, M. (1996), *The Rise of the Network Society*, Blackwell, Oxford.

Chan, D. (2000), The Story of Singapore Airlines and the Singapore Girl, *Journal of Management Development*, 19, pp. 456–73.

Conway, P. (2007), 'Driven to the Edge', Air Cargo World, October, pp. 21–7.

De La Pedraja, R. (1992), *The Rise and Decline of US Merchant Shipping in the Twentieth Century*, Twayne Pyblishers, New York.

Fishman, C. (2006), *The Wal-Mart Effect: How the World's Most Powerful Company Really Works – And How it's Transforming the America Economy*, Penguin, New York.

Friedman, T.L. (2005), *The World is Flat: A Brief History of the Twenty-First Century*, Farrar, Straus, Giroux, New York.

Friedman, T.L. (1999), *The Lexus and the Olive Tree*, Farrar, Straus, Giroux, New York.

Jeziorski, A. (1999), 'Humbled Korean Air Stages Management Upheaval', *Flight International*, 28 April.

Kumar, N. (1996), 'The Power of trust in manufacturer-retailer relationships' in Harvard Business Review on Managing the Value Chain, Harvard Business Press, Boston. pp. 91–126.

Levinson, M. (2006), *The Box: How the Shipping Container made the World Smaller and the World Economy Bigger*, Princeton University Press, Princeton.

Lynn, M. (1998), *Birds of Prey: Boeing versus Airbus-The Battle for the Skies*, Four Walls Eight Windows, New York.

Muller, G. (1995), *Intermodal Freight Transportation*, 3rd edition, Eno Transportation Foundation, Lansdowne, Virginia.

Nelms, (2007), 'Oversized ambition', Air Cargo World, April, pp. 16–20.

Newhouse, J. (2007), *Boeing versus Airbus: The Inside Story of the Greatest Competition in Business*, Alfred A. Knopf, New York.

Niemann, G. (2007), *Big Brown: The Untold Story of UPS*, John Wiley & Sons, San Francisco, CA.

Oum, T.H. and Yu, C. (1998), *Winning Airlines: Productivity and Cost Competitiveness of the World's Major Airlines*, Kluwer Academic Publishers, Boston.

Serling, R.J. (1992), *Legend and Legacy: The Story of Boeing and Its People*, St. Martin Press, New York.

Websites

Deutsche Post World Net, http://www.dpwe.de
Federal Express, http://www.fedex.com
Lufthansa Cargo, http://www.lhcargo.com
UPS, http://www.ups.com
WOW alliance, http://www.WOWtheworld.com

PART III
Facing the Future (2000–Present)

Chapter 14
Searching for Profits

Old Dogs

In an industry notorious for "boom-or-bust" and "no stranger to bankruptcy court", the post 9/11 situation looked strikingly familiar (Arndt and Woellert, 2001). If the losses were higher or the causes not entirely the same, still the basic issues remained: increasingly price sensitive consumers, overexpansion in the boom leading to overcapacity in the bust, high costs, contentious labor, and competition from low-cost and foreign carriers (Costa, Harned, and Lunquist, 2002; Derchin, 1995; Wolf, 1995). These issues were identified as key components of the financial crisis of the 1990s when the losses in the US reached a new record of US$13.1 billion for the period 1990–94 (Bond, 2002). In response to past crises, the industry created the hub-and-spoke system as a means of funneling and managing traffic, developed complex holding structures to manage debt, renegotiated labor contracts to manage wages and benefits, retired fleets and cut marginal routes to reduce capacity, merged and consolidated as weaker players faltered and stronger ones strived to position themselves for the next boom, and looked for marginal ways to reduce costs. Then with the next boom, the dominant logic of the industry becomes expand and spend (Rosen, 1995). While the industry has done a better job this time around of avoiding the "temptation of capacity", record new orders for aircraft were set for 2005 and 2006 (IATA, 2007).

Other troubling signs still persist. First, it is not clear if the high yield business traveler will ever come back to the traditional carriers in their former numbers. According to the Business Travel Coalition, many corporations intend to make their post 9/11 travel cuts permanent (Mecham, 2002). This trend began before 9/11 with business traveler complaints that fares were too high, restrictions too confining, and service too low, but the events of 9/11 and the "hassle factor" of additional security accelerated the domestic exodus from traditional carriers. Many business travelers switched to one of the low-cost carriers or discovered the benefits of flexjet and leasing options. Some may even have found themselves attracted to the new boutique, business class only airlines. Second, the gains that low-cost carriers made on their more traditional brethren during this downturn show no signs of diminishing or retreating. Projections shortly after 11 September suggested that the low-cost market share would rise from 20 to 40 percent in the US national market (Velocci, 2002; Haddad and Zellner, 2002). Following 11 September only low-cost carriers Southwest, JetBlue, and Airtran significantly increased the size of their fleet (Nelson and Francolla, 2008). Europe's low-cost carriers are also gaining ground led by Ryanair and are projected to capture

25 percent of the market, up from 7 percent in 2001 (Binggeli and Pompeo, 2002). Airlines in developing regions are also feeling the pressure from the low-cost carriers. There are currently six low-cost carriers in Mexico alone and they appear to be having an impact on the traditional carriers who are struggling to compete and become profitable (Ezard, 2008). While most of the globe's airlines returned to profitability within two years, US airlines continued to struggle and engage in the same old strategies of the past (IATA, 2008a). Table 14.1 illustrates this struggle. The problem with the old strategies, of course, is whether you believe that they truly worked in the past. An increasing number of individuals and organizations are beginning to question the old strategies and ask themselves if it is possible to teach an old dog new tricks.

Old Tricks Under Fire

The events of 9/11 and the fallout for world airlines caused many to raise serious questions about the old model of doing business in the airline industry. Does size really matter? If so, is it the scale of the operations or the scope? Is size important for some factors of production but not others? What exactly does an airline produce? Is there such a thing as too big? Where does an airline add value and how can this value be enhanced and captured? What should an airline "look" like and what should it do? Answering these questions is the topic of this chapter and must begin with a little lesson in economics.

One of the arguments presented in the debate over deregulation of the US airline industry was that regulation prevented carriers from developing economies of scale. Economies of scale occur when average costs decline as the production of a good or service goes up. These economies can derive from several sources:

Table 14.1   US and global profits 2000–2006

	2000	2001	2002	2003	2004	2005	2006
US							
Operating	7.0	(10.3)	(8.6)	(2.1)	(1.5)	0.4	7.5
Net	2.5	(8.3)	(11.0)	(2.4)	(7.7)	(5.8)	3.1
Global	-	-	-	-	-	-	-
Operating	10.7	(11.8)	(4.8)	(1.4)	3.3	4.3	12.9
Net	3.7	(13.0)	(11.3)	(7.5)	(5.6)	(4.1)	(0.5)

Source: US figures from Air Transport Association, www.airline.org/economics/finances. Global figures from IATA www.iata.org/economics

technological, managerial, financial, marketing, commercial, and research and development. Technological economies may result when a larger firm is able to employ more expensive machinery and use it more intensively. Managerial economies arise when a firm is able to divide tasks and employ specialists. Financial economies result when a firm is able to borrow money at lower rates (primarily because size is usually associated with greater assets, age, credit record, and so on). Marketing economies occur when firms are able to spread the high cost of advertising across a larger level of output. Commercial economies are gained from buying supplies in bulk and receiving larger discounts. R&D economies may appear when developing new or better products if basic research can give rise to multiple applications (Bized, 2002). From this breakdown, it is obvious that a firm, industry, or strategic group within an industry may enjoy economies in one area and not in another. Technologically, the new generation of aircraft tend to be more economical and efficient, however, the hub-and-spoke system employed by the major carriers limits the utilization of aircraft that must sit and wait for banks of smaller airplanes to feed passengers into the system nor does it seem economical for larger carriers to operate these smaller aircraft themselves since higher wage scales make them less productive. It has certainly been hard to argue that the major US carriers enjoyed financial economies over their smaller competitors given their low stock prices, high leverage, and negative growth. While major carriers may continue to enjoy economies in marketing, commercial, and R&D development, the level of this advantage is probably declining as technology, market fragmentation, and other factors come into play in the airline industry.

Since economies of scale are concerned with unit costs, it is important to define the unit of production in airlines. In other words, what does an airline produce? Does it produce a seat, a trip from point A to point B (called a leg) or an end-to-end experience, that is, many consumers connect from A to B to C as the final destination? The answer to this question may well matter since not all seats or trips are equal. The proverbial widget factory of business lore mass produces a product that is assumed to be the same—widgets. Economies of scale exist if the unit cost of the 10,000th widget is lower than the 1,000th. In the case of an airline, the seat on an aircraft from Atlanta to Boston is not necessarily the same as a seat from Atlanta to Denver or Denver to Chicago nor are the costs involved in producing these seats the same since they involve different lengths, flight crews, landing fees, aircraft types, passenger facilities charges, and so on. Sophisticated systems can be employed to analyze costs by route, but this unit of analysis problem greatly complicates the economies argument for carriers. In part, this focus on unit costs is driven by the traditional approach to accounting which basically adds direct material costs, direct labor costs, and overhead (rent, utilities, insurance, and so on) then divides by the unit of output to determine per unit costs. Activity-based costing looks at costs from an activity standpoint. Business activities include "all of the processes that a company uses in order to conduct its business: order processing, procurement, engineering, production set-up, quality inspection, warehousing and material movement." Under this approach, firms would determine the activities it performs and analyze them to determine the cost drivers within that activity. Costs to products are assigned based on how often they require inputs from that particular activity. The benefits of activity costing are found in the detailed cost information it provides and the focus on cost drivers within activities.

The notion of increasing scale leads to the question of whether a carrier can be too big. With size comes complexity, vertically, horizontally, and geographically. Large firms have more layers of management separating the top where "decisions" get made from the bottom where "decisions" and the actual work of the organization gets carried out. These layers often mean that actions are delayed and communications are poor, leading to misdiagnosis of problems or misapplication of solutions. Horizontal complexity occurs when firms become increasingly divided into ever finer units of specialized individuals who lose touch with the work (and importance) of other units as well as the overall goals of the organization. Geographic complexity occurs when firms spread across time zones and cultures making collaboration difficult and product and managerial decisions culture-specific. A further complexity, external boundaries, is becoming more common as firms outsource functions and blur the lines between the firm and its external environment. In fact, each of these areas creates its own boundary within the firm. In many large (old) firms, these boundaries are clear and impermeable; what is inside stays inside and what is out can not get in! Such organizations are slow to act, rigid in response, and poor in adaptation. Size becomes a disadvantage if the firm lives in a rapidly changing environment with younger, faster competitors (Ashkenas, Ulrich, Jick, and Kerr, 1995; Galbraith, 1995).

Economies of scope differ from those of scale in that they are not derived from increases in volume, but occur as the result of circumstances that allow firms to achieve synergy in production, product development, and distribution. Economies of scope can occur in production when firms are able to lower the cost of producing one product by producing another one, that is, an airline flying both passengers and cargo. Economies of scope in product development arise when common knowledge or equipment is used to produce more than one product, that is, laser technology can be used in many applications from surgery to metal cutting, an aircraft used for passengers during the day and cargo at night, a computer revenue management system used to manage airline seats, hotel rooms, rental cars, and so on. This last example is a classic one, that is, an infrastructure system capable of distributing one type of product used to distribute others.

If size is creating diseconomies of scale or scope, the firm has several options in downsizing: retrenchment, downscaling, or downscoping (DeWitt, 1998). Retrenchment attempts to maintain scope and often even increases output by centralizing certain firm functions, changing supplier relationships, and realigning managerial functions. For example, firms may re-engineer processes to improve productivity or eliminate redundant facilities (Hammer and Champy, 1993). Downscaling operations entails the permanent reduction of human and physical resources to bring supply in line with demand (Harrigan, 1983, 1985; Mahoney, 1992). Downscoping involves efforts to actually shrink the boundaries of the firm by effecting permanent cuts in human and physical resources as well as simplifying the organization's structure by reducing vertical, horizontal, or product diversity (DeWitt, 1993). The path a firm takes to downsizing is a function of many factors, but one factor is clearly the barriers to exit and mobility. Exit barriers create an impediment to the removal of excess resources (Caves and Porter, 1976) while mobility barriers affect the ability of firms to move between segments in an industry (Caves and Porter, 1977). Firms make certain industry-specific investments that may make exit difficult or very costly. For example, labor contracts may lock a firm into maintaining certain levels of operation. Fleet acquisitions may mean that cutbacks will lead to underutilization in the short run, raising costs, and fleet sales may take time and not generate enough in certain market conditions to recoup costs. Likewise, a high-cost labor force with rigid work rules may prohibit a firm from shifting to a lower costs segment of the industry. The task ahead for airlines is figuring out how economies and value-adding activities can be used to shape a profitable airline in the new environment.

Searching for Profits

In the introduction to this book, Warren Buffet's comments on the industry were noted, that is, the total money made in the airline industry since the time of the Wright brothers was zero (Loomis and Buffet, 1999). Clearly, one challenge ahead for the airline industry in general is proving this wrong. There are few that would question the air transport industry's status as a mature industry. It is true that in some countries in the developing world growth rates are relatively high due to the prior lack of aviation infrastructure, but the rate of development in even these countries is far slower than the early development of air transport in general. In the lifecycle of industries, emerging industries are characterized by uncertainty about products, markets, and standards. Companies compete on functional performance with little concern for cost and greater concern for user needs. In the second stage of life, demand increases attracting new competitors and competition centers on product types leading to efforts to standardize products. Organizations begin to segment the market based on costs or product differences. Rivalry is usually not as intense in the early stages of this phase because the market is growing faster than demand; companies can grow without taking the customers of other firms, thus limiting direct competition. In the mature phase, demand levels off or even drops. Competition often becomes intensive and is based on cost, increasing efficiencies, and incremental innovations in products and processes (Nadler and Tushman, 1997). Profitability is a function of these cost reductions, efficiencies, and standardized but incrementally improved products or services. Firms in a mature industry are generally large, functionally organized, and bureaucratic, an excellent description of the airline industry. They are not known for radical product innovation, preferring to emphasize stability, formality, and cost reduction (Nadler and Tushman, 1997).

Don Carty, CEO of American Airlines, told a Congressional panel after 11 September that American's main objective was to achieve permanent structural cost reductions of at least US$3 billion within the next several years in order to return costs to more competitive levels (Fiorino, 2002). He singled out three factors for special attention: fuel, distribution, and labor (Zellner, 2002). Each of these factors deserves a closer look in order to identify the issues and possibilities for savings.

Fuel

At the time of Carty's testimony to Congress, fuel prices represented roughly 10–15 percent of airlines' costs. According to IATA, fuel will represent 30 percent of the total operating costs for airlines in 2008, surpassing labor costs as the single greatest expense (IATA, 2008b). Even before oil passed the US$100 barrel mark, airlines were looking to save money. There are several obvious things that airlines can do to reduce or stabilize fuel costs. First, newer, more fuel efficient aircraft reduce fuel costs as well as overall maintenance costs. Many of the aircraft "retired" since 9/11 fell into the less efficient category. Unfortunately, financially troubled airlines often find fleet renewal difficult. Second, airlines can seek to hedge fuel costs, although this is not guaranteed to save costs since it depends on the financial and forecasting skill of the airline. Southwest Airlines has been one of the US carriers that has benefited from substantial fuel hedging (USAToday, 2007). Unfortunately, hedging is difficult if there is no clear sense of the future trend in fuel. The question for many airlines is, will fuel prices fall and how far? Will they rise further making it important to lock in current prices now? Given the very thin margins, "guessing right" by even a few dollars could make a big difference. Third, there are a number of operational measures that can be employed. The first edition of IATA's *Guidance Material on Best Practices for Fuel and Environmental Management* was issued in 2004. The manual goes through detailed information for weight management, pre-flight planning, engine start-up and taxying, reduced thrust take-off, and so on. Finally, many US airlines are simply shrinking their operations, particularly their regional jet operations which may be flying at a loss because of the generally higher operating costs of smaller aircraft (Reuters, 2008a). In what may be a "wave of the future", Delta Air Lines has unveiled a plan to offer buyouts to 30,000 in an effort to cut up to 2,000 jobs. The reason given is soaring fuel costs and their decision to ground an additional 4 percent of their fleet (MSNBC News Services, 2008). Although neither Delta nor Northwest has indicated any plans to retire additional aircraft or shed employees with their announced merger, it is difficult to see how the merger can be successful without these types of actions (Air Transport News, 2008).

Distribution

Distribution systems are areas over which carriers have greater control than fuel costs, however, the issues are more complex. In its formative years, air transport growth and profit were driven by airmail revenues. As passenger traffic increased in importance, airlines needed a process to track seat sales on flights. Without such a system, two problems can occur. First, an airline may sell more tickets than it has available seats on a given flight. This overbooking leads to disgruntled passengers who will have to be placated in some way (free tickets, discounts, frequent flyer mile, upgrades, and so on) or potentially lost to another airline. Placating costs money, however, the second problem also costs money, namely not selling all available seats. Airlines need to return cancelled seats as quickly as possible to the available pool or risk losing the opportunity to maximize revenue. Airline seats, like cabbage, are perishable goods, meaning that at some point in time they become unusable and unsellable; once a flight takes off, the seat has perished.

The saga of airline distribution systems is a fascinating one and illustrates some of the potential issues facing airlines today. One of the earliest systems for tracking reservations was the Request and Reply system that required customers to contact ticket agents at the point of departure and wait for a reply confirming seat availability. The explosion in traffic following World War II, however, made this centralized point of departure system unwieldy. Agents in reservations offices soon used availability display boards to scan for seat openings and alternative flights. At the Chicago office of American Airlines, an observer would have been confronted by a wall covered with a large cross-hatched board filled with cryptic notes. Men and women sitting in row upon row of desks would continually check this board, compare it to thick reference books all the while talking on the telephone to potential customers and filling out cards. Clerks and messengers scurried around between the desks with cards and sheets of papers as the chatter of teletypes and card sorting equipment filled the air (McKenney, Copeland, and Mason, 1967). American Airlines would replace this scene of mayhem with a machine called the Reservisor System which used a matrix of relays in which the columns represented dates and rows represented flights. Shorting plugs were inserted in the matrix to indicate a sellout. The system permitted fewer agents to book more flights, but maintenance of the system proved expensive. The next innovation introduced into the system was a magnetic drum computer memory to store data. By 1956, the Reserwriter, a computer that read punch cards of passenger data, converted them to tape, and telexed data was in operation. However, even with these improvements, an estimated 8 percent of all transactions were incorrect and the process required 12 people, 15 steps, and three hours. To remedy these problems, American worked with IBM to produce the SABRE system. The Computerized Reservation System (CRS) was born (McKenney, Copeland, and Mason, 1967).

The CRS (now also called Global Distribution Systems or GDSs) was originally intended for use by travel agents and large corporate clients. By 1990, 93 percent of travel agencies were plugged into one of the major CRS/GDS systems

(Bartimo, 1990). Not all carriers had their own CRS system and eventually began to accept the services of other carriers with CRS systems, however, since the CRS was initially developed by specific airlines, the systems that they each developed tended to favor their own flights. CRS systems also required a specialized knowledge of codes and procedures which made it profitable for many agencies to develop interfacing software that allowed them to use the system more efficiently and perform operations that their own customers wanted such as searching for best price (McKenney, Copeland, and Mason, 1967; Davidow and Malone, 1992). The relationship between airlines and travel agents began to change in the mid-1990s as airlines began their next major assault on distribution costs. This time the focus was on reducing the travel agents' commissions on domestic and international ticket sales which had been as high as 10 percent for domestic and 15 percent for international sales. By 1997, the number of agencies in the US had declined for the first time and the industry began to witness a wave of consolidation (Cook, Goff, Yale, and Wolverton, 1999). Most of the CRS/GDS systems have been spun off from the airlines that gave them birth. The largest of these GDSs is SABRE, formerly a part of American Airlines. Galileo, now part of Travelport, recently received approval to merge with Worldspan. The last major player in the GDS world is Amadeus which was formed by Air France, Lufthansa, SAS, and Iberia as an alternative to the US controlled GDSs. It is the largest system in Europe (Michels, 2007).

The popularity of the internet opened up new possibilities for carriers to further cut distribution costs by selling directly to consumers. E-business became a new airline strategy. Orbitz was founded in 1999 by United, Delta, Continental, Northwest, and American as an online travel agent providing direct booking with the participating airlines and is now the online arm of Travelport. Newer entrants such as JetBlue and easyJet are making extensive use of e-booking and seat assignments via the World Wide Web (Methner and Rospenda, 2001). The internet has allowed carriers to reduce the fees to travel agents as well as to computer reservation systems which have now by and large been spun off by the carriers into separate operating companies. Carty had estimated that American alone paid over US$400 in CRS/GDS charges in 2001 (Fiorino, 2002). The fact that American is currently targeting a system to travel agents, however, points up at least two problems with the latest drive to reduce distribution costs. First, traffic on the internet itself "was supposed to double every three months, but was growing at just a quarter of that pace" as late as 2002 (Rosenbush, Crockett, Haddad, and Ewing, 2002). The dream of eliminating major costs by shifting a significant portion of customers to a system whereby they booked their own flight over the internet, printed out their own boarding pass and baggage tags, and deposited their own bags at a designated airport conveyor belt has not yet arrived. Second, the airlines who once owned and benefited from the GDS providers find themselves at odds over costs. At one point many airlines threatened to stop doing business with the GDSs unless costs came down (Field, 2007).

It would seem that for the foreseeable future the internet will not be "the answer" to the distribution question, at least for the major carriers. Reducing distribution costs in any significant way may require more radical solutions requiring extensive investment in new equipment and software, money which most of the major carriers do not currently have and can not likely raise in the current environment. The truth of the matter is that the distribution systems of many large carriers are still heavily mainframe based, using PCs as dumb terminals whose sole function is inputting data into archaic programs that have been grown internally through haphazard means. The industry that represents "high tech" to many outsiders is in fact using old hardware and bad software to link to the high tech internet.

Labor

The third area of costs targeted for savings by American Airlines CEO Don Carty was labor, however, little or nothing was mentioned specifically in regard to how these costs would be cut (Fiorino, 2002). Labor was the single largest cost of major US carriers at roughly 40 percent prior to 11 September and many experts had suggested that labor costs needed to drop by 20 percent to return the airline industry to profitability. Unfortunately, in the absence of a major crisis there was often little probability of gaining union agreement to these reductions. Bankruptcy is just such a crisis. Following 11 September, four major US carriers entered bankruptcy: United (2002), US Airways (2002, 2004), Delta and Northwest (2005). United emerged from bankruptcy in 2006. US Airways emerged from its second bankruptcy to merge with America West. Delta and Northwest emerged from bankruptcy in 2007. Meanwhile, American Airlines was able to avoid bankruptcy by signing agreements with its three key unions to lower costs (Nelson and Francolla, 2008). According to the Air Transport Association's Quarterly Cost Index (2008), labor for the US industry as a whole now constitutes 23.4 percent of the cost, almost where experts had suggested it needed to fall. Perhaps even more significant is the fact that many of these airlines were able to get out from under massive defined benefits pension plans.

There are still things that airlines can do to improve productivity such as changing work rules or investing in additional information technology, but these are unlikely to achieve the level of cuts that many still consider essential, particularly in the face of rising fuel costs. Mergers or acquisitions have been seen in the past as a way to lower labor costs by "rationalizing" the workforce. There is little evidence that it has succeeded in the highly unionized airline industry. Unions have historically complicated airline mergers and acquisitions at the outset as the recent pilot talks between groups from Delta and Northwest demonstrate. The two pilots unions reportedly agreed to a comprehensive joint contract, equity stake for pilots, and big pay rises for some groups but could not agree on a combined seniority list (Weber, 2008). Reported plans for major labor cuts at Alitalia in the event of a takeover by Air France/KLM also prevented this deal (Reuters, 2008b).

These realities may place greater stress on airline management to consider more radical measures to reduce costs and raise productivity.

More Radical Approaches

Every industry can be said to have a value chain or a sequence of activities (processes) that create value. In a total quality sense, the value created is from the consumer's perspective and consumers determine the value (price) placed on these activities. The analysis of value-chain activities is based on the work of Michael Porter (1985). Once the value-chain is examined, firms use it to develop strategies to "create additional value" for their consumers. It can also be the basis for the decoupling of an industry. Decoupling is the reverse of the vertically integrated model that firms once pursued (referred to as the GM model in Chapter 10). Rather than perform all of the activities necessary to produce a good or service, firms outsource activities to other firms that specialize in that activity. In essence, firms choose an activity to perform based on their expertise, knowledge, or strategic vision. Figure 14.1 presents one model of a value-chain for airlines.

At the end of this process is the consumer of airline services. Given this value-chain, it is conceivable that the industry could become increasingly decoupled. There has already been a move among a number of carriers to outsource maintenance to other airlines or companies. Decoupling would also seem to encourage a shift in accounting toward activity-based costing. This shift could enable the decoupled segments to focus more on cost reduction in activities, increasing the cost competitiveness of the segment as a whole. Within airline alliances, carriers have begun to shift some of these roles as well (Feldman, 1999). However, the extent to which decoupling can take place in alliances is constrained at the present time by antitrust/competitive rules, national laws on related issues, that is, labor, safety, and so on, and general trust issues within alliances themselves.

The decoupling of an industry raises a number of other questions as well. First, where does the most value get added in the process? This is obviously the site of greatest profit and the most desirable location to be for prospective firms. Galbraith (1995) has suggested that the firm that performs the integrator role would benefit from the highest profit. The integrator is the firm that coordinates the decisions and actions of the many companies making up the network. It is responsible for overall strategy, member firm selection, and network linkages. Boeing performs this role for the multitude of firms involved in the "creation"

Figure 14.1   Airline value-chain

of the "Boeing aircraft." In addition, the integrator decides on which function or functions it will perform and which will be outsourced. Again, these decisions are based on the integrator's perception of its own strengths, expertise, and role. In addition to answering the questions of where value lies and who integrates, there is a third question. Is there enough value in each of the decoupled segments to attract sufficient numbers of firms to insure a competitive segment? Given that not all steps in the process generate the same level of value, and hence, profits, they should at least generate enough profits to attract firms into them and/or the decoupling should allow firms to find ways to increase profits through economies of scale, and so on. In a decoupling industry, there is also the possibility of gaining economies of scope by using the same knowledge, machinery, and systems in other industries. The same system that distributes airline tickets could conceivably distribute cruise ship rooms or concert tickets. The firm that manages one type of fleet could conceivably manage another.

On the topic of "enough profits", Chrysler, the integrator for its value chain, has an expression: "My enemy is my supplier's cost, not my supplier's margins. Therefore, what can I do to help my suppliers reduce their (and ultimately my) costs" (Galbraith, 1995: 127). This comment brings up one key pitfall of decoupling, namely the ability and willingness of network partners to work together in a non-adversarial way. There is ample evidence from research in Western firms that the objective of traditional supplier relations was to minimize vulnerability to supplier opportunism. This lack of trust leads to problems in attempting to increase informal, that is, non-contractual ties within networks (Mudambi and Helper, 1998; Spekman, 1985, 1988a, 1988b; Sako, 1992). This distrust will also tend to affect the strategic decisions of firms on the question of what gets outsourced to whom; technologically complex or proprietary-knowledge-based activities will tend to be kept in-house rather than outsourced for fear of losing these assets to others (Monteverde and Teece, 1982; Morten, 1984). This obvious lack of trust has broader implications for the ability of the network to operate as a "well-oiled machine."

The decoupling of the aviation industry also creates the possibility of a virtual airline. During the May 1997 meeting for the International Civil Aviation Organization, Dr. Kotaite described the virtual airline as follows:

The Virtual Airline owns no aircraft – they are leased.

The Virtual Airline employs no cockpit or cabin crew – they too are leased.

The Virtual Airline has no engineering facility – maintenance is contracted out.

The Virtual Airline does no ground handling – that too is contracted out.

The Virtual Airline also contracts out accounting and reservations, and may use electronic ticketing (ICAO, 2002).

In a decoupling world, the virtual airline becomes a possibility. What is left of the "airline" may well be nothing more than a small corporate office that retains some small equity as assets of the Virtual Airline. The chief concern of ICAO (and the national regulatory agencies), of course, is safety and security because "regulation of safety and security is the responsibility of individual States and, while Article 83bis of the Chicago Convention will provide for the transfer of responsibility in the case of lease, charter and interchange of aircraft among States, national reach beyond international borders is in practice limited, particularly where airlines are privately owned and national human, technical and financial resources for regulatory activities are frugal. Fully effective assurance of many aspects of safety and security can only be achieved by reciprocal arrangements or joint agreements, which only exist in certain areas of the world, or by world-wide co-operation." (ICAO, 2002). Lyle (1997) has offered the following example of a decoupled, virtual world in which "an airline from country A operating code-shared flights to country B on behalf of an airline from country C, which is in turn a franchisee of an airline from country D...uses leased aircraft which are on the register of country E and for which the maintenance is carried out in country F" (6). This globalization of aviation creates a host of safety, security, and political issues that have yet to be resolved. It can, however, create opportunities for improvement as well. For example, in the area of outsourced maintenance many carriers already consider it a non-core activity and have outsourced to other maintenance facilities or original equipment manufacturers. Over the last ten years, US airlines have increased outsourced maintenance expenses from 26 to 64 percent with the largest growth coming from foreign repair facilities (Business Travel Coalition, 2008). With greater oversight by firms, these outsourcers may in fact be able to create economies and competencies that will improve the quality of maintenance and in a concentrated industry this could improve the ability of national aviation authorities to oversee the process (Ebbs, 1997; Smith and Culley, 1997). Greater economies of scale on the part of maintenance facilities can also reduce the price of maintenance (Seidenman and Spanovich, 1997). However, without sufficient oversight, safety could become a major issue for carriers and their passengers. This is particularly true for foreign repair stations. In the case of the US FAA, there are only 103 inspectors for the 692 foreign repair stations, making adequate oversight problematic (Business Travel Coalition, 2008).

Aside from the issues of safety and security, there are further problems with decoupling and virtual airlines, namely the actual transition. It is relatively easy to imagine a start-up carrier with a small, limited market pursuing a virtual airline as a way to overcome some of the capital and labor costs inherent in the industry, however, it is much more difficult to imagine a path that would take a United toward virtual status. The coordination needs of such a vast network would be immense, although the network of a Boeing or Airbus is probably no less complex. Even if this problem can be surmounted, there is likely to be tremendous resistance from labor organizations. In general, labor has opposed any efforts to outsource jobs including the wet leasing. There has also been substantial resistance in recent years to two-tier wage agreements, that is, agreements that create a separate, lower wage scale for certain groups of employees. These agreement were relatively popular in the US in the years immediately following the financial crisis of the early 1980s, but evidence from the American Airlines' acquisition of Reno Air and negotiations between American and American Eagle unions indicates resistance to any type of system that creates pay inequity or creates the possibility of substituting lower wage employees for higher wage employees as a means of reducing labor costs.

Studies of wage levels in the airline industry indicate that by far, pilots have the highest level of wages among non-management employee groups and are most likely to "hold on" to wage gains in tough times (Johnson, 1995). In a decoupled industry, there would have to be some segment that handled labor for other firms to outsource this resource. This would appear to be the least attractive (possibly most costly) segment of a decoupled industry. Labor in the airline industry is highly unionized and labor-management relations highly polarized. Decoupling at this time does not seem to offer a solution, at least for the likes of United. A small, virtual carrier can find firms from which to outsource their labor needs, in many cases at a reduced cost since these pilots would not be paid benefits by the airline itself and are more likely to work for a lower wage. Outsourcing the total labor needs of United does not appear possible at this time. It is also not clear how such an outsourcing company would acquire a labor pool of this size willing to work for a wage likely to make it attractive for this firm's operating margins or interested outsourcers. Of course, the bankruptcy of one or several large carriers could free up a sizable pool of labor that might be available for outsourcing, but this assumes that governments would be willing to accept not merely bankruptcy but the possibility of liquidation. As noted in Chapter 1 by Wolf (1995), liberal bankruptcy laws in the US certainly have allowed carriers to continue operating without shedding sizable portions of their labor force.

Basic strategic logic suggests that any effort to reduce costs should first focus on those factors representing the highest levels of expenditure. For airlines, this would be labor costs, particularly pilots. Clearly, the incentives exist to find ways to reduce these costs either by reducing the overall numbers of workers employed, increasing the utilization of the labor force, improving the productivity of labor, or reducing the wages of existing labor. Given the power of airline labor, particularly pilots, there is certainly an incentive to deskill the laborer as a means of reducing the wages of existing labor. Adam Smith in the work that established the field of economics and defines the general terms of capitalism offers the classic example of the pin factory where:

A workman not educated to this business (which the division of labor has rendered a distinct trade), nor acquainted with the use of machinery employed in it (to the invention of which the same division of labor has probably given occasion), could scarce, perhaps with his utmost industry, make one pin in a day, and certainly could not make twenty. But, it is [now] divided into a number of branches, of which the greater parts are likewise peculiar trades. One man draws out the wire, another straights it, a third cuts it, a fourth points it, a fifth grinds it to the top for receiving the head (Smith, 1776. Reprinted in 1952 edition, R. Hutchins (ed.): 3).

Smith goes on to discuss how this division allows fewer men to do more work by specializing in a single task. While this is true, the process of division of labor also takes a skilled craftsman and deskills him. In the process, the value of his labor is decreased; skilled trades command higher wages, whereas the unskilled grinder of the pin above does not warrant such wages. New technology, like the machines that Smith spoke of in the pin factory, have been replacing workers for years by increasing the productivity of fewer workers or eliminating them entirely. These machines have reduced the skilled craftsman to a low wage operator. One of the key issues behind the longshoreman's strike on the US West Coast is the computerized technology that would replace hundreds of workers. Ironically, both sides in the dispute agreed that this new technology would increase the efficiency of port operations and allow for greater volumes of traffic with higher quality in handling (The Mercury News, 2002). While there is currently no accepted technology to replace pilots, many aircraft do operate on a fly-by-wire technology that is computer based and recent events have led to suggestions for systems that would allow ground operators to override an aircraft in flight (in the case of hijacking, for example) and land it safely.

Of course, there are more traditional ways to reduce the power of labor groups such as bankruptcy, however, these means have provided only short-term relief from high labor costs. If the industry were to decouple by spinning off units like what occurred in the auto industry, old labor contracts could be rewritten and additional changes in work rules and environments could be instituted. After the union experience in the auto industry, this is not likely to go unnoticed in the airlines and would likely provoke labor unrest. In short, while a decoupled industry with virtual airlines may be a sound concept theoretically, there are major impediments to creating this future in the airline industry.

Looking Ahead

In a 1988 book on international aviation, Taneja described the "prevailing attitude" of the North American airline industry as one that forced a carrier to choose one of three options: (1) become a megacarrier; (2) become a feeder to a megacarrier; or (3) fill a small niche in the marketplace. With the exception of carriers such as Southwest, the answer of the other major carriers was to become a megacarrier. A megacarrier, according to Taneja, has five key attributes. First, it has a large national and international route network. Second, it maintains a sufficient number of strategically located hubs with cost-effective feeder systems. Third, labor agreements are designed to provide low costs and high productivity in the long run. Fourth, an in-house automation system provides computerized reservations and the capability to manage yield and capacity cost-effectively. Finally, it possesses an attractive frequent flyer program. The events of 9/11 and the questions that it has given rise to are now challenging these attitudes and demanding that carriers in North America and around the world rethink the way they do business. The growing success of low-cost carriers is also challenging the great international carriers to redefine their place in the market and the ways that they generate value for consumers.

The questions have been asked, but there are as yet no clear answers. In fact, there is no "one right answer" to the questions posed here in this chapter. Each airline and region may arrive at their own solution to these challenges and it will remain for the marketplace to determine the "winners and losers." Whether the great names of airline history will be able to meet the challenges facing them or fall to the younger, smaller, faster competitors rising up before them has yet to be determined. They clearly face some very difficult choices and their "normal" options are constrained by an inability to quickly adjust capacity, lower labor costs, and readjust route networks. While bankruptcy does increase the range of options for carriers in some ways, it also carries definite risks. In the absence of government intervention, some carriers may simply not survive the process. While the "death" of one or two carriers in certain markets might actually benefit the industry overall by reducing capacity, freeing up valued resources, and opening opportunities into new markets, the widespread loss of carriers can lead to serious economic problems in the broader economy. As if the problem of profitability were not enough for carriers to face in the new environment, there is another question that is waiting to be asked, namely—what is the future of global aviation liberalization? The industry before 9/11 was on a steady path toward greater freedom to enter, exit, set prices, and establish capacity based on market forces. After a pause, it has lurched ahead finally with the new EU–US Open Skies agreement, but there remain many issues to be resolved. This topic will be the subject of Chapter 15.

References

Air Transport Association (2008), 'Quarterly Cost Index: US passenger Airlines', Available at: http://www.airlines.org/economics/finance/cost.

Air Transport News (2008), 'Delta Air Lines, Northwest Combining to Create America's Premier Global Airline', Available at: http://www.airtransportnews. aero.pl?id=1549.

Arndt, M. and Woellert, L. (2001), 'What Kind of Rescue: Cash won't Solve Air Carriers' Long-term Woes', *Business Week*, October 1, pp. 36–7.

Ashkenas, R., Ulrich, D., Jick, T., and Kerr, S. (1995), *The Boundaryless Organizations: Breaking the Chains of Organizational Structure*, Jossey-Bass Publishers, San Francisco.

Bartimo, J. (1990), 'Wanted: Co-Pilots for Reservation Systems', *Business Week*, April 9, p. 79.

Binggeli, U. and Pompeo, L. (2002), 'Hyped Hopes for Europe's Low-cost Airlines', *The McKinsey Quarterly*, Number 4.

Bized (2002), 'Economies of Scale', www.bized.ac.uk.

Bond, D. (2002), 'Back to Capital Hill: Airlines Seek More Relief', *Aviation Week and Space Technology*, September 30, pp. 38–47.

Business Travel Coalition (2008), 'Aircraft Maintenance Outsourcing Issue Analysis', March 18, Available at: http://bctnewswire.com.

Caves, R.E. and Porter, M.E. (1977), 'From Entry Barriers to Mobility Barriers: Conjectural Decisions and Contrived Deterrence to New Competition', *Quarterly Journal of Economics*, vol. 91, pp. 241–61.

Caves, R.E. and Porter, M.E. (1976), ' Barriers to Exit', in D.P. Qualls and R.T. Masson (eds), *Essays in Industrial Organization in Honor of Joe S. Bain*, Ballinger, Cambridge, MA, pp. 39–69.

Cook, R.A., Goff, J.L., Yale, L.J. , and Wolverton, J.B. (2000), 'Fasten Your Seat Belts: Turbulence Ahead for Travel Agencies,' in M.L. Taylor (ed.) *Case Set A to Accompany Dess & Lumpkin Strategic Management*, McGraw-Hill/Irwin, Boston, MA., pp. 32–41.

Costa, P.R., Harned, D.S., and Lunquist, J.T. (2002), 'Rethinking the Aviation Industry', *The McKinsey Quarterly*, Number 2: Risk and Resilience.

Davidow, W.H. and Malone, M.S. (1992), *The Virtual Corporation: Structuring and Revitalizing the Corporation for the 21st Century*, HarperCollins Publishing, New York.

Derchin, M. (1995), 'What went Wrong?', in P. Cappelli (ed.) *Airline Labor Relations in the Global Era: The New Frontier*, ILR Press, Ithaca.

DeWitt, R.L. (1998), 'Firm, Industry, and Strategy Influences on Choice of Downsizing Approach,' *Strategic Management Journal*, vol. 19, pp. 59–79.

DeWitt, R.L. (1993), 'The Structural Consequences of Downsizing', *Organization Science*, vol. 4, pp. 30–40.

Ebbs, G. (1997), 'Supporting Roles,' *Airline Business*, April, pp. 58–60.

Ezard, K. (2008) 'Focus: The Mexican Airline Sector', Air Transport Intelligence, January 15, Available at: http://www.rati.com/news/item.asp?id=237348.

Feldman, J.M. (1999), 'Disappearing Act', *Air Transport World*, February, pp. 25–30.

Field, D. (2007), 'Uneasy truce', *Airline Business* vol. 23 (3), pp. 40–44.

Fiorino, F. (2002), 'Carty to Analysts: AA Aims to Survive', *Aviation Week and Space Technology*, September 20, pp. 47–8.

Galbraith, J.R. (1995), *Designing Organizations: An Executive Briefing on Strategy, Structure, and Process,* Jossey-Bass Publishers, San Francisco.

Haddad, C. and Zellner, W. (2002), 'Getting Down and Dirty with the Discounters', *Business Week*, October 28, pp. 76–7.

Hammer, M. and Champy, J.S. (1993), *Reengineering the Corporation: A Manifesto for Business Revolution*, HarperBusiness, New York.

Harrigan, K.R. (1985), *Strategic Flexibility*, Lexington Books, Lexington, MA.

Harrigan, K.R. (1983), *Strategies for Vertical Integration*, Lexington Books, Lexington, MA.

IATA (2008a), 'Fact Sheet – Fuel', Available at: http://www.iata.org/pressroom/ facts_figures/fact_sheets/fuel.htm.

IATA (2008b), 'Financial Forecast: Cyclical Downturn Ahead in 2008' December. Available at: http://www.iata.org/economics.

IATA (2007), 'IATA Economic Briefing: Passenger and Freight Forecasts 2007–2011', October. Available at: http://www.iata.org/economics.

IATA (2004), 'Guidance Material on Best Practices for Fuel and Environmental Management', Available at: http://www.iata.org/nr/rdonlyles/66a62927-d1cb-474c-821e-16f68fb.

International Civil Aviation Organization (ICAO) (2002), *Launch of the Strategic Action Plan*- 1997, ICAO, May 22, pp. 1–9.

Johnson, N.B. (1995), 'Pay Levels in the Airline Since deregulation', in Peter Cappelli (ed.) *Airline Labor Relations in the Global Era: The New Frontier*, ILR Press, Cornell, pp.101–15.

Loomis, C. and Buffet, W. (1999), 'Mr. Buffet on the Stock Market', in *Businessman of the Century*, Fortune, vol. 140.

Lyle, C. 1997), 'Global Safety: Can Advice Overcome Diplomatic Caution?' Presentation at the European Air Transport Conference on Airline Globalization, Brussels, Belgium, October 8.

Mahoney, J.T. (1992), 'The Choice of Organizational Form and Vertical Financial Ownership versus Other methods of Vertical Integration,' *Strategic Management Journal*, vol. 13, pp. 559–84.

McKenney, L., Copeland, D.G., Mason, R.O. (1967), 'American Airlines SABRE System,' Harvard Business School Case No. EA-C.

Mecham, M. (2002), 'Are There Too Many Aircraft Even With the Desert Full?' *Aviation Week and Space Technology*, April 22, pp. 40–41.

Methner, B.E. and Rospenda, C.J. (2001), 'Airline Strategy in a Digital Age: What Does 'e' Mean to Me?', in Gail F. Butler and Martin R. Keller (eds), *Handbook of Airline Strategy*, McGraw-Hill Companies, New York, pp. 389–406.

Michels, J. (2007) 'Travelport', Aviation Daily, August 22, Available at: http:// www.aviationweek.com/aw/generic/story_channel.jsp.

Monteverde, K. and Teece, D. (1982), 'Supplier Switching Costs and Vertical Integration in the Automobile Industry,' *Bell Journal of Economics*, vol. 13, pp. 206–13.

Morten, S. (1984), 'The Organization of Production: Evidence from the Aerospace Industry,' *Journal of Law and Economics*, vol. 27, pp. 403–17.

MSNBC News Services (2008), 'Delta to Offer Buyouts to Some 30,000', MSNBC, March 18, Available at: http://www.msnbc.com/id/23690403.

Mudambi, R. and Helper, S. (1998), 'The 'Close But Adversarial' Model in the U.S. Auto Industry', *Strategic Management Journal*, vol. 19, pp. 775–92.

Nadler, D.A. and Tushman, M.L. (1997), *Competing By Design: The Power of Organizational Architecture,* Oxford University Press, Oxford.

Nelson, A. and Francolla, G. (2008), 'Airlines: A Tale of Mergers and Bankruptcy', CNBC.com, February 21, Available at: http://www.cnbc.com.

Porter, M. (1985), *Competitive Advantage*, Free Press, New York.

Reuters (2008a), 'Big US Airlines Look to Shrink to Save Money', CNBC.com, March 17, Available at: http://www.cnbc.com.

Reuters (2008b), 'Air France-KLM Chief warns Alitalia deal at Risk', CNBC. com, March 19, Available at: http://www.cnbc.com.

Rosen, S.D. (1995), 'Corporate Restructuring: A Labor Perspective,' in P. Cappelli (ed.) *Airline Labor Relations in the Global Era: The New Frontier*, ILR Press, Ithaca.

Rosenbush, S., Crockett, R.O., Haddad, C., and Ewing, J. (2002), 'The Telecom Depression: When Will It End', *Business Week*, October 7, pp. 66–74.

Sako, M. (1992), *Prices, Quality and Trust: Inter-Firm Relations in Britain and Japan*, Cambridge University Press, Cambridge.

Seidenman, P. and Spanovich, D. (1997), 'Global Competition Drives Maintenance Market', *Aviation Maintenance*, January, pp. 8–14.

Smith, A. (1952), *An Inquiry into the Nature and Causes of the Wealth of Nations*, in Robert Maynard Hutchins (ed.) *Great Books of the Western World* series, no. 39.

Smith, T.W. and Culley, J. (1997), 'Gently Down Stream', *Airline Business*, October, pp. 2–55.

Spekman, R.E. (1985), 'Competitive Procurements Strategies: Building Strength and Reducing Vulnerability', *Long Range Planning*, vol. 18, pp. 75–81.

Spekman, R.E. (1988a), 'Strategic Supplier Selection: Understanding long-term Buyer Relationships', *Business Horizons*, vol. 31, pp. 75–81.

Spekman, R.E. (1988b), 'Perceptions of Strategic Vulnerability Among Industrial Buyers and its Effects on Information Search and Supplier Evaluation', *Journal of Business Research*, vol. 17, pp. 313–26.

Taneja, N.K. (1988), *The International Airline Industry*, Lexington Books, Lexington, MA.

The Mercury News (2002), 'Longshoremen's Union Pitches Adding Tech Workers', *The Mercury* News, October 9.

USA Today (2007), 'Southwest Airlines' Fuel Hedging Pushes Profits', USAToday Online, Available at: http://www.usatodat.com/pt/cpt?action=cpt&title=South west+Airlines%27.

Velocci, A.L. (2002), 'Can Majors Shift Focus Fast Enough to Survive?', *Aviation Week and Space Technology*, November 18, pp. 52–4.

Weber, H.R. (2008), 'Delta Pilots Say No Deal With Northwest', WTOPnews.com, March 18, Available at: http://www.wtopnews.com/?nid=111&sid=1347940.

Wolf, S.M. (1995), 'Where Do We Go from Here: A Management Perspective', in Peter Cappelli (ed.) *Airline Labor Relations in the Global Era: The New Frontier*, ILR Press, Cornell, pp. 18–23.

Zellner, W. (2002), 'What's Weighing Down the Big Carriers', *Business Week*, April 29, p. 91.

Websites

Air Transport Association, http://www.airline.org
IATA, http://www.iata.org

Chapter 15

Seeking Liberal Markets

Truly Open Skies

Europeans have long complained that open skies is an "American term" that does not in fact truly involve open markets, but represents an extension of what bilateral air service agreements have always been about, namely negotiating to achieve maximum national benefit (Lobbenberg, 1994; Sorenson, 1998). In other words, they did not believe the rhetoric of open skies; they have charged that open skies bilaterals are simply another attempt by the US to dominate their aviation systems without allowing them an equal opportunity to compete (Wallerstein, 1991). In the aftermath of World War II, the inequality was largely due to external factors relating to the destruction of commercial aircraft and aviation infrastructure. Today, the inequality is created by a bilateral system that grants US carriers greater access to European markets than European airlines receive into the US or even into their own markets. For example, the European Cockpit Association (ECA) pointed out that the bilateral system with open skies EU countries prevented European companies from taking full advantage of the European market, but allowed US carriers to string together the fifth freedom (beyond) rights included in open skies agreements to serve the European market in a more profitable way (European Cockpit Association, 2000).

Given these perceived disparities in access, it was not surprising that many of the European nations that had been opposed to an open sky in Chicago (1944) now called for more liberal markets in aviation. Further, they wanted issues of ownership and domestic market access addressed as well the elimination of any remaining barriers within the aviation market place. With the aviation barriers dropping in the EU with the 1997 Single Sky, they saw the US exercise of fifth freedom rights as cabotage and wanted the same privileges in the US (Sorenson, 1998). The European vision has been to extend the single aviation market created by the 15-nation European Union across the Atlantic, the so-called Transatlantic Common Aviation Area (TCAA). Clearly, the rhetoric of liberalization is now in the "best interest" of European carriers. The question is whether it will benefit US and Canadian carriers and individual consumers and local communities on both sides of the Atlantic. Of course, the events of 11 September momentarily took this transatlantic fight off the table, but the stakes were too high to leave it off for long and the US would eventually find a need for its EU allies, however, it would be a long road to agreement. Even the 30 March 2008 start of the new multilateral EU–US open skies agreement is seen by the Europeans as only one step in a process whose next stage was set to begin 30 May 2008 with the next round of negotiations toward an "Open Aviation Area" (EurActiv.com, 2007).

The Long Road

In a 1995 policy paper on European Union (EU) external aviation relations, the Association of European Airlines (AEA) put forth a proposal for a new regulatory framework between Europe and the US The following year the Council of Ministers for the European Union issued a mandate to the Commission's work toward establishing a "Common Aviation Area." This Common Aviation Area proposed that air carriers from both sides of the Atlantic be allowed to provide their services within a common commercial framework that ensured competition on a fair and equal basis within an equivalent regulatory regime (AEA, 1999). Under a TCAA, the US and Europe were expected to "harmonize" the following key areas: (1) rules governing market entry, access, and pricing, (2) rules governing airline ownership and the right of establishment, (3) rules governing competitive behavior and policies, and (4) rules governing leased aircraft.

Entry, Access, and Pricing

The basic objective of a TCAA was to insure unrestricted commercial opportunities allowing carriers (and market forces) to determine routes, markets, capacity, and pricing without discrimination anywhere within the countries party to a TCAA agreement. Under the proposal, a distinction would be made between TCAA countries as a group and third parties with whom the traditional bilateral air service agreements would still apply. In other words, the two parties to the bilateral would be the TCAA (as a single unit) and the third party. This was a general principle behind economic integration. One of the problems of a free trade area (FTA) (the first step in economic integration) is that although members of the FTA have eliminated internal barriers to the movement of goods, the external tariff barriers to third party goods remains in place and may vary in such a way that third parties can benefit by selectively entering the FTA country with the most favorable tariff conditions and then gaining access from there to other member states (Hill, 2001). The AEA suggested a phased approach to establishing this new single aviation area that is similar to the EU liberalization that took place through a series of three packages (Chapter 9). The envisioned approach would have allowed EU countries the flexibility to negotiate with the US subject to achieving some minimum standards set by the overall parties (AEA, 1999).

Ownership and Right of Establishment

The right of establishment is a legal term relating to the national control of companies. In other words, TCAA proposed granting firms that are 1) majority owned or controlled by nationals of any of the TCAA parties or their governments or 2) incorporated and have their principale place of business within the territory of a TCAA country equal rights and recognition. With the right of establishment comes the end of "foreign national" restrictions on cross-border mergers, acquisitions, and entry. Under the second definition, airlines from third party countries could begin operations in a TCAA country and then gain the right to operate throughout TCAA airspace. It would, of course, be possible under option one for a country to apply for membership into the TCAA, thus opening up their aviation system to all TCAA members in the process.

Competition Policy

In Chapter 11, the issue of antitrust or competitiveness policy was discussed as it related to strategic alliances. From that discussion, it should be clear that although the basic concepts underlying both the US and EU policies are similar, the application of these policies has differed in a number of significant ways. The Association of European Airlines (1999) suggested that common standards should be developed in the following areas:

- Basic criteria for granting exemptions, and in particular means of reconciling the relevant criteria of the EC competition rules and the US concept of the "public interest";
- The definition of the "relevant market";
- The concept of "market power" as distinct from "market share";
- The notion of "predatory behavior";
- The question what "essential facilities" airlines would have to share with each other;
- The treatment of airline co-operative arrangements;
- The nature of remedies and sanctions to be applied (AEA, 1999).

The AEA argued in their proposal that strategic alliances whose objectives were to create TCAA airlines that were competitive in world markets should be considered by both EU and US standards to contribute to economic progress, the interests of consumers, and the interest of the public at large (AEA, 1999). Further, they believed that code sharing, blocked space, franchising, and other cooperative agreements including activities involving tariff (fare) consultation for interline purposes should be considered indispensable to the operation of strategic networks.

Leasing Aircraft

There are differences between the US and Europe over the question of wet leasing aircraft. The US prevents US airlines from wet leasing non-US registered aircraft from other airlines and requires that non-US leasers have route authority for the operation concerned. EU rules require registration in a member state but permit this to be waived for short-term lease arrangements or other exceptional circumstances. The Association recommended that the US–EU rules be modified to allow any TCAA carrier to lease from or to any other TCAA carrier and that, if third party leasing were permitted, a maximum percentage of fleet standard be set. These rules would be contingent upon all parties complying with established safety standards.

Raising Objections

The European Cockpit Association which represented over 2,600 pilots from EU countries endorsed TCAA with several reservations. First, they were concerned that relaxing ownership and leasing rules might create "flags of convenience" in aviation similar to those existing in the maritime industry. In the United States, for example, the Jones Act requires that ships carrying cargo from one domestic port to another be built, maintained, and operated (and flagged) in the US, but does not have such a requirement for ships coming from a foreign port. There are a number of countries that allow open registries whereby ships owned by individuals or corporations in other countries may be flagged in their country rather than the country of the ship's owner. Critics charge that the practice of open registries allows owners to avoid the fees, taxes, safety requirements, and manning rules of their home country and poses a risk to crews, the marine environment, and the ports into which they enter (Morris, 1996; Ryan, 1996). If TCAA included countries with safety and social standards below EU/US standards, there would be a cost incentive to flag aircraft in that country leading to lowered safety standards for airline operations and the shifting of operations to common aviation areas offering lower taxes, wages, benefits, and so on. This would obviously affect employment opportunities, local tax bases, and merchants in affected areas. The ECA also expressed concern that liberalized ownership would result in the conversion or merging of alliances into mega-airlines dominated by US carriers and that route structures and associated carriers could be manipulated for cost-cutting purposes (ECA, 2000).

TCAA did not provoke a significant reaction from US aviation groups. Labor delegates at a 1999 aviation summit in the US cautioned against rapid change and any liberalization that failed "to maintain the integrity of companies and to protect jobs" (Ott, 1999: 45). Their reasoning and concerns were very similar to the position stated by the ECA, although they did not indicate even a conditional endorsement of TCAA. By and large, US airlines cautiously ignored the proposal. Meanwhile, the US government was lukewarm to TCAA. At the 1999 aviation summit mentioned above, Rodney Slater, then US Secretary of Transportation, committed the US to examining the TCAA proposal. This US reaction of "committing to study the issues" was repeated when the President and CEO of Air Canada, Robert Milton, proposed a single aviation market for North America saying that he "urged the two governments to build on the success story of the 1995 Canada–US Open Skies

Agreement by progressively removing all restrictions in order to arrive at a fully integrated, common air transport market with the United States" (Melnbardis, 2001: 1). Reacting to the Canadian proposal, American Airlines and United Airlines indicated that they supported the principle of liberalized air policy, but needed time to study the specifics (Chase and McArthur, 2001).

The whole matter of Atlantic liberalization fell by the wayside with the events of 11 September. Not only did the US feel that it had more important issues to consider but security considerations suddenly loomed much larger on everyone's agenda. The fact that US airlines were particularly hard hit by these events did not encourage US airlines or the government that represented them in efforts to open up the US market. The US Congress also became increasingly concerned about issues of foreign ownership and control of important US industries and assets.

Balancing Acts

Before looking specifically at the possible winners and losers in an open aviation market, it is important to examine several broader issues. First, TCAA was the first time that the United States had been officially asked (or considered) to trade in roughly equivalent domestic markets. A quick look at Table 8.2 shows that the open skies agreements of the past essentially involved countries with small domestic markets. Ideology aside, it never made "economic sense" for the United States to trade access to its large domestic market for the domestic markets of Singapore, The Netherlands, or even Germany. The size differences were simply too great. The population of the United States is estimated at roughly 300,000,000. Calculating the estimated EU population from Chapter 9 yields a total EU population of roughly

490,000,000 (CIA Factbook, 2007). Given some of the differences between US and EU transportation markets noted in Chapter 9, namely more developed EU intermodal competition and charter market and the higher domestic departures of the US (Sinha, 2001), these markets appear to be roughly similar in size, particularly if we add in the estimated population of Canada (CIA Factbook, 2007). This "equivalent markets" argument raises a question about the potential single North American market proposed by Air Canada. While the two countries have roughly equal land masses (9,976,140 square kilometers for Canada and 9,629,091 for the US), there is a major difference in the population size (CIA Factbook, 2007). Much of the Canadian land mass is in the far north where the Canadian government has declared many communities in need of essential services, particularly in winter months, when air service is a vital link to the outside world. US carriers would have little interest in gaining access to these markets and under open skies have already gained access to the southern Canadian markets. Air Canada, on the other hand, would seem to have a great deal to gain from single markets. The Air Transport Association of Canada which represents a number of Canadian carriers has said that it supports the idea of "modified sixth-freedom rights" between the US and Canada, but this wording appears to be only a limited endorsement of the single market concept. The chairman of WestJet Airlines has gone on record as opposing the concept of a single market arguing that it would do nothing to lessen the grip of Air Canada on the domestic market and would put Canadian carriers at a disadvantage since they pay much more for fuel than their US counterparts (Chase and McArthur, 2001). In short, it does not appear that any North American carrier has anything to gain except Air Canada. While the Canadian government considered a single market as a way to deflect consumer complaints over the decision to allow Air Canada to become a monopoly, the US government was always likely to receive a great deal of pressure from the US airline industry to oppose a deal.

A second issue that argued in favor of TCAA was that the safety and security levels of European carriers are equal, if not higher, than their US counterparts. European airports have historically incorporated security designs and policies that limited access in gate areas to ticketed passengers, encouraged bag matching, and other sophisticated screening techniques. In a post-9/11 environment, this was likely to be an important consideration and TCAA could facilitate closer cooperation on improving these areas. It is true that recent efforts by the US to gain access to more personal information from EU flyers into the US has raised opposition in the EU from privacy advocates, but this would not argue against generally high EU security standards.

Finally, the European Commission has committed itself to implementing a multilateral aviation approach for the EU to end the current system of bilateral air service agreements. The Commission launched a case in 1998 against eight member states with US open skies agreements claiming that these agreements breached single market rules because they disadvantaged other member nations. Further, they charged that the bilateral agreements infringed on the EU external competence in foreign affairs. In January 2002, the European Court of Justice ruled that these countries had broken EU laws in signing such bilateral. The key issue is the nationality requirements (contained in Article 52) and Article 307 of the EC treaty that requires states to make every effort to amend international agreements that violate EC law. In effect, the EU has declared themselves a single market for external purposes and reiterated their belief that extensive fifth freedom rights exercised by US carriers are cabotage. The Commission demanded reciprocal access to the US for their carriers as well as ownership privileges. A 2005 compromise was opposed by the US Congress, throwing the matter back to the respective governments. The EU was clearly determined to keep the pressure on the US concerning liberalization.

Winners and Losers

Calculations were and continue to be made on both sides of the Atlantic about the costs and benefits of single markets. These calculations include consumer groups, airlines, employee organizations, local communities, and national governments. In this section, the issues relating to these group-specific calculations will be discussed.

Consumers

General economic theory suggests that consumers benefit from having more choices of products, services, and firms. Single aviation markets do promise to broaden the choices of consumers. However, the same problems may arise in this next phase of liberalization that occurred in earlier deregulation efforts. First, the heightened competition of the early period could be jeopardized by failures to enforce laws on predatory behavior and merger/acquisition leading to high failures rates of "new entrants" and mergers that result in the concentration of the market in a few select carriers. Second, consumers in some markets may lose service as US–EU carriers re-deploy their fleets to new, more lucrative markets. Given the cost structure of the entering international carriers, they would likely concentrate on higher yield markets with the all-important business travelers. Markets vacated by these carriers in Europe would be open for low-cost carrier entry. In any event, neither the North Americans nor Europeans are likely to drop their right to insure that essential services are provided to local communities. The difficulty lies in harmonizing the implementation of the rules and policies that define relevant markets, frequency requirements, carrier types, and so on, in the determination of essential services.

Airlines

Sorting out the potential winners and losers among the airlines is in large part the function of two factors: relative costs and relative service levels. The last major study to examine the cost competitiveness of international airlines was conducted by Oum and Yu (1998). They examined the cost of airline inputs (labor, fuel, aircraft, capital, and materials) and the revenue of airlines (outputs) from passengers, freight, and mail to determine the efficiency of carriers and their cost competitiveness. As mentioned briefly in Chapter 8, almost thirty years of deregulation in US markets created carriers with much lower costs and higher levels of productivity and cost competitiveness. In the Oum and Yu (1998) study, only British Airways and KLM were close to achieving a level of cost competitiveness comparable to their US counterparts. Of course, if many of the European carriers began operating in the US they would likely be able to reduce many of these costs, at least in US operations, since fuel prices, the benefits component of labor costs, and many related fees tend to be lower in the US The Oum and Yu (1998) study did not consider the low-cost European carriers such as Ryanair and easyJet who may well have costs structures more comparable to Southwest in the US From a firm point of view, single markets increase strategic flexibility by allowing firms to move assets as well as perform work where it makes the most sense to do so from a cost and logistical standpoint. This flexibility is precisely the concern of labor groups, as we will see in a minute. The fact that European airlines recovered more quickly from 11 September and have been able to post profits well in advance of their US counterparts probably alleviates the old concern about US carrier dominance in alliances, possible mergers, and so on, although US airlines have used bankruptcy to lower their own costs and improve performance. However, as Chapter 14 highlighted, US carriers have suffered greatly in the wake of 9/11 and as a group are far weaker than their EU counterparts which may alleviate ECA fears of US airline dominance but does little to reassure the US government or US airlines.

The second issue is relative service levels between US and European carriers. At least some of the cost differences between US–EU carriers are probably the result of the generally higher levels of service provided by EU carriers. In an environment where carriers are free to operate anywhere within the single market, there are some carriers that may clearly be disadvantaged by high cost structures and poor quality. At the margin, consumers will decide the issue of price and service level. In general, the trend in the US has been toward viewing air transportation as a basic commodity that is cheap and relatively indistinguishable from one provider to another. Indications are that European markets are beginning to move more in this direction with the success of their own low-cost carriers such as Ryanair. Nationality issues aside, single markets increase the competition on international routes where service level issues are considered more important and would tend to favor the European carriers.

Labor Groups

Single markets open up the very real possibility that firms will shift operations from one region to another or utilize labor from one area over another as a means of reducing costs. This shift has occurred in other liberalizing industries and is very likely to occur in aviation. Most at risk may be pilots who account for greater labor costs than do mechanics and flight attendants. With or without single markets, however, the losses of recent years will force carriers and labor groups to make some very hard choices in their efforts to bring costs and capacity down to competitive levels. It should be noted that the cost of labor is not the only issue that managers should consider; the productivity of labor can balance this cost in the long run. Oum and Yu (1998) found that while Thai Airways had input costs that were 52.1 percent lower (22.4 percent of which were attributable to labor) than American Airlines, however, in terms of overall efficiency (outputs to inputs) Thai was 42.9 percent less efficient. A higher cost but more efficient labor force can still be cost competitive. In many western countries, productivity gains have been achieved through the adoption of improved information systems, but productivity can also be improved through more flexible work rules, attention to work flows, cross-functional team implementation, and other redesign options. Bankruptcy has allowed most of the major US carriers to reduce their labor (and pension) costs even further. US network carriers have also shed 150,000 jobs since 2001 and may well lose more in a series of mergers (Air Transport News, 2008).

Local Communities

If we define local communities broadly as nations, then there are clearly risks involved in single markets. High cost, low productivity, and low service carriers will probably not survive without government assistance. As we discussed in Chapter 1, airlines have historically been closely associated with national pride, power, and prestige. The EU is currently struggling with this issue as we speak and the debate over whether the Sabenas of aviation should be allowed to continue to serve "their communities." More narrowly defined, there may be some city and city-pair markets that will see reduced service as carriers adjust their route structure toward higher margin routes. Many of these markets will continue to receive service from the entrance of low-cost carriers, but the quality and frequency of service is likely to change for some communities.

National Governments

There is a saying that "all politics is local." Given the historic attachment of localities to their airlines and the strategic flexibility that single markets give to airlines, there will be pressure on governments to intervene in the process to influence local outcomes. Economists talk about long-run equilibriums and structural adjustments; politicians are concerned about the next election. Predicting the outcome of this political wrangling is far more difficult, particularly when questions of local, national, and supranational jurisdiction, responsibilities, and calculations come into play.

Moving Ahead

After four years of negotiations and several setbacks, the EU and US finally reached a multilateral agreement that opened up the transatlantic routes beginning in March 2008. The agreement removed restrictions on the number of carriers allowed to fly transatlantic routes. EU carriers will be able to fly from any EU city to any American city and onward to a third destination. The US has full rights to fly from any US city to any EU city and beyond. EU airlines can fly between the US and non-EU countries that are members of the European Common Aviation Area. From the US perspective, it achieved one of its major goals in opening up Heathrow airport, but not until the long awaited Terminal Five was opened. The Europeans did not get the right of cabotage in the US, although they may establish subsidiaries in the US under a number of restrictions. EU owners can buy up to 100 percent of the non-voting stock in US companies but voting stock is still limited to 25 percent. Given this restriction, the EU set a 25 percent limit on US companies and insisted on a suspension clause should the US fail to comply with an agreement to open a second round of talks 60 days after this agreement goes into effect. While government officials have suggested that the new deal will create 80,000 jobs and generate 12 billion euros in economic benefits others are not so certain (EurActiv, 2007). According to some industry watchers, after a few introductory low fares, consumers are not likely to see significant reductions in fares and the vast majority of new flights will be targeted to the already well-trafficked, high-yield markets. In fact, the airlines are expected to focus on the high-yield business and leisure travelers as a way to improve their financial positions (Wilen, 2008).

In short, there will be no "Big Bang" approach to transatlantic liberalization. While the Europeans would have preferred an agreement that went farther than the current one, most EU groups were satisfied with greater initial access. The US moved reluctantly on the issue given the lukewarm reception in the industry and broader security and terrorism concerns, feeling that they needed to appease the EU somewhat to gain support in other non-aviation areas. It is too early, of course, to see how the process of harmonizing policies on predatory behavior and merger/acquisition will go, but it is not unreasonable to assume that it might take a number of years to resolve.

References

Air Transport News (2008), Available at: http://www.airtransportnews.aero/article. pl?mcateg=&id=12041.

Association of European Airlines (1999), *Towards a Transatlantic Common Aviation Area: AEA Policy Statement,* September.

Chase, S. and McArthur, K. (2001), 'US Warm to Proposed Increased Air Competition', *Global Interactive*, December 8.

CIA Factbook (2002), www.odci.goc/cia/publications/factbook.

European Cockpit Association (ECA) (2000), *From EASA to TCAA: The Flight Crews View on a New Regulatory Framework in Aviation*, ECA, Brussels, Belgium.

EurActiv (EU News, Policy Positions) (2007), 'EU-US Open Skies Agreement', Available at: http://www.euractiv.com/en/transport/eu-us-open-skies.

Hill, C.W. (2001), *Global Business*, 2nd edition, Irwin-McGrawHill, Boston.

Lobbenberg, A. (1994), 'Government relations on the North Atlantic: A case Study of Five Europe-USA Relationships', *Journal of Air Transport Management*, vol. 1, pp. 47–62.

Melnbardis, R. (2001), 'Air Canada Wants Open U.S.-Canada Air Market', Reuters Newswire, December 6.

Morris, J. (1996), 'Flags of Convenience give Owners a Paper Refuge', *Houston Chronicle online edition, www.chron.com.*

Ott, J. (1999), 'Aviation Summit Yields EU Plan for Open Market', *Aviation Week and Space Technology*, December 13, pp. 43–5.

Oum, T.H. and Yu, C. (1998), *Winning Airlines: Productivity and Cost Competitiveness of the World's Major Airlines*, Kluwer Academic Publishers, Boston.

Ryan, G.J. (1996), 'Testimony by George J. Ryan, President-Lake Carriers' Association', presented before the House Subcommittee on Coast Guard and Maritime Transportation, June 12, Washington, D.C.Sinha, D. (2001), Deregulation and Liberalization of the Airline Industry: Asia, Europe, North America, and Oceania, Ashgate, Aldershot.

Sorenson, F. (1998), 'Open Skies in Europe', *FAA Commercial Aviation Forecast Conference Proceedings: Overcoming Barriers to World Competition and Growth*, March 12–13, Washington, D.C., pp. 125–31.

Wallerstein, I. (1991), *Geopolitics and Geoculture: Essays on the Changing World-system,* Cambridge University Press, Cambridge.

Wilen, J. (2008), 'Open Skies: More Flights, Same Fares', Available at: http://biz.yahoo.com/ap/080326/open_skies.html.

Chapter 16
Spreading the Promise

Problems and Promises

Aviation and the globalization movement of which it is an integral part promised to transform domestic and global economies by linking distant communities in an ever shrinking, complex web of interaction. Along these links flow a vast variety of goods, services, and people. As the flow increases, so does the income, standard of living, and general welfare of the people connected to this great web. This is the promise of globalization and aviation, but the reality is that there are a number of countries and regions around the world that have yet to collect on the promise. Three areas in particular have yet to experience the full benefits of this transformation: Africa, the Middle East, and Latin America. These areas have not yet been fully linked to the rest of the world, either virtually through the internet or physically through transportation. The purpose of this chapter is to explore the reasons why these areas have not yet benefited from civil aviation and to address various means by which the world community and national governments can work to spread the promise.

Africa—Understanding the Problems

Africa is the second largest continent in the world and possesses the population base and the geographically challenging terrain to make it ideal for air transportation. Unfortunately, these advantages are outweighed by a number of factors that have prevented the development of a viable civil aviation industry in Africa. The first factor is the underdeveloped state of the national economies of most of Africa (Graham, 1995; Taneja, 1988). As Table 16.1 demonstrates, the majority of the nations in Africa are poor. According to the World Bank Group, over 50 percent of the population in all of the 18 nations for which data was available were living on US$2 or less a day (World Bank Group, 2002). While the gross domestic product of Africa rose 3.2 percent in 2000, African economies will need to grow at an average of 7 percent a year to halve the poverty level by 2015. This may be difficult for a region heavily dependent on foreign aid and investment. According to the 2005 World Bank African Development Indicators report, the average income in Sub Saharan Africa, excluding South Africa, was US$342. Twenty-four of the thirty-two countries with the lowest level of human development were in Africa. There was some good news, however; net aid increased 40 percent in 2003 and debt service relief rose to US$43 billion (World Bank, 2005). Still, the level of poverty in Africa means that most of these nations can not afford the necessary level of

Table 16.1   Information on African countries (A through Z)

Country	Area*	Population**	Airports (Paved)***	GDP $****
Algeria	2,381,270	33,333,216	150 (52)	$8,100
Angola	1,246,700	12,263,596	232 (31)	$6,500
Benin	112,620	8,078,314	5 (1)	$1,500
Botswana	600,370	1,815,508	85 (11)	$14,700
Burkina Faso	274,200	14,326,203	33 (2)	$1,200
Burundi	27,830	8,390,505	8 (1)	$800
Cameroon	475,440	18,060,382	45 (11)	$2,300
Cape Verde	4,033	423,613	8 (8)	$7,000
Central African Republic	622,984	4,369,038	51 (3)	$700
Chad	1,284,000	9,885,661	55 (7)	$1,600
Comoros	2,170	711,417	4 (4)	$600
Congo, Democratic Republic of the	2,345,410	65,751,512	237 (26)	$300
Congo, Republic of the	342,000	3,800,610	31 (5)	$3,700
Cote d'Ivoire	322,460	18,013,409	34 (7)	$1,800
Djibouti	23,000	496,374	13 (3)	$1,000
Egypt	1,001,450	80,335,036	88 (72)	$5,400
Equatorial Guinea	28,051	551,201	5 (5)	$44,100
Eritrea	121,320	4,906,585	18 (4)	$1,000
Ethiopia	1,127,127	76,511,887	84 (15)	$700
Gabon	267,667	1,454,867	53 (10)	$13,800
Gambia, The	11,300	1,688,359	1 (1)	$800
Ghana	239,460	22,931,299	12 (7)	$1,400
Guinea	245,857	9,947,814	16 (5)	$1,000
Guinea-Bissau	36,120	1,472,780	27 (3)	$600
Kenya	582,650	36,913,721	225 (15)	$1,600
Lesotho	30,355	2,125,262	28 (3)	$1,500
Liberia	111,370	3,195,931	53 (2)	$500
Libya	1,759,540	6,036,914	141 (60)	$13,100
Madagascar	587,040	19,448,815	104 (27)	$1,000

Table 16.1 *Concluded*

Malawi	118,480	13,603,181	39 (6)	$800
Mali	1,240,000	11,995,402	29 (8)	$1,200
Mauritania	1,030,700	3,270,065	25 (8)	$1,800
Mauritius	2,040	1,250,882	5 (2)	$11,900
Morocco	446,550	33,757,175	60 (27)	$3,800
Mozambique	801,590	20,905,585	147 (22)	$900
Namibia	825,418	2,055,080	137 (21)	$5,200
Niger	1,267,000	12,894,865	28 (9)	$700
Nigeria	923,768	135,031,164	70 (36)	$2,200
Rwanda	26,338	9,907,509	9 (4)	$1,000
Sao Tome and Principe	1,001	199,579	2 (2)	$1,200
Senegal	196,190	12,521,851	20 (9)	$1,700
Seychelles	455	81,895	15 (9)	$18,400
Sierra Leone	71,740	6,144,562	10 (1)	$800
Somalia	637,657	9,118,773	67 (7)	$600
South Africa	1,219,912	43,997,828	728 (146)	$10,600
Sudan	2,505,810	39,379,358	101 (16)	$2,500
Swaziland	17,363	1,133,066	18 (1)	$4,800
Tanzania	945,087	39,384,223	124 (10)	$1,100
Togo	56,785	5,701,579	9 (2)	$900
Tunisia	163,610	10,276,158	30 (14)	$7,500
Uganda	236,040	30,262,610	32 (5)	$1,100
Western Sahara	266,000	382,617	9 (3)	N/A
Zambia	752,614	11,477,447	107 (9)	$1,400
Zimbabwe	390,580	12,311,143	341 (19)	$500

* Square Km. ** Estimated July 2007 figures *** Data from 2006 **** Estimated 2006
Source: CIA Factbook

investment in aviation infrastructure to create an aviation system competitive on the international level.

This lack of aviation infrastructure is reflected in a number of ways. First, the Flight Safety Foundation has reported that Africa has the highest level of accidents per departure of any region in the world at nearly 9.8 accidents per one million departures, compared to a world average of 1.2 accidents per one million departures. This rate of accidents is attributed to poor training for pilots, controllers, and regulatory officials, poor to non-existent radar coverage, high numbers of non-precision approaches, and non-enforced or non-existent legislation (Phillips, 2002). In many developed nations, revenues generated by aviation activity are placed in designated funds for the upgrade infrastructure, however, in Africa this is generally not true; aviation revenues go into the general coffers and are spent on other needs (Phillips, 2002).

Second, there is not a substantial internal demand for air transportation due to the general level of poverty and the increasingly competitive global market has not been kind to African airlines. Almost all of Africa's airlines remain wholly or partly state-owned. The traffic patterns of these carriers reflect Africa's colonial past running north to south, unfortunately placing African airlines at the wrong end of the route, that is, principal flows originate in the northern, wealthy nations of Europe where passengers tend to fly on European national carriers (Graham, 1995). In order for African carriers to compete effectively with these European carriers they must provide equal or superior service in a number of areas including flight punctuality, in-flight service, superior aircraft, comfortable seats, clean cabin, seats, and washrooms, good food, efficient reservation systems, competitive pricing, good check-in, attractive frequent flyer programs, and superior first and business class accommodations. At least seven of these areas are heavily dependent on the quality of the aircraft. Unfortunately, the aircraft of many African airlines are aging and investment for new aircraft is often non-existent. These aging aircraft also do not meet the noise restrictions imposed by many countries and are, therefore, not eligible to land at many international airports. Aircraft leasing is not well developed in Africa, making the acquisition of new aircraft difficult for many carriers who might find this a preferred way to modernize their fleets (Abeyratne, 1998).

Addressing the Issues

Given the lack of domestic demand, the need to compete globally with larger, better established carriers, and the limited funding for aviation development, African nations have attempted to join together. In 1961, ten African nations signed the Treaty on Air Transport in Africa, popularly known as the Yaounde Treaty. Under Article 77 and 79 of the Chicago Convention which provides for joint or international operating organizations, these nations established Air Afrique to operate international service between contracting states and other nations and to provide domestic service within the territories of contracting states. The second major event in African aviation was the Yamoussoukro Declaration on a New African Air Transport Policy (1988). The Yamoussoukro Declaration committed African states to achieving the total integration of their airlines through the liberal exchange of air traffic rights, use of an unbiased computer reservations system, and other joint aviation infrastructure developments. The first phase of the declaration was expected to last two years and result in recommendations for integrating African airlines with the rest of the world. Phase two was to be a three-year effort dedicated to the commercial aspects of aviation including the integration of computer reservation systems (CRSs), joint purchasing of spare parts, maintenance, and overhaul equipment, training of personnel, and so on. In phase three, African carriers were to be integrated into a consortium of competitive entities that would bring about sustained progress in air transport in Africa (Abeyratne, 1998: 34). Progress has been made in a number of areas including the development of the Gabriel Extended Travel Service (GETS) CRS, the establishment of the Air Tariff Coordination Forum of Africa to assist airlines in adapting to international air tariff policies, the opening up of South Africa to intra-African aviation, and efforts to establish an African financing and leasing company (Abeyratne, 1998).

Challenging the Promise in Africa

Unfortunately, one area in which Africa has not made significant progress is the integration of airlines. Air Afrique, one of the oldest jointly owned airlines, declared bankruptcy in 2002 after years of financial crisis. The company's troubles had been blamed on 1) the difficulty of managing an airline owned by 11 states, and 2) Air Afrique mismanagement (BBC News, 2002a). One area of mismanagement cited by critics was the fact that many people with family links to government members and senior officials were allowed to travel free (BBC News 2002b). Other efforts at joint ownership include East African Airlines, a joint venture between the governments of Kenya, Tanzania, and Uganda, which dissolved in the 1970s and Alliance Air, jointly owned by South Africa, Uganda, and Tanzania, which ceased operations in 2000 (BBC News, 2002e). A joint service agreement between Air Mali and Cameroon Airlines also ended in 2001 (BBC News, 2002e). These failures should not be attributed solely to the joint nature of the airlines. Like young, small market carriers around the world, African airlines have often struggled. In 2000, Uganda Airlines went into liquidation after South African Airways withdrew its bid (M2 Communications Ltd, 2000). Nigeria Airways announced a cut of 1,000 employees in January 2002 in a "right-sizing exercise" (BBC News, 2002c). Ghana Airways announced in June 2002 that its debt had risen to US$160 million and creditors were threatening to seize assets (BBC News, 2002d). In short, airlines continue to struggle and that struggle is likely to continue as fuel prices climb to new heights.

Several events raised hopes that Africa was finally beginning to emerge from the old pattern of tightly restricted air service agreements and government ownership that have plagued them in the past. First, activity accelerated to form new airlines that were privately owned and financed by groups of African entrepreneurs. The catalyst was the collapse of Air Afrique, Sabena, and general reductions in service following 9/11 that created a vacuum in air transport service that appeared to leave room to support new-carrier entry (BBC News, 2002b; BBC News, 2002g; BBC News, 2002f). Unfortunately, Africa One, one of the first to get off the ground, suspended operations a year after beginning service to restructure its operations (Wakabi, 2003). It seems that the struggle to create viable African carriers will continue. However, another sign of the changing times in Africa has been the growing movement toward privatization with carriers such as Air Tanzania, Kenya Airways, and Air Mali opening up to private investment (BBC News, 2002e; BBC News, 2002g; Godwin, 2002). In 2004, Virgin Nigeria was formed with Nigeria investors holding 51 percent of the equity and UK-based Virgin Atlantic holding the remaining 49 percent (virginnigeria.com, 2008). Liberalization in bilateral service agreements is also taking hold in Africa. As of the end of 2001, 10 of the 56 nations signing open skies agreements with the United States were from Africa. In December 2007, Delta Airlines became the first major US carrier to offer direct flights between the US, Ghana, Senegal, and Nigeria. Plans call for additional African destinations in 2008, including Kenya, Egypt, and South Africa (Delta, 2007). As US major carriers continue to shift from domestic to international flights, this first foray into Africa might be the beginning of a new trend that would benefit consumers from both North America and Africa even if it puts even more pressure on African airlines themselves.

Prospects for the Future

While traffic growth for the world as a whole declined 2.9 percent in 2001, Africa posted a 1.4 percent gain (ICAO, 2002). Unfortunately, the 3 percent growth in African passenger traffic for 2007 still lags behind the industry average of 6.7 percent (IATA, 2008a). Boeing's 2007 market outlook predicts that the market value of new aircraft in Africa will be only about 2 percent, the lowest value for any region (Boeing, 2007). IATA had predicted that the annual growth rate for Africa through 2011 would be 5.6 percent due to strong GDP growth and new capacity, however, in its most recent financial forecast operating profits for the region's airlines were expected to be zero for 2008 (IATA, 2007; IATA, 2008b). Several developments are essential if Africa is to take advantage of the current growth in traffic and increasing liberalization in international markets. First, the continent must make a commitment to improving aviation safety. Projects continue with the US Federal Aviation Administration, the American Association of Airport Executives, and the US Trade & Development Agency as well as their counterparts in the EU. The goal of these efforts is "to provide the full universe of what they need, a road map to upgrade safety and security and ATC and to put them in touch with funding sources" (Ott, 2001: 108). The International Federation of Air Line Pilots Associations (IFALPA) has worked to document deficiencies in the aviation system and suggest remedies. ICAO funding has been provided to eight African nations through their Technical Cooperation Program (Ott, 2001). Second, African nations need to continue the privatization of airlines. This privatization not only has the potential to create viable, competitive airlines, but removes the government incentives to offer preferential treatment to the state's flag carrier. Third, African nations need to continue to sign liberal bilateral agreements within Africa and with the outside world. The newly created carriers of Africa cannot survive if they are not granted access to outside markets.

Latin America and US Challenge

ICAO groups 32 nations into the Latin American region. This region covers approximately 15 percent of the earth's landmass and is expected to account for roughly 5 percent of world passenger traffic in 2011, unchanged from the 2001 figures (IATA, 2007; ICAO, 2002).

Compared to Africa, Latin America and the Caribbean are more affluent (Table 16.2), support larger domestic markets, attract more tourists, and possess larger, more modern fleets of aircraft. Like Africa, the transportation network tends to be dominated by colonial and imperialist forces with international traffic focused

Table 16.2   Information on South American countries

Country	Area*	Population**	Airports (Paved)***	GDP $****
Argentina	2,766,890	40,301,927	1,272 (154)	13,000
Bolivia	1,098,580	9,119,152	1,061 (16)	4,400
Brazil	8,511,965	190,010,647	4,263 (718)	9,700
Chile	756,950	16,284,741	358 (79)	14,400
Colombia	1,138,910	44,379,598	934 (103)	7,200
Costa Rica	51,100	4,133,884	151 (36)	13,500
Cuba	110,860	11,394,043	165 (70)	4,500
Dominican Rep	48,730	9,365,818	34 (15)	9,200
Ecuador	283,560	13,755,680	406 (104)	7,100
El Salvador	21,040	6,948,073	65 (4)	5,200
Guatemala	108,890	12,728,111	402 (12)	5,400
Guyana	214,970	769,095	93 (9)	5,300
Honduras	112,090	7,483,763	112 (12)	3,300
Jamaica	10,991	2,780,132	34 (11)	4,800
Mexico	1,972,550	108,700,891	1,834 (231)	12,500
Nicaragua	129,494	5,675,356	163 (11)	3,200
Panama	78,200	3,242,173	116 (54)	9,000
Paraguay	406,750	6,669,086	838 (13)	4,000
Peru	1,285,220	28,674,757	237 (54)	7,600
Puerto Rico	13,790	3,944,259	29 (17)	19,600
Surinam	163,270	470,784	50 (5)	7,800
Uruguay	176,220	3,460,607	60 (9)	10,700
Venezuela	912,050	26,023,528	390 (128)	12,800

* Square Km. ** Estimated July 2007 figures *** Data from 2007 **** Estimated 2001
Source: CIA Factbook

primarily on North–South US routes and European links funneled through former imperial capitals (Graham, 1995). Latin America also tends to be far more urbanized than is true for Africa (Taneja, 1988). A review of the airline traffic numbers for selected Central and South American carriers since 11 September shows a very mixed picture (Table 16.3). However, revenue passenger traffic grew by 14.4 percent in 2007 for the region, higher than any other area of the world (IATA, 2008a). As the table shows, some carriers did very well. LAN Airlines not only grew in Chile, but expanded in Latin America with LANArgentina, LANDominica, LANEcuador, and LANPeru. TAM of Brazil appears set to follow this pattern of growth. Its Brazilian sister airline, Varig, declared bankruptcy in 2005 and was eventually purchased by GOL (Air Transport Intelligence, 2008).

Nuutinen (1993) has identified three key problems facing Latin American carriers. First, they compete directly with the aggressive US mega-carriers. With their large domestic base, highly sophisticated yield management systems, and lower cost structures, these mega-carriers have presented their Latin American counterparts with a very difficult challenge. Second, the terms of US bilateral agreements are heavily biased in favor of US interests. Ten Latin American nations have now signed open skies treaties with the United States (Table 8.1), while many others have liberalized their bilateral air service agreements in recent years. The experience with liberalized markets has not been kind to many Latin American carriers. In Chile, the first Latin country to sign an open skies agreement in 1997, LAN-Chile (now LAN Airlines) and Ladeco suffered heavily at the hands of US competitors, American and United Airlines (Graham, 1995). Roughly 14 percent of American's operating revenue comes from Latin America which is currently the highest level for a US carrier (American Airlines, 2001). This clearly makes them a serious challenger, however, LAN Airlines has recovered well since 1995 posting the third highest growth rate of any carrier in the world

Table 16.3   Central and Latin American passenger traffic (000s)

	2006	2005	2004	2003	2002
Aeromexico	8,750	9,160	9,090	8,780	9,220
Avianca	8,000	7,100	5,400	4,880	-
LAN Airlines	8,880	7,970	6,580	5,510	-
Mexicana	9,000	8,900	8,400	8,000	7,800
TACA	3,010	3,160	2,950	3,890	3,710
TAM	25,020	19,570	13,550	11,200	-
Varig	5,780	12,750	12,310	11,040	-

Source: Air Transport Intelligence, www.rati.com

with a 44.8 percent increase in sales. They posted record profits in 1997 and 1998 entering into an alliance with American Airlines (LAN-Chile, 2002). In November 2001, they opened a new cargo terminal in Miami. Cutbacks by US carriers on marginal routes opened up even more opportunities after 9/11. While the more liberal bilateral between the US and Mexico has increased the number of tourists traveling between the two countries and lowered fares, it has also decreased airline yields. Both Aeromexico and Mexicana suffered a combined loss of US$371.5 million in 1992–93 (Graham, 1995). The 1994 Mexican financial crisis sent both carriers to the brink of bankruptcy, however, a planned merger between the two was blocked by the Mexican competition authorities. Both have now been privatized, but are facing competition from the countries new low-cost carriers (Air Transport Intelligence, 2008). Aeromexico joined the SkyTeam alliance while Mexicana became a member of STAR (Moody's Transportation Manual, 2000). Third, less than one-third of Latin America's carriers are now state owned. While this is generally a good trend, the fact that many Latin American governments rushed into the sale of loss-making carriers as part of the general shift toward market economies in the 1990s did nothing to help these carriers adjust to the new realities of industry deregulation and liberalized international operations. In fact, this rush to privatize and throw open markets may have done as much or more to destabilize the Latin American carriers as US mega-carrier competition. The success of efforts by LAN and TAM could lead the way to profit and stability, although the IATA forecast for 2008 predicts the region will suffer an overall loss for 2008. Further, IATA is predicting that the growth through 2011 will be a slow 4.4 percent, slightly ahead of their key North American market with 4.2 percent growth (IATA, 2007; IATA, 2008b).

Caribbean nations in particular have struggled in international aviation. Of the 44 developing nations identified by the Commonwealth Secretariat/World Bank Joint Task Force (2000) as vulnerable small states, that is, population below 1.5 million people, 33 are in the Caribbean region. The United Nations Conference on Trade and Development has also addressed the problem of small island developing states (SIDS). Both reports cited similar concerns and issues for these nations. According to the UN report, SIDS not only face problems associated with their smallness but are 1) more susceptible and vulnerable to natural disasters, 2) geographically remote and dispersed, 3) ecologically fragile, and 4) constrained in terms of transportation and communication infrastructure (Abeyratne, 1999; UN General Assembly, 1993). Tourism is a key component in the economy of most of these nations. Given the generally inaccessible nature of SIDS, air transportation is vital in developing tourism. Many of these nations would benefit from direct non-stop service from their major tourist markets, however, these nations tend to lack the fleet or market access to offer these services themselves forcing their carriers to engage in island hopping (Abeyratne, 1999; Antoniou, 2001). Abeyratne (1999) has suggested that air services in these regions may qualify as natural monopolies and would, therefore, not benefit from the effects of competition, that is, improving efficiency, lowering costs, and so on. Caribbean nations could, however, benefit from a greater focus on regional cooperation and/or integration in a number of areas like aviation.

Turbulence in the Middle East

The Middle East is composed of 14 nations that accounted for roughly 3 percent of the world scheduled passenger traffic in 2001. These 14 countries range widely in size and income (Table 16.4). Like the region of Africa, most aviation activities are focused on international travel rather than domestic service which accounts for less than 20 percent for the region as a whole (Feiler and Goodovitch, 1994). This figure actually hides a great deal of variation; Saudi Arabia has a domestic market that has increased at an average annual rate of 15 percent from 1970 to 1994 carrying over 1.6 million passengers (Ba-Fail, Abed, and Jasimuddin, 2000) while the Gulf States and Kuwait have essentially no domestic air services (Taneja, 1988). In 1982 ICAO identified three attributes of the Middle East that affected

Table 16.4   Information on selected Middle Eastern countries

Country	Area*	Population**	Airports (Paved)***	GDP $****
Bahrain	665	708,573	3 (3)	34,700
Egypt	1,001,450	80,335,036	88 (72)	5,400
Iran	1,648,000	65,397,521	331 (129)	12,300
Iraq	437,072	27,499,638	110 (76)	3,600
Israel	20,770	6,426,679	53 (30)	28,800
Jordan	92,300	6,053,193	17 (15)	4,700
Kuwait	17,820	2,505,559	7 (4)	55,300
Lebanon	10,400	3,925,502	7 (5)	10,400
Oman	212,460	3,204,897	137 (7)	19,100
Qatar	11,437	907,229	5 (3)	75,900
Saudi Arabia	2,149,690	27,601,038	213 (77)	20,700
Syria	185,180	19,314,747	90 (26)	4,500
UAE	83,600	4,444,011	39 (22)	55,200
Yemen	527,970	22,230,531	50 (17)	2,400

* Square Km. ** Estimated July 2007 figures *** Data from 2007 **** Estimated 2007
Source: CIA Factbook

the demand for air travel. First, there is a relatively large movement of people to, from, and within the area. Second, the population density of the area is comparable to North and Latin America. Third, two-thirds of the area's population lives in oil producing nations. In fact, oil and tourism have been key factors in the traffic growth in the Middle East (Graham, 1995; Taneja, 1998).

Many Middle Eastern nations have invested heavily in infrastructure improvements in recent years, particularly airport expansion and fleet renewal. In a virtuous cycle, this passenger traffic and this investment have helped to foster at least two of the fastest growing airlines in the world (Table 16.5). In their most recent report, IATA is predicting traffic growth for the region through 2011 of 6.8 percent (IATA, 2007). Dubai International Airport, located in the UAE, served over 12 million passengers in 2000, making it the busiest airport in the region. King Abdulaziz International Airport in Saudi Arabia served over ten million in that same year (Airports Council International, 2002). Emirates Airline, based out of Dubai, has been one of the fastest growing and highest quality rated carriers in the world. El Al, the Israeli carrier, is considered one of the most efficient carriers in the world. In short, as a whole, the Middle East enjoys a number of advantages over the other two regions discussed in this chapter. While the wealth is still unevenly distributed in the region, efforts have been made by richer nations to assist their neighbors. The single greatest factor limiting the ability of the region to prosper has been political instability and conflict (Graham, 1995).

Table 16.5   Middle Eastern passenger traffic (000s)

	2006	2005	2004	2003	2002
El Al	3,550	3,590	3,210	2,800	2,730
Emirates	17,540	14,500	12,530	10,440	8,500
Etihad	2,750	1,010	340		
Gulf	7,100	7,400	7,490	6,050	5,460
Qatar	7,100	6,040	4,500	3,200	2,300
Saudi Arabia	17,790	16,900	15,770	14,490	14,880

Source: Air Transport Intelligence, www.rati.com

Helping the Developing World

In addition to providing funding and technical advice, developed nations can also contribute to the success of civil aviation in these regions by considering the adoption of a number of recommendations by international agencies and scholars. ICAO addressed these issues in a 1996 report on preferential treatment for member states who are at a competitive disadvantage in international markets. The following is a list of their recommendations for preferential treatment:

1. The asymmetric liberalization of market access in bilaterals with developed countries, including access to more cities and greater fifth freedom rights.
2. More flexibility for air carriers in changing capacity and gauge between routes in bilaterals.
3. Trial periods for carriers of developing nations to operate under liberal arrangements for an agreed period of time.
4. Gradual introduction of more liberal market access over longer periods of time for developing country carriers.
5. Use of liberalized arrangements.
6. Waiver of nationality requirements for ownership.
7. Special allowances for developing national carriers to use more modern, leased aircraft.
8. Preferential treatment for the purpose of slot allocation.
9. More liberal policies for ground handling, conversion of currency, and employment of foreign personnel. (ICAO, 1996)

Several scholars have made some additional recommendations. Abeyratne (1998) has suggested that developed nations consider allowing an air carrier from one country to exercise the air traffic rights on behalf of another carrier in the event that no carrier from that country were able to launch service to that route for economic reasons. Other recommendations by aviation scholars in Findlay, Sein, and Singh's (1997) book on policy reforms in Asian markets include opening freight and charter markets between countries in a region, relaxing code sharing and ownership rules, liberalizing markets before airline privatization, and expanding multilateral agreements with regional neighbors. Longer term, these expanded multilateral agreements could become regional open skies and general trade agreements, even inclusion in General Agreement on Trade in Services (GATS). (These ideas summarize the recommendations of Oum, Forsyth, and Trethaway in Findlay et al, 1997.)

References

Abeyratne, R.I.R (1999), 'The Environmental Impact of Tourism and Air Transport on the Sustainable Development of Small Island Developing States', *Journal of Transportation World Wide*, vol. 4, pp. 55–66.

Abeyratne, R.I.R. (1998), 'The Future of African Civil Aviation', *Journal of Transportation World Wide*, vol. 3, pp. 30–48.

Air Transport Intelligence (2008), 'Focus: The Mexican Airline Sector'. Available at: http://www.rati.com/news/item.asp?id=237348.

Air Transport Intelligence (2008), Available at: http://www.rati.com.

Airports Council International (2002), 2001 Worldwide Airport Traffic Report, ACI, Geneva.

American Airlines (2001), 'Annual Report-2001', www.sec.gov

Antoniou, A. (2001), 'The Air Transportation Policy of Small States: Meeting the Challenges of Globalization', *Journal of Transportation World Wide*, vol. 6, pp.65–92.

Ba-Fail, A.O., Abed, S.Y., and Jasimuddin, S.M. (2000), 'The Determinants of Domestic Air Travel Demand in the Kingdom of Saudi Arabia', *Journal of Air Transportation World Wide*, vol. 5, pp. 72–86.

BBC News (2002a), 'Air Afrique Finally Goes Bust', www.bbc.co.uk, February 7.

BBC News (2002b), 'Pan-African Airline Takes off', www.bbc.co.uk, April 29.

BBC News (2002c), 'Nigeria Airways Halves Workforce', www.bbc.co.uk, January 4.

BBC News (2002d), 'Ghana Airways Seeks Outside Help',www.bbc.co.uk, June 13.

BBC News (2002e), 'Air Mali Strikes Egyptian Alliance', www.bbc.co.uk, May 8.

BBC News (2002f), 'New Airline for West Africa', www.bbc.co.uk, September 6.

BBC News (2002g), 'Air Tanzania Sell-off Delayed'www.bbc.co.uk, August 5.

Boeing (2007) 'Current Market Outlook 2007', Available at: http://www.boeing. com/commercial/cmo/regions.html.

CIA Factbook (2007), www.odci.gov/cia/publications/factbook.

Commonwealth Secretariat/World Bank (2000), *Small States: Meeting the Challenges in the Global Economy*, A Report of the Commonwealth Secretariat/ World Bank Joint Task Force on Small States, London, March.

Delta Airlines (2007), 'Delta expands Africa presence with first nonstop flights between Lagos and New York', Available at: http://news.delta.com/print_doc. cfm?article_id=10917.

Feiler, G. and Goodovitch, T. (1994), 'Decline and Growth, Privatization and Protectionism in the Middle East Airline Industry', *Journal of Transport Geography*, vol. 2, pp. 55–64.

Findlay, C., Sein , C.L., and Singh, K. (eds), (1997), *Asian Pacific Air Transport: Challenges and Policy Reform*. Institute of Southeast Asian Studies, Singapore.

Godwin, N. (2002), 'Kenya Airways Comes to N. America to "do Business", *Boston Ventures Management, Inc.*, June 17.

Graham, B. (1995), *Geography and Air Transport*, John Wiley & Sons, New York.

IATA (2008a), 'Strong 2007 traffic growth set to slow', Available at: http://www. iata.org/pressroom/facts_figures/traffic_results/2008-01-31-01.

IATA (2008b), 'Financial forecast: cyclical downturn ahead in 2008', Available at: www.iata.org/economics.

IATA (2007), 'IATA Economic briefing: passenger and freight forecasts 2007 to 2011', Available at : www.iata.org/economics.

ICAO (2002), 'Press Release: One Year After 11 September Events ICAO Forecasts World Air Passenger Traffic will Exceed 2000 levels in 2003', October 2.

ICAO (1996), *Study on Preferential Measures for Developing Countries*, ICAO Doc AT-WP/1789, August 22.

LAN-Chile (2002), 'Our History', www.lanchile.com.

M2 Communications Ltd (2000), 'Uganda Airlines Corporation to go into Liquidation', www.findarticles.com, March 31.

Moody's Transportation Manual (2000), Mergent FIS, New York.

Nuutinen, H. (1993), 'Fighting to Beat Back the US Majors', *Avmark Aviation Economist*, vol. 10, pp. 11–8.

Ott, J. (2001), 'Rising African Safety Culture Paves Way for New Projects', *Aviation Week and Space Technology*, March 19, pp. 106–9.

Phillips, E.H. (2002), 'Africa Leads in Hull Losses: FSF Cites Challenges to Flying', *Aviation Week and Space Technology*, April 22, pp. 44–5.

Taneja, N.K. (1988), *The International Airline Industry: Trends, Issues, and Challenges*, Lexington Books, Lexington.

United Nations General Assemby (1993), Resolution 47/186, A/RES/47/186, February.

Wakabi, M (2003), 'Africa One Suspends Flights to "Restructure"', *The East African,* Available at: http://www.nationaudio.com/News/EastAfrican/17032003/Regional/Regional1703200336

World Bank (2005), 'African Development Indicators', World Bank, Washington, DC.

World Bank Group (2002), 'Making Monterrey Work for Africa: New Study Highlights Dwindling Aid Flows, Mounting Challenges', Press Release no. 2002/273/S.

Website

Virgin Nigeria, http://www.virginnigeria.com

Chapter 17
Fighting Carbon Emissions

In the Spotlight

A strange thing happened to the airline industry on the way to recovery: the world, particularly the US, was suddenly reminded that aviation had been left out of the debate on carbon emissions and global warming. The 19 December 2006 cover story of *USAToday* rectified this oversight, proclaiming that "Concern grows over pollution from jets: Aviation emissions will take off along with worldwide air travel." The article pointed out that each passenger on a commercial jet from New York City to Denver would generate between 840 and 1,600 pounds of carbon dioxide, roughly the same amount of carbon as a Sports Utility Vehicle (SUV) driven over the period of a month. With air travel projected to continue to increase in the coming decades, aircraft emissions could become one of the largest contributors to global warming by 2050 (Stoller, 2006). The European Commission, already responding to the concerns of its citizens, has proposed including emissions from civil aviation into the European Union (EU) Emissions Trading Scheme (ETS) by 2011 for all internal EU flights and by 2012 for all flights to and from EU airports. The issue has not made its way onto the agenda of the US government which is not surprising given that the Bush administration has only recently acknowledged that the evidence does suggest some warming is occurring that might be related to human activity. US airlines are strongly opposed to the EU action (Pilling and Thompson, 2007). In the EU, the issue has received so much attention that Britain's Prince Charles was forced to defend his decision to fly to New York in January 2007 to accept the Global Environmental Citizen Prize (Reuters, 2007). Meanwhile, the British parliament is considering measures to limit the growth rate of aviation to the rate at which the industry improves its fuel efficiency. At the local level, citizens are rejecting planned increases in aviation activity such as new airport runways or additional flights due to concerns over the environment and global warming (Stoller, 2006). Such complaints stalled for years the expansion efforts at Heathrow Airport in London which just recently added a fifth terminal and still operates with only two runways (Michaels, 2008). Groups such as Sustainable Aviation are working to insure that aviation becomes part of the solution to the problem of greenhouse gases (GHG) through 1) full industry commitment to GHG reduction, 2) incorporation of aviation into a global policy framework, and 3) reduction in the environmental footprint of aviation (Sustainable Aviation, 2006).

With the United States now poised to "go green" and the price of oil over US$100 a barrel, the time appears to be ripe for change (Adler, 2006; Kaihla,

2007; Stone, 2006). The world consumes 85 million barrels of oil every single day (Tertzakian, 2006). The US accounts for roughly 25 percent of total daily consumption, consuming approximately 22 million barrels a day for the week of August 18, 2006 (Energy Information Administration, 2006). Oil accounts for almost 40 percent of the energy needs in the US. Transportation accounts for almost two-thirds of total oil consumption (National Energy Policy Development Group (NEPDG), 2001). Until recently, aviation barely merited an honorable mention in the debate over global warming; the Kyoto Protocol did not include aviation emissions as they were believed to be a minor contributor to global warming when the agreement was first negotiated (Stoller, 2006).

An airline industry that finally posted solid profits after 11 September has proven remarkably reluctant to address carbon emissions and has been even less thrilled with the predictions of some geologists and environmentalists such as Colin Campbell, author of *Oil Crisis* and a chief proponent of an early peak for oil production. Campbell has suggested that the "airline business will go into near extinction as fuel costs soar. Very few people actually need to travel by air. Modern communications makes most business travel unnecessary" (2005: 298). Lester R. Brown, president of the Earth Policy Institute, has offered a less dire prediction for the aviation industry, but he still suggests that cheap airfares, fresh fruit transported by aircraft to out-of-season consumers, and citizens willing to "subsidize this high-cost mode of transportation for their more affluent compatriots" will soon be a thing of the past (Brown, 2006: 234).

The aviation industry has made air travel accessible to millions of consumers in such a safe and reliable manner that most people have come to take it for granted. Only the occasional bankruptcy or accident has thrown it into the spotlight in the past. As the world moves toward a consensus on global warming and carbon emissions, the industry is likely to find itself right in the middle of the debate and challenged on all sides to come up with solutions.

Subject to Debate

The debate about the reality of global warming and its causes has largely been settled in much of the world, but it remains a topic of dispute in the US as the recent visit by former US Vice-President Al Gore to the US Congress illustrated (Kluger, 2007). The EU has put in place a plan to cut energy use by 20 percent by 2020 and increase the share of renewable energy to 12 percent by 2010. The US has no comprehensive plan to address the issue of energy use, carbon emissions or renewable energy. It is counting on markets to drive change (Brown, 2006; McKinnon and Meckler, 2006). Most of the attention in the US has been focused on automobile use. In the electricity generation industry which relies on coal for almost half of its needs, there have been calls for greater use of nuclear power or "clean coal." As for the automobile, renewed interest in ethanol production mostly from corn has already raised food prices without making any serious dent in oil consumption (Grunwald, 2008). The primary concern of the aviation industry has been the cost of petroleum-based jet fuel, not carbon and other emissions and their primary focus has been on technological improvements and air traffic modernization (Pilling and Thompson, 2007).

Growing Impact

The Federal Aviation Administration (FAA) is predicting that the number of US passenger aircraft will increase by 47.3 percent between 2005 and 2020. The projected fuel consumption is expected to increase even more at 68.7 percent for airlines in passenger and cargo service. General aviation fuel consumption is predicted to triple over the same period due to the development and projected popularity of very light jets (Bond, 2007). Currently, all transport modes are believed to be responsible for 23 percent of the total carbon emissions with air transport accounting for 12 percent of this total (Ott, 2007). The jet engine is the chief source of carbon emissions. A jet engine emits more carbon dioxide than the actual weight of the fuel that creates combustion within it (Bond, 2007). According to Environmental Defense, burning a gallon of jet fuel will produce 21.1 pounds of carbon dioxide or about half a pound per passenger per domestic mile or one pound per passenger per international mile. Further complicating the issue is the fact that these emissions tend to take place at high altitude which may represent a greater problem for global warming than those that occur at sea level (Environmental Defense, 2007; Stoller, 2006). Some sources suggest that non-carbon dioxide greenhouse gas (GHG) emissions may be even more significant. These include nitrogen oxide, sulfur oxide, soot, and water vapor (Stoller, 2006).

The aviation industry can roughly be divided into six segments: airlines, manufacturers, airports, general aviation, airspace, and air cargo. These segments exist to some extent throughout the world, although there are some important structural differences. US airlines and air cargo operators are privately owned. Almost all are publicly traded stock companies and subject to financial as well as operational reporting. Airports, on the other hand, are owned by the city or county in which they are located with the exception of some small general aviation airports and military airfields. All but a small number of airports are open to general aviation traffic. The airspace in the US is tightly regulated with an air traffic system managed by the US Federal Aviation Administration. Controllers are public employees who while unionized have limited ability to engage in work actions. For the rest of the world, full or partial government ownership of airlines is common. Airports, on the other hand, are increasingly being privatized or the management of the airport outsourced. General aviation is much less common and many airports are closed to this type of traffic. Airspace is less restricted and in some case such as Africa radar coverage is limited (Rhoades, 2003). These differences may not be the primary factor in driving sector contribution to carbon emissions, but they may affect future support for carbon constraint. Currently, each segment contributes to carbon emissions in a multitude of ways and each is approaching (or not approaching) the issue of emissions at their own pace and in their own way.

Flying Green

Currently, US airlines alone use 53.4 million gallons of jet fuel per day for a total of US$19.5 billion gallons a year. Fuel constitutes 20–30 percent of the total operating costs of an airline, surpassing labor as the single largest expense (Air Transport Association, 2007). Aircraft emissions standards are set by the US Environmental Protection Agency. Responsibility for enforcement of the standards rests with the Federal Aviation Administration. The US guidelines roughly mirror the old international standards set by the International Civil Aviation Organization (ICAO). ICAO's Committee on Aviation Environmental Protection recently approved new guidelines that include recommendations on emissions trading, however, like all ICAO actions, these guidelines are not binding on any nation (Ott, 2007). An aircraft emits carbon dioxide and nitrogen oxide on the ground and while in flight. On the ground, fuel may be burned when the aircraft backs from the gate under power, taxis to the runway, or is repositioned on the airport, either to a new gate or a maintenance hangar on airport property. On the ground, fuel burn has tended to raise concerns about local air and noise pollution rather than carbon emission and has been the subject of complaints from citizens surrounding busy commercial airports. It is the in-flight, upper atmosphere emissions and the creation of contrails (condensed water vapor formed in the wake of an aircraft which are believed to contribute to cloud cover) that has raised the most concern from scientists and environmentalists. These concerns are also the most difficult to address (McKinnon and Meckler, 2006).

Making it Green

Aircraft engines have continued to increase the efficiency of their fuel burn, doubling fuel efficiency over the past 40 years. Engine manufacturers are committed to a further improvement of almost 50 percent (Sustainable Aviation, 2006). These technologies would also reduce carbon dioxide emissions, but are estimated to increase nitrogen oxide emissions by about 40 percent over the same period (McKinnon and Meckler, 2006). Aircraft and their engines are long-lived assets. The replacement of existing fleets with newer more fuel efficient aircraft is a slow process given the cost to aircraft operators. Modifications to existing aircraft would likely yield only modest improvements in efficiency (Bond, 2007). Another option for airlines intent on reducing carbon emissions is the use of alternative fuels. The turbine engine of a large commercial jet uses a high octane form of diesel fuel, commonly called Jet A. Jet A must perform under extreme temperature conditions, particularly the cold of high altitude. Smaller general aviation aircraft use what is called Avgas. As the name implies, Avgas is more closely related to gasoline than diesel (US Department of Energy, 2005). It should be noted that Virgin Atlantic recently tested jet biodiesel on a demonstration flight from London to Amsterdam. No statements on the specific performance of the aircraft have been released, but the plane did successfully make the short flight (United Press International, 2008).

Greening the Neighborhood

Airports have been a focal point for resident and environmental groups concerned about environmental impacts arising from noise and air pollution. In addition to the activity of the aircraft themselves, airports utilize powered vehicles for baggage transfer, aircraft maintenance, emergency response, terminal-to-terminal transportation, terminal-to-parking transportation, and so on. In the US, most airports are accessed through private automobile which adds to the local pollution levels. Since parking fees represent a substantial source of revenue, airports are often reluctant to tamper with this aspect of the airport. Although airport master planning in the US requires that intermodal transportation issues be addressed through the design of parking facilities, rental cars, and public transportation access, the reality is that only 14 airports in the US are linked to rail systems, one of the least polluting forms of transportation, leaving the rest to rely on other forms of surface transportation. (Airport Council International (ACI) and Air Transport Action Group (ATAG), 1998).

Airspace is restricted to a certain extent in all countries due to noise, security, safety, and radar coverage. Examples of restrictions include military facilities, residential neighborhoods, and key public buildings. In the US, airspace is more tightly controlled than in many other regions and is the responsibility of a single entity, the FAA. In regions such as the European Union (EU), multiple air traffic control systems increase the inefficiency of the airspace. Another source of global inefficiency are country limitations on the entry of foreign aircraft either by closing entrance to foreign aircraft or charging fees for entry or overflight, thus encouraging aircraft operators to fly around restrictions which adds to flight times and fuel consumption. The current system of air traffic management also utilizes step-down approaches that require progressive altitude changes and thrust applications in descent to landing, adding to fuel burn (Hughes, 2007).

Freight Green

World air freight growth is closely linked to the overall growth in world GDP and has recovered slowly since 2001, however, recent forecasts predict the annual growth to be 6.8 percent through 2015. Asia, particularly China, is expected to see the highest growth (Graham, 2006). Air freight is carried either as belly cargo on commercial airlines or on dedicated freighter aircraft, some of whom are operated by the airlines themselves. As airlines have struggled to return to profitability, many increased their reliance on air cargo, particularly on Asian to North American routes. Cargo revenue for the world's airlines has increased from a-post 2001 low of US$38 billion in 2002 to roughly US$56 billion for 2006 (Putzger, 2006). Many all-cargo operators act as air freight forwarders, handling the air segment of a shipping operation. This includes operators handling oversized cargo such as Volga-Dnepr. Oversized carriers use some of the largest aircraft in the world, for example, the C-17 and An-124 to ship large industrial equipment. These services have been attractive to firms in industries such as oil and gas where the time saved by shipping equipment by air rather than slower modes of transportation may prove an ideal trade-off to get operations up and running quickly or keep them up and running (Nelms, 2007).

The best-known global shippers are the so-called integrated carriers such as UPS, FedEx, and DHL. While air forwarders such as airlines and all-cargo operators are responsible for only the air portion of travel and require shippers to make their own arrangements to get freight to and from the airport, the "integrated" carriers combine all modes of transportation to provide seamless, door-to-door shipping. FedEx started life as an overnight air freight delivery company while UPS began as a ground delivery company that expanded into air freight later in life. This has not stopped either company from amassing an air fleet that would rank them among the largest airlines in the world (Niemann, 2007).

And the Answer is...

The aviation industry is pursuing a number of actions to reduce GHG emissions. The primary hope for significant reduction lies in new technologies, but certain sectors are currently engaged in actions to change existing processes and/or pursue a holistic approach to the GHG issue. Aircraft and engine manufacturers are currently working on technologies to redesign aircraft wings to reduce drag and fuel burn, utilize advanced lightweight composite materials, and replace existing technology with fuel cells (Sustainable Aviation, 2006). In Europe, the Advisory Council for Aeronautics Research (Acare) has established a goal of reducing nitrogen oxide emissions by 80 percent and carbon dioxide by 50 percent by 2020 (Norris, 2007). The two major US engine manufacturers, General Electric (GE) and Pratt & Whitney, part of United Technologies (UTC), are founding members of the Pew Center Business Environmental Leadership Council (BELC), an organization dedicated to addressing global climate change (Pew Center on Global Climate Change, 2006). UTC, part of the Dow Jones Sustainability index, was named one of the top 100 sustainable companies at the 2005 World Economic Forum in Davos. UTC and Pratt & Whitney have announced a commitment to reducing GHG by 12 percent over the next four years. The company includes key performance indicators for air and carbon dioxide emissions in their public reporting (United Technologies, 2007). GE has also committed to reductions in the intensity of GHG emissions 30 percent by 2008 (Pew Climate, 2007).

The only "drop" in alternative fuel for Jet-A is synthetic jet fuel. It is manufactured through a conversion process from natural gas or coal that produces 1.8 times the carbon dioxide of conventional jet fuel production. Other alternative fuel technologies require engine modification. The use of 100 percent bio-fuels is not currently viable as they freeze at the normal cruising temperatures of large commercial aircraft (Daggett, Hendricks, Walther and Corporan, 2007). The Renewable Aviation Fuels Development Center (RAFDC) at Baylor University has run a series of experiments using alternative fuels for aviation. RAFDC tests examined biodiesel blends of 5, 10, 15, 20, and 25 percent. The best results were obtained for the 20 percent blend. Beyond this level of blend, major changes in engine configuration would be required and significant clouding at cold temperatures is likely. The recent biodiesel test run by Virgin Atlantic used a 20 percent blend. Airbus has also conducted a trial run of the A380 from Filton, UK to Toulouse, France. The A380 was using Rolls-Royce Trent 900 engines and a 20 percent blend as well (Next Energy News, 2008; United Press International, 2008). Boeing is currently exploring the use of cryogenic hydrogen and liquid methane (Daggett, Hendricks, Walther and Corporan, 2007).

General aviation includes all non-commercial, non-military aviation. Most of this segment relies on piston-powered, propeller engines. These craft use Avgas rather than Jet-A fuel. Avgas is more closely related to ethanol. There are over 320,000 general aviation aircraft including helicopter, single, piston engine craft, and turbo-props. In the US, general aviation aircraft fly over 27 million hours annually (General Aviation Manufacturers Association, 2006). RAFDC has tested ethanol and Eythyl Teriary Butyl Ether (ETBE) against avgas in the piston engines commonly used in general aviation propeller aircraft. While some engine modification is required, tests showed that engine efficiencies were higher for ethanol than avgas. These improve even more with increased compression. Mileage per gallon of ethanol was lower. Tests indicated that at 80 percent power ethanol consumed 11 percent more fuel than avgas. Ethanol and ETBE were shown to produce lower emission of carbon monoxide and unburned hydrocarbons, but to increase the emission of carbon dioxide and nitrogen oxide because of lower energy conversion rates, a fact reflected in the level of fuel consumed (Shauck and Zanin, 2001). A modified piston aircraft was flown without significant problems across the Atlantic using ethanol (Shauck and Zanin, 1990). During the transatlantic flight no fuel-related problems were encountered. Considering the price of ethanol in the US at the time of the flight, the cost of the ethanol for the transatlantic crossing was US$160 compared to US$230 for Avgas, even including the reduced mileage (Shauck and Zanin, 2001). Results also indicate that ethanol burns more completely and cleanly than gasoline. The observed reduction in range (mileage) was between 10 and 15 percent (Johnson, Shauck and Zanin, 2000).

There are a number of technologies that can be implemented to improve airport arrival and departure procedures (See Chapter 20 for more information). The Next Generation Air Transportation System (NGATS) is looking at technologies such as 4D Trajectory Management. This technology would involve runway-to-runway planning with auto negotiation equipment in the aircraft that would allow flight crews to adjust the flight plan as necessary to accommodate weather, aircraft separation, airport delays, and so on. Air traffic management (ATM) technologies combined with Global Positioning Satellites (GPS) and Automatic Dependent Surveillance-Broadcast (ADS-B) to implement proper spacing could be used to replace the step-down descents with Continuous Descent Arrivals (CDAs). It is estimated that CDAs could save between 100 and 300 pounds of fuel (Hughes, 2007). The US Air Transport Association, a trade organization representing US airlines, and the FAA support an airspace management initiative called Secure America's Future Energy (SAFE). SAFE would link a satellite-based air traffic system to ground-based technologies in order to reduce delays and shorten travel. SAFE has estimated that implementation of these actions could save 400,000 barrels of oil daily by 2030 and reduce carbon emissions by 57.5 million metric tons per year (Air Transport Association, 2007). The European equivalent of this program is the Single European Sky ATM Research Programme (SESAR) and the Advisory Council for Aerospace Research in Europe (ACARE).

While there are a number of technological solutions being studied, changing processes can also have an impact on carbon emissions. Airlines are taking a number of actions that reduce fuel burn and emissions on the ground, primarily out of concern with rising fuel costs. These actions include the elimination of power backing (backing the airplane from the gate using its engines) in favor of small tugs that push the aircraft back from the gate and "supertugs" that can be used to tow aircraft around the airport itself (repositioning it to another gate or a maintenance hanger). EU airlines are addressing government and customer concerns by developing explicit plans to manage and report on a range of environmental issues. For example, British Airways has a section on their website that reports on their environmental actions in the area of noise, air quality, waste and biodiversity. There is also a way to calculate and offset your carbon dioxide emissions. Most of the EU airlines have affirmed their support for the Emissions Trading Scheme and called for action on an international scheme for emissions trading. Although not stated, a widely adopted international emissions scheme would insure that no airlines are unduly disadvantaged in pursuit of GHG emission deduction (British Airways website). Air France also reports on their actions toward sustainable development including their tracking reports for emissions and efforts to reduce emissions through fleet renewal, alternative fuel ground vehicles, and air-rail link options (Air France, 2007). In contrast to these examples, US airlines do not include any information of this nature in their investor reports or on their websites. A few US airlines do mention environmental issues, but usually only to affirm their "commitment" to the environment. Recently, some sites have included information directing concerned customers to outside websites such as GoGreen to explore means of offsetting carbon emissions.

Unlike their airline counterparts, US airports have been more aggressive in their approach to environmental issues. Three examples highlight the types of action that airports are employing. Dallas-Fort Worth Airport (DFW) is the world's third busiest airport with 1,900 flights per day. DFW has taken a very proactive approach to environmental issues and was recently recognized by the US Environmental Protection Agency as part of their National Environmental Performance Tracking program. Over the past five years, DFW has reduced its air emissions by 95 percent and converted 100 percent of its light-to-medium vehicles on airfield fleet as well as bus and shuttle operations to alternative fuels (DFW News Release, 2007). The Port of Seattle which includes the Sea-Tac airport as well as the seaport in Seattle is another example of a committed and proactive local entity. The port has a staff of 22 individuals responsible for environmental issues and compliance and has converted most of their on-airport vehicles to natural gas. In addition, they have redesigned field operations to reduce the number of tanker trucks needed on the airfield (Port of Seattle, 2006). The Airport Carbon Management Group (ACMG), based in the UK, was created to explore ways to reduce carbon emissions, primarily through improved energy use. To date, the efforts of this group have reduced carbon emissions by 13,000 tons per year (Sustainable Aviation, 2006). Unlike the US, there are also over 40 airports in Europe with air-rail links and an additional 49 links planned. It has been estimated that the Heathrow Express removes over 3,000 cars a day from London roads (ACI–ATAG, 1998).

The integrated freight carriers are making some of the greatest efforts to address environmental issues, including carbon emissions. DHL has launched its GoGreen program that allows shippers to select low carbon emission modes of shipping. This option was provided to delegates attending the World Economic Forum in Davos as part of the Forum's carbon neutral goal for the 2007 conference. DHL has entered a joint venture with Lufthansa Cargo called AeroLogic. AeroLogic will utilize the more fuel efficient B777 primarily to Asia. DHL is also exploring the use of biogas, hybrid, and fuel cell vehicles for ground shipping and packaging options that reduce GHG emissions (DHL website; Turney, 2008). FedEx is also exploring alternative fuels for its ground vehicles and has recently launched 18 Optifleet E700 hybrid vehicles to its fleet. On the aviation side, FedEx has retired its remaining B727 aircraft and hush-kitted older aircraft, both of which reduce the overall fleet emissions and noise levels. Beginning in 2009, FedEx will begin acquiring B777 freighters which provide 18 percent greater fuel efficiency. The FedEx Oakland, California, facility has one of the largest industrial solar operations in the US (FedEx website, 2007; Moorman, 2008). UPS was the launch customer in the mid-1990s for the low emission version of the GE CF6-80C2 engine and is installing ADS-B in all its aircraft. It expects to save a million gallons of jet fuel a year and reduce noise and nitrous oxide emissions (Moorman, 2008). UPS has also taken a number of actions to reduce fuel consumption and emissions from its ground fleet including trailering trucks onto railcars and optimizing driving routes. In addition, they deployed 50 new hybrid vehicles to their fleet in 2006. These hybrids join a fleet of 12,000 low emission vehicles already in operation (Niemann, 2007). UPS has established key performance indicators (KPI) for environmental performance that include ground and aviation emissions targets. These are reported on their website (UPS, 2007).

Aviation in Green

With the exception of US airlines, other sectors of the aviation industry are taking important steps to address GHG and climate change. While it would be incorrect to say that the airline industry has taken no actions to reduce energy use, to switch to renewable fuels, or to reduce emissions, these actions have been driven largely by higher fuel prices rather than other concerns. This may not be surprising given that airlines as a group (and US airlines in particular) are only now beginning to recover from the effects of 11 September. This segment of the industry has also struggled over time to post a consistent profit (Loomis and Buffet, 1999). Unfortunately, airlines have tended to react to their external environment rather than taking a proactive stance. This is not the case with much of the rest of the industry. The Bali Conference, recently held to discuss a post-Kyoto regime, will probably be the first of many conferences to come and it is unlikely that aviation will be given a "pass" this time in the fight against global warming. The world will be expecting it to do its part.

References

Adler, J. (2006), 'Going Green', *Newsweek*, July 16: 43–52.
Air France (2007), 'Sustainable Development', Available at: www.airfrance.us/US/en/local.
Air Transport Association (2007), 'US Airlines Support Development of Alternative Fuels', *ATA Issue Brief*, Available at: www.airlines.or/government/issuesbrief/alt+fuels.htm.
Air Transport Association (2007), 'ATA and 'Safe' Agree that Modernized ATC will Significantly Reduce Fuel Consumption and US Oil Dependence', *ATA News Release*. Available at: www.airlines.or/government/issuesbrief/alt+fuels,htm
Airport Council International (ACI) and Air Transport Action Group (ATAG) (1998), *Air Rail Links: Guide to Best Practic*, Geneva: ACI-ATAG Press.
Bond, D. (2007), 'Green is for Go', *Aviation Week and Space Technology*, August 19: 52–5.
Brown, L.R. (2006), *Plan B 2.0*, London: W.W. Norton & Company.
Campbell, C.J. (2005), *Oil Crisis*, Essex, UK: Multi-Science Publishing Company Ltd.

Daggett, D.L., Hendricks, R.C., Walther, R., and Corporan, E. (2007,), 'Alternative Fuels For Use in Commercial Aircraft', Boeing Company, Seattle.

DFW News Release (2007), 'DFW International Airport's Environmental Success Lands EPA Recognition – Earns Participation in National Environmental Performance Track Program', Available at: www.dfwairport.com

Energy Information Administration (2006), 'Prime Supplier Sales Volumes', Available at: www.tonto.eia.doe.gov/dnav/pet/pet_cons_prim_dcu_nus_m.htm.

Environmental Defense (2007), 'How Your Pollution is Calculated', Available at: http://www.fightglobalwarming.com/content.cfm?contentid=5043.

General Aviation Manufacturers Association (2006), 'Industry Facts', Available at: www.gama.aero/aboutGAMA/industryFacts.php.

Graham, M. (2006), 'Emerging Markets Drive Growth', *Air Cargo World*, May: 21–34.

Grunwald, M. (2008), 'The Clean Energy Scam', *Time*, 7 April, pp. 39–45.

Hughes, D. (2007), 'ATM is no Silver Bullet', *Aviation Week and SpaceTechnology*, August 19: 66–8.

Johnson, G., Shauck, M.E. and Zanin, M.G. (2000), *Performance and Emissions Comparison Between Avgas, Ethanol, and Etbe in an Aircraft Engine*, Renewable Aviation Fuel Development Center, Baylor University, Available at: http://www3.baylor.edu/bias/publications/avgasethanol/etbe.pdf.

Kaihla, P. (2007), 'Go Green. Get Rich: Problem #1-Global Warming', *Business 2.0*, January/February: 68–9.

Kluger, J. (2007), 'What Now?' *Time*, April: 50–60.

Loomis, C. and Buffet, W. (1999), 'Mr. Buffet on the Stock Market', *Fortune*, Special Issue, vol. 140 (10): 212–220.

McKinnon, J.D. and Meckler, L. (2006), 'Bush Eschews Harsh Medicine in Treating US Oil "Addiction"', *The Wall Street Journal*, August 9, pp. A1, A9.

Michaels, D. (2008), 'Heathrow Makeover to Heat Up Airline Wars', *The Wall Street Journal* Online, March 6.

Moorman, R.W. (2008), 'Greening the Fleet', *Air Cargo World*, January, pp. 21–7.

National Energy Policy Development Group (NEPDG) (2001), *Reliable, Affordable, and Environmentally Sound Energy for America's Future*, Washington, DC: US Government Printing Office.

Nelms, D. (2007), 'Oversized Ambitions: The Outsized Air Cargo Market is Growing Rapidly', *Air Cargo World*, April: 16–20.

Next Energy News (2008), 'Airbus A380 Becomes First Commercial Jet to Use Biofuel', Available at: http://www.nextenergynews.com/news1/next-energy-news2.4d.html.

Niemann, G. (2007), *Big Brown: The Untold Story of UPS*, John Wiley & Sons, San Francisco.

Norris, G. (2007), 'Green Machines', *Aviation Week and Space Technology*, August 19: 62–4.

Ott, J. (2007), 'Clearing the Air', *Aviation Week and Space Technology*, August 19: 54–5.

Pew Center on Global Climate Change (2006), *Getting Ahead of the Curve: Corporate Strategies that Address Climate Change*, (ed.) Hoffman, A.J., University of Michigan.

Pew Center on Global Climate Change (2007), *Business Environmental Leadership Council*, www.pewclimate.org/companies_leading_the_way_belc.

Pilling, M. and Thompson, J. (2007), 'Carbon storm', *Airline Business*, February, pp. 54–6.

Port of Seattle (2006), 'Environmental Programs', www.portseattle.org/community/environment.

Putzger, I. (2006), 'Can Cargo Yield Profits', *Air Cargo World*, June: pp. 21–5.

Reuters News Agency (2007), Price Charles Cancels Ski Trip to Help Save Planet, www.enn.com/today_PF.html?id=12068.

Rhoades, D.L. (2003), *Evolution of International Aviation: Phoenix Rising*, Aldershot, UK: Ashgate Publishing.

Shauck, M.E. and Zanin, M.G (2001), *The Present and Future Potential of Biomass Fuels in Aviation*, Renewable Aviation Fuel Development Center, Baylor University. www.baylor.edu/bias/publications/bomassfuels.pdf

Shauck, M.E. and Zanin, M.G. (1990), *The First Transatlantic Flight on Ethanol Fuel, Renewable Aviation Fuel Development Center,* Baylor University, www.baylor.edu/bias/publications/trasnatlanticflight.pdf. Accessed February 3, 2007.

Stoller, G. (2006), 'Concern Grows Over Pollution From Jets: Aviation Emissions Will Take Off Along With Worldwide Air Travel', *USA Today*, December 19, pp. 1A–2A.

Stone, B. (2006), The Color of Money, *Newsweek*, November 13, pp. E10–E15.

Sustainable Aviation (2006), *Sustainable Aviation Progress Report 2006*, www.sustainableaviation.co.uk Accessed April 30, 2007.

Tertzakian, P. (2006), *A Thousand Barrels a Second: The Coming Oil Break Point and the Challenges Facing an Energy Dependent World, New York: McGraw-Hill.

Turney, R. (2008), 'Virtual Air, Air Cargo World', March, pp. 13–14.

United Press International (2008), Virgin Atlantic to Test Jet Biofuel, Available at: http://www.upi.com/NewsTrack/Top_News/2008/02/06/virgin_atlantic.

United Technologies. (2007), 'Responsibility', Available at: www.utc.com/responsibility/environment.htm.

US Department of Energy (2005), Biofuels Encyclopedia, USDOE, Washington, DC.

Websites

British Airways, www.britishairways.com/travel/crenv/public/en_gb

DHL, www.dpwn.de

GoGreen, www.gogreeninitiative.org

FedEx, www.fedex.com/us/about/responsibility/environment.html

UPS, www.ups.com

Chapter 18
Diverging Visions

Getting From Here to There

A strange thing happened in the closing years of the twentieth century—the vision of the two remaining large commercial aircraft (LCA) makers began to diverge in ways that seem to suggest that both can not be right. For its part, Boeing sees a world in which passengers will decide to skip the overcrowded hub with its security lines and airline transfers. Passengers, they believe, will prefer to fly point-to-point to their destination in an airplane with the range to reach distant shores without stopovers. In short, the market of the future is fragmenting, not concentrating passengers and the airlines of the world need an aircraft that can serve this need at an economical cost. The Boeing solution is the B787, a mid-sized, twin-engine, wide-body aircraft that they believe will use 20 percent less fuel than a comparable sized aircraft. On the other hand, Airbus sees a world where continuing population growth in major hub cities, time-zone differences, and pressures on airport capacity will necessitate a more intense, efficient use of the hub-and-spoke system. To achieve this efficiency, they believe that airlines will need larger aircraft in order to land more passengers with fewer flights. The Airbus solution is the A380. The story of how these two giants of the aerospace world came to their visions depends on who is telling the tale. Only time will determine who is right in this high stakes game of aviation forecasting. Whatever the outcome, the process reveals a great deal about the players and the industry they call their own.

Downturns and New Visions

The early years of the 1990s were not good for the airlines or the people who supplied them with aircraft. As the economy slowed, airline losses mounted and airlines engaged in all the usual responses cited in Chapter 14. It seemed to both aircraft makers as though the answer to the cost pressures on world airlines was a bigger plane with the lower seat miles costs that size would bring. By this time, Airbus had a family of aircraft that could compete with their Boeing rival in every class except the top where the B747 dominated. Airbus was convinced that it was at this end of the market that Boeing was making its biggest profits. In fact, Aris (2002) has put forth the claim that Boeing makes US$30 million per B747 although Newhouse (2007) disputes this notion and claims that Boeing's most profitable aircraft was the extended range B767. Whatever the truth of the matter,

Airbus believed these profits allowed Boeing to undersell Airbus on competing models. Further, Airbus felt that they could not achieve their stated goal of 50 percent market share without an aircraft to compete with the B747. With these considerations in mind, Airbus was determined to enter the market with what they first called the ultra-high-capacity aircraft. They knew that the cost of development would be high and had considered various partnerships, however, it was not until new Boeing CEO Phil Condit mentioned in an interview one month before the Farnborough Air Show that they were exploring "larger aircraft" that Airbus decided to put their planning into high gear and contact Boeing about a possible joint project to study the concept (Aris, 2002).

The results of this joint study would be the subject of much debate while the motives of the two players would result in endless speculation. Both players calculated the cost of development at between US$14.5 and US$15.5 billion, but they did not agree on the market size. Airbus forecast a market for 500 to 600 aircraft over a ten-year period. Boeing saw a much smaller market between 300 and 350. This difference is significant because it determines the all-important breakeven number that is often the key factor in deciding whether to proceed with an aircraft project. To Boeing, the analysis meant that "for some unknown period of time these airplanes, if built, would be sold for much less than it had cost to develop them because the various factories building them would not yet have come down the learning curve" (Newhouse, 2007; 149–50). It is difficult to determine at this stage whether the Boeing reluctance to proceed with the project was because they truly did not see a market for the very large aircraft or because the rising costs of the B777 and the need to modernize the B737 made the company averse to assuming the risk of this new endeavor. Some inside Boeing even claim that their initial interest was simply a way to trap Airbus in a losing proposition (Newhouse, 2007).

Meanwhile Boeing's behavior during this period seemed to indicate to many observers that the company did not have a strategy for moving forward. Boeing would explore a series of new B747 versions with prospective customers before announcing their intention to proceed with the so-called Sonic Cruiser, an aircraft capable of flying just below Mach 1 over extended ranges. Unfortunately, this aircraft met with even less interest than the slight modifications proposed to the B747 because trans-sonic flight would save little time and use far too much fuel to do so. Ultimately, Boeing would decide to produce the B747-800, an aircraft with a new wing and a number of advanced features including lighter construction materials and higher-performance engines that would make it a much bigger leap in design than the earlier proposed derivations, and a totally new aircraft, the B787. For their part, Airbus would push on alone with the A3XX as it came to be called. As the 1990s slump turned into a booming new economy, Boeing attempted to ramp up its production and bury Airbus only to be caught in a production nightmare. This disarray and the confusion of its earlier efforts to come up with a strategy certainly helped Airbus in their marketing efforts, their attempt to get launch aid from various European governments, and their reorganization of the Airbus structure itself. The starting gun for the great aircraft order race was fired in

April 2000 with the Emirates Airline order of 10 A-3XX aircraft, soon to be given the name A380 (Aris, 2002)

Comparing Cases, Comparing Planes

The Airbus case for a very large jet was built on several issues. First, the 747 was nearing the natural end of its life. The design had been conceived in the 1950s and developed in the 1960s. The oldest were now approaching 25 years of age. These aging aircraft would have to be replaced by the world's airlines with a craft of equal or larger size that utilized the newest in aviation technology. Second, Airbus looked to the rapidly growing regions of Asia with their large mega-cities and eight of the ten top airports as an ideal market. The vast time differences also meant that an airline catering to passenger preferences for arrival would bunch flights around these preferences making fewer, larger planes a matter of capacity for airports. Third, Airbus reasoned that the operating costs of the A380 would be 15 to 17 percent better; the plane would have almost 50 percent more space in the cabin but would only require 12 to 15 percent more to lift this weight into the air, thus the cost per seat mile would be less (Aris, 2002). Fourth, Airbus believed that the A380 would help to protect the A340 which was not faring well against the B777. The A340 was a longer-range mini-jumbo with four engines while the B777 could fly a similar range with two fewer engines making it more economical to operate. Airbus hoped that fleet commonality would encourage "Airbus customers" to choose the A340 despite this operating cost issue. Fifth, Airbus countered critics concerned with the size (and potential engineering challenges associated with size) with the argument that the A380 was really only 35 percent bigger than the B747 (Newhouse, 2007).

In addition to their concerns about market size resulting from fragmentation of the market itself, Boeing is betting that the A380 with its 550 seats will be too large for many markets, making the B747-800 with 450 plus seats a better option. Further, they believe the freighter version of this aircraft will prove a better cargo carrier than the A380 and cost much less. In effect, they believe that the A380 will be even further squeezed at the top of the market, further stretching out its time to profitability. Publicly, Boeing is convinced that they have "guessed right" and that their line-up of the B747-800, B777, and the new B787 will outperform the A380 (Newhouse, 2007). Table 18.1 shows the vital statistics on the latest entrants into the large commercial market.

Whose Down Now?

It is interesting to compare the conclusion of the recent entrants into the Airbus/ Boeing book saga: Lynn (1998), Aris (2002), and Newhouse (2007). The Lynn (1998) book *Birds of Prey* concludes by noting that Airbus was then taking between

Table 18.1   Comparison of B787 and A380

	B787	A380
Seating	290–330	525–853
Range	2,500–3,000 nautical miles	8,200 nautical miles
Wing Span	170 feet	261.8 feet
Length	186 feet	239.3 feet
Cruising Speed	Mach 0.85	Mach 0.89
Maximum Take-off Weight	364,000 pounds	1,235,000 pounds
Cargo Volume	4,400 cubic feet	650 cubic feet
Fuel savings	20 % < per comparable plane	12 % < per passenger
Orders to date	369	189

Source: Boeing website www.boeing.com. Airbus website www.airbus.com

30 and 35 percent of the market and posting steady profits while Boeing had dropped out of the superjumbo race and blinked over the trade war started by their effort to sign exclusive contracts. Several years later, Aris (2002) would end his book on the great battles with a list of the latest Boeing scandals—US$1.1 billion charge for their satellite business, investigation for misappropriation of confidential document by Boeing from Lockheed-Martin, and the Boeing tanker contract with the Air Force. Newhouse (2007) would close the latest installment of this saga with the observation that Airbus had "begun mixing complacency with an arrogance of the kind usually associated with Boeing" (222) and was showing signs of the same lack of strategy and leadership that had plagued Boeing in the 1990s. In short, the race continues with the two key players trading the lead, highlighting each "sale", and spinning their tales in the trade wars. The reality is that neither of these companies could (or should want) to supply the whole market for LCAs. If by some chance one disappeared tomorrow another challenger would arise. Despite the talk, competition is good and "good competitors" are priceless; they push you to achieve your very best. Without the Airbus leap into composite materials and fly-by-wire, it is doubtful that Boeing would have sought to incorporate this technology in the B777 or extend its use in the B787. Without the clear knowledge that the competition is "breathing down your neck", the arrogance of the "I build it, you buy it" manufacturer would continue; the airlines themselves would be clamoring to find a new manufacturer. In the latest round, however, the US Air Force has decided that the future of their tanker program lies with Northrop Grumman Corp and their European Partner, EADS, the parent company of Airbus. The potential US$35 billion deal went to them over rival bidder Boeing who has supplied the

Air Force's tanker needs for over 50 years (Tessler, 2008). If EADS can firmly establish itself in the lucrative military market, then it will have a further cushion against vagaries of commercial aviation and the opportunity to apply research and development activities funded by "the government" to civilian aviation.

Still, there will be a few interesting decades ahead to see which of the LCA manufacturers has guessed right about the market—fragmenting or concentrating around major hubs. The 2007 market outlook issued by both companies clearly highlights their differing visions of the future (Table 18.2). Note the big differences in the estimated market for intermediate twin and large aircraft. According to Newhouse (2007), the next big battleground will be around the replacement for the single aisle aircraft (B737 and A320). These aircraft make up the bulk of the market. This end of the market is also most vulnerable to potential competition from the number three and four players in commercial aviation, Embraer and Bombardier. Both of these firms already produce aircraft in the 110–120 seat range and could well move in to compete with their larger Boeing/Airbus cousins. Then there is Asia!

The Asia Airbus

The question of an Asian competitor in the LCA market has been around for years. While Airbus does its share of outsourcing, typical of aerospace manufacturing, Boeing has relied heavily on Asian companies for manufacturing and, increasingly,

Table 18.2   Boeing/Airbus 2007 market outlook

	Boeing	Airbus
Passenger traffic	4.5 percent	4.9 percent
Cargo	6.1 percent	
Passenger delivery		
Total	28,600	24,300
Single aisle	17,650	16,620
Small twin	3,700	4,008
Intermediate twin	6,290	1,936
Large	960	1,698

Source: Company websites

design work as well. The Japanese "heavies" helped to design the fuselage for the B767 in 1978. By the time it came to designing the B777, Japanese companies were working side by side with Boeing engineers for critical component design. The electronic, paperless design of the B777 saved time and money, but it also facilitated the free flow of design information that in the past would have been unthinkable. To many people in Boeing, the real value-added skill is systems integration, the broad systems understanding of how things work. As long as Boeing retained this position, they believed the competitive risks of information sharing were minimal, however, this close collaboration has periodically raised concerns from others inside Boeing who fear that the company is training a future competitor and losing vital knowledge and skills in its push to outsource more of its operations. Ultimately, many in Boeing believe that the Japanese are too risk averse to strike out on their own and will be content with the role Boeing allows them to play (Newhouse, 2007). This belief may have been in error as whilstHonda, Mitsubishi, and Toyota have announced plans to enter the market, Honda and GE have announced a joint effort to produce a jet engine for a new generation of small, low-cost business jets (Woodyard, 2008). Mitsubishi Heavy Industries is not only entering the regional jet market in the 70–90 passenger range but has announced that All Nippon Airways will be the launch customer (Reuters, 2008). Toyota has agreed to invest 10 billion yen in the Mitsubishi project (Watanabe, 2008). It appears that Boeing (and now Airbus) may have underestimated the potential for competition from Japan.

The same can not be said for the Chinese who have shown themselves capable of moving rapidly into high-tech manufacturing and design. The Chinese are now manufacturing the complete wing for the A320 as well as landing gear. Plans call for an assembly plant to be built in Tianjin for the A320. Airbus and the China Aviation Industry Corporation (AVIC I) have announced a joint venture engineering center with the ultimate goal of making China a full-risk-sharing partner capable of assuming complete responsibility for design as well as manufacturing (Newhouse, 2007). In 2003, AVIC I signed a formal contract with GE to supply engines for the first homegrown commercial aircraft, the ARJ21-700. The ARJ21-700 was originally designed as a 70–90 seat aircraft, but the AVIC I Commercial Aircraft Company (ACAC) has announced that the base model will have 90 seats. An even longer version, the ARJ21-900, is expected to makes its maiden voyage in 2008 (ACAC Press Release, 2006; GE Press Release, 2003). While these aircraft currently compete against the regional jets of Embraer and Bombardier, there is no reason to believe that the Chinese are not interested in expanding their line of aircraft. From a Boeing/Airbus perspective, the most dangerous combination might be a joint Chinese/Japanese venture into LCA manufacturing; this would combine the financial resources of the Chinese with the extensive aerospace background of the Japanese (Newhouse, 2007). Further, this Asian Airbus would be well positioned to take market share in one of the most rapidly growing aviation regions of the world. It is true that in China itself there is only one buyer of aircraft, the Chinese government. As noted throughout this book, the link between aviation, economics, and politics is always close. If China is successful in re-establishing its ancient hegemony over the Asian region, then the aircraft it produces are certain to benefit, directly and indirectly, inside and outside of China.

At the present time, the Asian efforts are targeted at the lower end of the commercial jet market and are not a threat to the LCA manufacturers, however, this end of the market appears to be getting very crowded. If the trend toward small aircraft and point-to-point operations continues, then there may be room for all of these new players. On the other hand, two other possibilities are clearly possible. The most immediate threat comes from the prospect that Embraer or Bombardier will continue to move up the food chain to produce aircraft to compete with the successor to the B737/A320. Given their expertise and existing facilities it would seem to be a less difficult move than for either the new Japanese or Chinese competitors. Further down the road is the potential for competition from the Asia players who, like Airbus before them, may not be content with the lower end of the market. In any event, neither Boeing nor Airbus can afford to underestimate the potential competition as Boeing learned in the case of Airbus. A firm backed by the resources and will of its government is not to be taken lightly.

Real Men Sell Big Engines

There is an old joke in the aviation industry that men sell engines but real men sell big engines. (The same, of course, can be said of plane.s) It is certainly true that the twenty-first century would see the big three LCA engine makers producing engines for big planes. All three have a version for the biggest commercial plane ever produced, the A380 (Table 18.3), but in some ways the times are changing. The old way of doing business in the aerospace industry was driven by an engineering mentality that said that if you built it to some engineering ideal of performance and standard then they (the airlines) would buy it; real men would sell it in the great game of high stakes/high politics aerospace. Increasingly, the engine manufacturers are finding that customer service is the driving factor in sales. For the men selling these engines, this is a profound change. The job no longer centers on dazzling "them" with specifications and performance data; it is all about finding out what the customer wants, listening to their concerns, addressing their needs. In short, customer service, not engineering specs win the day. Further, the money is not in the engine sale itself but in the aftermarket services. As an example, GE offers OnPoint Solutions, a comprehensive program to meet operational, financial, and technical needs. The program will collect historical data, establish baselines for use and performance, identify upcoming changes in demand, and forecast future needs costs. The program offers "lower, predictable, guaranteed pricing", asset management, leasing, engine swaps, and spare parts control (GE website). Given the critical nature of the aircraft engine, airlines find that outsourcing the maintenance to the Original Equipment Manufacturer (OEM) only makes sense. The engine makers find that over the life of the engine itself they make far more money in the afterlife service.

Table 18.3   Large commercial aircraft engines

Manufacturer	Engine	In-Service Date	Aircraft Example
Pratt & Whitney	GP7000	TBD	A380
	PW6000	2007	A318
General Electric	GP7000	2007	A380
	GEnx	TBD	B787
Rolls-Royce	Trent 900	2007	A380
	Trent 1000	TBD	B787
	Trent XBW	TBD	A350

Source: Company websites

Flying Forward

In what Newhouse in a previous book called the sporty game, the future still looks like a high stakes competition to make really big sales. Each side will announce the total sales after each air show as proof that they are winning, closing the gap, meeting customer needs, and so on. If the past holds true in the future, both Airbus and Boeing will be "surprised" when a new competitor challenges them for a share of the market. The B787 and A380, while touted as "changing the experience of flying", will likely end up packing the seats in so that airlines can get the most out of their assets. Presidents and Prime Ministers will still go out around the world privately pitching "their" aerospace company. However, sometimes things really do change. The industry faces a number of challenges in this new century—carbon emissions limits (Chapter 17), new technology and capacity demands (Chapter 20), rising costs, particularly for fuel (Chapter 14), and liberalizing markets (Chapter 15). If it can keep its eyes on the skies and not on the current sales numbers, then the future may be bright.

References

ACAC (2006), 'ACAC ARJ21 Chinese Regional Jet Aircraft Production Starts, Adds Seats', Available at: http://www.acac.com.cn/News/Media/20060222C110831.html.
Aris, S. (2002), *Close to the Sun: How Airbus Challenged America's Domination of the Skies*, Arum Press, London.

GE Press Release (2003), 'GE Signs Definitive Agreement with Cina for Regional Jet Engines', Available at: http://www.geae.com/aboutgeae/presscenter/cf34/cf34_20031112.html.

Lynn (1998), *Birds of Prey: Boeing vs. Airbus – A Battle for the Skies*, Four Walls, Eight Windows, New York.

Newhouse, J. (2007), *Boeing versus Airbus: The Inside Story of the Greatest Competition in Business*, Alfred A. Knopf, New York.

Reuters Limited (2008), 'ANA weighs Buying 30 Mitsubishi Regional Jets, Report Says', *USAToday* online edition, Available at: http:///www.usatoday.com/pt/cpt?action=cpt&title=ANA+weighs+buying.

Tessler, J. (2008), 'Northrop, EADS win $35B Air Force deal', ABCNews, Available at: http://abcnews.go.com/print?id=4367303.

Watanabe, C. (2008), 'Toyota Asked to Invest in Jet Project', *USAToday* online edition, Available at: http:www.usatoday.com/pt/cpt?action=cpt&title=Toyota+asked+.

Woodyard, C. (2008), 'Honda, GE Build New Jet Engine', *USAToday* online edition, Available at: http:www.usatoday.com/pt/cpt?action=cpt&title=Honda+GE+build+.

Chapter 19

After the Revolution

Trading Time for Money

Like all of the aviation and aerospace industry, the air cargo world was rocked by the events of September 11. Unfortunately, nearly seven years after these events the industry is still facing many unanswered questions, specifically over cargo security requirements and fuel prices. While companies tout the newest and latest technologies for tracking and screening cargo, many industry experts wonder how reliable the new technologies will prove to be, how quickly they can be deployed, and who will pay for them. Further adding to cargo industry uncertainty is the prospect of a world economic slowdown and the rising price of oil. Both of these issues threaten the phenomenal growth of air cargo by raising questions in the perennial debate of speed versus cost. Long security lines are slowing the flow of freight while increasing regulations (with the mass of paperwork that this usually entails) are adding to overall costs. These factors might make buyers and suppliers rethink their international versus domestic sourcing options. The disadvantage of a tightly linked, time-sensitive system is that it is easily disrupted. Rising prices for transportation (related to the price of oil) and slowing sales have many firms re-thinking the need for speed, opting for lower-cost shipping solutions or suppliers closer to home, and building up emergency inventories (or pushing these demands onto suppliers as logistics-leading WalMart has continued to do). It appears that air freight, the only major mode of transportation whose average length of haul fell during the 1990s, may witness a reversal in this trend as slower modes supplant it due to cost (Bureau of Transportation Statistics, 2005). If falling transportation costs helped to create the logistics revolution, then the rising cost of fuel and security could bring the revolution to an end. Of course, rising costs could also prompt a classic, economic response—consolidation. Consolidation is one of the ways that industries try to lower their costs by creating economies of scale. As we will see in this chapter, all of these challenges are creating a variety of responses and the jury is out on which "answer" will prevail.

Securing the Goods

In the US, the 9/11 Commission made a number of recommendations for securing cargo entering the United States, including a requirement for 100 percent physical inspection of all cargo. Of most concern was the cargo carried on passenger aircraft, however, the Commission envisioned the requirement applying to all types and forms of cargo, surface and air. While the concept received wide support when it was first released, it has faced a number of obstacles on the road to implementation. Legislation in the US House of Representatives is calling for a three-year phase-in to 100 percent screening to be fully implemented by 2009. Still, the Bush White House has argued that the technology does not yet exist to handle the level of cargo entering the US without substantially impeding the flow of trade. A debate has even developed over the wording between the House and US Senate versions, that is, how does 100 inspection differ from 100 screening. Air cargo operators have argued that they already screen all of their freight shipments in one fashion or another. Further complicating the matter, auditors for the US Congress have suggested that full physical inspection of all cargo on passenger aircraft alone would cost approximately US$3.6 billion over ten years (Moorman, 2007a).

The initial efforts of the Transportation Security Administration (TSA) to improve cargo security were severely criticized in a recent report by the US Department of Homeland Security's Office of Inspector General who cited the TSA for having too few cargo inspectors, vague regulations, and an ineffective database for tracking violators (Moorman, 2007b). The TSA has proposed creating a cargo version of the Known Traveler program. Shippers would be certified by forwarders. An expedited system would then be established for cargo from shipper facilities that meet specific, comprehensive security standards identified by the TSA (Moorman, 2007a). Cargo executives, however, have complained that this program does not make sense if a parallel program for 100 percent inspection is also required. The industry favors a multilayered approach to cargo security that includes random physical inspection, X-rays, explosive detection systems, and canine screening. These elements would be combined with a certified shipper program and improved intelligence gathering (and communication) on possible threats involving cargo (Moorman, 2007b).

The International Air Transport Association (IATA) and the International Federation of Freight Forwarders (FIATA) formed a Global Air Cargo Security Industry Task Force in April 2007 with the stated goal of seeking to promote harmonization of security regimes across countries and airports. The group is also concerned that some of the national laws being proposed, particularly in the US, are "not proportionate to the threat." John Edwards, IATA head of cargo security, has suggested that governments avoid comparing security for passengers to air cargo because most air cargo travels on pallets or in containers that have been packed under secure conditions. Like much of the air cargo industry itself, the Task Force is arguing that the security focus should be shifted to the point of origin rather than the point of departure (airport) and that mandating costly, unproven equipment will be prohibitively expensive and damaging to world trade and economies (Doyle, 2007).

In 2005, the TSA launched a study into eight technologies proposed for cargo screening. The technologies ranged from trace element sensing to high-energy computer tomography. Under development are technologies such as L-3 Communications' neutron resonance radiography screening to detect explosives,

Omni's high-energy X-ray to penetrate densely loaded containers, AS&E's Z Backscatter imaging technology to provide photo-like images of interior spaces, and ENSCO's Microsearch Human Detection System to identify possible human presence in cargo spaces. In other security-related work, Telair International is working on hardened containers for the shipment of elevated risk cargo. These containers would in theory contain a small explosive event, protecting an aircraft's hull from damage (Moorman, 2007a). Another technology that could be utilized for identifying, tracking and certifying cargo is radio frequency identification devices (RFID). According to the 2006 Unisys Global Shippers' Survey, only about one percent of current shipments utilize RFID technology, although this was expected to rise to 8 percent in 2007 and 25 percent in 2009. Several factors were cited in the survey as impeding the adoption of RFID technology including the initial cost, lack of industry standards, and possible legal challenges.

Future of Fuel

The airlines have reported an overall rise of 90 percent in their costs since 2000 with fuel costs now representing 26 percent of the total operating expenses, higher than labor costs (23 percent) (Associated Press, 2008). Table 19.1 shows the cost of a barrel of oil, the cost percent mile for US domestic air travel, and the price of jet fuel from 2000 to 2007. It should be noted that the cost to fly has gone down slightly over the period while jet fuel prices have soared. The Air Transport Association (ATA) estimates that every penny paid for jet fuel costs the US airline and air cargo industry US$190 to US$200 million annually (ATA, 2007). As noted in Chapter 14, fuel prices are one of the many costs over which carriers have little leverage. Aside from hedging strategies, fleet renewal, weight reduction, and operational flight changes, there is little that carriers can do to affect fuel costs.

The Air Cargo Management Group wass forecasting that global air freight traffic would fall between 5 and 8 percent in the first quarter of 2008 as average monthly jet fuel costs of $2.769 a gallon forced cargo carriers to increase fuel surcharges. These surcharges rose from 50 cents in early 2007 to 80–85 cents by January 2008 (Air Cargo World, 2008). Unfortunately, there is a limit to the level of charges that can be levied on customers before they actively seek lower cost options. How price sensitive shippers might be is uncertain, however, higher fuel prices have already encouraged a number of American and Canadian airlines to operate "truck flights" that shift cargo that might have moved by air to trucks (Seemuth, 2008). Both UPS and FedEx have warned that economic slowdown in the US, rising fuel prices, and credit worries will lead to slower than expected growth and earnings in 2008. The weakness appears to be spreading to other world markets as well (Center for Asia Pacific Aviation, 2008).

Table 19.1   Price of fuel and air travel

Year	Crude Oil*	Domestic Travel**	Jet Fuel***
2000	30.38	14.57	90.1
2001	25.98	13.25	74.7
2002	26.18	12.00	70.9
2003	31.08	12.29	85.7
2004	41.51	12.03	120.8
2005	56.64	12.29	172.7
2006	66.05	13.01	197.0
2007	72.34	TBD	216.5

* price per barrel ** cents per mile *** cents per gallon

Source: Air Transport Association website. Data available at: http://www.airlines.org/economics/energy/

3PL

In an era in which cost and time considerations are driving logistics and supply chains to new levels of sophistication, it is not surprising to discover that many firms are outsourcing these activities to firms who specialize in these areas, freeing themselves to make or retail the products themselves. These third-party logistics providers (3PLs) may specialize in everything from warehousing and inventorying to single or multi-mode transportation. Taking the concept even further are the so-called 4PLs who re-engineer a firm's entire logistics process but frequently do not provide services directly; they contract with other service providers on behalf of their clients and manage the supply chain (Anderson and Leinbach, 2007). The Unisys Global Shippers' Survey found that most shippers prefer multiple providers as a means of avoiding single-source dependence. Even the largest shippers reported using medium-sized or niche logistics providers who covered only a limited geographic region or provided a limited set of services. Many corporations provided an approved list of transport and logistics provider to regional units who were free to select the ones that best fit their needs.

A 2003 survey of the 3PL industry in the US found that the top 25 firms had annual gross revenues of approximately US$40 billion during the survey period (www.eyefortransport.com/3pl/NA_3PL_Jul04.pdf). Not surprisingly, many of these firms got their start in one of the specialized areas discussed above. Kitty Hawk Cargo, an air freight forwarder, went into ground transportation in 2005 because many of its customers and competitors had already moved into ground transportation. It did so by purchasing Air Container Transport, a West Coast trucking company, however, the street goes both ways. Cargo-Master, a surface freight company, decided in 2006 to open an air freight forwarding unit. For trucking companies, air freight operations offer a way to get more high yield business and meet specialized time-sensitive shipping demands. Many air cargo operators believe that ground shipping will help them compete with lower priced trucking services (Page, 2006). Sadly, strategies and tactics that seem to make sense on paper often fail to produce the desired results when faced with the realities of intense competition and uncertain operating conditions; Kitty Hawk, who reported losses in both 2006 and 2007, was forced into bankruptcy as they found competition with Forward Air, Towne Air Freight, and BAX Global, the leading air freight truckers, particularly daunting. In the complex new world of transportation and logistics, even a company such as Forward Air, the dominant trucker in the airport-to-airport trucking market, will struggle when faced with North America traffic growth of 0.2 percent (Seemuth, 2008).

Hard Times and New Friends

As the new century opened, the venerable US Postal Service (USPS) announced that it would have a $300 million loss for the fiscal year. Reasons given for the loss included a decline in first class cards and letters, increased gasoline prices, and additional labor costs (Robinson, 2000). Although the loss proved to be only US$199 million, the USPS was clearly struggling under the weight of growing competition and changing times. Some of the challenges facing the USPS are well known to older established firms such as growing fixed expenses for pension plans, worker compensation, health benefits, and the interest expense of debt. Further adding to these challenges are concerns that postal volumes will continue to decline due to competition from other express and parcel companies as well as new electronic alternatives. Unfortunately, the USPS has a limited ability to deal with these issues. Even postal rate changes must be approved by the Postal Rate Commission who often hears arguments from "interested parties" for lower rates. The USPS attempted to address these basic problems through a number of classic business tactics: restructuring, lay-offs, asset sales, accounting adjustments, and outsourcing (Ho, 2001; Robinson, 2000). It is ironic that one outcome of these struggles was a June 2006 announcement that the USPS had signed a US$100 million deal with UPS to carrying US mail on its jets. The threeyear contract makes UPS responsible for delivering mail to 96 US cities. UPS would also appear to be a prime contender for the US$1.3 billion Express and Priority mail contract. After years of battling the USPS for the right to deliver packages across the US, UPS has now made a "pact with the devil" in a sign of the changing world of airmail and small packages (Niemann, 2007). Also in 2006 the Postal Accountability Enhancement Act was passed separating the USPS services into market-dominant and competitive products. Under this legislation, the USPS can make and retain profits on competitive product offerings and is prohibited from cross-subsidizing between the two categories. The USPS could cut some of its cost in international markets if it were allowed to include foreign carriers in the bidding process, but at the present time, they are prohibited from doing so unless the services of US carriers are deemed "inadequate."

Meanwhile in Europe, Deutsche Post, who had gone public in 2000 and acquired Danzas Holding, a Swiss logistics company, was beginning further expansion by acquiring Air Express International, the remaining shares of DHL, and Excel. It would now be transformed into Deutsche Post World Net (www.dpwn.de). In fact, these acquisitions were simply the largest in a series of acquisitions as noted in a 2007 feature in *Aviation Week & Space Technology* entitled "Evolution of the Air Cargo Industry." In a center fold out, the article traces the history of the key players among the integrators, forwarders, and airlines since the 1980s. It visually displays the name, size, and region where each player was acquiring companies and assets. In the middle of all of this activity was a very busy Deutsche Post (CRA International, 2007).

Logistics in Brown

While the deal with the USPS was a sweet one for UPS, they also began a series of acquisitions in 2000 that would strengthen their ground and logistics operations (CRA International, 2007). During the five-year period, 2002–06, UPS completed 11 acquisitions. Some of these acquisitions were designed to strengthen their operations in key regions such as China, Japan, and Europe. Other acquisitions were undertaken to broaden their capabilities in freight-forwarding, heavy freight and less-than-truckload services. Overall, UPS grew during this period at a compound rate of 4 percent a year. Domestic package delivery accounted for 64 percent of their 2006 revenue with international package delivery accounting for another 19 percent. The remaining 17 percent of their revenue came from their supply chain and freight division (UPS Annual Report, 2006).

In 1999, their logistics/supply chain services become known as UPS Logistics Technologies. The company's transportation and logistics software, ROADNET, would help firms like Frito-Lay, Costco, and SYSCO optimize routes, plan territories, dispatch vehicles, and track deliveries. In other cases, UPS helped manufacturing companies with their supply chains. It redesigned Ford Motor Company's system for getting cars from the assembly plant to showroom floors, helped Harley-Davidson Motor Company track and inventory inbound parts and accessories, and improved the logistics of the service center of European medical supplier, Royal Philips Electronics (Niemann, 2007). Integration of several acquired units in 2006—the Motor Cargo unit of Overnite and Menlo Worldwide Forwarding—led to some disappointing revenue results for that year but overall revenues for the freight and supply chain unit were up 33 percent from the prior year (UPS Annual Report, 2006).

Table 19.2 provides an overall snapshot of the operational results for UPS, a company that still defines itself by its primary business of time-definite delivery even as it expands into the broader area of logistics and supply chain. The post-9/11 trends continued upward for UPS driven primarily by international growth. Express package deliveries continue to rise as does the revenue of the firm overall. The only downward measure was fleet size. Like the passenger carriers, there was a post-9/11 movement to retire older, less fuel efficient aircraft that reduced capacity, primarily in the domestic market. Fleet numbers began to climb again in 2005 and 2006. It is too early to determine what impact rising fuel prices might have on fleet size.

Related Diversifications?

The year 2000 marked a new evolution at Federal Express whose corporate identity changed in 1994 to simply FedEx and who now established a separate until called FedEx Express to oversee development in its express-specific service offerings. Ground operations which began in 1985 with Roadway Package System, a division of Roadway and later Caliber System, became FedEx Ground in 2000 with the acquisition of Caliber. FedEx acquired American Freightways in 2001, adding to earlier acquisitions of Viking Freight (part of Caliber) and Caribbean Transportation Services (1999). In 2006, FedEx acquired Watkins Motor Lines a ground, freight forwarding company. These units created FedEx Freight which became a leading provider of next- and second-day, less-than-truckload freight services. FedEx entered the world of supply chains and services with new units in these areas. With the 2004 acquisition of Kinko's, FedEx boasted of 1,500 store locations in 11 countries (www.fedex.com). Like rival UPS, FedEx is strengthening its presence in China and other rapidly growing Asia markets as well as strengthening key ground and logistics operations.

Table 19.3 shows the growth at FedEx from 2000 to 2006. Like rival UPS, there was a post-9/11 fleet reduction, but the overall trends have remained positive.

Table 19.2   UPS growth 2000–2006

	2000	2001	2002	2003	2004	2005	2006
Revenues	29,771	30,646	31,272	33,485	36,582	42,581	47,547
Express Package	3,190	3,246	3,228	3,370	3,460	3,706	4,057
Fleet	622	599	583	582	569	577	607
Employees	359,000	371,000	360,000	355,000	384,000	407,000	428,000

Source: Company website, www.ups.com

Table 19.3   FedEx growth 2000–2006

	2000	2001	2002	2003	2004	2005	2006
Revenues	18,257	19,269	20,607	22,487	24,710	29,363	32,294
Express Package	3,251	3,263	3,075	3,118	3,264	3,255	3,283
Fleet	663	640	647	643	645	670	671
Employees	163,324	176,960	184,953	190,918	195,838	215,838	221,677

Source: FedEx website, www.fedex.com, Annual Reports

FedEx has not witnessed the kind of growth in express package volumes that UPS has experienced. In fact, the number of packages has fluctuated over this period and remains relatively static. With the various acquisitions, there has been an overall rise in the number of employees, although FedEx has yet to reach the levels of UPS.

Is it Over?

It is probably too early to declare the logistics revolution over, but there is little doubt that rising fuel prices and possible security costs do threaten to slow the predicted growth of the industry. A further uncertainty is the state of the US economy. If the recession that appears to be underway is deep or protracted, then the volume of goods from Asia is certain to slow. The first operators to feel the pain are likely to be the smaller freight forwarders. The integrated carriers will be able, if necessary, to shift customers to cheaper modes of transport, but can still be expected to see some impact in the event of economic slowdown. Still, it is far too early to count air freight out of the aviation picture. As noted previously, it was air cargo that "made" the aviation industry and as long as aviation survives, there will be a need for air freight.

References

Air Cargo World (2008), 'Freight's on-off peak', January, p. 4.

Air Transport Association (ATA) (2007), 'Quarterly Cost Index: US Passenger Airlines', Available at: http://www.airlines.org/economics/finance/Cost+index. htm.

Anderson, W.P. and Leinbach, T.R. (2007), 'E-commerce, Logistics, and the Future of Globalized Freight' in *Globalized Freight Transport: Intermodality, E-commerce, Logistics, and Sustainability* (Thomas R. Leinbach and Cristina Capineri eds), Edward Elgar, Cheltenham, UK.

Associated Press (2008), 'Airlines' Costs Rose in 3Q Led by Fuel-price Jump; Soars 91 percent above 2000 Levels', Available at: http://biz.yahoo.com/ap/080129/airlines_costs_index.html.

Bureau of Transportation Statistics (2005), 'National Transportation Statistics 2004', Available at: www.bts.gov.

Center for Asia Pacific Aviation (2008), 'US Exports Economic Weakness,' *Air Transport News,* Available at: http://www.airtransportnews.aero/analysis. pl?acateg=experts.

CRA International (2007), 'Evolution of the Air Cargo Industry', *Aviation Week & Space Technology* May 7–14, pp. 48–53.

Doyle, J.M. (2007), 'Intervention prevention', *Aviation Week & Space Technology*, May 7–14, pp. 63–4.

Ho, D. (2001), 'Post Office May Stop Saturday Mail Delivery', Associated Press, April 3, Available at: www.apwu73.com/bulletin/Post%20may%20stop%20S aturday%.

Moorman, R. (2007a), 'Drawing New Security Lines', *Air Cargo World*, March, pp. 20–24.

Moorman, R. (2007b), 'Secure Funding', *Air Cargo World,* October, pp. 10–11.

Niemann, G. (2007), *Big Brown: The Untold Story of UPS*, Jossey-Bass, San Francisco, CA.

Page, P. (2006), 'Cargo's Trading Places', *Air Cargo World*, August, pp. 27–32.

Robinson, A.M. (2000), 'USPS Finances: Are We on the Road From Universal to Invisible?, Available: at http://www.aircargoworld.com/features/0208_1.htm.

Seemuth, M (2008), 'Cargo's Truck Factor', Available at: http://www.postcom. org/public/articles/2000articles/101000a.htm.

Unisys (2006), Unisys Global Shippers' Survey 2006, *Fastforward Q3*, Available at: www/Unisys.com/eprise/main/admin/micro/doc/FF_2006Q3.pdf.

UPS Annual Report (2006), 2006 Annual Report, Available at: http://www.ups. com.

Websites

Deutsche Post World Net, http://www.dpwn.de
FedEx, http://www.fedex.com

Chapter 20
A Twenty-First Century Airspace

Crowded Skies

The International Air Transport Association (IATA) has reported that international passenger traffic year-on-year was up 9.3 percent in November 2007, the fastest growth in over 18 months. Passenger growth in North America and Europe was up slightly less at 7.6 and 7.8 percent. Latin America and the Middle East posted double-digit rates of growth—20.1 and 18.3 respectively (IATA, 2008). Longer term, IATA and the Airports Council International (ACI) are predicting growth rates of more than 4 percent a year between 2005 and 2020 resulting in 7.4 billion people flying annually by 2020. According to IATA, North America will post the slowest growth through 2011 with an annual rate of 4.2 percent (IATA Fact Sheet, 2008; ACI, 2005). A 4 percent annual growth may not seem like a major increase, but the actual numbers are impressive. According to the 2006 annual report of the Air Transport Association (2007), US carriers enplaned 744.6 million passengers in 2006. Given the size of the current base, a 4 percent annual increase will add up quickly. In fact, the Federal Aviation Administration (FAA) is predicting that traffic levels will rise by a factor of two to three by 2025 (FAA Fact Sheet, 2007). In Europe, 2020 is expected to bring passenger traffic of two billion per year (ACI, 2005).

Accommodating these levels of air traffic will require the nations of the world to make some very significant investments in aviation infrastructure, otherwise the current capacity shortfall will grow to critical levels, threatening growth and the safety of the system. In developing nations, the current emphasis is on building the basic infrastructure of an aviation system—airports (runways, terminals), radar stations, and supporting infrastructure (access roads, warehouses, intermodal links, maintenance facilities). These regions will also have to address the need for trained personnel to man the system. Some of these nations are making rapid strides in their efforts while others are struggling, usually for the lack of money. Specific regional issues have already been covered in earlier chapters. Here it is important to note that the nations that can and are investing now have the opportunity to take advantage of technological advances in airspace management without facing the difficult and sometimes wrenching transitions that more developed regions are facing. In some ways the situation is similar to the industrial rebuilding that took place in Europe and Asia after World War II. A new steel mill would incorporate the new closed hearth rather than the less efficient open hearth technology. In a similar way, developing nations can leapfrog to a satellite-based system rather than the old ground-based radar of the Post-WWII era.

For the early pioneers in aviation (mostly those in United States and Europe), the problems are different—maintaining an aging infrastructure while transitioning to a new system of organization. James C. May of the Air Transport Association has noted that Charles Lindbergh, who made history in 1927 with his solo transatlantic flight, would be surprised to discover that 80 years later "we still rely on old technology that forces aircraft to fly inefficient, less direct routes, with unnecessarily inefficient separation requirements" (May, 2006). In fact, the ground radar, voice communication system in use today dates from the period just after World War II. The system has been modernized over the decades, but is essentially based on the same general technology and framework. These nations must make the transition to a new system in the face of rising traffic, active environmental movements, vocal consumer rights groups, and traditional carriers under pressure from new international and low-cost competition. Key indicators that the aviation systems of North America and Europe are struggling with capacity issues include slot controls at airports, flight delays, and flight cancellations. Although North America has the space to construct more basic infrastructure, that is, airports and runways, doing so raises environmental concerns as well as the more general not-in-my-backyard (NIMBY) reaction. The closing of a number of US military bases had raised the hope that some of these facilities could be converted to civilian use, but in many cases local opposition halted these plans (FAA, 2006).

In this chapter, we will explore the technologies that are expected to shape the airspace and aviation system of the twenty-first Century in the context of the developed systems of North America and Europe. While some of the conditions and constraints vary, both regions are facing the difficult task of changing the tires on a rapidly moving vehicle. Further, each region is dealing with a set of political and economic problems that threaten to derail deployment.

Creating the Future

In the US, the Next Generation Air Transportation System (NGATS), commonly referred to as NextGen, is the air transportation solution for the twenty-first century. In Europe, the roughly equivalent concepts fall under the Single European Sky Air Traffic Management (ATM) Research (SESAR) program, although European efforts are also an attempt to integrate the airspace in the EU in accordance with the single sky concept. The definition phase (2005–08) of SESAR was jointly funded by EUROCONTROL and the European Commission. It was tasked with delivering a European ATM Master Plan based on future aviation requirements as defined by key stakeholders in the system. Further, it is expected to identify the actions needed to achieve the objectives of SESAR. SESAR and NextGen envision a totally new architecture that will allow information integration, combining new technologies on the ground and in the sky to create a more efficient system. They are expected to "create" new capacity by allowing air traffic to more efficiently utilize the existing airspace. The proposed new systems will also help to address many of the economic and environmental concerns facing the industry and the public. More efficient, direct continuous descents and ascents use less fuel, thus contributing less carbon and other greenhouse gases to the environment and reducing the national dependence on petroleum. Improved utilization of existing airspace relieves some of the need for more airport construction with the environmental impacts that such construction almost always entails. Both US and European efforts began at roughly the same time and are planned for full implementation around 2020–25.

As with all things aviation, the discussion is filled with acronyms. To avoid confusion, the technological discussion that follows will try to broadly identify the systems and concepts. According to the FAA Research, Engineering & Development Advisory Committee (REDAC), the NextGen system will require the development and implementation of nine capabilities: network-enabled information access, performance-based services, advanced air traffic automation services, aircraft trajectory-based operations, weather assimilation into decision loops, broad-area precision navigation, equivalent visual operations, super density operations, and layered adaptive security (FAA REDAC, 2006). There are at least two key technologies:

1. *Automatic Dependency Surveillance-Broadcast* (ADS-B) is a satellite-based system that allows aircraft to broadcast their position to others. ADS-B *out* will replace many ground radars with ground-based transceivers. ADS-B *in* would allow aircraft to receive signals from the ground-based transceivers as well as from ADS-B equipment onboard other aircraft.

2. *System-Wide Information Management* (SWIM) is a new system architecture that would allow airspace users to access a wide array of data on the National Air Space (NAS) and weather. SWIM is a net-centric link between air traffic management, customers, and the departments of Homeland Security and Defense which would provide full automation and data convergence across all authorized users on a common display format.

In essence, the old system of ground-based radar and positive voice control would be replaced with an "intelligent" aircraft capable of using satellite technology to finds its own position, calculate its best flight path, communicate and coordinate its position with other craft in the airspace, and integrate multiple streams of information. Working within this overall system, specific tools such as broad-area precision navigation will allow for continuous descent approaches while 4D trajectory flight management will allow for time-based arrival/departure planning. The system would create the kind of precision necessary to allow for reduced aircraft separation and the simultaneous use of closely spaced parallel runways. In addition, new groundside technologies will detect runway and intruder incursions, improve taxiway and ramp management, and permit improved all-weather operations (Burkle and Montgomery, 2007). These new Surface Management Systems will generate moving maps of the airport surface, provide data-linked taxi instructions, and allow flight planning feedback and negotiation (Joint Planning and Development Office (JPDO), 2006).

The US and NextGen

In the US, the last major airport constructed was Denver International Airport (DIA) which opened in 1995. While DIA is the largest piece of real estate dedicated to commercial aviation in the world, it can not make up for capacity shortfalls at other key airports (Dempsey, Goetz, and Szyliowicz, 1995). The FAA Annual Service Volume plan has called for the construction of eight new runways through 2008 to increase capacity at other airports (FAA, 2008). The US Federal Aviation Administration's report *Future Airport Capacity Task* has projected that 14 airports and eight metropolitan areas will require new capacity to meet air traffic growth projections for 2025 including Atlanta, Philadelphia, Los Angeles, San Diego, and Las Vegas (Wilson, 2007). Atlanta, the busiest airport in the US, has recently added a fifth runway which is predicted to increase airport arrival capacity by almost 30 percent while the Las Vegas area is in the early stages of planning a reliever airport for McClerran (Yu, 2006).

Although new airport construction will help the situation, it alone will not solve the current (and predicted) capacity crunch. Another area requiring major investment is the air traffic management system and related ground-based systems at airports. In the highly complex New York/New Jersey area which hosts three large international airports, John F. Kennedy (JFK), Newark, and La Guardia, the FAA has announced plans to cap flights into JFK to reduce delays at peak times and is suggesting some form of capacity pricing to encourage airlines to adjust flight schedules, however, this is seen as a short-term fix for the delays and cancellations caused by the capacity crunch (Schofield, 2008). The long-term solution is to increase the efficiency of the existing airspace, that is, to implement NextGen.

In 2003, the US Congress passed Vision 100, Century of Aviation Reauthorization Act. This act created the Joint Planning and Development Organization (JPDO) to manage work related to the creation of the next generation air transportation system (NGATS). JPDO is also responsible for coordinating with partner agencies:Department of Transportation (DOT), Department of Commerce (DOC), Department of Defense (DOD), Department of Homeland Security (DHS), Federal Aviation Administration (FAA), the National Aeronautics and Space Administration (NASA), the White House Office of Science and Technology Policy (OSTP), and the Office of Management and Budget (OMB). JPDO is a planning and coordinating body with no authority over the human and financial resources necessary to create and deploy the system.

Funding NextGen

There is almost universal agreement that the "FAA's funding structure is obsolete and unpredictable." In fact, special commissions such as the so-called Mineta Commission have called for reform for over 20 years (May, 2006; Oster and Strong, 2006). However, beyond this recognition, there is no agreement on a new means of funding the FAA or NextGen. While some FAA funding comes from the General Fund, most of their funding comes from the Airports and Airways Trust Fund whose revenues are generated through excise taxes (Table 20.1). Roughly 70 percent of the 2004 revenues came from the passenger ticket tax, flight segment tax, rural airport tax, and frequent flyer tax (Oster and Strong, 2006). Given the other obligations of the US government and the current deficit, it is likely that General Fund contributions will decrease in the future. Further, the trend in the US has been for low-cost carriers (LCCs) to drive down average fares and LCCs are predicted to increase their share of the domestic market over the next few years (Cordle and Poole, 2005). The 2004 uncommitted balance in the Trust Fund was US$7.3 billion. By 2006, the uncommitted balance had dropped to US$1.2 billion (May, 2006).

The actual cost of NextGen is also a subject of debate. The FAA had originally "estimated that its ATC modernization efforts would cost $12 billion and could be completed over 10 years. Now, two decades and $35 billion later, the FAA expects to need another $16 billion through 2007 to complete key projects, for a total of $51 billion." (General Accounting Office (GAO), 2004). The FAA 2007 reauthorization bill proposed moving from the current system of excise taxes to a cost-based user fee system in which the aircraft operator would pay for the air traffic services they used. The reauthorization legislation ran into early trouble over contract talks with the air traffic controllers' union (NATCA). NATCA, angered over the FAA imposed contract in 2006, also charged that the FAA had neglected facilities maintenance, creating unsafe conditions, and wasted money in air traffic organization (ATO) reorganization and modernization efforts (NATCA, 2008a, 2008b, 2008c). Further opposition to reauthorization came from the general aviation community because the proposed charge would be levied whether the aircraft carried two or 200 people. The general aviation (GA) community argues that many GA flights operate in uncongested airspace under visual flight rules and hence do not use significant air traffic services, however, several studies have estimated the GA share of ATC costs at between 10 and 25 percent, well above their 3 percent contribution to the Trust Fund (Oster and Strong, 2006). Unfortunately, the FAA has been unable or unwilling to deal with the issue of cost of service. The FAA can account for its inputs—labor, facilities, equipment and supplies—and it can provide a broad list of outputs from its activities—aircraft movements, and departures—but it has not clearly connected the cost of inputs to the cost of specific outputs. The FAA's (1996) report, *A Cost Allocation Study of FAA's 1995 Costs* (CAS), assigned costs to various services, but these appear to be based more on the ability to pay than on the actual cost of the services provided. This inability

Table 20.1   US aviation excise taxes

Domestic passenger ticket tax	7.5% of ticket price (10/1/99 through 9/30/2007)
Domestic flight segment fee	Rate is indexed by the Consumer Price Index starting 1/1/02
	$3.00 per segment during calendar year (CY) 2003
	$3.10 per segment during CY2004
	$3.20 per segment during CY2005
Passenger ticket tax for rural airports	7.5% of ticket price Flight segment fee does not apply
International arrival & departure tax	Rate is indexed by the Consumer Price Index starting 1/1/99
	Rate during CY2003= $13.40
	Rate during CY2004 = $13.70
	Rate during CY2005 = $14.10
Flights between continental US Alaska and Hawaii	Rate is indexed by the Consumer Price Index starting 1/1/99
	$6.70 international facilities fee + applicable domestic tax rate (during CY03)
	$6.90 international facilities fee + applicable domestic tax rate (during CY04)
	$7.00 international facilities fee + applicable domestic tax rate (during CY05)
Frequent flyer tax	7.50%
Domestic cargo/mail	6.25% of amount paid for the transportation of property by air
General aviation fuel tax	AvGas: $0.193/gallon
Jet fuel: $0.218/gallon	Jet fuel: $0.218/gallon
Commercial fuel tax	$0.043/gallon

Source: Oster and Strong (2006)

to clearly identify the usage and cost of service has seriously hampered the FAA's ability to make an argument for user fee charges.

Broadly speaking, the FAA has six key services that it provides to external customers—air traffic control, regulation and certification, civil aviation security, airport development, and commercial space. Air traffic control accounts for almost two-thirds of the total FAA budget while airport development is roughly 18 percent (FAA, 1996). In 2005, the FAA outsourced the Automated Flight

Service Station (AFSS), formerly a part of their air traffic services program, to Lockheed-Martin. The AFSS provides weather briefings, flight plan filing services, and other assistance to private pilots. This contract is expected to save the FAA $2.2 billion over the next ten years and may help lead efforts to change the way the US approaches aviation systems and funding, including providing a better understanding of the cost-of-service questions (Cordle and Poole, 2005). The Oster Report (2006) suggested that there were really only two options for advancing the NextGen vision: 1) leave air traffic services with FAA under a user fee structure (essentially the approach of the most recent FAA reauthorization bill) or 2) remove the system from the FAA and establish an autonomous agency similar to NAV CANADA and NATS. Option 1 does not resolve the fact that the FAA has yet to determine the cost of its services, has a poor record of performance, and lacks the organizational independence to pursue a market-based rather than politically based strategy. Option 2 avoids these problems but faces opposition because of the user fee issue as well as the more generalized opposition to privatization

To date, neither the US Senate nor the House has endorsed the user fee concept. The Senate has proposed a $25 surcharge, extension of current ticket taxes, and a rise in the international arrival/departure and aviation fuel excise taxes. The House has proposed extending the current taxes and raising the aviation fuel rate (FAA Fact Sheet, 2007). In essence, Congress appears unwilling to consider any new concepts for aviation funding and until the Senate and House can reconcile the FAA reauthorization bill the organization will operate under a continuing resolution. This is clearly not likely to further the deployment of NextGen.

Deploying NextGen

In 2004, air traffic control function was reorganized into the Air Traffic Organization (ATO) with a newly appointed chief operating officer. The ATO was billed as a "performance-based organization" that breaks the existing "stovepipes" within the FAA bringing the key units responsible for management and modernization together. While this reorganization changes the reporting lines of ATS-related branches within the FAA, the ATO remains an agency within the FAA subject to the annual budget appropriations process of Congress. In 2005, the ATO was reorganized from nine to three service areas and staff support services for En Route, Terminal and Technical Operations were placed in shared service centers in the three service areas. Both this reorganization and the original one were contrary to the recommendations of the FAA hired consultant Booz Allen Hamilton which called for ATO headquarter consolidation into five service and two staff units and greater cuts in managerial staff (NATCA, 2008b).

In addition to the structural issues complicating deployment, the FAA must contend with its own poor performance record on previous projects. Specifically, they have been cited for "(1) promising more capability than they ultimately deliver, (2) being completed later than promised, and (3) costing far more by the time they are completed than the initial cost estimates" (Oster and Strong, 2006).

A 2005 report by the USDOT inspector general noted "that cost growth, schedule delays, and performance shortfalls with major acquisitions continue to stall air traffic modernization." Eleven of the 16 projects appeared to be experiencing total cost growth while over half were experiencing schedule slips from two to 12 years. In short, planned deployment is in serious doubt. One example is the development and implementation of the Wide Area Augmentation System (WAAS). WAAS was projected in 1994 to cost $509 million. In 2004, the Inspector General testified to Congress that the projected cost of the yet-to-be-implemented program was over $2.9 billion. This represents a 227 percent increase in the cost of a program whose implementation has been extended by 13 years (NATCA, 2008c).

Europe and SESAR

In Europe, physical expansion of infrastructure–new airports and new runways–is expected to be very difficult because of space, environmental or social constraints. Yet, the EU recognizes that "Europe's airports are currently the main bottleneck in the air transport chain" (Eurocontrol, 2008: 40). The answer to the dilemma is to unlock the latent capacity in the system through the application of new technologies to air and groundside operation. In other words, Europe too must create and deploy their answer to a twenty-first century airspace system. As noted above, the SESAR concept embodies not only the European answer to the aviation system of the future but the first ever European effort to involve all of the aviation stakeholders (civil and military, legislators, industry, operators, users, ground and airborne) in the process of defining, committing to and implementing a pan-European program consistent with the Single European Sky legislation. As currently envisioned the process will proceed in three phases: definition (2005–07), development (2008–13), and deployment (2014–20). The definition phase, funded equally by EUROCONTROL and the EC transport directorate for 50 million euros, will deliver the European ATM Master Plan with a roadmap of actions for development and deployment.

Funding SESAR

In order to develop the system, a legal entity was created under EC law, the SESAR Joint
　　　　Undertaking (JU). The SESAR JU will 1) secure the appropriate funding and concentrate the necessary research and development resources into SESAR, 2) define and update the work program, including allocating tasks and organizing calls for tender, 3) ensure technical progress, and 4) report on the development phase. The first phase of tender contracts wa set to close on 29 February 2008 (EUROCONTROL, 2008).

"Final Answer"

There is very little disagreement over the general shape and technologies needed for the twenty-first century aviation system. All parties also agree that the current system can not meet the traffic demands of the future and must be replaced as soon as possible. Unfortunately, this is as far as the general agreement goes. In the US, it does not appear to be enough to overcome fundamental disagreements over questions of structure and funding. While these issues remain unresolved, NextGen work on the technologies proceeds in a haphazard, stop-and-start way because of funding uncertainty. The basic framework exists for almost all of the key components in the system, but few, if any, have been widely deployed (NATCA, 2008d). Meanwhile, industry vendors tout their twenty-first century solutions to government and other key stakeholders who marvel at its possibilities and baulk at paying the bill. The existing system continues to age and deteriorate while the FAA, scrambling to meet current operational and maintenance budgets, reduces the number of facilities set for modernization and extends the deployment dates of planned new technology for the remaining sites. In Europe, it is too early to judge the results of the first definition phase, although definition has NOT been the main problem in the US. It is far too early to assess the success of development and deployment, the major stumbling blocks for the US. Decades of efforts at European integration might work in favor of a smoother process for Europe, but this is far from certain. The EU could also benefit from prior work in the US on various components of the system, but past experience would tend to suggest that harmonizing systems, rules, and standards between the US and Europe will be difficult at best. National/regional self-interest can easily hide under the cloak of technical specification on system performance.

In the US, there are three key, closely linked recommendations that must be undertaken if NextGen has any hope of deployment.. First, an effort must be undertaken to develop a clear set of cost-of-service parameters. This effort can NOT be led by the FAA. They have shown neither the willingness nor the ability to undertake such an effort. Further, poor planning, cost overruns, and mismanagement have eroded what little credibility the agency had with its stakeholders. Second, a concerted, sustained effort must be made to involve all of the key stakeholders in the process of shaping and deploying NextGen. This recommendation is not new. The GAO (2004) cited this lack of input as one of the factors contributing to cost overruns and implementation delays. NATCA, representatives of the primary users of any air traffic system, has complained that their input is rarely sought and often only after serious problems arise. Recent collaborative efforts between the FAA and controllers on the Domestic Reduced Vertical Separation Minimum (DVRSM), the Airport Surface Detection Equipment—Model X (ASDE-X), and Advanced Technologies and Oceanic Procedures (ATOP) have proven that cooperation is possible and productive (NATCA, 2008c). Of course, these projects are relatively narrow in scope. For NATCA, a more fundamental issue is related to working conditions and employee attrition. Air traffic controllers are leaving in numbers not seen since the Professional Air Traffic Controllers Organization (PATCO) strike of 1981. There are several reasons for these departures: normal baby boomer attrition, general working conditions, and the newly imposed work rules and pay cuts of the September 2006 contract. The attrition in 2007 was 33 percent higher than FAA projections (NATCA, 2007). The US is now at a 15-year low in fully certified controllers (Hall, 2007). This staffing crisis can be added to projected shortages in airline pilots. Like air traffic controllers, the baby boom generation of pilots is retiring. Instability in US airlines and attractive wages from expanding international carriers are driving many pre-retirement pilots out of the US market (Darby 2008). Given the direct impact that NextGen systems have on the job of this group, they also deserve a voice in the way forward.

Other groups that need a seat at the table for these discussions include the General Aviation Manufacturers Association (GAMA) and the National Business Aviation Association (NBAA). Both groups represent the general aviation community in the US. The primary concern of the GA community is, of course, the question of funding and its impact on private and business flyers. Their goal is to keep their contribution as low as possible, however, if capacity is not increased in the system, then they may find themselves increasingly shut out of airports that are struggling to accommodate commercial traffic. The introduction of the Very Light Jet (VLJ) and the per-seat-on-demand concept, if it succeeds, will place even more pressure on the existing system. The large commercial airlines, individually and through the Air Transport Association (ATA) and the International Air Transport Association (IATA), have exercised their political voice in these matters. Their concern is that they should not be singled out as a source of funding over the GA community because they are perceived to have a greater "ability to pay." Airports have a stake in the system as well. The failure to implement NextGen seriously impairs their ability to grow capacity and meet the service quality levels demanded by customers. The New York–New Jersey airports are a case in point.

The third recommendation is to settle, possibly as part of the stakeholder process in recommendation two, on a structure as soon as politically possible. In 2006, an extensive report on ten major international air navigation service providers (Australia, Canada, France, Germany, Ireland, Netherlands, New Zealand, South Africa, Switzerland, and the United Kingdom) found that there was an increasing movement toward corporatizing or privatizing Air Navigation Systems (ANS) due to considerations of cost, efficiency, procurement, capacity constraints, and the desire to access private capital markets. Most of the ANS providers reviewed utilized user fees and were expected to be self-sufficient. Some were allowed to make a profit directly, although most could establish for-profit subsidiaries. All ANS providers reviewed could issue bonds securing the debt with revenue streams. Only a few could issue government-guaranteed debt (Dempsey, Janda, Nyampong, Saba, and Wilson, 2006). The two examples most often cited as models for the US are Canada and the United Kingdom. NAV CANADA was the first private sector company to use a non-share capital structure to commercialize a government function and is governed by a stakeholder cooperative with

Transport Canada, a government entity, assuming safety oversight. NATS is a public–private partnership in which the government owns 49 percent while the remaining ownership is split between an airline consortium (42 percent), NATS employees (5 percent), and British Airports Authority (BAA) plc (4 percent). The UK Civil Aviation Authority (CAA) is responsible for safety regulation. Both rely on user fees for revenue. It seems contradictory to many observers outside of the US that a nation that has devoted much of its recent efforts to promoting free market ideas and policies should so strongly resist privatizing or corporatizing any aspects of the aviation system, but this debate will be long, hard, bloody, and absolutely necessary for any long-term progress to be made. As Jim Hall, former Chair of the National Transportation Safety Board (NTSB) and member of the Gore Commission tasked with cutting the aviation fatality rate has noted: "It is time for the federal government and the aviation industry to focus on – and not hide – the next generation of risks. A failure to respond to new hazards endangers the safety culture that we have worked so hard to create" (Hall, 2007). The failure to move forward now on NextGen will seriously jeopardize the ability of the US aviation system to meet projected air travel demands as we move further into the twenty-first century. A nation without the infrastructure to compete in the coming century may be doomed to emerge from it as an international follower in aviation and economic performance. This would be a sad position for a nation that led the aviation revolution.

Conclusion

The technology exists to create a more efficient, environmentally friendly aviation system. What is needed now is the political will and public support to implement this system BEFORE the twenty-second century arrives. A solution would seem to be in the best interest of all parties, but in the highly contentious aviation industry it is often difficult to get "agreement" on issues even when the parties do agree. Further, NextGen will find itself competing with a host of other funding priorities both in the transportation area and outside of it—education, health care, social safety nets, energy dependence, and so on. Still, this is a debate that can not be delayed much longer.

References

Airports Council International (ACI) (2005), 'Eurocontrol and ACI Europe: A vision for European aviation', Newsdesk Communications Ltd, London.

Air Transport Association (2007), 'Economic Report: Balancing the Aviation Equation', Washington, DC.

Associated Press (2007), 'Airline Passengers Dissatisfied With Service', 15 May, online edition, www.msnbc.com/id/18661797/print/1/displaymode/1098.

Burkle, M.W. and Montgomery, T.E. (2007), 'The Integrated Airport – A Next Gen Test Bed', Lockheed Martin Corporation, Washington, DC.

Cordle, V. and Poole, R.C. (2005), *Resolving the Crisis in Air Traffic Finding*, Reason Foundation, Washington, DC, Available at: www.rppi.org/ps332.pdf.

Darby, K. (2008), 'How Will Growth in Pilot Demand be Met in the Future', *TRB 87th Conference*, Washington, DC.

Dempsey, P.S., Janda, R., Nyampong, N., Saba, J. and Wilson, J. (2006), The McGill Report on Governance of Commercialized Air Navigation Services, *Annual of Air and Space Law*, Vol. XXXI, pp. 214–349.

Dempsey, P.S., Goetz, A.R., and Szyliowicz, J.S. (1995), *Denver International Airport: Lessons Learned*, McGraw-Hill Publishers, New York.

EUROCONTROL (2008), Available at: http://www.eurocontrol.int/sesar/public/ subsite_homepage/homepage.html.

FAA (2008), 'Capacity: Annual Service Volume', Available at: www.faa.gov/ about/plans_reports/portfolio_2008/media/annaul%20service%20volume.pdf.

FAA (2007), 'Fact Sheet', Available at: http://www.faa.gov/news/fact_sheets/ news_story.cfm?newsId=8807.

FAA (2006), 'The New England Regional Airport System Plan', New England Region ANE-600, Washington DC.

FAA REDAC (2006), Financing the Next Generation Air Transportation System Working Group Presentation to NGATS Institute Workshop, 27 April, Washington DC.

FAA (1996), 'A Cost Allocation Study of FAA's 1995 Costs', US Department of Transportation, Washington, DC.

GAO (2004). 'Air Traffic Control, FAA's Modernization Efforts—Past, Present, and Future, Statement of Gerald L. Dillingham, Director, Physical Infrastructure Issues', GAO-04-227T.

Hall, J. (2007), 'Despite Advances, More Must be Done', *Tennessean*, Available at: www.tennessean.com/apps/pbcs.dll/article?AID-/2007/1030/ OPINION1/71/1030034.

International Airline Transport Association (IATA) (2008), ' Fact Sheet: Industry Statistics', Available at: www.iata.org/fact-sheets.

International Airline Transport Association (2008), 'News Release: Passenger Demand Surges to 18-month High', Available at: www.iata.org/pressroom/ pr/2008-01-04-01.htm.

Joint Planning and Development Office (JPDO) (2006), Summary Description of the JPDO Portifolio, 7 April, NGATS Institute, Washington, DC.

May, J.C. (2006), 'Speech by James C. May: Smart – and Fair – Skies: Blueprint for the Future', International Aviation Club, Washington, DC, Available at: www.airlines.org/news/speeches/speech_4-18-06.htm.

National Air Traffic Controllers Association (2008a), 'NATCA Opposes the Nomination of Bobby Sturgell for FAA Administrator', Press release, Available at www.natca.org/mediacenter/press -release-detail.aspx?id=460.

National Air Traffic Controllers Association (2008b), 'ATO Service Area Restructuring: When Change May Not Guarantee Progress', Available at: www.natca.org/legislationcenter/ATOService.msp.

National Air Traffic Controllers Association (2008c), 'Modernization: Still Doing Today's Work With Yesterday's Tools', Available at: www.natca.org/legislationcenter/Modernization.msp.

National Air Traffic Controllers Association (2008d), 'Modernization Cutbacks', Program Descriptions, Available at: www.natca.net/safetytechnology/modernizationcutbacksdetails.msp.

National Air Traffic Controllers Association (2007), 'Controller Staffing Crisis: Fact Sheet', Available at: www.natca.org.

Oster, C. V. and Strong, J.S. (2006), *Reforming the Federal Aviation Administration: Lessons from Canada and the United Kingdom*, IBM Center for the Business of Government, Virginia.Schofield, A. (2008), 'Debate over JFK Delays Sparks Talk of Congestion Pricing', *Aviation Daily*.

USDOT (2005), 'Status of FAA's Major Acquisitions: Cost Growth and Schedule Delays Continue to Stall Air Traffic Modernization', Federal Aviation Administration, Report Number AV-2005-061, date issued: May 26, 2005.

Wilson, B. (2007), 'Flight Delays Top the List of Pax Complaints New Study Finds', *Aviation Daily*, Washington, DC, vol. 369 (35). p. 4.

Yu, R. (2006), 'A Chance to Unclog Atlanta: New Runway Will Increase Airport's Arrival Capacity by 30%', *USA Today*, McLean, VA,

Chapter 21
Wave of the Future

Waves of Change

In *The Third Wave* (1980), Alvin Toffler, noted futurist, talks about wave-front analysis or the examination of history as a succession of waves of change that represent the discontinuities or breakpoints in the pattern. The goal of the futurist or forecaster is, of course, to identify the wave-front, the leading edge of the approaching wave; the goal of the firm is to position itself to ride the 'wave of the future.' Unfortunately, the present sometimes resides between two waves of change or, worse still, the trailing wave has begun to overtake the earlier wave creating a clash of currents that makes it difficult to see the wave-front, much less to catch it. In the 1960s an observant watcher of aviation might have detected the rolling motion that would eventually become the breaking wave of change once the bottom began to shallow. On this wave, among other things, rode the principle of deregulation. Even as this wave approached the shore in the early 1990s, another wave was gathering momentum that carried with it the possibility to change the way we see aviation, international liberalization. The international airline industry was already swimming hard to catch the trailing wave before 9/11, trying to prepare its national carriers for global competition. For a moment, 11 September seemed to freeze this scene, but after catching a long, slow breath the wave is moving again. Adding to the seeming chaos of water are two more trends that promise to bring great change: rising fuel prices and emissions concerns related to global warming.

Before the ink was dry on the first edition of this book, United Air Lines was swamped by the turbulent seas of the post-9/11 ocean. It was the second US carrier to file for bankruptcy since those events; US Airways who filed in 2002 was the first. Suddenly, the industry was faced with the prospect that the world's second largest airline with 1,700 flights a day and 20 percent of the total flights in the US would cease to exist. In fact, many industry experts at the time had given the company less than a 50 percent chance of avoiding Chapter 7 liquidation. Of course, it did emerge after a lengthy bankruptcy which included labor cuts, fleet reductions, pension changes, schedule cutbacks, and charges that its continued operation was spreading a 'bankruptcy virus.' (Arndt and Zellner, 2002; Holmes and Matlack, 2002; Wolf, 1995). Still, before the bankruptcy wave was over US Airways would file for a second time in 2004, emerge and then merge with America West in 2005. Delta and Northwest would enter bankruptcy in 2006 and emerge in 2007 (Nelson and Francolla, 2008). US Airways would pursue a merger with Delta, but be strongly rebuffed by that carrier whose employees could be seen wearing buttons saying "Keep Delta My Delta" (Steffy, 2007). By April 2008, Delta and Northwest would work out the details of a merger plan that will (temporarily) create the world's largest carrier (Grantham and Tharpe, 2008). 11 September, war, economic downturn, and SARS affected the rest of the aviation world as well. However, the major players in the global industry would recover faster than their US counterparts and emerge apparently stronger from the turbulent seas. They will need this strength to face the rising price of fuel.

On other aviation fronts, global economic development continues to support healthy growth in air cargo operations as just-in-time firms need material NOW from suppliers around the world and affluent consumers want exotic products from faraway places. The large commercial manufacturers (Boeing and Airbus) have placed their bets on very different visions of the future and are waiting for the judgement of the marketplace to decide the 'winner.' At the lower end of the commercial jet market, new competitors are coming and this may increase the incentive for the existing players to move up market. Aviation growth is placing greater demands on infrastructure, lending new urgency to calls for a twenty-first century air transportation system. The world is coming to a consensus on the need to control carbon emissions and is giving the role of aviation in emissions control a new look.

Forecasting is a dangerous and thankless job, however, the purpose of this final chapter is to summarize what 'we think we know' about what is happening in the aviation industry and where 'we think it is going.' There are no certainties and miraculous turnarounds do occasionally happen, but the odds-makers in Las Vegas and the practitioners of hindsight in industry and academia will have to deal with these issues when the future becomes the past and 'prediction' becomes easy.

Not Dead Yet!

It certainly appeared that the legacy mega-carrier concept in North America was dead (or at least dying) when the first issue of this book went to press. The mega-carrier concept as articulated by Taneja (1988) and pursued by the large US carriers demanded the creation of large domestic and international route networks linked at key hubs to a low-cost feeder system of regional airlines that many of the majors eventually acquired. The system was managed by an automation system of mainframe, legacy technology with some add-on 'new' hardware. Software (often designed in-house using the extensive historical data of these carriers) sought to maximize revenues (yields), manage capacity, match aircraft to routes, crew flights according to 'established work rules', and recover as quickly as possible from disruption. Carriers consolidated their hold on these strategic hubs utilizing large aircraft that waited at the gates for banks of smaller feeder aircraft to arrive with passengers to fill the available seats. These large aircraft allowed carriers to spread their higher-cost worker salaries over more passengers, giving them a somewhat better productivity per worker. On the other hand, these crews waited at the gates, often for extended periods, for the arriving bank of passengers. The revenue system which 'managed' these passengers often had as many as ten different fare classes with attached rules and restrictions. The system was run frequently to determine if the pre-assigned numbers of seats in each class were filling up to expectations. If not, adjustments were made in fares to achieve maximum yield. These two factors created conflicting demands on the mega-carrier. First, the pressure of low-cost price competition necessitated cuts in airline spending, many in the visible area of service quality, fare restrictions, meal quality, and so on. Second, the revenue system placed consumers in the same cabin who were receiving the same service but at very different fare levels. This gave rise to the ultimate airline shopper, the individual whose mission in life was to shop until they had achieved the lowest fare possible and 'beaten the system.' In the past, these 'shoppers' were primarily leisure travelers who could, and did, arrange their travel around deals. Business passengers had continued to pay higher fares in exchange for the ability to book with little notice and travel at certain times of the day or week.

The events of 9/11 did not create the problems that the industry is facing, but it did accelerate many of the trends; two trailing waves were already rapidly overtaking the mega-carrier concept. The first change was the growth of low-cost carriers (LCCs) who have increased their expansion rates in North America and Europe. As major carriers around the world pulled out of marginal markets in an effort to improve profitability, low-cost carriers moved in to fill the gaps. These carriers offered simplified fare structures, few restrictions, and, in many cases, reliable, consistent basic service. In Europe, 'doing a Ryanair' has become a catch phrase for buying a cheap ticket to some out-of-the-way location for a weekend jaunt (Creaton, 2005). Communities across the US that had lost service in the early years of deregulation or struggled along with high fares from one or two legacy carriers intent on flying them miles out of their way to the closest hub before putting them on a bigger plane to their final destination actively courted the LCCs (Grossman, 2007). The second change was the flight of the traditional business traveler away from the high fare–high restriction traditional carriers and toward either less travel overall, LCCs, or one of the new boutique international carriers offering single, business class cabins and better service. Domestically, the per-seat-on-demand (PSOD), air taxi concept is now trying to lure the domestic business passenger away with promises of more convenience and less hassle. These business travelers had subsidized the cost-minded, post-deregulation leisure traveler for years and accumulated more frequent flyer miles than they could ever use. They had sat in lounges around the world drinking little bottles of wine while reading the financial publications of a dozen nations. They did not need any more gifts from the frequent flyer magazine or little salt and pepper shakers with their meals. If the business traveler of bygone days is truly gone in sizeable numbers, then the high-cost legacy carrier is in serious trouble.

It appears that the death of the US mega-carrier was greatly exaggerated as the new merger wave illustrates, however, a number of the world's carriers have faced the end, hoping for some government intervention or white knight to save them.

Some of these carriers were from small market nations where they were unable to generate enough long-term traffic to survive in the face of greater competition generated by international liberalization. Other carriers fell victim to more efficient, low-cost carriers or to their own mistakes: overexpansion of routes, industry high labor costs, uncompetitive route structures, and so on. It can be argued that some carriers have fallen victim to 'bad timing', that is, starting up in a capital intensive business just as fuel prices have risen to new heights. Fuel prices have been the primary reason cited for four recent US bankruptcies: Aloha Airlines, ATA, Skybus, and Frontier (Associated Press, 2008). Even more damning for the airlines may be the harsh realities of the industry itself. Robert Crandall, former CEO of American Airlines, has said that, "If some of the steps that have been proposed to restore the industry's health are implemented, such as reducing labor costs and rationalizing fleets, US carriers would stop hemorrhaging cash. But that's different from saying [the industry] can be economically and financially successfu—which is to say, earn its cost of capital" (Crandall's Rx for Airlines, 2002). In a free market system, it seems inconceivable that firms could continue to exist without the ability to earn the cost of their own capital, but the airline industry does. After 9/11, the stock value of the major US carriers dropped sharply, many into the single digits. With the exception of Southwest, these carriers were downgraded below the junk bond level status of BBB. The debt leverage rate of the major US carriers after 9/11 was 93 percent, meaning that 93 cents on the dollar was borrowed (Air Transport Association (ATA), 2002). Bankruptcy has allowed the legacy carriers to reduce labor costs, rationalize fleets, and re-capitalize. The industry has not yet fallen victim to the temptation to add capacity. In Europe, the airline consolidation that the EC had wanted to occur is happening with the Air France–KLM deal and, possibly, the new deal with Alitalia. Three questions remain: Is this enough? Will the changes hold or be lost in the next cycle of 'good times'? Will rising fuel prices destroy any gains?

Dire times require dire measures and the airline industry has tried many things. American Airlines (and others) experimented with a new 'rolling hub' system that spreads flights out during the day to increase the utilization of planes and flight crews. Fare structures at the legacy carriers simplified (Arndt and Zellner, 2002). The system of rigid work rules is beginning to change and will hopefully raise productivity (Velocci, 2002a, 2002b). The 'carrier-within-a-carrier' concept has been revisited as Delta Air Lines launched Song and United announced the formation of TED (Haddad and Zellner, 2002). While Song is 'officially' gone, TED struggles on at United raising new questions about the whole concept. Theoretically, it makes sense to focus on the segment of the industry that is growing, particularly when your carrier is facing some of the stiffest competition from this group of carriers. Unfortunately, few if any carriers have been able to match the success of the Southwest (Ryanair) low-cost, no-frills strategy even when they start out with the concept; traditional full-service, high-cost carriers have a history of failure: the United Shuttle, USAirways' MetroJet, Continental's Lite, and British Airways' Go. Aside from the very real difference in mindset inherent in a cost-focus strategy, there are two other significant problems. First, in order to be successful the low-cost unit needs low-cost labor. Differences in wage scales tend to create dissension among employees of 'one company.' Any reasonable thinking employee of the low-cost unit has to at least consider strategies for moving up in the company world. Second, if the two units are set up to run independently, then competition is likely to arise between the two units as both attempt to appeal to the same customer groups to 'grow their market share.' Again, any 'right-minded' low-cost unit of 'one company' would have to be considering how best to lure the dissatisfied business traveler to their operation. While it would be nice to think that they were luring these passengers away from the competition, some will inevitably come from their higher-cost, traditional operations. The answer to this problem might be to establish some artificial competitive boundaries between the units. For example, the US car company Saturn, part of the General Motors Company, was restricted to selling 'compact' cars. Only recently was it allowed to produce mid-size cars and the popular Sport Utility Vehicles (SUVs). In the case of the major carriers, a domestic–international split might make the most sense. Certainly in the US, domestic service is increasingly seen as a commodity and price as the driver of consumer choice. International service demands larger aircraft and generates higher yields based on consumer desires (and willingness to pay) to receive higher levels of service on international flights. The domestic battleground is likely to be the few high density, high yield routes, although Robert Crandall has suggested that fewer than 500 of the roughly 6,000 routes in the US might qualify for non-stop service (Crandall's Rx for Airlines, 2002).

If the 'carrier within a carrier' concept did not work well, then another questionable concept is the ability of legacy airlines to reposition themselves from high-cost, traditional carriers to low-cost competitors. Two bankruptcies did allow Continental Airlines to achieve lower input costs (primarily labor costs) than their major traditional competitors, but this is not the same as repositioning to achieve the cost structure of a Southwest (Oum and Yu, 1998). At the present time, America West and US Airways are attempting to lower costs through changes in labor costs and purchased meal options. Delta, in fact, has suggested that Song did not die but transform Delta itself. Still, there is no evidence yet that they can or will become true low-cost carriers. Under CEO Ron Allen, Delta had a 'Leadership 7.5' program designed to get their available seat mile costs down to Southwest Airlines levels. His successor, Leo Mullin, blamed this program for declining morale, customer service, and falling financial performance, instituting his own program. In a stinging indictment of all of these efforts, Nolan (2005) has suggested that the end result of all the savings claimed by Allen, Mullin, and Grinstein (Mullin's successor) "has been thousands of people without a job, tens of thousands of people with their pensions at serious risk and a company in bankruptcy – and wealthy retired CEOs" (182).

It's Always Something

In a report to the US Congress, the General Accounting Office (GAO) has called the airline industry inherently unstable because of the structure of the industry and its economics (GAO, 2005). Even as the industry has made progress with labor and overall unit costs, the price of fuel began to rise and, in a related area, the world began to notice the carbon emissions related to aviation fuel use. While the airlines have suffered the most in the turbulent seas of change, they were not alone; air cargo operators, manufacturers, and related suppliers have also felt the tension and experienced many a sleepless night. After all, without airlines what would these industry players do? These latest changes challenge aviation as a whole to come up with solutions or become 'extinct' as Colin Campbell, peak oil advocate, and some environmentalists have suggested. While 11 September was a discrete event from which many claimed to see a clear path to recovery (even if the road turned out to be longer than some had predicted), these latest challenges have been building for some time and 'timeline to recovery' is not yet clear.

Thinking the Unthinkable

The industry has tried cost cutting before only to give back these advantages when times improved. They have tried some incremental shifts in market focus and marginal tinkering with revenue systems. If the airline industry is indeed inherently unstable, then these are all short-term solutions to long-term systemic problems. Deregulation has been praised for the dramatic lowering of fares and damned for creating the destructive price competition that has been a part of the financial crisis experience by the industry in each of the last three decades. International liberalization is likely to face similar charges, however, industry 'experts' do not seem to think that the new open skies agreement between the US and EU will do much to lower fares given fuel prices (Wilen, 2008). Of course, the Europeans will charge that this agreement falls far short of the single sky that they proposed. The truth is that the industry is still subject to a number of regulations; it is not regulation-free. The question becomes not whether you have regulation or not, but what you choose to regulate. The airline industry will never achieve the ideal of perfect competition extolled by economists, but how many competitors are necessary to insure 'workable' or 'contestable' markets. Should governments intervene to save failing carriers? Should the government act to change bankruptcy laws to allow the market to adjust overcapacity more quickly or will investors and lenders self-adjust to the realities of a failing market? Should the governments change their position on consolidation, foreign ownership, and right of establishment in the industry? There are as many answers to these questions as there are 'experts' in aviation and economics. Let's consider the following possibilities:

No Action at All

In almost any situation, one possible response is to 'do nothing.' Sometimes doing nothing turns out to be better than 'doing something wrong.' The problem is that governments generally want to be seen as 'doing something.' In the case of troubled national airlines or aerospace manufacturers, there is also likely to be tremendous pressure from citizens groups and other stakeholders to act. This pressure can be seen in the noise over the Air France–KLM and Alitalia deal and the Northrop–EADS tanker contract (Reuters, 2008; Tessler, 2008). In the United States, many will try linking their preferred action (or inaction) to terrorism and preventing another victory for terrorism; politics and aviation have never been strangers. In the case of the airlines, there are signs that the arguments are wearing thin, even within other segments of the industry. The recent debate on FAA funding and 'who should pay' for system upgrades illustrates this frustration (Chapter 20). If governments choose to act, there is a range of actions that they could attempt.

Consolidation

The first type of government action would be to allow further consolidation to occur in domestic markets. This option has a long history in aviation. Weaker carriers can either be acquired outright or, as in the case of TWA, another carrier may acquire the assets (not the liabilities) of the failing company. This is a market solution that has the potential to save some jobs, airports/local communities, and so on. It could reduce some of the overcapacity (prevent more capacity from entering) in domestic markets while saving, hopefully, the valuable assets of the failing companies. Even if possibilities exist, governments will not, and should not, approve 'any merger.' Mergers between very similar competitors generally result in greater competitive losses than mergers between complementary carriers. The effect of mergers between carriers with very similar route structures has the potential to severely reduce capacity (and competition) in certain markets, resulting in higher prices, fewer choices, and lower capacity. In almost any conceivable merger or consolidation, there is likely to be some loss of jobs, cutbacks on redundant service or unprofitable routes, and closure of redundant facilities. This is simply the nature of such transactions whose aims are lowering costs through economies of scale, elimination of redundancy or synergistic sharing between the units of the 'new company.' Consolidation, of course, does not guarantee that any of these things will occur. The proposed merger of United and US Airways would not have created a better, higher quality carrier; it would have combined two high-cost, poorly managed carriers into a bigger higher-cost carrier. It remains to be seen if the US Airways/America West merger will achieve its goals of creating a viable, profitable low-cost carrier.

This merger did not kick off further consolidation in the US as some had predicted, but the Delta–Northwest deal is already giving rise to talk of a United–Continental merger. Of course, the Delta–Northwest merger has not yet been approved, but some have suggested that it will be approved simply because "businesses in a bad way must do something and merging is something" (Jenkins, 2008). This is not to suggest that it will be successful at achieving the goal of realizing "$1 billion in annual gains through the merger, including about $700 million in additional revenue and $300 to $400 million in cost savings" (Grantham and Tharpe, 2008: 3). In fact, the carriers have officially stated that they will not be closing any of the seven hubs or laying off any frontline employees. Further, they expect to improve aircraft utilization from the combined carrier's 12 different aircraft types, an extraordinary feat indeed. They will also be faced with problems from the Northwest pilots' union who were unable to agree on the merged seniority lists (Air Transport News, 2008; Grantham and Tharpe, 2008; Weber, 2008). Unfortunately, only one of the 20 major airline merger/acquisitions since the 1978 deregulation has been judged by experts a 'success.' The majority have fallen "victim to runaway costs, dissatisfied passengers and labor disputes" (Steffy, 2007: 1).

Foreign Ownership

Changes to rules on foreign ownership would open up the pool of potential investors and bring new money into the industry, but only if these investors are allowed the control that goes with stock ownership. As Richard Branson has noted, only a fool would invest in a company without some assurances of control. He has dived into the pool anyway with Virgin America. As noted in the introduction to this book, governments have historically resisted this option for a number of reasons, most notably national defense, but it could be a reasonable option for governments as long as they feel that they are able to retain the right to approve the proposed merger and can create mechanisms to 'control' the actions of these companies. In a separate, but related area, governments could grant the right of establishment in domestic markets allowing foreign companies to establish operations in domestic markets and operate as domestic competitors with the same rights, privileges, and obligations as 'true' domestic firms. The first action could save airlines that cannot attract domestic investment, however, it would not increase the number of competitors in domestic markets. The second action has the potential to actually increase the number of competitors in domestic markets, although if these new competitors prove more efficient than existing domestic competitors, there could be long-term reductions in the number of competitors.

The EU continues to pressure the US to open up domestic markets to foreign ownership, but the recent open skies agreement continues to limit foreign owners to 25 percent voting stakes while at the same time stepping back and placing a specific limit on US ownership of airlines in Europe. It remains to be seen whether further pressure in the follow-up meetings will produce a way forward toward a single sky. In essence, sixty years after the Chicago Conference the Australian–New Zealand proposal could come to pass if the single sky can be achieved (Chapter 5). Domestic markets might then be left to low-cost carriers. International service would become the province of large multinational entities. The European fear that such an entity would be dominated by the US mega-carriers is growing less likely by the minute given the financial weakness of US carriers. Governments tend to follow rather than lead, but for such a transition to occur there would have to be substantial changes in the rules and regulations governing not only ownership, but safety, airworthiness, licensing, and so on.

Government Loans, Guarantees, and so on

Governments have intervened in great and small ways in the post-9/11 industry. The US Airline Stabilization Board has provided loans to eligible airlines. The Belgian government intervened in the case of Sabena as did the Swiss with Swissair, however, governments seem to be losing their taste (and the resources) for major interventions. This may not stop some national governments from attempting to creatively aid their struggling carriers, but it should prevent major, overt bail-outs. While the US government has historically preferred to intervene in indirect ways to aid their national carriers, the debate over the extent of government intervention became a hotly contested issue during the United bankruptcy. In its bankruptcy filing, United acknowledged that it was losing US $20 million a day. Worse still, the business plan that had failed to convince the Ait Transport Stabilization Board (ATSB) to intervene also failed to convince the private lenders of capital that United could return to profitability in a reasonable timeframe (McCartney, 2002). Ultimately, the US government (and taxpayer) did play a significant role in saving United when the US government took over the pension plan obligations through the Pension Benefits Guaranty Corporation. The obligation for United and US Airways alone totaled US$9.6 billion (GAO, 2005).

Given this action, we may never know if the sudden and rapid fall of a carrier responsible for roughly 20 percent of the domestic flights in the US would have proved too disruptive to endure. There was enough capacity in the US system to adjust to the loss of United. Certainly, American Airlines would have benefited in Chicago and a number of other major cities. Regional and low-cost carriers have certainly proved that they can move rapidly into abandoned markets. Internationally, it might have taken longer to adjust capacity only because of the restrictive nature of some bilaterals, but given the decline in both Atlantic and Pacific traffic to the US right after 9/11 this might not have posed a pressing problem. In both the domestic and national context, a reduction in capacity could have benefited existing carriers, many of whom were struggling under the combined effects of 9/11 and the economic slowdown. Bankruptcy laws are "designed to serve two fundamental purposes: (1) to relieve an honest debtor from over-burdensome financial obligations and give him or her a fresh start, free of claims of former creditors, and (2) to provide for equitable treatment of creditors who are competing for the debtor's limited assets" (Roszkowski, 1989: 603). They were not intended to relieve a company's management from the responsibility for their own actions or inactions nor to save companies without the resources, assets, or abilities to achieve future success. In any event, we have yet to test the result of a major airline liquidation.

Re-regulation

The crisis following 9/11 did cause some governments to re-examine the question of deregulation itself. Joseph Stiglitz, the 2001 Nobel Prize winner in Economics, has pointed out that deregulation episodes tend to give rise to a bubble-and-bust cycle, a description that certainly seems to fit the airline industry (Stiglitz, 2002). The self-interest of airlines who focus on growing their companies in the good times works to benefit consumers, especially when economic downturn creates overcapacity; it does not benefit the airlines faced with excess capacity, the aircraft leasing companies faced with returned aircraft, the investors holding worthless stock, the employees faced with worthless pensions, or the local communities faced with service cutbacks. Where you stand on the issue of re-regulation depends on where you sit, as the saying goes. Even those who might favor some form of re-regulation will not necessarily agree on what form that regulation should take. Does the government set service level standards? Does it control entry into the industry, establishing a maximum number of carriers or market share limits? Does it intervene to establish minimum/maximum prices? Does it intervene in labor issues, financial practices, alliance arrangements? The list of possible interventions is legion and the pros and cons of each action can, and will, be debated. Whatever the outcome in various countries, an ultimate judgement must be made on whether air transportation is an essential service that can be provided in a safe, economical way by a free market. A radical, minority view of the industry has suggested that it suffers from an 'empty core' and is inherently unable to make a long-term profit. The solution would be to 'suspend' antitrust rules when the times are tough and allow carriers to "collude over fares and routes in order to maintain service levels without bleeding each other to death" (Jenkins, 2008). In other words, they would be allowed to fix prices and divide up markets. The view is probably no more far-fetched than the idea that most of the new mergers will result in profitable, efficient carriers, but it seems too radical for an industry that remains determined to try the same things that failed the last time.

A Buffet Ending?

It is difficult to imagine a near-term future without some form of commercial air transportation. Air transportation is simply too vital to the growth and prosperity of the world economy and the nations that make up our world. This is the good news for those who have loved this industry for so long. The bad news may be that the aviation world as we know it may be ending and what emerges may not be the industry we would wish for our successors. The tragedy is that unless the industry applies the same ingenuity and daring to recreating itself in the aftermath of its latest crisis as it did in the early years of its development, it may be doomed to fulfill Warren Buffet's prophesy of making zero long-term profit. The challenge facing the airline industry is to prove Buffet wrong through thinking outside of the box that has been its home for so long. This is a challenge worthy of the next generation. It is my hope that the students of today will take up this challenge, not forgetting the past but not bound to its old ways and conventional wisdom.

References

Air Transport Association (ATA) (2002), *State of the US Airline Industry: A Report on Recent Trends for U.S. Air Carriers, 2002–2003*, Air Transport Association, Washington, DC.

Air Transport News (2008), 'Delta Air Lines, Northwest Combining to Create America's Premier Global Airline', Available at: http://www.airtransportnews. aero.

Arndt, M. and Zellner, W. (2002), 'How to Keep United Flying', *Business Week*, December 23, pp. 34–5.

Associated Press (2008), 'Frontier Airlines Files for Bankruptcy', 11 April, Available at: http://www.cnbs.com/id/24060605.

Crandall's Rx for Airlines (2002), *Aviation Week and Space Technology*, November 18, p. 54.

Creaton, S. (2005), *Ryanair: How a Small Irish Airline Conquered Europe*, Arum Press, London.

GAO (2005), 'Structural Costs Continue to Challenge Legacy Airlines Financial Performance', GAO-05-834T, Washington, DC

Grantham, R. and Tharpe, J. (2008), 'NWA Merger Agreement Keeps Delta in Atlanta', *The Atlanta Journal-Constitution*, Available at: http://www.ajc.com/ pt/cpt?action=cpt&title=NWA+merger+agreement.

Grossman, D. (2007), 'Bringing a Low-cost Airline to Town', USAToday.com, Available at: www.usatoday.com/pt/cpt?action=cpt&title=Bringing.

Haddad, C. and Zellner, W. (2002), 'Getting Down and Dirty with Discounters', *Business Week*, October 28, pp. 77–8.

Holmes, S. and Matlack, C. (2002), 'Caught in United's Downdraft: How will Boeing's Finance and Leasing Business be Affected?', *Business Week*, December 23, p. 35.

Jenkins, H.W. (2008), 'Plane Wreck', *The Wall Street Journal*, 16 April, p. A18.

McCartney, S. (2002), 'For United, Liquidation is a Very Real Possibility', *The Middle Seat*, December 20.

Nolan, H.L., Jr (2005), *Airline Without a Pilot: Lessons in Leadership*, Targetmark Books, New York.

Nelson, A. and Francolla, G. (2008), 'Airlines: Tale of Merger and Bankruptcy', CNBC.com, 21 February, Available at: www.cnbc.com/id/23260075.

Oum, T.H. and Yu, C. (1998), *Winning Airlines: Productivity and Cost Competitiveness of the World's Major Airlines*, Kluwer Academic Publishers, Boston.

Reuters (2008), 'Delta, Northwest Merger faces Another Hurdle', CNBS.com, Available at: www.cnbc.com/id/23289650.

Roszkowski, M.E. (1989), *Business Law: Principles, Cases, and Policy*, HarperCollins, New York.

Steffy, L. (2007), 'Airline Mergers Usually Don't Fly', Houston Chronicle, Available at: http://www.chron.com/disp/story.mpl/business/steffy/5309876. html.

Stiglitz, J. (2002), 'The roaring nineties', *Atlantic Monthly*, October, pp. 76–89.

Taneja, N.K. (1988), *The International Airline Industry: Trends, Issues & Challenges*, Lexington Books, Lexington, MA.

Tessler, J. (2008), 'Northrop, EADS win $35B Air Force deal', ABCNews, Available at http://abcnews.go.com/print?id=4367303.

Toffler, A. (1980), *The Third Wave*, William Morrow and Company Inc., New York.

Velocci, A.L. (2002a), 'Can Majors Shift Focus Fast Enough to Survive,' *Aviation Week and Space Technology*, November 18, pp. 52–4.

Velocci, A.L. (2002b), 'No Silver Bullet Seen for Airlines' Dilemma,' *Aviation Week and Space Technology*, November 18, pp. 52–4.

Weber, H.R. (2008), 'Delta Pilots Say No Deal with Northwest', WTOPnews.com, Available at: www.wtopnews.com/?nid=111&sid=1347940

Wilen, J. (2008), 'Open Skies: More Flights, Same Fares', Available at: http://biz. yahoo.com/ap/080326/open_skies.html.

Wolf, S.M. (1995), 'Where Do We Go from Here: A Management Perspective', in P. Cappelli (ed.) *Airline Labor Relations in the Global Era: The New Frontier*, ILR Press, Cornell.

Index

Other titles from Ashgate

Introduction to Air Transport Economics:
From Theory to Applications
Bijan Vasigh, Thomas Tacker and Ken Fleming
2008 • 400 pages
Hardback/Paperback
978-0-7546-7079-7/ 978-0-7546-7081-0

Aviation Markets:
Studies in Competition and Regulatory Reform
David Starkie
2008 • 246 pages
Hardback/Paperback
978-0-7546-7360-6/ 978-0-7546-7388-0

Air Transportation:
A Management Perspective, 6th edition
John G. Wensveen
2007 • 590 pages
Hardback/Paperback
978-0-7546-7165-7/ 978-0-7546-7171-8

Airline Marketing and Management, 6th edition
Stephen Shaw
2007 • 336 pages
Hardback/Paperback
978-0-7546-4819-2/ 978-0-7546-4820-8

ASHGATE